'Never Had the Like Occurred':

Egypt's view of its past

UCL

PRESS

Institute of Archaeology

Encounters with
Ancient
Egypt

Titles in the series

ENCOUNTERS WITH ANCIENT EGYPT

'Never Had the Like Occurred':

Egypt's view of its past

Edited by

John Tait

PRESS
Institute of Archaeology

First published in Great Britain 2003 by UCL Press,
an imprint of Cavendish Publishing Limited, The Glass House,
Wharton Street, London WC1X 9PX, United Kingdom
Telephone: + 44 (0)20 7278 8000   Facsimile: + 44 (0)20 7278 8080
Email: info@uclpress.com
Website: www.uclpress.com

Published in the United States by Cavendish Publishing
c/o International Specialized Book Services,
5824 NE Hassalo Street, Portland,
Oregon 97213-3644, USA

Published in Australia by Cavendish Publishing (Australia) Pty Ltd
45 Beach Street, Coogee, NSW 2034, Australia
Telephone: + 61 (2)9664 0909   Facsimile: + 61 (2)9664 5420

British Library Cataloguing in Publication Data
Tait, W. J.
'Never had the like occurred': Egypt's view of its past –
(Encounters with ancient Egypt)
1 Historiography – Egypt 2 Egypt – Historiography
I Title
932'.0072

Library of Congress Cataloguing in Publication Data
Data available

ISBN 1-84472-007-1

1 3 5 7 9 10 8 6 4 2

Designed and typeset by Style Photosetting, Mayfield, East Sussex
Email: style@pavilion.co.uk

Printed and bound in Great Britain

Cover illustration: The creation of humankind by the God Khnum seated before his potter's
wheel (digital colour version by Stuart Laidlaw based on eighteenth Dynasty representation at
Deir el-Bahri; Arnold 1974b: pl. 48).

Series Editor's Foreword

This series of eight books derives from the proceedings of a conference entitled 'Encounters with Ancient Egypt', held at the Institute of Archaeology, University College London (UCL) in December 2000. Since then, many new chapters have been especially commissioned for publication, and those papers originally provided for the conference and now selected for publication have been extensively revised and rewritten.

There are many noteworthy features of the books. One is the overall attempt to move the study of Ancient Egypt into the mainstream of recent advances in archaeological and anthropological practice and interpretation. This is a natural outcome of London University's Institute of Archaeology, one of the largest archaeology departments in the world, being the academic host. Drawing on the Institute's and other related resources within UCL, the volumes in the series reflect an extraordinary degree of collaboration between the series editor, individual volume editors, contributors and colleagues. The wide range of approaches to the study of the past, pursued in such a vibrant scholarly environment as UCL's, has encouraged the scholars writing in these volumes to consider their disciplinary interests from new perspectives. All the chapters presented here have benefited from wide-ranging discussion between experts from diverse academic disciplines, including art history, papyrology, anthropology, archaeology and Egyptology, and subsequent revision.

Egyptology has been rightly criticized for often being insular; the methodologies and conclusions of the discipline have been seen by others as having developed with little awareness of archaeologies elsewhere. The place and role of Ancient Egypt within African history, for example, has rarely been considered jointly by Egyptologists and Africanists. This collaboration provides a stimulating review of key issues and may well influence future ways of studying Egypt. Until now, questions have rarely been asked about the way Egyptians thought of their own past or about non-Egyptian peoples and places. Nor has the discipline of Egyptology explored, in any depth, the nature of its evidence, or the way contemporary cultures regarded Ancient Egypt. The books in this series address such topics.

Another exceptional feature of this series is the way that the books have been designed to interrelate with, inform and illuminate one another. Thus, the evidence of changing appropriations of Ancient Egypt over time, from the classical period to the modern Afrocentrist movement, features in several volumes. One volume explores the actual sources of knowledge about Ancient Egypt before the advent of 'scientific' archaeology, while another explores knowledge of Ancient Egypt after Napoleon Bonaparte's expeditions and the unearthing of Tutankhamun's tomb. The question asked throughout these volumes, however, is how far fascination and knowledge about Ancient Egypt have been based on sources of evidence rather than extraneous political or commercial concerns and interests.

As a result of this series, the study of Ancient Egypt will be significantly enriched and deepened. The importance of the Egypt of several thousands of years ago reaches far beyond the existence of its architectural monuments and extends to its unique role in the history of all human knowledge. Furthermore, the civilization of Ancient Egypt speaks to us with particular force in our own present and has an abiding place in the modern psyche.

As the first paragraph of this Foreword explains, the final stage of this venture began with the receipt and editing of some extensively revised, and in many cases new, chapters – some 95 in all – to be published simultaneously in eight volumes. What it does not mention is the speed with which the venture has been completed: the current UCL Press was officially launched in April 2003. That this series of books has been published to such a high standard of design, professional accuracy and attractiveness only four months later is incredible.

This alone speaks eloquently for the excellence of the staff of UCL Press – from its senior management to its typesetters and designers. Ruth Phillips (Marketing Director) stands out for her youthful and innovative marketing ideas and implementation of them, but most significant of all, at least from the Institute's perspective, is the contribution of Ruth Massey (Editor), who oversaw and supervized all details of the layout and production of the books, and also brought her critical mind to bear on the writing styles, and even the meaning, of their contents.

Individual chapter authors and academic volume editors, both from within UCL and in other institutions, added this demanding project to otherwise full workloads. Although it is somewhat invidious to single out particular individuals, Professor David O'Connor stands out as co-editor of two volumes and contributor of chapters to three despite his being based overseas. He, together with Professor John Tait – also an editor and multiple chapter author in these books – was one of the first to recognize my vision of the original conference as having the potential to inspire a uniquely important publishing project.

Within UCL's Institute of Archaeology, a long list of dedicated staff, academic, administrative and clerical, took over tasks for the Director and Kelly Vincent, his assistant as they wrestled with the preparation of this series. All of these staff, as well as several members of the student body, really deserve individual mention by name, but space does not allow this. However, the books could not have appeared without the particular support of five individuals: Lisa Daniel, who tirelessly secured copyright for over 500 images; Jo Dullaghan, who turned her hand to anything at any time to help out, from re-typing manuscripts to chasing overdue authors; Andrew Gardner, who tracked down obscure and incomplete references, and who took on the complex job of securing and producing correctly scanned images; Stuart Laidlaw, who not only miraculously produced publishable images of a pair of outdoor cats now in Holland and Jamaica, but in a number of cases created light where submitted images revealed only darkness; and Kelly Vincent, who did all of the above twice over, and more – and who is the main reason that publisher and Institute staff remained on excellent terms throughout.

Finally, a personal note, if I may. Never, ever contemplate producing eight complex, highly illustrated books within a four month period. If you *really must*, then make sure you have the above team behind you. Essentially, ensure that you have a partner such as Jane Hubert, who may well consider you to be mad but never questions the essential worth of the undertaking.

Peter Ucko
Institute of Archaeology
University College London
27 July 2003

Contents

Note: No attempt has been made to impose a standard chronology on authors; all dates before 712 BC are approximate. However, names of places, and royal and private names have been standardized.

Contributors

Sally-Ann Ashton is Assistant Keeper in the Department of Antiquities at the Fitzwilliam Museum, University of Cambridge. Her publications include *Ptolemaic Royal Sculpture from Egypt* (2001), contributions to the exhibition catalogue *Cleopatra of Egypt: from history to myth* (2001), and *The Last Queens of Egypt* (2003). She received her PhD from King's College, London University.

Whitney Davis is Professor of the History and Theory of Ancient and Modern Art and Chair of the Department of History of Art at the University of California at Berkeley. His interests include prehistoric art and archaeology, ancient Egyptian art, the classical tradition, and the history and theory of archaeology and art history. His books include *The Canonical Tradition in Ancient Egyptian Art* (1989), *Masking the Blow: the scene of representation in late prehistoric Egyptian art* (1992), *Replications: archaeology, art history, psychoanalysis* (1996), and *Pacing the World* (1996). He is currently working on the theory of visual culture and on eroticism and aesthetics in the 19th century. He received his PhD from Harvard University.

Hans-W. Fischer-Elfert is Professor of Egyptology at the University of Leipzig. He is particularly interested in ancient Egyptian literature and magic and is currently working on a book about 'outsiders'. His works include *Die Satirische Streitschrift des Papyrus Anastasi I* (1986), *Die Vision von der Statue im Stein. Studien zum Altägptischen Mundöffnungsritual* (1998) and *Die Lehre eines Manner für seinen Sohn: Eine Etappe auf dem 'Gottesweg' des loyalen und solidarischen Beamten des Mittleren Reiches* (1999). He received his PhD from the University of Hamburg.

David Jeffreys is Lecturer in Egyptian Archaeology at the Institute of Archaeology, University College London and is Director of the Egypt Exploration Society's Survey of Memphis. His publications include archaeological reports and discussions of excavation and surveys at Memphis, discussions of the topography of the Memphite area, and archaeological sources for the regional survey. He has made a special study of the work of Joseph Hekekyan, who made geological soundings at a number of sites in Egypt in the early 1850s. He received his PhD from the University of London.

Antonio Loprieno is Professor of Egyptology at the University of Basel, Switzerland, after having served for 10 years as Professor of Egyptology and Chairman of the Department of Near Eastern Languages and Cultures at the University of California, Los Angeles. His research topics include comparative Afroasiatic and Egyptian linguistics as well as Egyptian history and literature. His publications include *Das Verbalsystem in Ägyptischen und im Semitischen* (1996), *Topos und Mimesis* (1988), *Ancient Egyptian: a linguistic introduction* (1995), *La Pensée et l'écriture* (2001) and, as editor, *Ancient Egyptian Literature: history and forms* (1996). He received his PhD from the University of Turin, Italy, and his Habilitation from the University of Göttingen, Germany.

Ludwig D. Morenz is Privatdozent in Egyptology at the University of Leipzig. His current research interests include the origins of writing and the emergence of an Egyptian complex society, the uses of visual poetry and the Renaissance and Baroque constructions of Ancient Egypt. His publications include *Beiträge zur ägyptischen*

Schriftlichkeitskultur (1996), and *Herrscherpräsentation und Kulturkontakte* (2003, jointly with Bosshard-Neoustil). He received his doctorate from the University of Leipzig and his Habilitation from the University of Tübingen, Germany.

Robert Morkot works as an independent scholar, combining teaching, principally for the University of Exeter, with writing and museum work. His publications include *The Black Pharaohs: Egypt's Nubian rulers* (2000), and 'Egypt and Nubia' (in Susan Alcock *et al.*, *Empires: perspectives from archaeology and history*, 2001). His special research interests include the relationship between Egypt and other ancient societies, and the intellectual development of Egyptology and ancient history. His postdoctoral studies were undertaken at the Humboldt University, Berlin and at University College London, from where he received his PhD.

David O'Connor is Lila Acheson Wallace Professor in Ancient Egyptian Art and Archaeology at the Institute of Fine Arts of New York University, Professor Emeritus of the University of Pennsylvania, and Curator Emeritus of the Egyptian Section of its Museum of Archaeology and Anthropology. He has excavated extensively in Nubia and at Malkata, Thebes, and at Abydos in southern Egypt since 1967. His publications include *Ancient Egypt: a social history* (1983), *Ancient Nubia: Egypt's rival in Africa* (1993), *Ancient Egyptian Kingship* (1995, with David Silverman) and *Amenhotep III: Perspectives on his Reign* (1998, with Eric Cline). He received his PhD from the University of Cambridge.

John Tait is Edwards Professor of Egyptology at the Institute of Archaeology, University College London. He has edited hieroglyphic, hieratic, demotic and Greek papyri, and studies Egyptian literary traditions. His publications include *Papyri from Tebtunis in Egyptian and in Greek* (1977), and *Saqqara Demotic Papyri* (1983, with H. S. Smith) and he has made several contributions to the work of the Project for the Publication of the Carlsberg Papyri (Copenhagen). He received his D Phil from the University of Oxford.

Eric Uphill is an Honorary Research Fellow of the Institute of Archaeology, University College London, and formerly a tutor in Egyptology at Birkbeck College, London. He has taken part in excavations at Saqqarah in Egypt and at the Buhen fortress in the Sudan. His publications include *Who Was Who in Egyptology* (1995, with W. R. Dawson), *The Temples of Per Ramesses* (1984), *Egyptian Towns and Cities* (1998), and *Pharaoh's Gateway to Eternity: the Hawara labyrinth of King Amenemhet III* (2000). He obtained his PhD from the University of London.

Dietrich Wildung is Professor of Egyptology at the Free University in Berlin, Director of the Egyptian Museum and Papyrus Collection, Berlin and Director of the Naga Excavation Project in the Sudan. His special areas of interest are art history and the Sudan. His publications include *Die Steine der Pharaonen* (1981), *Egyptian Saints: Deification in Pharonic Egypt* (1977), *Sudan: ancient kingdoms of the Nile* (1997), and *Imhotep and Amenhotep* (1977). He received both his doctorate and Habilitation from the University of Munich.

List of Figures

COLOUR SECTION

A note on transliteration from ancient Egyptian

The ancient Egyptian scripts convey 24 consonants, no vowels. Fourteen of these occur in modern English, written with one letter: b, d, f, g, h, k, m, n, p, r, s, t, w, y. Three more are also found in English, but usually written with two letters: to keep transliteration as direct as possible, these are transliterated by Egyptologists as follows:

š   'sh' as in 'sheep'

ṯ   'ch' as in 'chin'

ḏ   as in 'j' and 'dg' of 'judge'

The other seven Egyptian consonants do not occur in written English, and are transliterated by Egyptologists as follows:

ꜣ   the glottal stop (faintly heard if you start a sentence with a vowel in English)

i   a sound varying between glottal stop and y

ꜥ   the 'ayin' of Arabic, a deep guttural clenching of the throat

ḥ   a stronger 'h', found in modern Arabic

ḫ   found in Arabic, the 'ch' of Scottish 'loch'

ẖ   a sound varying between *ḥ* and *š*

q   a form of 'k' pronounced deeper in the throat, and found in Arabic

CHAPTER 1

INTRODUCTION – '... SINCE THE TIME OF THE GODS'

John Tait

Time and time again, and in response to a variety of challenges and problems, Egyptians of the dynastic period made use of the past to confirm – and to explore – their own identity. Therefore these ideas of identity need to be understood before the kind of past the Egyptians had in mind can be seriously investigated.

Dynastic Egypt has usually been seen by scholarship since the early 19th century as a very self-confident culture: the Egyptians were sure that Egypt was where the cosmos came into being, and that foreign lands were merely useful appendages provided and overseen by the gods for the purpose of helping to maintain the world-order within the only part of the world of any significance – Egypt. This attitude may be perceived in the whole range of 'official' religious and royal texts that survive, although these texts do not often state the totality of this view in any explicit way, as it was not open to question. The Egyptians had no idea of any need for 'faith', or expressions of faith.

Nevertheless, there are some texts which apparently saw a necessity to defend the Egyptian worldview. The last sections of the Middle Kingdom (earlier second millennium BC) 'Tale of Sinuhe' can be interpreted as a deliberate assertion that Egypt (and above all the royal court) was the only place where it was worthwhile living (Baines 1982; Loprieno 2003: 38; Morenz, Chapter 6). The 'Tale of Wenamun', which represents an official of the Karnak temple of Amun as sent upon an errand to claim a load of timber for the construction of a replacement for the sacred boat of the god, has often been interpreted as a faithful representation of the decline of Egyptian power and prestige in the Levant at the opening of the first millennium BC (Loprieno 2003: 45–48). Some recent studies (Baines 1999; Eyre 1999) have seen its statements more in terms of literary discourse. There could be no doubt, however, that the words in the 'Tale of Wenamun' put in the mouth of the ruler of Byblos, addressing the Egyptian Wenamun, concerning the supremacy of the Egyptian 'state' god Amun, were meant to show – or rather to consider the view – that Egypt was at the heart of the cosmos: "Amun has established all lands; but he established them only after he had first established the land of Egypt, from whence you (that is, Wenamun) have come" (2.19–2.21).

This text shows an Egyptian concern about Egypt's own place in an increasingly complex world at a particular point in time (even if the precise point in time is debatable: 10th century BC, ninth century BC?). The text specifically looks to the past:

"He (that is, the ruler of Byblos) had the ledgers of his ancestors brought, and had them read out to me (that is, Wenamun)." In the fictional world of the text, the ruler's purpose is to establish what had been the tradition of proper diplomatic practice, in order to extract payment from Wenamun. On another level, it suggests that one cannot act properly without reference to the past.

Traditionally, Egypt's own view of its past has been studied primarily in works that treat a particular period, or a particular kind of evidence. For example, recently, Manuelian (1994) has concentrated upon the Saite period (664–525 BC), while Vernus (1995) has essentially exploited textual sources. In this book, the time-range covered is (deliberately) vast, and some contributors are chiefly concerned with texts, while others concentrate upon material culture. Overall, the authors try to combine and to use in conjunction the two types of evidence, whatever the chronological period.

The focus of this book is the Egyptians' view – down to the end of the first millennium BC – of their own past. It is possible for a society to conspire to forget its past, above all the recent past, especially if this has been inglorious or miserable – or simply to be indifferent to it. One theme that emerges from the following chapters is that the Egyptians did not ever take these paths, unless this is what happened in the Coptic period – that the past became irrelevant, and was ignored.

Egyptian identity and foreigners

In terms of lexicography, the Egyptians did not have an emotive term for their own 'country' or 'nation': there is no equivalent to concepts such as 'Greek', 'Macedonian', or 'Arab'. It is a commonplace in modern discussions to state that the Egyptian term for their own country was *kmt*, and that this meant 'the black (land)', that is, the cultivatable flood plain of the Nile Valley and Delta, as opposed to the 'red', the desert. The Egyptian for 'Egyptians' was *rmṯ(.t) n(t) kmt*, 'people of Egypt' (Erman and Grapow 1926–1950: ii, 423), a term that remained standard into the Coptic stage of the language (Crum 1939: 110). Yet the term presents a problem, since *rmṯ(.t)* can be seen to mean 'real people' (civilized persons?), so that the Egyptians' view of themselves could be argued to be exclusive: to be *rmṯ(.t) n(t) kmt* you had to be a *real* Egyptian, and speak Egyptian. Nevertheless, there are abundant indications that the Egyptians in one sense saw as 'Egyptian' anyone who lived in Egypt: that is, within the Nile Valley from the Mediterranean coast in the north to the First Cataract in the south. Herodotus (II.18) in the fifth century BC reported what has every appearance of being an Egyptian tradition concerning the inhabitants of the western Delta region (or perhaps it should be called a 'myth') that states the idea very explicitly. It is also very relevant to the topic of Libyan ethnicity discussed further below (and see Cline and O'Connor 2003).

> Those from the city of Marea and that of Apis, living in the part of Egypt neighbouring Libya, reckoned themselves to be Libyans and not Egyptians. They felt aggrieved at the religious observances that required them not to touch the meat of cows. They sent to (the Oracle of) Ammon, saying that they had nothing in common with the Egyptians, and that they themselves lived outside the Delta, and did not at all agree with them. They wished to be allowed to taste everything. However, the god did not allow them to do this, saying that 'Egypt' was whatever the Nile irrigated in its course, and

'Egyptians' were those who lived downstream of the city of Elephantine and drank from that river.

To have an idea of what makes one Egyptian, one has to know what is *not* 'Egyptian'. O'Connor (Chapter 9) suggests as a starting-point for discussion the apparent 'brutality' that Egyptians considered (throughout the dynastic period) as appropriate behaviour towards those who patently were not Egyptian. Such reported action might, of course, have been 'metaphorical' rather than actual. No doubt the situation varied from case to case. Also, it seems clear that Egyptian attitudes to foreigners outside Egypt varied according to how – how well – they were seen to 'choose' to behave. There may well not have been one fixed mode of behaviour, but rather a variety of attitudes and responses. For example, the attitudes towards foreigners were significantly different in periods when Egypt was unified and had strong central control from the attitudes when the country was fragmented. Further, some differences in the stance taken towards different foreign peoples seem to have lasted over long periods of time, even though in scenes of offering 'tribute', the attitude seems uniform. An extreme case is the Puntites (Harvey 2003; Meeks 2003). The well-known depictions of their culture in the mortuary temple of Queen Hatshepsut at Deir el-Bahri have often been discussed as if they were an ethnographic record (Herzog 1968; Kitchen 1999), but it is difficult to know if these are stereotypes of the representation of 'others' (not otherwise explicitly attested) that are being depicted. The representation of the Queen of Punt, often described as grotesquely obese, is accompanied by a routine textual caption, and there is no hint as to whether the viewer is supposed to see her as bizarre or just as a Puntite queen.

It is very commonly suggested that foreigners who entered Egypt and became fully Egyptianized were fully accepted into Egyptian society. This must be at least in part a realistic view, although it is difficult to argue whether or not it might have applied at all levels of society. It is also doubtful whether such Egyptianization was always an available option, and assimilation may sometimes have been enforced. This is presumably not a matter that Egyptian texts would have wished to involve themselves with.

What *is* mentioned is the special case of the education of the children of conquered rulers of Syria-Palestine in the Egyptian palace school, with the intention that they should in due course return to rule their territories with a favourable attitude towards Egypt. This is quite the reverse of the case of the Egyptian abroad. In the Middle-Kingdom 'Tale of Sinuhe' (Fischer-Elfert, Chapter 7; Loprieno 1988; Loprieno, Chapter 8; Morenz, Chapter 6), Sinuhe spends many years in Syria-Palestine with the ruler of Upper Retjenu, and comes to adopt the appearance, dress, and whole way of life of a local ruler. Eventually he returns to Egypt, and is re-accepted into Egypt and the Egyptian court; but he has to be divested, almost ritually, of all the marks of 'foreignness' acquired during his years in Syria-Palestine. The text clearly involves conscious reflection on 'Egyptianness'. It can perhaps be taken more to reflect a view that an Egyptian always remains an Egyptian, rather than a fear that it is dangerously easy to turn into a foreigner.

The later periods of Egyptian history show a number of better documented crises in the Egyptian view of themselves and their own past. In the Third Intermediate Period, the (earlier first millennium BC) Libyan rulers and officials appeared in art highly Egyptianized, and yet retained some clear outward indications of their Libyan origins. They essentially stemmed from disparate Libyan groups settled in the Delta, an area of Egypt always in the ancient world difficult to unify politically. No textual evidence survives that expresses an anti-Egyptian view: their wish to retain distinctive identities was conceivably more related to a desire to differentiate themselves from other Libyan groups (Cline and O'Connor 2003) (as Egyptian representations had always indicated the 'Libyans' had done) than to show themselves as not quite Egyptian. The situation was very different in the case of the Kushite conquerors (twenty-fifth Dynasty, 751 BC until the 660s/650s). In royal public display, at any rate, they had long adopted much of Egyptian practice (Morkot, Chapter 5). However, they chose to regard the contemporary Egyptians as failing properly to keep up Egyptian religious practices, and they therefore strongly maintained various distinctive Kushite features, for example of royal iconography, while also initiating, within Egypt itself, a new era of 'archaizing' in art based on Egyptian models of several periods (Morkot, Chapter 5). Thus the Kushites seem to present a unique phenomenon among catalysts for change in the Egyptians' view of themselves and their past. They aggressively presented themselves as both Egyptian and not Egyptian, and they did this, not in distinct contexts, but consistently. The solid evidence for any difference between the impact of the Libyan and Kushite periods on Egypt is limited: official texts of the Kushite period take an aggressive stance. In his 'Victory Stela', Piye is represented as telling the defenders of the besieged Egyptian town of Per-Sekhemkhepera:

> O you who live in death, you who live in death; you poor wretches, you who live in death! If the moment passes without your opening to me, you will be counted slain according to the King's judgement.
>
> (Lichtheim 1980: 74)

In royal iconography, the use, for example, of the double uraeus must surely be seen as an overt comment on Egyptian kingship. One can also look to later Egyptian reactions to the plight of Egypt in these periods (Bresciani 2001; Loprieno, Chapter 8).

The immediate reaction to the Kushites, under the Saite dynasty, was not a simple one. The most distinctively 'Kushite' features of royal iconography, for example, disappear, but the apparent enthusiasm for archaizing is continued and taken to greater lengths. There does not appear to have been any attempt to erase the Kushites from memory. The dismantling of their monuments, even within a short period of time, should not be misinterpreted; this was an indignity suffered by many kings, without any necessary indication of disapproval. Later traditions reported by Greek authors imply that each of the Kushite rulers was remembered on their merits or their faults. The traditional set of views of Nubian foreigners returned, and remained into the Roman Period. There is nothing to suggest that the experience of Kushite rule resulted in any new attitudes towards Nubia, although it must presumably have led to a sharper and more self-conscious interest in the nature of being Egyptian and in the Egyptian past and identity.

The Persians of the first Persian period (525–404 BC) were a very different case (Cook 1983; Kuhrt 1995, ii: 647–701; Ray 1988). In general, the Persian king was not resident in Egypt, making it difficult for the Egyptians to see him as fulfilling the role expected of an Egyptian king. 'Collaborators' among the Egyptian elite may have persuaded themselves – or sought to persuade others – that Darius the Great or Cambyses really was of divine descent (Lloyd 1982: 170–175), but there is no indication that this was effective, certainly not in the longer term: the later Egyptian view that we can detect was not a positive one, even if the very negative Greek views of the Persian occupation of Egypt were coloured by Greek attitudes to their own struggle with Persia. The Great King is depicted on some Egyptian stelae and monuments as an Egyptian king, but in general the Persians themselves seem to have had little interest in exporting the trappings of Egyptian royal display, or Egyptian culture in general. Egyptian craftsmanship may have been a different matter, and it has been suggested that artisans were transported to Persia in considerable numbers. A statue of Darius I found at Susa seems to have been of Egyptian workmanship and may have been made in Egypt. It depicts him in purely Persian form. The sole Egyptian feature is the row of the names of the peoples subject to Persia around the base, carved in good Egyptian hieroglyphs, in the traditional Egyptian manner, such as we see in the lists of foreign subject states at Karnak: the head of a foreign captive surmounting a cartouche containing the name. The Persian occupation, then, offered little enduring threat to the Egyptians' ideas of their self-identity: the Persians were viewed simply as foreign invaders. In several ways it seems to have promoted an interest in the past. Assmann (1996: 6) has suggested that the Persian period was crucial to developments in Egyptian views of the past: that stronger ideas emerged of the need to categorize and to canonize the knowledge of the past.

The Ptolemaic period presented the Egyptians with quite new problems of identity. The Macedonian rulers in Alexandria and their immediate court maintained a style that was not just Greek, but Macedonian (La'da 2003). Yet they were depicted on Egyptian temple walls and stelae and in statuary as Egyptian kings and queens (Ashton, Chapter 12), and they were given royal titles that overtly linked them with the Egyptian past (already Alexander had been given a cartouche name partly based on one of those of the last native ruler of Egypt, Nectanebo II). A portion of Alexandria (and other cities) was very Greek. More importantly, Greeks and other foreigners lived up and down Egypt in great numbers and some at first had no intention of Egyptianizing themselves, in the sense of deliberately trying to be assimilated into Egyptian culture. For Egyptians above the lowest levels of society, it became essential to learn Greek, and advantageous to adopt some kind of Greek identity, even if they could not, and perhaps did not wish to, match the culture and status of the Greeks of Alexandria and the few other great Greek cities of Egypt. That is, they could not establish their own gymnasia as foci of education and culture, and seemingly did not want to attempt to construct large-scale 'civic' buildings, such as existed at Hermopolis. Egyptian priests in the temples of the traditional gods on the one hand laboured to maintain Egyptian religion and general culture, with a strong interest in the past, but on the other could switch to a degree of Greek identity. This could be expressed by the use of 'Greek' names as alternatives to Egyptian names, and by an interest in Greek literature (van Minnen 1998).

Ashton (Chapter 10) looks at a problematic group of material, perhaps all from Memphis, which nevertheless has implications for the Egyptians' relationship with foreigners. Petrie published a number of small terracotta heads which he asserted deliberately represented the ethnicities to be found there in the Ptolemaic period. Contrary to this interpretation of the material, ideas that it was foreigners who were being represented are problematic – and so are ideas of manufacture by foreigners. For much of the material, the chief interest lies in what it reveals about the reaction to foreign art, particularly Greek, of Egyptian craftsmen, at a humble level of craftsmanship, while working essentially within Egyptian traditions.

Aside from the issue of the recognition of who was Egyptian and who was a foreigner, it is difficult to find in Egyptian texts any interest in the history of foreign peoples. Clearly the Egyptians must have been well aware that the foreigners they faced changed over time, but this is not directly reflected in written sources, nor commented upon. Manetho allegedly spoke of the Hyksos as a new threat: Josephus claims to quote the actual text of Manetho when writing:

> Tutimaeus. In his reign, for what cause I know not, a blast of God smote us; and unexpectedly, from the regions of the East, invaders of obscure race marched in confidence of victory against our land.
>
> (Waddell 1940: 79)

There is, however, no clear equivalent in Egyptian rhetoric.

When was the past?

Chronology has always haunted traditional Egyptology. Its study has usually aimed at determining at what absolute date BC events happened (above all the beginnings and ends of kings' reigns). Sometimes it is comparative or relative dating that is sought. Notorious examples would be: when was the Exodus, and so who was the 'pharaoh of the Exodus'? and clearly it would be convenient for the analysis of the Amarna period if the co-regency question of various possible overlaps (or none) between the reigns of Amenophis III and IV (Akhenaten) could be resolved.

However, the time-honoured investigation of Egyptian chronology starts (apart from astronomical records) from the tattered remains and reflections of Egyptian king lists, most substantially the Palermo stone, the Turin Canon, and the various traditions derived from the text of Manetho (Loprieno, Chapter 8). Manetho himself wrote in Greek for the royal court in the early Ptolemaic period, allegedly under the direct patronage of Ptolemy II (third century BC), and his work took the form of a history. The earlier Egyptian-language sources could all be seen as belonging within a narrow 'scholarly' tradition specific to Egypt itself. They were celebrations of kingship rather than practical, administrative documents, and their audience would have been the royal court and the priestly elite, and the scribal elite which had a predilection for texts in the form of lists. The Turin Canon and Manetho listed kings in sequence, giving the length of the reign of each. A brief entry for the Kushite dynasty in Manetho, as preserved in Eusebius, reads:

> The twenty-fifth Dynasty consisted of 3 Ethiopian kings
> 1. Sabakôn, who, taking Bochchôris captive, burned him alive, and ruled for 12 years
> 2. Sebichôs, his son, 12 years
> 3. Tarakos, for 20 years
> Total, 44 years
>
> (cf. Waddell 1940: 167)

The Turin Canon recognized the beginning of major epochs by signalling the names of outstanding kings (Malek 1982). It also gave totals for the reign lengths of significant sequences of kings. This raises the question of whether these figures derive from a practical interest in absolute chronology, or relate to the ideas discussed by Uphill (Chapter 2). Other 'eras' fleetingly known include the 'era of Memphis' and the '400 Year Stela'. The '400 Year Stela' found at Tanis (Kitchen 1996: 116–117) states that it was explicitly set up on the orders of Ramesses II "bearing the mighty name of his forefathers, in order to maintain the name of the father of his fathers". It then puzzlingly names Ramesses' immediate predecessor (Seti I), and proceeds extraordinarily with a date in the standard formulation for a royal date: "Year 400, 4th month of Shomu, Day 4", but the 'King' in question is the god Seth (Kitchen trans. 1996). The presentation is problematic, but no doubt Ramesses II is celebrating his immediate two predecessors, and his family line, presented as stemming from the god (a god especially recognized by the Ramessides). How realistic the figure of 400 years was is debatable, but it reveals that there was a tradition of dead reckoning of time from the foundation of Tanis, or from some other significant family event.

Manetho, to judge from the excerpts from his text that survive, divided his listing fundamentally into the dynasties that are still basic terminology today (as in the passage given above). Neither the Turin Canon nor Manetho indicated when they were listing contemporary or overlapping sequences of kings (as is today agreed some must be), and it is difficult to find any indication as to whether the Egyptians were oblivious to this (as we would see it) flaw, or welcomed it, or had other textual resources to circumvent it. Modern scholarship has tried to reconcile or explain away both these problems and also the numerous clearly conflicting statements about the lengths of reigns, a procedure that has sometimes been criticized as unrealistic. One important theme of the present volume, however, is that there were within Egypt traditions of looking at the past other than these scribal practices of compiling 'lists'.

Uphill (Chapter 2) suggests how the Egyptians approached talking about the very remote past (and indeed the very remote future). The time when the god or gods ruled the universe had a long tradition in Egypt. There is a distinction between a vague reference to "the god", and the solemn setting out of a sequence of gods in the manner of a king list. The sections of the Palermo Stone that deal in this way with the rule of gods or demi-gods have often been seen as an embarrassment, and ignored. Throughout dynastic history, texts refer to a time before the rule of conventional kings. The word *pȝwt* "primeval time" is clearly related to the root *pȝw*, "to have done (something) before", that is, to a concept of the past. A brief demotic text of the Ptolemaic period refers to very lengthy reigns of the gods. Classical authors seem to show some awareness of Egyptian ideas of the rule of the gods (Tait 2003: 32–34), although there is the problem as to whether they were in fact imposing Greek ideas.

Uphill suggests that the Sothic cycle could eventually have played a part in Egyptian speculation about the distant past. The actual discourse of cycles for remote eras of time involved the pair of terms *nḥḥ* and *ḏt*. These most frequently occur together as a pair, although not always. They also occur in a restricted number of types of context, which is one way in which the understanding of terms in a dead language can present virtually insoluble problems. They have been discussed on numerous occasions. Otto (1954) considered the Egyptians' concepts of time and their terminology, and the widespread though problematic view that the Egyptians, more than other cultures, had a special tendency to perceive time in terms of repeated cycles. Otto regarded *nḥḥ* as signifying 'recurring time', while *dt* signified 'unchanging time', an interpretation often debated since (e.g. Assmann 1975, 1983; Zabkar 1965). Otto (1960, 1964) was an especial protagonist of the idea that the Egyptians had a dualistic view of the world, while Englund (1987; cf. Westendorf 1975: 183–184) suggested that a male-female contrast between *nḥḥ* (grammatically masculine) and *dt* (grammatically feminine) was fundamental to Egyptian thought. Hornung (1965) regarded it as mistaken to try to see any meaningful distinction between the terms, although he attempted to suggest an etymology for *dt* ('horizon'). Iversen (1963), in discussing Horapollo's comments on the Egyptians' use of snakes to signify "eternity" and "the whole universe", pointed out that *dt* can have a hieroglyph for 'land' as its determinative. Thus yet another view is that *dt* refers to space, while *nḥḥ* refers to time (Westendorf 1975, 1983). This does not exhaust the catalogue of interpretations, let alone the bibliography. Some discussions have concentrated on the evidence of just one kind of text, and it is far from impossible that the terms (together or apart) might have been used in different senses in different contexts. In considering *conscious* Egyptian reflections upon the immensity of time, Uphill (Chapter 2) suggests that here a past-future distinction is appropriate, a conceptual application not extending before the creation or after the end of the created world. These terms gave the overall context in which the Egyptians saw what we regard as their 'historical' past (Assmann 1975; Kákosy 1978).

The 'eras' mentioned above are not hints of practical schemes for reckoning past time, but belong in the same category as official, religious, priestly, and royal texts. This is well exemplified by the '400 Year Stela', which served the interests of the prestige of the Ramessides. Documentary texts and narratives may not accurately report the speech of daily life, even in the case of the simplest and briefest phrases. However, they suggest, at least, that the Egyptians may in real life have spoken freely of events 'two years ago' or 'six years ago', where 'year' presumably means a period of 365 days, but that counting back substantially larger numbers of years was not normal. Official texts could refer to quite recent dates by the formal apparatus of regnal years. Notoriously, Akhenaten complains

> It was worse than those which I heard in regnal year 4
> It was worse than [those] which I heard in regnal year 3
> It was worse than those which I heard in regnal year 2
> It was worse than [those which I heard in regnal year 1]

He then states that three predecessors had not heard worse, concluding "[It was] worse [than] those heard by any kings who had assumed the White Crown" (Amarna Boundary Stelae K, X and M: Murnane 1995a: 78). In the 'Demotic Chronicle', Darius is said to have ordered the recording of Egyptian law "down to regnal year 44 of Amasis" (that is, barely a year before the Persian take-over) (Spiegelberg 1914: 30–32).

In the demotic 'First Setna Story', Setna seeks, on behalf of a long dead magician, to discover the location of the tomb, long lost from view, that contains the bodies of the magician's wife and son. He encounters an aged priest (in fact the magician himself), and addresses him:

... Setna said to the old man 'You have the look of an aged man: do you know the tomb in which lie Ahwera and her son Merib?' The old man said to Setna 'The father of the father of my father said to the father of my father that the father of the father of his father said to the father of his father "The tomb of Ahwera and her son Merib is at the south corner of the house of the chief of police"'.

(First Setna 6.10–6.13)

The location in time of Setna as a son of Ramesses II seems secure in the story. However, just how far back in the past the magician he encounters was supposed to have lived is problematic. The magician's father was a king, named as Mernebptah; Loprieno (Chapter 8) mentions the general problems of the names given to kings in later literature. This passage from 'First Setna' raises the question of the use of counting generations and of the use of genealogy in viewing the past. Unlike the attitude in many cultures, the Egyptians do not appear to have attached great importance to being able to give a detailed account of their ancestry. Of course, kings often needed to be able to legitimize themselves by showing lists of their predecessors, a kind of genealogy, either in great detail, as in full king lists, or in summary, concentrating upon the most famous figures of the past. However, outside royalty, Egyptians seem to have concerned themselves mostly with their most recent ancestors, one, two, or perhaps three generations at most. This changed over time: the stating of a genealogy became increasingly common through the Late Period. However, it was not until the Roman Period that, for example, a need to prove priestly descent was required in order to be accepted by the administration as a priest – or at any rate, as a priest qualified to gain from priestly tax concessions.

Questions about the perception of time itself are raised by Loprieno (Chapter 8). His discussion raises the issue of multiple ideas of where people or events lie in the past. He writes of the 'multilayered' structure of a narrative. This is one approach that may bring some order to the understanding of many Egyptian texts and their reflections in classical (and perhaps later) writers.

Text and memory

One factor contributing to the difficulties in understanding how the Egyptians knew about their own past is that textual material survives from Ancient Egypt in relatively small quantities. The quantity may seem generous in comparison with material from, say, the rest of north Africa in the same periods, but appears meagre in comparison with that from Mesopotamia. More importantly, the Egyptian material survives in a very uneven fashion. Any kind of inscription upon stone has survived the risk of re-use as building material or (in the case of limestone) the limekiln purely by accident. The everyday writing materials, papyrus and ostraca, are not normally found at settlement sites until the Greco-Roman period, when the material preserved becomes abundant, although often fragmentary. Papyrus from earlier periods survives when it has been stored or thrown away at the dry desert margins, and ostraca require almost equally special conditions if the ink is not to be lost from the surface. The unevenness of survival comprises both time and space. Little from any period has been discovered from within the Delta itself, while western Thebes is heavily over-represented. There is sparse evidence from the Libyan period, and puzzlingly little from the first Persian

Period (and see Aston 1999). In consequence, it is unsafe to assert that a type of text or a particular idea did not exist, just because no trace of it has survived. There are many examples of Egyptian literary texts that, as far as is known, have been preserved in only a single copy: for example, from the Middle Kingdom, the 'Shipwrecked Sailor' (Morenz, Chapter 6); or many narratives of the later New Kingdom; or the 'Tale of Woe' from the Third Intermediate Period (Caminos 1977); or the demotic 'Second Setna' story from the early Roman Period (Griffith 1900; Lichtheim 1980: 138–151). Indeed, the 'Tale of Woe' could be seen as the solitary surviving example of a whole genre, and similarly only a single known demotic hymn is in poetical (that is, verse) form (Zauzich 1991). Nevertheless it is possible to make general statements about developments and trends (Assmann 2001; Baines 1989b).

It is virtually inconceivable that oral traditions of tales and songs – and religious and magical material – did not exist in Egypt. Even though the indications are very slight (cf. Morenz, Chapter 6), it is simply assumed here that literary works may derive, more or less closely, from oral traditions, or may self-consciously exploit the manner or material of oral tradition (cf. Baines 1990b; Morenz, Chapter 6). It is also perfectly likely that a literary work crosses over into oral tradition (e.g. 'Thousand and One Nights' stories which, after being fixed in written form, later became a staple of coffee-house story tellers). Some of the possible complexities of the situation may be judged from the Inaros-Petubastis stories (Tait 1994), where there is a clear awareness of the fragmented nature of the country in the ninth to seventh centuries BC, from a period perhaps some 500 years before the stories assumed anything like their surviving form.

Some have seen in Egyptian narrative texts a somewhat cavalier and/or confused attitude to the past. For the periods down to the Late Period as well as in demotic narratives, ammunition for this kind of view can be seen from the fact that kings' names may be distorted, and chronology may be very vague (Fischer-Elfert, Chapter 7; Loprieno, Chapter 8; Morenz, Chapter 6). There is no attempt to place the stories within precise historical settings or exploit known events in the past. Thus, although Kitchen (1973: 455–461) and others have tried to trace what real similarities there are to the political shape of the Delta in the Late Period literature as compared to actual political events, no one has tried to argue that one particular period is consistently portrayed. The texts used memories of the Third Intermediate Period as a suitable setting for stories that commented on the nature of Egyptian culture and religion of the current time. When the texts reached written form, and possibly when they first took shape, the problems preoccupying those who thought of themselves as Egyptians were not a divided country, nor foreign enemies, nor a king who could scarcely keep his own elite supporters under control, as portrayed in the texts, but a country firmly under foreign rule, and a threat to their culture from foreign cultures. Clearly, those among whom these stories circulated had not consulted texts such as king lists carelessly; they had constructed a detailed past on the basis of a memory of history.

Herodotus frequently reported that he had been "told" things in Egypt, often specifically by priests (Lloyd 1975: 89–100), and for the remoter past the kind of information he gained seems to be of the same kind as can be seen in the demotic stories. The connection between some of the substantial tales in Herodotus and

Egyptian literature has long been suggested (Griffith 1900). Memories of the past can survive for long periods: it is not necessary for a whole population, or indeed even any large proportion of it, to keep a remembered past alive. It can survive, waiting to be called upon when needed.

Archaism

The modern recognition of archaism in Egyptian art began with material of the Saite Period, where the mechanics of copying past works was most evident. The word is often now used as a kind of technical term to refer to the nature of the art specifically of the Kushite and Saite Periods, when the very widespread imitation of an enormous range of past sculpture, relief and architecture is wholly apparent. For example, Robins (1997) does not raise the issue of archaism in her general study of Egyptian art until her chapter on the Late Period. A significant problem in studying archaism in the Late Period is the continuing uncertainty over the dating of the evidence, particularly sculpture. Although confusions are not as great as they were before the publication of Bothmer (1960b), if the Egyptians were continually referring to works of the past, with no continuous tradition of internal development in its archaizing work, then difficulties of dating some un-provenanced works must continue to be insurmountable. In the Saite period, works of the past were clearly studied in detail, but the general tendency was to reinterpret and to adapt. In the Ptolemaic period, there was probably a greater inclination to copy (Ashton, Chapter 12). This could be seen as some Egyptians wishing under foreign rule not only to keep Egyptian culture alive, but also to preserve it. Throughout the later periods, there are real issues as to whether a feature of art was taken from the Egyptian past or borrowed from abroad: Smith and Simpson (1998: 232) seriously consider whether the heavy musculature of much Kushite period statuary and relief might be borrowed from Assyrian art rather than from Egyptian exemplars; and Ashton mentions similar debates for the Ptolemaic period; Thissen (1999) has discussed the nature of possible foreign 'influences' on Egyptian literature of the Greco-Roman period.

Morkot (Chapter 5) takes the debate on archaism back into the New Kingdom, while Wildung (Chapter 4) compares practice over the Middle and New Kingdoms. Yet another problem for dating is the re-use and the usurpation of earlier work, typically sculpture, which is essentially transportable (Ashton, Chapter 12; Wildung, Chapter 4). There is perhaps little difference to be seen between temple sculpture and the more portable case of heirlooms (Jeffreys, Chapter 11). In sculpture, sometimes the traces of previous inscriptions, particularly royal names, are plain, but sometimes the obliteration has been complete. In these cases, the grounds for dating the original work may be straightforward, but there are instances where uncertainty remains (Wildung, Chapter 4). Such re-uses of material could be explained as simply based upon a wish to save the effort of making a new piece; however there are several grounds for doubting that this is a satisfactory explanation. Thus, Wildung points out that statues were sometimes displayed without any change to their inscriptions. Re-use appears chiefly to occur at times of prosperity and regeneration, when royal resources could presumably have best been able to order new work. An element of royal display was precisely the ability to overcome the difficulties of quarrying in the

Egyptian deserts, and to fetch home quantities of significant minerals. In some cases, it therefore seems highly likely that there was a wish to gain legitimacy from an association with the past (just as also with the repeated location of pyramids close to the Step Pyramid of Djoser at North Saqqarah, and even the several instances of the re-adoption of the pyramid form as tombs). In other cases, the intention may have been to affirm that the present matched or surpassed the glories of the past. These two ideas were, of course, not mutually exclusive.

Archaism does not require a long past to explore. Some Ptolemaic sculpture looks back to the very recent past (Ashton, Chapter 12), while Davis (Chapter 3) explores the very meaning of the concept, and takes as a case study the famous wooden panels from the tomb of Hesy-Ra at North Saqqarah, of early Old Kingdom date. The panels offer unique opportunities. There are five relatively well-preserved examples, from a secure context, but showing the work of more than one artist, and there is roughly contemporary work to compare. The use of archaism and modernism in such a tomb may have had different intentions from the essentially royal uses of archaism usually discussed in the literature. Davis presents a set of possible scenarios which could have applied at different moments in the perception of the panels as seen by different viewers. His examples also raise wider questions concerning archaism in Egyptian funerary practice in general. In tomb-scenes, specific borrowing from ancient models is one phenomenon, but notoriously it is an idealized world that is always depicted.

Conclusions

That the Egyptians made deliberate use of the past is beyond all doubt. It was clearly embedded in central features of Egyptian culture. It appears that a view of the creation of the cosmos, the divine ordering of the world, and the king's role as intermediary between the sphere of the gods and that of the Egyptian people, and all humankind, was crucial. The core of this worldview remained unchanged until the last traditional Egyptian temple had closed. This mythical perspective led directly to a feature that plays an important part in most of the contributions to this volume. In theory, every king who could claim to be the Horus (and, for most of dynastic history, son of the sun god) was the equal of any other. His essential role was to maintain the smooth running of the cosmos in the manner the gods intended. He was not ordained to achieve anything new or different. It so happens that we have evidence of rulers who clearly *did* attempt something different, notoriously Hatshepsut and the Amarna kings, and to varying extents they were both reviled and written out of history. To set against this are numerous royal assertions of having achieved more than their predecessors, or of having done something that had never been done by anyone in the past. Perhaps the earliest royal example is Sesostris III's claim in the Semna Stela of year 16 (in a problematic phrase) "I have gone further south than my forefathers". That particular assertion on that occasion could be seen as justifiable. It is fitted into the broader myth of the king's role, as Sesostris' achievements are ascribed to the will and the assistance of the god: "As my father (the sun god) lives for me ...", he swore. This approach was universally – and even more explicitly – taken by later kings. However, other boasts, such as Hatshepsut's claim that her Punt expedition was the first ever, bore no relation to reality. If the Egyptians had taken a *purely* cyclical view of the past, it would have been possible to appeal to a supposed unchanging past only in order to lament or oppose present change. The Egyptians did of course also do this. Yet a consistent feature is the recognition that some kings were more significant than others. By the Late Period, some of these figures were invented, but this type of view of the past remained essentially the same. Another factor is the apparently monolithic institution of scribal training and practice in Egypt. Although the cuneiform tradition was equally, if not more, impressive, the Egyptian had many distinctive features. The Egyptian scribes constructed their own view of the history of the role of scribes and of the 'authorship' of texts. By the Late Period, the tradition was entirely maintained by members of temple elites, which profoundly affected the kind of past that was sought for.

The reasons for shifts over time in the view of the past are complex and debatable – they cannot be detached from broader developments in Egyptian society. If it is appropriate to look for particular causes of change at any one time, then these must concern political and social change. From at least as early as the Kushite period, it became a strain to adhere to the traditional view of Egypt's foreign enemies, and the king's role towards them. Similarly, foreigners had their own histories, and their own concepts of the past. It was evident that the position of Egypt as central to the whole cosmos could no longer be taken for granted. It was necessary to convince foreigners of the value of the Egyptian past; worse still, it had to be protected even within priestly communities who saw themselves as Egyptian.

The whole phrase "Never had the like occurred ..." (and its many variants), although formulaic and usually divorced from reality, itself reveals an expectation that it should be possible to know about the past, and even the remote past. This book reveals a constant tension between these two ideas: first, that knowledge of the past was problematic – P. Westcar (the 'Tales of the Magicians'), a manuscript dating from before the New Kingdom but a story set firmly in the Old Kingdom, has Prince Hardedef complaining of the stories of magicians of the past (as opposed to a magician of the present day) that "one cannot distinguish truth from falsehood". Second, the view that the past was accessible: that it had left monuments, and that it had been recorded. How it had been recorded, and what questions should be asked of it, were matters specific to Egyptian culture.

CHAPTER 2

THE ANCIENT EGYPTIAN VIEW OF WORLD HISTORY

E. P. Uphill

Broadly speaking we recover human history backwards.

(Glanville 1942: xiii)

This conclusion, expressed many years ago, is not only true of information relating to history and prehistory when derived from archaeology or related studies, such as astronomy, but can be detected in the methods employed by ancient peoples when reconstructing their origins.

In fact the Egyptians, like the Babylonians and, indeed, modern astronomers, clearly worked backwards in time from fixed points observed from star positions. Meyer's old premise that the date 4241 BC in prehistory marked the first 'historical' date when expressed as a calendric feature is unwarranted, as is Pliny's statement (*Historia naturalis* VII.193) citing Epigenes:

> Epigenes, a most important author, teaches that among the Babylonians, observations about the movements of the stars have been preserved on baked clay tablets for 720,000 years. Berossos and Kritodemos, however, give a shorter period, 490,000 years.

Neither Meyer's postulated Sothic date nor Pliny's vastly earlier one were, in reality, derived from contemporary astronomical observations, but were both projections backwards in time. As Pliny himself said, such calculations had been recorded over a long period of time in Mesopotamia, but not during these remote periods of prehistoric myth. These great totals of years are merely postulated datings designed to cover the phases of human development envisaged by the Sumerians as having elapsed after the creation of the world. These ages were represented in the Sumerian King List by either eight or 10 antediluvian kings, according to the version favoured by the scribal copyists. The lengths of these fabulous reigns also varied, that of the first ruler, called Aloros of Babylon by Berossos, lasting for 10 *sars*, or 36,000 years, while the traditional list calls him Alulium of Eridu, and accords him only 28,800 years. Hence there is a large discrepancy in the dynastic totals, the list used by Berossos having 10 kings ruling 120 *sars*, or 432,000 years, in all, and the shorter Sumerian list of eight kings aggregating only 241,200 years. From an analysis of these figures each of the rulers was given a reign whose total duration was computed in round numbers of *sars*, or units of 3,600 years. This system of counting is thus not even really cyclic but purely arbitrary reckoning in round numbers.

By contrast, the period of 24,510 years after the Flood that was accorded to the First Dynasty of Kish that followed this event is no longer set in round numbers of years, but is also comparable in length to the 23,200 + x years given in the Turin Canon as the period when the gods and prehistoric kings ruled in Egypt before King Menes. How this total was arrived at is not known, but there seems to be some indication that the method used may have been by projecting back in time from a fixed point in history. If so then this method, when used in Egypt, most probably used Sothic cycles as units for measuring this great time span.

The use of other means of calculating long periods of time by means such as 'precession' has been suggested by some writers (cf. Sellers 1992), but has not as yet proved to have been used by the Egyptians. Precession is caused by the conical motion of the earth's axis, which traces a circle on the heavens and is directed to different Pole stars through many millennia as the visible sky changes. As the point of indication moves westward where the equator cuts across the path of the sun (the ecliptic), the positions of all the stars change, hence the point is described as 'precessing'. The time taken to complete a circuit round the full circumference of the sky, or 360°, is therefore called a 'Great Year' or a 'Precessional Year'. The length of this Great Year is equal to 25,920 ordinary solar years. The most convincing case for the ancients having understood precession before its discovery by Hipparchus in ca. 146 BC is that advanced by Sellers, who cites reasons for believing knowledge of it preceded this date. Despite her important evidence relating to star charts found in the Theban royal tombs, the case for actually dating events forwards or backwards in time by such means is as yet unconfirmed by any textual evidence.

She also makes the point that the Precessional Year length would apparently not be the same as in modern estimates, due to certain factors relating to Hipparchus' observations. Consequently, even allowing that the Egyptians or Babylonians had some knowledge of such a long period, their estimates, like that of Hipparchus, must have been different, thereby rendering any system using modern estimates unworkable.

It is safer to assume at present that dating involving long periods was arrived at by means of observing the rising of Sirius. This view is supported by the fact that a number of these Sothic observations have survived after being recorded on Egyptian documents from widely different periods.

The Sothic cycle therefore remains the most probable method used by the Egyptians for back-dating historical events, and especially phases of prehistory. But in using dates based on such a Sothic cycle framework, it is very important to remember first that the place where observations were taken affects the year reading to a certain extent, and second that the Egyptians, like other ancient peoples, were not as accurate in these observations and resultant calculations as modern observers. Hence, as Parker (1950) pointed out, if the writer of the Old Chronicle as cited by Syncellus is to be believed (Waddell 1940), a cycle of exactly 1,460 years followed by an intercalated year was used to adjust the calendar, not the cycles of 1,456 and 1,458 years he himself suggested as the lengths of the last two known ones. Using the possible terminal date supplied by Censorinus for the final cycle, that is, AD 139, the previous cycles would have ended in 1322 BC and 2782 BC following the uniform 1,460 year period. But since

Sirius itself is moving, then allowing for this factor, Parker suggested that 1317 BC and 2773 BC would be more accurate readings in real astronomical terms.

But there is no uniformity even among present-day writers as to the precise dates that cycles began. In a recent study reviewing the evidence, Depuydt (1997) gives an update on the relevant material and cites the computations made by Ingham (1969) as regards fixing the dates when Sothis (Sirius) rose at the time of the New Year. These assume that if the rising was seen on the Egyptian New Year's day in AD 139, it would be observed at the beginning of the new year 1,452 years earlier, in or about 1314 BC, and 1,454 years earlier, in about 2768 BC. If so, in 1314 BC the new year, i.e. *ȝḥt 1*, fell in modern terms on 18 July 1314 BC, and 16 July in 2768 BC. These figures give an eight year and 14 year difference to those of the Old Chronicle system. It is therefore suggested that, to the Egyptian historians writing in later periods, while the last used cycle ended in either AD 139 or AD 143, the margin of discrepancy for the periods covered by the previous one may have increased. Prior to the date of commencement of the earlier cycle, ranging from a traditional 2782 BC to a lower postulated 2768 BC, it is not certain what system was used for long-period dating as in the Turin Canon or Manetho, but it would have been possible for historians to have projected backwards using a perfectly logical extension of the cyclical system.

If this was the case then a whole series of preceding Sothic cycles could have been used to cover the period now termed predynastic and prehistoric Egypt. Given this possibility, the modern datings of 2773 BC or 2768 BC, if adopted as a basis for counting, require all dates prior to this time to be adjusted for the Early Dynastic period, albeit this makes very little difference to periods prior to the unification of the Two Lands.

How, then, was this fixed date of either 2773 BC or 2768 BC arrived at? It would seem from the evidence of a late period text at the temple of Edfu, that a war took place between what are termed the Seth people and the Horus rulers, in what is referred as the 363rd year of the "Era of Horakhti". As the famous High Priest Imhotep is shown reading an account of this event, it must have preceded his time. Some Egyptologists have seen in this a reference to wars recorded on statues of King Khasekhemui of the second Dynasty, and thus originating during his reign, or up to 28 years before the establishment of the third Dynasty under which Imhotep functioned (Sewell 1942).

Significantly, in the context of this era linked to the sun god and thus perhaps having a solar or astronomical derivation, the Palermo Stone Annals also record the periodic celebration of a Festival of *ḏt* or Eternity, enacted at what would seem to have been regular intervals.

The first of these festivals took place in year nine of a king whose name is missing, but whose year entries are the first surviving ones post the unification of Egypt. It has been generally taken that this ruler could have been either King Aha or King Djer, his successor, the second or third kings of united Egypt. Allowing this to be so, figures of reign lengths derived from Manetho would indicate a period of up to 62 years covering the reign of Menes (Narmer) – the first king is missing on the stone. Or, if other versions of Manetho are followed that give shorter reigns of only 30 years for Menes and 27, not 57, years for his successor, then a period of nearly 60 years is indicated. The position on the stone shows that if restored, the year of the festival would come at approximately 70 years from the beginning of the line recording first Dynasty regnal years.

Two other Djet festivals are recorded later in the Palermo Stone Annals, one of which fell in the later first Dynasty period and is called the second one, while the last surviving entry has its number missing but is dated to the reign of King Nineter in the earlier part of the second Dynasty. No more festivals are recorded in the Annals from the time of the third Dynasty onwards, nor elsewhere in contemporary inscriptions, suggesting that it had ceased to have any significance later.

If this festival equates with the Era of Horakhti as suggested, then it is probable that year 365 of the Era dating may not only have fallen in the reign of Khasekhemui, but also near to the beginning of the Sothic cycle running from 2773 or 2768 BC. Seventeen kings are recorded for the first two dynasties of Egypt, of whom Khasekhemui was the last, their reign totals, where known, suggesting an aggregate of between 300 and 400 years. A generation average of 22 years would indicate a duration of 374 years for both dynasties, a total very close to the years accorded to this Era of Horakhti. Thus the inauguration of a calendric system related to Horakhti, and perhaps termed _dt_ because it was linked with "Eternity", may have taken place at the time of the accession of Menes or else his unification of Egypt. A periodic festival celebrated every 71 to 72 years, allowing some possible odd months and days added at the beginning and end of the missing reigns in the Annals, allows five of these to have been held in a period of 360 years. If the interval was 73 years, or with a 72-year gap between the actual years of each festival, a total of 365 years would elapse. Hence the addition of a quarter of a day would make exactly one quarter of a Sothic cycle of 1,460 years.

The first full day after this quarter cycle would have inaugurated the first full cycle to be used for dating. In fact this quarter cycle might represent a period of trial and adjustment instituted at the beginning of Egyptian history, in order to perfect the subsequent system of Sothic dating, and correct other calendars in use earlier.

Another possibility is that the calendric system represented by the Era of Horakhti, and instituted by Menes for use in his kingdoms of Upper and Lower Egypt, had fallen into abeyance due to civil wars at the end of the second Dynasty which may have interrupted astronomical observations. If so, then at some period after the fifth (?) _dt_ festival, Khasekhemui renewed the taking of observations by starting the cycles in use in later pharaonic times. Or this abandonment of the earlier Era method could have been due to both of these factors.

Once such a system was firmly established, the Egyptians would possess a perfect method for projecting backwards into the past to explain chronologically periods of development pre-Menes. On this method the date for the beginning of the first Dynasty would be fixed by adding 365 years to 2782, giving 3147 BC as the traditional time, or, if added to 2773, then 3138 BC, and added to 2768, then 3133 BC, as the modern projected dates. That this date must be lowered if the reigns of the kings of the first two dynasties amounted to less than this total does not, of course, affect the traditional dating. Recent C14 dating for materials dated to the beginning of the first Dynasty tend to confirm a dating around 3150 BC.

Working backwards, the Egyptian figures for the number of years covered by the preceding predynastic and prehistoric periods must now be examined. For the period after the rule of the gods, the Turin Canon (Gardiner 1959: pl. I, I–II) lists an age designated as the rule of the Spirits or Horus, and following them, government by specific different parts of Egypt. To this phase it allots a total of 13,420 years plus a small number of missing single years, the entry being damaged, as opposed to the rather more precise but lesser figure of 11,025 years in Manetho (see Table I, p. 27 for a breakdown on this figure). The Turin Canon total is in fact very close to 9½ Sothic cycles of 1,460–1,461 years, i.e. 13,505 years, a difference of 80 years at most.

Following on from this, the total number of years for the combined rule of the gods and these later dynasties is given in the Turin Canon as 23,200 + x years. This total is close to 16 cycles, or 23,376 years, a difference of about 170 years. Given the damaged state of the papyrus as regards a whole number of these prehistoric period entries, these totals could have been even closer.

Going further back in time, it is clear from many Egyptian textual references that this period – termed the rule of the gods – has nothing to do with their own ages or that of the universe itself, but only relates to settled life in Egypt and on earth generally. Gods like Horus were considered to be millions of years old, as is proved by a number of references in the 'Book of the Dead'. Typical of these is the following: "Horus the son of Isis and the son of Osiris has repeated millions of Sed-festivals" (Allen 1974: 35). Given the use of the plural for the number millions, this must denote at least three of them. As a heb-sed, or jubilee, was normally celebrated after 30 years, and repeated after that at three-year intervals if the king lived long enough, then the total years indicated must be very great. In fact, it implies a figure of either three or more million 30-year periods, or at least 90,000,000, or a minimum total of three million times three years, or 9,000,000 years.

This huge total of years constitutes but a moment in time when compared with the stupendous duration accorded to the god Atum and the universes he personified. In P. Ani the owner as an Osiris figure asks what shall be the length of his future lifetime, and Atum answers him thus (Allen 1974: 184; Budge 1913, 1: pl. 29, 2: 563–564; Wilson 1969: 9): "Thou art (destined) for millions of millions (of years), a lifetime of millions." The god then adds what will be the end of all life and the entire cosmos: "I have caused that he send out the Elders. And I will destroy all that I have made; this land shall return into Nun, into the floodwaters, as it was in its first state. I (alone) shall survive together with Osiris, when I have made my form in another state, serpents which men know not and gods do not see" (see also Allen 2003).

The meaning of this at times obscure text can be seen to link the soul of the deceased to the creator god and the physical earth and universe in its cycle of creation and destruction. Like Atum, Osiris, here representing the dead, is destined to survive the return of the physical elements to the primordial waters, or god Nun, from whom Atum and the universe came forth, and then undergo a transformation into cosmic serpents perhaps analogous to Mehen, or the 'Great Encircler' snake, shown coiled round the shrine of the sun god in the barque 'Millions of Years'.

Given that Atum is destined to exist in modern terminology for a trillion years into the future on this reckoning, it may be inferred that the Egyptian scribes considered that he had already lived for a comparable time in the past, otherwise how could such aeons of time have been computed? As already shown, Horus was considered to be millions or even tens of millions of years old, so logically the creator of the cosmos, Atum, must have far exceeded him in duration at the time that these texts were written. This vast lifetime accorded to the universe and its creator seems to have been divided into phases of active development of life followed by dormant periods. Scenes frequently depicted in the tombs in the Valley of the Kings and contemporary funerary papyri relate the passage of the sun god across the sky and through the underworld, with the passage of the soul of the deceased to future heavenly life (Figure 2:1 col. pl.). The scene showing the great serpent Mehen referred to above can best be explained by Spell 131 in the 'Book of the Dead' texts. It is captioned "Spell for existing beside Ra", thereby making the link between the dead and the sun god in his voyaging (Allen 1974: 107 n. 222; cp. Faulkner 1977: 290). "This encircler-snake is millions, even two millions in length starboard to port."

At first reading this figure might appear to indicate length in cubits or even *iteru* measures, an *iter* being a river measure of approximately 10.5 kilometres or 20,000 cubits. Against this rendering is the fact that the text goes on to refer to the "ways of fire", recalling the more complete texts accompanying a mysterious scene painted on the coffin of the twelfth Dynasty general Sepi. Here, the text written round the ovals showing these roads of fire separated by parallel concentric rings of darkness suggests, as Faulkner thought, that years rather than linear measures were intended (Lacau 1914: 170–199). "The paths of fire. These paths guard the larboard side of the 'Coiled One', who makes a circle in a million after a million (years)."

This can only refer to the great serpent associated with the god Ra-Atum and the cosmos itself, with whom the dead person's soul would join in the solar barque, participating in a long voyage that was perhaps a duplication of his daily one across the sky. The latter journey involved a following trip through the underworld during the hours of night; here it may represent a much more vast cosmic journey undertaken through the universe, which took two million years to complete.

In the centre of the Sepi scene a god is shown seated on his throne holding a sceptre denoting power in his right hand, and the sign of life in his lowered left hand. This deity, identified as an Osiris figure wearing the Atef crown by Lacau (1914: 170–199), but as Ra by Faulkner (1977), is certainly linked with the future life of Sepi. Alongside the ankh-sign (Figure 2:2) is written "millions", thus denoting "millions of years of life". Three 'million' signs are also written on the god's throne, also suggesting millions of years. Round the periphery of this scene run four red cartouche-shaped oval rings (alternating with rings of other colours), indicating the ways of fire. The inference from this would possibly be that a journey round one of the rings took a million years to complete along the left side, followed by another million years along the right. The four rings therefore denote that these journeys were repeated a number of times, each one lasting "a million after a million years". In one such period lasting half the circuit, or "day", the earth produced life in the form of flora, fauna and human beings, while in the other half, or "night", it would have lain dormant.

If one of these circuits took two million years to complete, we can comprehend how the immense totals of years relating to future life-spans were reckoned as lasting a million of a million years. While probably coincidental, the Egyptians believed the

Figure 2:2   Detail of the painted wooden coffin of general Sepi of the twelfth Dynasty from el-Bersheh (Cairo Museum 28083; ht. 69 cm). The deity is shown holding the sign of life and is seated on a throne bearing the signs of 'millions of years', surrounded by circles of fire.

sun's daily circuit that was completed during the night by a journey underground from west to east would have to be repeated 532,900 times during a Sothic cycle lasting 1,460 years. In other words, if each journey was expanded to two million years' duration, a total of just over one million million years would elapse before this gigantic cycle would terminate.

Whatever may have been the exact belief of the Egyptians about these great periods of time, the duration of Atum must have been considered by them to have resembled that of the god Brahma in ancient Indian religious texts. Brahma also had his life reckoned in countless millions of years, and, like Atum, not only created the physical universe, but was identified with it, and thought to exist alongside it.[1] A recent analysis by Cremo (1999) expresses these important points very clearly. As he says, according to Hindu belief: "life is only manifest on earth during the day of Brahma." This concept is further reinforced, "With the onset of Brahma's night the entire universe is devastated and plunged in darkness. When another day begins life again becomes manifest". This cyclic scheme of creation followed by darkness and destruction seems to be an almost exact parallel to that indicated by the Egyptian accounts in relation to Ra-Atum. When it is remembered that a "day" of Brahma is the equivalent of 4,320,000,000 human years, the resemblances to the passages from the 'Book of the Dead' are striking. The end of the god Atum and the reversion of the universe to the primal waters of Nun find a close analogy in the Indian universe ending in destruction by both fire and water.

Other parallels abound, thus whereas ordinary Indian deities were considered to have lives in which one of their years was equal to 360 human years, the *kalpa* or "day" of Brahma was reckoned as lasting for a period very similar to current estimates of the earth's age. These shorter divine life-spans recall the periods associated with the lesser deities who succeeded the eight great gods ruling on earth in Egyptian mythology, and also the ages occupied by demi-gods, or Spirits of Horus, that followed. Another similar tradition in Indian beliefs sets each Brahma's life-span at exactly 100 years, each of which comprised all 360 *kalpa* days, or a 15-figure total of human years.

In Ancient Egypt also, even the immense duration of Atum and the universe may not have been their complete vision of cosmic development. In India there was thought to be a series of Brahmas and associated universes, and the gods Siva and Vishnu were later considered to have a much greater duration, apparently running concurrently with them. Similarly, some Egyptian texts refer to the god Ra-Atum becoming aged and unable to function effectively. This is shown in the story of the Duel of Horus and Seth when the god Baba said to the presiding Pre'-Harakhti: "your shrine is empty", meaning his power was no longer evident. Even more revealing is the story of how Isis found out the secret name of Ra, of whom it is said, "a divine old age had loosened his mouth. He cast his spittle upon the ground and spat it out, fallen upon the earth". Like Atum spewing out Shu (Air) and Tefnut (Moisture) when creating the universe, this spittle is the source of power, in that Isis moulded it with the earth to make a poisonous snake. The snake bites Ra and poisons him. To effect his cure the god tells Isis his name. This legend shows Ra-Atum as being old, while texts in the New Kingdom royal tombs might suggest that the god was thought to be reborn at the end of each universe, in other words, that there are a series of such creations.

The Papyrus of Ra has a version of Spell 175 that increases the hoped-for future life of the owner by a million times. The deceased interrogates Thoth and Atum and is then told: "Osiris N shall exist as thou exist, he shall endure as thou endurest, his (years) are like thy years and *vice versa* on earth for a million of a million of a million (years)" (Naville 1886: 1, pls. cxcviii–ix). Naville (1886: 100) noted that the deceased here interrogates Thoth then Atum, here described as deities "who are both coming into existence as the children of Nut". The specific link with the sky or heaven here gives it a cosmic significance, apparently intended to be applied to the dead man's soul now thought to be in heaven.

This immense total could have been arrived at by simply multiplying the smaller previously quoted total a million times, but if it was a cyclic progression it could have been arrived at by multiplying the total by another Sothic cycle of days and nights. In other words, a duration reaching $1,000,000 \times 532,900 \times 2 \times 532,900 \times 2$ in all.

Such immense periods of future life for the soul of the dead person may seem to be, in some senses, mere abstractions, like the ages accorded to some Bodhisattvas living on a spiritual plane (Agrawal *et al.* 1999). These mythical figures had life-spans resembling the great temporal periods accorded in Indian beliefs to the gods and universe. Their ages could therefore reach to as much as 10^{32} years in length. But the condition of being on a spiritual level may not apply to Egyptian belief regarding the lives of deities such as Atum or the universes co-existent with him. The texts suggest that a long sequence of creations may have been considered to have taken place in the aeons before the present time, and also to be continuing into the future for a stupendous number of years.

These immense spans of time, however, do not express in the ultimate sense the solution to the problem of duration. To do this the Egyptians used two words, *dt* and *nhh*, meaning eternity. These are often coupled together in a manner suggesting that one leads to the other, i.e. *dt r nhh* "Eternity to Eternity", rather along the lines of present day "For ever and ever", but with a clear separation, unlike the modern phrase. On examination of the many examples of this frequently used phrase, it appears that the Egyptians generally used *dt* to stand for past eternity, and *nhh*, by contrast, for 'future eternity', and thus followed a logical sequence in the statement. Their meaning can be shown by several representative examples. First, the very often used epithet applied to the king when seen in company with the gods, *di ˁnh mi Rˁ dt*, "given life like Ra forever", demonstrates the past meaning and application of this kind of eternity. From the context, it has already been awarded to the king in addition to the god who already possessed it. Whether the king's "past eternity" comprised the whole of past time, as did the god's, or was simply a small part of it that had been given at a certain period in his life, is not entirely clear. Either of these gifts could have been intended, but in both cases the meaning must denote past and completed life at the present time of reference. A typical example of this statement can be found on a re-used Middle Kingdom granite sphinx usurped by Ramesses II and later kings: "Ramessu given life like Ra forever, on the throne of Atum" (Uphill 1984: 94). As the living representative of Horus on earth, and also as the "Son of the Sun God", it is logical to assume that the reigning pharaoh had also existed in spirit form since the beginning of time.

Two further scenes from the temple of Queen Hatshepsut at Deir el-Bahri help to clarify the distinction. A representation in the Anubis shrine shows Tuthmosis III before Sokar, a god who is a funerary deity and thus associated with the future life of the deceased here. Sokar says to the young pharaoh: "I give to thee the celebrating of millions (of years) in very many heb-seds like Ra forever (*dt*)." Here, while the gift to the king is for the future, the eternity mentioned is in the past, as it refers to Ra who had already lived and ruled for countless millions of years. By contrast, on the east wall of the Funerary Chapel of Tuthmosis I, there is another speech written behind the god Ptah, who is shown standing in his shrine, that states, "I give to thee years (*rnpwt*) of eternity (*nḥḥ*)". This is therefore as a gift for the future life of Queen Hatshepsut, thus denoting eternity to come.

This time distinction can best be illustrated by two diagrams depicting the passage of time horizontally and vertically as a continuous progression.

dt   ◄— PRESENT —►   *nḥḥ*

PAST OF ENDLESS   FUTURE OF ENDLESS
DURATION   DURATION

This shows how the historian worked both back and forward from the present moment, conceived as a fixed point in time, thereby dividing eternity into two parts of infinite length that would meet at the exact instant in which s/he was writing.

The second concept suggests the passage of time from infinite past to infinite future in an unbroken sequence:

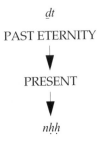

dt

PAST ETERNITY

▼

PRESENT

▼

nḥḥ

FUTURE ETERNITY

Just as day follows night to the Ancient Egyptian, particularly after burial in the tomb, so *nḥḥ* follows *dt*. Spell 17 in the 'Book of the Dead' relates this unequivocally to eternity: "As for eternity (*nḥḥ*) it means day, as for eternity (*dt*) it means night" (Allen 1974: 28).

It is significant that in these scenes it is the god Ptah and the related Memphite deity Sokar who give eternal life, rather than any other deities. In the Memphite Theology Ptah, in what must be a later synthesis of both the Heliopolitan and Hermopolitan creation stories, is made both a primal cause of creation and an amalgam of all the major deities associated with the process involved (Sethe 1928). In this text he is said to have created all the deities as well as the physical universe: "through this heart (or mind), by which Horus became Ptah, and through this tongue (speech) by which Thoth became Ptah." The wording implies a higher, more abstract method of creative process, manifested through thought and utterance, that brings into existence what is conceived by the creator. The text later says what happened at the end of the process: "And so Ptah rested (*htp*), after he had made everything, as well as all the divine order." While this could be rendered as 'Ptah was satisfied', the statement suggests a quiescent period followed in the universe after the activity of creation, and that this still continues up to the present.

This passage has often been likened to the biblical account of the creation in which Yahwe is said to have rested on the seventh day, as recorded in the book of Genesis. Other Egyptian references suggest that this phase of less active development will last until the final destruction of the present existing cosmos.

From these concepts, it seems that to the Ancient Egyptians all the past, when considered as "night", or in the completed or perfective state, is linked with *dt* eternity, and all the future continuing state, when considered as forming the "Day" following, is tied to *nhh* eternity. Put in terms of the creator deity, a night of Ptah would be the whole of *dt*, and a day the whole of *nhh*, both these periods being of limitless time. Expressed in present-day terminology, such a day and night would be the figure 1 followed by an infinite number of zeros, or expressed as a mathematical abbreviation 10^{∞}.

The full intention of the above speeches put into the mouths of the gods Ptah and Sokar can now be understood. As the creator god *par excellence*, Ptah is better suited than any other deity to award the king life comprising infinite years of future eternity (*nhh*), and is raised beyond even Ra-Atum and the sequence of universes linked to him.[2] This concept of the god Ptah being considered beyond ordinary methods of year counting, such as Sothic cycles, may be reflected in a statement found in the Old Chronicle, ascribed by Syncellus to Manetho but possibly by another later compiler. In this very inaccurate historical chronological framework, the compiler gives a period of 25 cycles of 1,461 years, or a total of 36,525 years exactly, stated to have elapsed since the beginning of the reign of Helios the sun god, whose rule is here extended to 30,000 years. Interestingly, the sun god is called the son of Hephaestus (Ptah), who is stated to have had "no period assigned, because he shines night and day". This reference therefore appears to have had a purely cosmic significance, here related to a deity who, as suggested, was linked with eternity in time rather than with specific periods of years. This is, of course, not the case with the standard versions of Manetho or the Turin Canon where Ptah is accorded a fixed period of rule.

The textual evidence suggests that the Egyptians may have thought of the past as being divided into two different phases. The first, what can be termed cosmic ages, relates only to the creation of the universe and its possible precursors, and its symbolism, as seen in the form of deities representing physical elements, is shown in summary form in Table IIa (p. 28). The second is again symbolized by the sequence of deities listed in the Turin Canon as ruling over what may be termed settled life on earth, thought to have begun 23,000 years before Menes. This phase also includes the first human rulers after the gods and demi-gods, and clearly relates to the earliest known human inhabitants on earth as known to the Egyptians. Table IIb (p. 29) relates the identifications and attributes of the deities, again using the order followed in the

Turin Canon and Egyptian records, of what scribal historians may have conceived to form the order of major human discoveries, here expressed in modern terminology.

Ptah, as is shown by countless references in Egyptian texts, was the deity most associated with crafts and craftsmen. Hence, the discovery of fire, regarded by ancient peoples as of supreme importance, would fit very well into this part of the prehistoric period, well before such advances as the formation of states or even, perhaps, agriculture. Stone and metal tools as used by craftsmen would also fit into this period in the sequence of discoveries. Indeed, the actual title of the High Priest of Memphis, the greatest centre of arts and crafts in later times, was "Great Overseer of Craftsmen" (wr ḥrp ḥmwt). Ra was, by contrast, the god of priests and learning, linked with astronomical observation and knowledge, whose High Priest bore the title "Greatest of Seers" (wr mȝw), thus proclaiming this link. Osiris, Isis and Horus all relate to the formation of kingship in later predynastic times, as opposed to tribal chieftainship, while Thoth represents a whole range of advances relating to writing and mathematics, and studies such as calendric division and architectural planning that were associated with them.

From this evidence, it would seem that the Ancient Egyptians, like the early Indian chroniclers of the gods, tended to lose themselves in a fabulous system of inconceivably long ages, involving countless aeons of time, but one possibly reckoned by the use of cycles of years, such as those calculated from the rising of Sothis. It would also seem that they had a more complete set of beliefs regarding what is now called the prehistoric period, and its possible steps in human advancement, than any other ancient people possessed.

Notes

1   Cremo (1999) gives a useful summary of the use of Indian yuga or age cycles of years, and other methods of counting time. While some of the views expressed here as to human life having existed in remote periods dated to as much as nine million years ago are highly controversial and not in accord with current views in archaeology, the similarities between these ages and Egyptian periods of time linked with the Mehen serpent are striking. Every yuga age of the world is preceded by a twilight period and followed by another of equal length lasting one tenth of a yuga. The four Yugas constitute 12,000 gods' years, or 4,320,000 human years, each succeeding one being of shorter duration, the first of 1,728,000 years down to the last of only 432,000 years.

2   The time span covered here (Waddell 1940: 229–230) ends with the thirtieth Dynasty, allowing one king – not three – in this dynasty wrongly designated as a king originating from Tanis. This ruler is accorded 18 years, thus agreeing with the Africanus version of Manetho for Nectanebo I, the founder of the dynasty ruling at Sebennytus. Perhaps this was the time when these 25 Sothic cycles were conceived to have ended, i.e. ca. 361 BC.

Note on the Dynasties in Phase 6 of Table I (p. 28)
Three dynasties of human rulers are listed, and recall that the Palermo Stone Annals have room for about 100 names before Menes. If the dynasties were contemporary and not in sequence, as shown in the Turin Canon, they would cover a period of at least the 2,431 years accorded to the Delta rulers. This figure, added before 3150 BC, almost exactly parallels the earliest thermoluminescence dating of Badarian pottery, i.e. 5531 BC, and the comparable C14 dating for the earliest Nabta Playa pottery phase of ca. 8100 BP.

More realistically, the Turin Canon only lists for this period 10 kings of Upper Egypt, who on a generation count of 22 years would have ruled for about 220 years. The dynasties of Memphis and Lower Egypt, with 19 and about 20(?) rulers, suggest a maximum period of 420–440 years. The first would equate with Naqada III period, and the others with both Naqada II and III in archaeological terms. They would therefore have existed at the time of the beginnings of writing, and simple royal names could have been recorded. Assuming that these kings really existed and reigned in succession, and were not all contemporaries, they represent the earliest recorded dynastic framework in Egypt.

Table I. Chronological Framework

Period	Description	Duration
1. Ptah	Creator and Summation of all deities. Eternal *dt*. Limitless past time existence. Night	Duration of Period to present: 10^∞ BP
2. Ra-Atum	Creator of the sequences of universe past, present and future. Identity as 'everything' in existence	Duration of life reckoned in millions of millions of years, or in units of 1,000,000,000,000 years
3. Ra	The aspect of the solar god as ruler of the existing universe	Life subdivided into phases of 1,000,000 year-long "days" and dormant period "nights" of equal length, recurring in cycles

Establishment of settled human life on earth – ca. 26338+ BC

4. Reign of the Gods		Duration of period 9,780+ years (from the Turin Canon)
Ptah		100+ years of rule
Ra-Atum		? total missing
Shu		103+ years
Geb		736+ years
Osiris		? total missing
Seth		200 years
Horus		300 years
Thoth		7726 years
Maat		200+ years
Hor		? missing
Anubis		? total missing
Total		*Eleven plus ? deities ruling 9,365 + x years in all*

5. Spirits of Horus or demi-gods		Rule commenced ca. 16558+ BC
Total		*7,716 years in all. Rule ended ca. 88422 BC*

6. Human rulers and dynasties (from the Turin Canon)

Spirits of Horus (kings)	20	Ruled for 1,110 years
Kings. Location unspecified	10	Total regnal years missing
Kings. Location unspecified	ca. 12	Ruled for 330 years
Kings of Upper Egypt (*nsw*)	10	Ruled 1,000 + x years
Kings of Memphis (*Inbw ḥḏ*)	19	Ruled 11 + x years 4 months; 21 days
Kings of Lower Egypt (*bity*)	19 + x	Ruled for 2,431 years
Total	*6 dynasties*	*4,882+ x years**
7. Menes	Unification of Egypt	Traditional date ca. 3147 BC, adjusted here to ca. 3138

* The Turin Canon aggregate is 5,704 + x years hence the figures include about 822 missing years.

Table II. Prehistoric Phases

Phase	Significance
a. Cosmic Significance	
1. Ptah	Primal cause. Among eight sub-elements are Ptah-Nun, father of Atum, Ptah-Naunet, mother of Atum, Ptah the Great Heart (Horus), Ptah the Tongue (Thoth), of the Ennead, representing Creative Mind and Speech.
2. Ra-Atum	Creator of the physical universe as Khepri. Light in general as the sun god, heat, life and sustainer of everything in the universe.
3. Shu:	Second creative cause as Air and Cosmic Space.
Tefnut	Partner of Shu, Moisture and Rain elements.
4. Geb	Earth, minerals, vegetation hence flora and crops.
Nut	Heaven, sky and galaxy, stars, sun, moon, planets.
5. Osiris. Sahu (Orion)	Departed spirits of mankind in heaven. Renewal of animal life on earth.
Isis. Sopdet (Sirius)	Sothis goddess "Opener of the Year".

6. Seth. Khepesh (Taurus)	Destruction in heaven, storms and devastation on earth. Also at times animal life.
7. Horus	Heaven. Sky Spirit, creative aspect of Ptah.
8. Thoth	Creator of the Ogdoad as an aspect of Ptah. These eight elements are:
Amun and Amaunet:	Hidden elements.
Huh and Hauhet:	Formlessness.
Nun and Naunet:	Primeval Waters.
Kuk and Kauket:	Darkness.
Also the Moon God	Compare also Khonsu, son of the first pair here, as another lunar deity.

b. Significance after the Establishment of Settled Human Life

1. Ptah	Fire, crafts, stone and metal working.
2. Ra	Priestly learning, astronomy and calendar years, law and divine judgment. Father of Maat in the context of world order.
3. Geb	Farming and food production.
4. Osiris	Kingship, primogeniture, civilized arts.
5. Isis	The throne, queenly status.
6. Seth	Kingship, pre-primogeniture succession, god of Upper Egypt.
7. Horus	Pharaonic kingship as opposed to other forms, primogeniture. Lower Egypt.
8. Thoth	Speech, writing, mathematics, calendar, architecture.

CHAPTER 3

ARCHAISM AND MODERNISM IN THE RELIEFS OF HESY-RA

Whitney Davis

Archaeological and art-historical investigations explicitly focused on 'archaism' offer little of analytical use because the concept of archaism in art history does its most profitable work when it is seen as an aspect of a *modernism* (Rather 1993). Moreover, cultural temporalities – such as archaism and modernism – should be distinguished from replicatory histories such as the survivals and revivals that seem, in some Egyptological accounts, to be virtually identical with archaism.[1]

On the one hand, survivals can survive into an archaism, a classicism, or a modernism, and revivals can be revived in, or as, an archaism, a classicism, or a modernism. On the other hand, a survival can be archaistic, classicistic, or modernistic – just like a revival. We must be prepared to recognize such possibilities as an 'archaistic modernist survival' or a 'modernist classic revival'. If it is to be archaistic at all, a form, style or motif must of course be a revival precisely because it had to be rediscovered (see Barkan 1999). But such a revival might also be a *survival* because the form, style or motif persisted from an earlier cultural period into the contemporary time of its rediscovery and revival – its archaistic replication (whether or not it did so *as* the archaic phenomenon constituted in its latest and specifically archaizing replication *in* that survival and revival).

Behind these considerations lies a crucial distinction between the *date* and the *age* of a form, style or motif. This recognizes the difference between the date and duration and the historical significances of stylization in depictive construction and configuration.

The date of depiction and the age of depiction

For the purposes of historical interpretation it is usually necessary to know the date of a work, whether in absolute or in relative terms. Velazquez's *Las Meniñas*, for example, was painted in AD 1656 – a secure absolute date. Picasso painted a series of paintings in response to it not only in 1957 (a secure absolute date) but also 'after' Velazquez's painting *and* in a 'modern' style relative to it – two kinds of relative dates that might be secured without knowing the absolute date(s) of the paintings. The second might be regarded as addressing the *age* of Picasso's paintings. This date could be taken to state that Picasso's paintings were made later than Velazquez's, a chronology measured by the difference between the two absolute dates. But the same 'date' specifies how Picasso's paintings placed themselves in relation to the prototype, or the source picture, to which they responded – a picture perhaps implicitly acknowledged to be *non*-modern for Picasso when he replicated it in his modern style.

Style as such cannot be the same thing as the age of the depiction. Picasso could have painted his series of replications as faithful reproductions of Velazquez's paintings: he could have produced replications in Velazquez's mid-17th century style, and not in his own or any other identifiably later-20th century style. Nevertheless, such imaginary paintings would still come 'after' the Velazquez. However similar they might be, the Picassos would remain resolutely modern in relation to the Velazquez: they are 'later' to its 'earlier'.

Their 'cultural temporality', however, would remain to be identified. On the one hand, the Picassos imagined to be virtually identical to the Velazquez might well manifest a modernism. On the other hand, the Picassos could manifest an archaism, namely, the return to the style of Velazquez – a style which we might know to be 'earlier' than Picasso's paintings. Indeed, in its cultural temporality Picasso's 'classicism' (a familiar aspect of many paintings produced throughout his long career) could be more 'modern' than his seemingly 'modern' style in his replications of a work. In the cultural temporality which embeds *both* Picasso's classicizing paintings *and* his modernist replication of Velazquez's *Las Meniñas*, it could well turn out that *Las Meniñas* had itself been constituted as 'older' than the 'classical' style that Picasso had earlier developed. For example, Picasso might have turned to Velazquez for replication in his modern work in order to discover aspects of the very origin of his classicism. So an archaistic and a modernistic Picasso could look exactly the same, but they would have dramatically distinct cultural temporalities. Therefore they would require different historical interpretations of Picasso's situation and intentions in painting the pictures.

Velazquez's *Las Meniñas*, though later than the classical Greeks in absolute terms, might be 'archaic' relative to the 'classicism' replicated in Picasso's modern art. Cultural temporalities cannot be the same as datings, absolute *or* relative. Instead they are 'histories' in a much deeper sense. For the purposes of historical understanding, knowing the mere date is not sufficient. To date a picture does not show whether the picture presumes and solicits an archaic, a classical, or a modern cultural temporality or significance. The latest picture could be the most archaic. One of the earliest could be extremely classical. A modern picture might have been produced by an archaizing classicist – and so on.

It is only as a legacy of the history of philosophies of consciousness that cultural temporality has been broken into Archaic, Classical, and Modern phases, or Prehistoric, Archaic, Classical, Mannerist, Modern, and Post-Modern ones – and so on. There really is no such thing as a picture that is 'archaic' *or* 'classical' *or* 'modern' (to use the terminology of relative dates) or that is 'archaizing' *or* 'classicizing' *or* 'modernist', 'modernistic', *or* 'modernizing' (to use the established terms of cultural temporality). Every depiction will (re)present aspects of *all* periods or strata of its internal sedimentation. All pictures – all coherent representations – will always manifest an interdetermination of archaizing, classicizing, and modernizing aspects relative to the cultural traditions and contemporary contexts to which they belong. In the terminology of relative dating, an 'archaic' work simply manifests the characteristics – technical, iconographic, rhetorical, stylistic – of early works in the traditions to which it belongs. But in the terminology of cultural temporality, an 'archaizing' or 'archaistic' picture manifests a classicizing/modernizing replication of aspects of depiction constituted by classicizing/modernizing works in the tradition *as* archaic, e.g. as pictures 'older-than-classical' in relative-dating terms *even if* they are not 'earlier-than-classical' in absolute-dating terms. In form and style and motif – in its depictive morphology – archaistic replication might look quite archaic *or* quite classical *or* quite modern.

All this is a far cry from what we typically find in Egyptology, classical archaeology, and other branches of style studies in non-art-historical disciplines. Typically they have not worried about their constant and perhaps even constitutive anachronism. One routinely finds putatively art-historical publications in Egyptology that cite 'parallels' for a stylistic trait or iconographical motif drawn from practically all later periods of the entire cultural tradition or cultural history in question. For an early fourth Dynasty sculpture or relief, for example, one might find citations to supposed similarities in sculptures or reliefs of the fifth and sixth Dynasties, the Middle Kingdom, and even the eighteenth and nineteenth Dynasties of the New Kingdom – i.e. supposedly comparable instances ranging over 1,500 years of cultural history. In principle this procedure must violate the tenets of iconological analysis – that iconography is 'disjunctive' from one replication to the next (Panofsky 1960; see Davis 1992: 24–27, 1996: 117–127 for examples in prehistoric and Egyptological archaeology). In the ancient Egyptian context, the procedure might be justified by a robust understanding of a 'canonical tradition' (see Davis 1989) – of persistent substitutability and comparability. But typically style studies in Egyptology have resisted this interpretation of the history they claim to reveal; instead, they assert that they identify stylistic variation and development. Their anachronistic methods, then, are all the more disturbing.

Canonical tradition and stylistic variation

When the standard distinction of cultural temporality into Archaic, Classical and Modern is used in what follows, I do not suggest that ancient Egyptian picture makers in the third Dynasty (or ca. 2600 BC) really discriminated the cultural temporality of depiction into just those three, and only those three, interdetermined phases. In adopting such traditional categories to describe any given 'dated' point in Egyptian cultural history, we may be obscuring temporalities which animated the same history 'from the Egyptians' point of view'.

Nevertheless, we can suppose that 'from the Egyptians' point of view' there would have had to have been some kind of Archaic (i.e. older-than-classical), Classical (i.e. younger-than-archaic, older-than-modern), and Modern (i.e. younger-than-classical) cultural norms and alternatives. One basis for this assertion is that Egyptian depiction manifested a 'canonical tradition' (Davis 1982, 1989). Within such a tradition, and partly as a function of its longevity, stability, and extensive history of replicatory variation, it must have been possible to distinguish not only earlier but also 'older' (archaic), and not only later but also 'younger' (modern), aspects of its normative traditional (classical) replication. Whereas any Archaic and Modern culture-times in a canonical tradition inherently imply a relative dating – relative to one another and to the classical norm – the classical culture-time has been constituted at least partly and in relative-chronological terms to be *timeless*. Even if cultural life displays older and younger ways to do it, the 'it' in question remains canonical – the same 'image' (Davis 1989: 192–224). Ancient Egyptian depiction must have manifested Archaic and Modern cultural temporalities insofar as it was possible within the tradition to identify its younger and older dates of replication.

Egyptian depiction was not entirely governed by unchanging and rigid rules (Davis 1982). Indeed, I have identified (Davis 1989: 93) six practices of variation in depiction – 'expansion', 'contraction', 'expressive magnification', 'division', 'equivalent substitution', and 'nonequivalent substitution'. These account for the self-evident fact that designers had "enormous flexibility in mediating the canonical image in, or more precisely, into its architectural context". Any identification of 'true innovation' (Davis 1989: 82–92) requires historical understanding of these or other processes of iconographic replication.

As the concept of a 'canonical' tradition suggests, ancient Egyptian depictions do replicate several interacting constructive and configurative techniques: section contour, proportioning, 'co-ordination of aspect', and register composition (Davis 1989: 7–37). Each of these elements may display considerable stylistic variation, but all of these were "straightforward variations on the main canon" (Davis 1989: 10–15, 20–27). The most important constructive technique was the canonical configurators' selection of certain so-called *geradansichtig-vorstellig*, or 'aspective' views of objects (Schäfer 1928, 1963). Schäfer's description remains valid, but it is imperative explicitly to reject the essentialist, even racializing, cultural psychology and cultural history implied in Schäfer's interpretation of his findings. The invariance of the 'canonical tradition' in my sense lay not in the stylistic variation or development of elements such as contouring (e.g. in modelling) or proportioning, but in the *interacting linkage*, the 'interdetermination' of constructive conventions – the creation of a particular, highly distinctive, and highly stable kind of whole depiction of figures and scenes, an 'image'. There is no 'alternative mode of representation' in any ancient Egyptian depiction produced for elite consumption or display, although the existence of 'pre-canonical' and 'non-canonical' depictions (Davis 1989: 116–191) help to pinpoint the social specificity and boundaries of canonical depiction. Of course, there was considerable and continuous stylistic variation and development *within* canonical depiction. But the maintenance of canonical construction *as* a style must be distinguished from routine stylistic variation.

Egyptological art studies have not properly investigated stylistic variation and development. Most of them shy away from any correlation between stylistic datings and cultural temporalities, even though their stylistic analysis assumes a culture-temporal process that seems to be its analytic object, its methodological presumption, *and* its supposed historical conclusion. For example, Russmann (1995) offered implicit reflections – though not in theoretical terms, and not followed up – on what she saw (following Vandier 1958: 140) as the "impulses of renewal and reaction against the past" (Russmann 1995: 271) in the distinctive style she identified. One cannot agree, however, that this "style provides us with *the earliest documented occurrence of deliberate stylistic change in ancient art*" (Russmann 1995: 173, emphasis in original; cf. Harvey

2001: 5). On the one hand, Russmann's formalism offers no criteria for distinguishing her 'deliberate' style from undeliberated or unintentional style, as art-historical connoisseurship would require (see Morelli 1892). On the other hand, it offers no demonstration that stylistic variation in late prehistoric, early dynastic, Archaic or Old Kingdom Egyptian depiction before the "second style" of the sixth Dynasty was *not* 'deliberate'.

Egyptological stylistic assumptions fill journals with self-perpetuating publications on dating and style. But they fail to distinguish between form and style, between *Grundform* (a maker's nondeliberated style) and conventional form (a social co-ordination of *Grundformen*), between morphological similarity and stylistic replication, between unique morphology and repeated morphology, between habit and mannerism, between style and convention, between unintended and intentional depictive activity, between configuration and motif, between reference and figuration, and between dating and temporality.

According to Baines (1990, 1994), what I call canonical Egyptian depiction was a social practice of 'decorum' – a propriety in depiction and other forums and practices of social life. Undoubtedly an ancient Egyptian scribe, painter or sculptor working for an elite patron would usually have tried 'to do the proper thing' in producing a depiction. Possibly he experienced a decorum in interacting with superior agents in elite or court culture, in honouring his social obligations and pursuing his social interests, and in fulfilling his religious convictions. But his self-description would tell us little about many aspects of the constructive and configurative systems of his depiction as such. To consider depiction as a kind of 'etiquette manual' tends to downplay the agency – the creative power – of intersubjective norms and interactions, and to reify an implied notion of individual interested agency vested in artists or other 'executants' and their patrons. In pharaonic Egypt individual agency was organized in interaction with canonical tradition, whether or not any aspect of tradition was present to the awareness of social actors or relayed their perspective. If Baines' prescription were to be adopted in Egyptological art studies, it would be impossible to conduct a connoisseurship of the objects, of the paintings and sculptures produced in ancient Egyptian culture. Connoisseurship requires the identification of formal and stylistic morphology produced entirely *outside* the maker's intentions, and wholly unconventionalized in his or her intersubjective or cultural interactions: the 'actors' or 'executants' remain entirely unaware of – and therefore could have no 'perspective' on – the constitutive features of their own replicatory activity in depiction. Knowing the 'actor's perspective' will be able to give us only part of the whole story. None of this is to dismiss the crucial identification of intentional stylistic variation. But intentional stylistic variation can only be identified by considering the context and the history of the entire determination of stylistic variation, intentional or not (and see Davis 1996: 94–127).[2]

Stylistic dating, cultural temporality, and the reliefs of Hesy

The acacia-wood reliefs of the royal official Hesy, taken from the western 'palace façade' niches in one of the inner corridors of his tomb (A3 = QS 2405) at Saqqarah, have long been regarded as prime examples – and artistic masterpieces – of 'Archaic'

Egyptian depiction in the archaeological or Egyptological sense of that term. Five panels were recovered by Mariette's workmen in 1860–1861. A sixth panel was retrieved and the "hopelessly decayed" remains of five other panels – there were eleven in all – were observed by J. E. Quibell in 1911–1912 (Quibell 1913; and see Porter and Moss 1978: 439–440; Wood 1978).[3]

William Stevenson Smith (1946) assigned the panels of Hesy to the first of three phases he claimed to identify within the Archaic horizon of Old Kingdom artistic culture – namely, the 'transition' from the second to the third Dynasty (for Smith it encompassed the reigns of Khasekhemuwy and Djoser), the third Dynasty, and the 'transition' from the third to the fourth Dynasty (for Smith it encompassed the reigns of Huni and Snofru and certain aspects of production in the reign of Kheops). His Archaic I or early/archaic Archaic can best be understood in culture-temporal terms as the modernist Archaic and his Archaic III or late/modern Archaic can best be understood in culture-temporal terms as the classicist Archaic (Smith 1946: 131–156). The datable place of the reliefs of Hesy in this scheme required Smith to emphasize contemporary parallels in the relief sculpture made for Djoser's building projects at Saqqarah and elsewhere. He conceived these royal works – the production of workshops making the most 'high quality' and 'advanced' stone statues and reliefs for the king's buildings – to be something like the *avant-garde* of Archaic culture. This advance distinguished the royal artistic culture of the early third Dynasty from the preceding artistic culture of the early dynastic period. In the later part of the third Dynasty, beginning with the Archaic II/III in Smith's sense, some – although not all – aspects of the technique, construction, style and iconography co-ordinated by the Djoserian *avant-garde* of Archaic I would become classical – the canonical art of the Old Kingdom (Smith 1946: 157–213).

Thus, at the same time as Smith specified an early Archaic date for the reliefs of Hesy he observed similarities between the *early* Archaic artistic culture and the later Archaic artistic culture of the third Dynasty. In this later phase of Archaic civilization, some works of stone relief sculpture in private mastabas at Saqqarah – Smith took them to be 'later' than Hesy's mastaba – provided apposite parallels to Hesy's wooden reliefs. Relative to the highly contemporary production of Djoserian artistic culture in the early Archaic period, this subsequent artistic culture could be seen as 'modern' in culture-temporal terms. It absorbed, and retrospectively rendered classical, what had already been constituted in an earlier (Djoserian) phase of artistic culture as new and original relative to a *pre*-Archaic (early dynastic) culture now in turn rendered 'pre-canonical' or even 'prehistoric' in relation to its modernized classical descendant. As noted, the 'modern' Archaic culture of the third Dynasty became the stable canonical culture of the Old Kingdom – though there too, of course, we can continue to observe relatively more 'archaic' and relatively more 'modern' cultural temporalities in depiction. The reliefs of Hesy in part culturally predated this 'classical' modernization of the early Archaic style in which they are chronologically placed – a modernization that Smith saw developing throughout the Archaic I/II/III artistic cultures into fourth Dynasty artistic culture. Thus, they could be seen from its retrospective vantage point to be culturally *as well as* chronologically archaic – even though in their *original* culture-temporal Djoserian context, in the artistic culture of the early Archaic, they were highly contemporary. In the end, then, at the cost of some anachronism Smith's account constituted the reliefs of Hesy as 'archaic' *not only* in the relative-chronological sense, that is, as belonging to the early Archaic phase of Archaic cultural tradition. The reliefs of Hesy were *also* 'archaic' in the culture-temporal sense: they were an 'older' but nonetheless directly ancestral form of the classical co-ordination achieved by Archaic artistic culture *after* – and partly stimulated by – the work of Hesy's sculptors pursuing a Djoserian *avant-garde*.

Smith's observations did not really conform to the accepted method of stylistic analysis in art history. Therefore the basic data of his account were not fully articulated in terms usable for the purposes of any subsequent art-historical paradigm of historical interpretation, such as the 'social history of art' and the 'New Art History' (Cheetham *et al.* 1996; Harris 2001; Nelson and Schiff 1996). Smith's idiosyncratic method of a putatively stylistic analysis was compromised by his tendency to confuse style with *form* and stylistic analysis with the procedures of *formal* analysis that tended to overemphasize the individual, rare, or unique properties of a picture at the expense of the expected, standard, or usual ones. Formalism of this kind tends to be coupled with style-periodization, in which the observer tries to identify those traits or features of an artefact or depiction that 'date' it. A museum curator naturally wants to know what is particular, and perhaps even different or unique, about an individual work on display. But pernicious art-market forces and modern ideologies of artistic creativity and the 'aesthetic' often contribute to the inflation of the cultural significance of particular attributes singled out in formal analysis.

Smith's stylistic observations routinely violated the minimum criterion for attribution through style – namely, that the *Grundform* identified as the habitual procedure of a maker at a particular point in time remains entirely unintended in the maker's co-ordination of the production of the whole artefact. Many of the features of depictions that Smith cited to effect his attributions to stylistic phases or cultural periods were clearly made intentionally. Therefore they have no bearing on the *Grundformen* that index a maker's habits at a particular point in time. Indeed, Smith's stated aim to reveal the conventions of Egyptian style and iconography – especially "its mode of representation of the human figure" (Smith 1946: 272–350) – runs counter to the requirement of stylistic analysis that *Grundformen* must be entirely *un*conventionalized.

Smith (1946) offers a bewildering labyrinth of 'formal' and 'stylistic' observations of uncertain methodological derivation and unequal theoretical value. Sometimes Smith claimed that the lack of a 'stylistic' parallel for a formal morphology constituted evidence for a maker's independence or innovation, and hence for cultural temporalities of variation, development and creativity in conventional Egyptian depiction. But if everything in the pool of formal morphologies, including unique morphologies, is 'stylistic', then nothing is. And if everything in the pool of formal morphologies, stylistic or not, *Grundform* or not, conventional or not, might 'date' a depiction, then nothing does. The real issues – to specify the date of morphology which has culture-temporal particularity, to specify the culture-temporal age of morphology which has chronological particularity – have simply not been joined.

It must be a measure of the culture-temporal challenge posed by the reliefs of Hesy that when Ludwig Borchardt (1937: 108–110) included them in the *Catalogue Général* of the Cairo Museum he dated them (without giving reasons) to the fourth Dynasty. In Smith's terms this could be his Archaic III, which he might have accepted as a date for the reliefs, or his fourth Dynastic artistic culture *after* Snofru and Kheops, which he would not have accepted. Borchardt must have believed that the reliefs manifested striking similarities with the pictorial procedures and styles of the fourth Dynasty, especially in certain aspects of the depicted figure of the tomb owner himself. No doubt he came down on the side of the fourth Dynasty partly because of the high quality, the technical and artistic confidence, and the stylistic and iconographic distinctiveness or uniqueness of some of the reliefs, which made it all the more difficult to associate them with Archaic artistic culture. Archaic culture tended to be associated not only with an 'older' form of the canonical or classical tradition in Egyptian depiction but also with a 'primitive' precursor to it. Indeed, Smith himself recognized that the artistic culture of his Archaic I inherited, even if it revised, the artistic culture of his Early (predynastic and early dynastic) period of Egyptian depiction. Because the reliefs of Hesy were clearly something like its most 'contemporary' and 'advanced' revision, Borchardt seems to have considered that they must be grouped – despite their distinctiveness – with the *post*-primitive cultural tradition to which they clearly belonged stylistically. The substantive point disputed between Smith and Borchardt was whether this post-primitive cultural tradition in the modernized 'classical' form manifested in the reliefs of Hesy had an 'early Archaic' (Archaic I = early third Dynasty) origin and temporality or could only be assigned a 'late Archaic' (Archaic III = later third Dynasty/early fourth Dynasty) context. The 'dates' they offered to rationalize this art history differed drastically in absolute chronological terms: Borchardt's date would place the reliefs at least two or three generations later than Smith's. Paradoxically, however, both datings, insofar as they were essentially independent of an archaeological date-context, tried to acknowledge the very same cultural temporality – namely, the 'archaic' precociousness or modern proto-classicism of the reliefs relative to the manifestations of later classical Egyptian depictive conventions. Neither Borchardt nor Smith stopped to consider whether the reliefs of Hesy might have been both 'archaizing' *and* 'modernizing' simultaneously.

The archaeological date-contexts of the reliefs of Hesy

In the 'rubbish' which Quibell's workmen (1913: 3, 12, 39, no. 23, pl. 18, no. 23) removed from the burial chamber of the mastaba, "robbed and half full of broken stone", two (or maybe three) fragments of a seal of the Horus Neterykhet appeared "in almost the last basketful of earth". This has been interpreted to mean that the seal fragments were recovered from the floor of the chamber in turn covered by fill and rubbish, possibly a fairly undisturbed context (Cherpion 1989: 24 n. 25, cf. 1999: 104 – where there are said to have been two seals). But the tomb had been robbed more than once in antiquity, and it was 'excavated' twice, first by the workmen of Mariette (who may not have reached the underground chambers) and then by Quibell – both teams working quickly and rooting about for objects. From the fill (though he did not say where) Quibell also recovered a bone dagger handle inscribed with Hesy's name (Quibell 1913: 38, nos. 8–9, pl. 18) as well as a much decayed bit of bone with an incomplete name and title which he did not take to be Hesy's (Quibell 1913: 38, no. 12, pl. 18), though in fact it does seem to give his title of "master of scribes of the king" (Kahl *et al.* 1995: 102–103). These objects, however, provide no evidence for the absolute date of the tomb equipment – as the seal seems to do. This seal has been widely used to constitute the entire tomb of Hesy, including all its decorations and depictions, as a fixed point in the morphological 'dating' and, to a lesser extent, the culture-temporal periodization of a good deal of the *other* production thought to belong to the third Dynasty. For example, Barta's (1963: 29) morphological and inscriptional typology and chronology of Archaic and early Old Kingdom offering lists accepts the seal-dated panel of Hesy at his offering table (CG 1426) as one of the most important 'fixed points' in a seriational arrangement used by art historians to help date the style and motifs of other table scenes of the third Dynasty (see Terrace and Fischer 1970: 40).

An even more serious problem in the archaeological dating is that the mastaba of Hesy – unlike most Archaic and Old Kingdom mastabas at Saqqarah and Giza – was not the product of a unified project in which the building can be treated architecturally as a single unit and its decorations can be treated as a single design assigned to one period. Instead, it underwent a series of modifications in which the wooden reliefs must have been located and conceivably even relocated. The resulting aggregation has often been described as the 'tomb of Hesy'. In fact, however, the later stages of the modification of the tomb likely postdated the death of Hesy by more than a generation. As Bolshakov (1997: 194–197, 209) reminds us, some part of the painted and sculpted decoration in an Old Kingdom tomb must have been planned or commissioned and made and perhaps even used ritually during the lifetime of the tomb owner – that is, in this case, *pre*dating the burial of Hesy with his tomb equipment. Thus the archaeological date for the wooden reliefs of Hesy in the 'tomb of Hesy' must range over a period of tens of years, perhaps as much as half a century. In their architectural location in the 'tomb of Hesy', the reliefs were situated in a part of the construction that certainly had not been included in the *earliest* conception of the architectural form, and perhaps of the decorative programme, of the tomb.

Unfortunately, information on the relative dates and the cultural temporality of the phases of construction in the tomb of Hesy is scanty. As Janosi (1999: 37 n. 5; cf. Kaiser 1998) has noted, "the building stages of [the tomb of Hesy] are still insufficiently investigated and documented". And as he goes on to say, "because Hesi-Re's monument is unique in the context of the few other known mastabas of the late third Dynasty, it is difficult to make a clear presentation of tomb development in this epoch based on its example". Most of our understanding derives from Quibell's (1913: pls. 1, 2, 1923: pl. 2) puzzling plans of the tomb (Figure 3:1), with brief and sometimes vague descriptions, in turn used by George A. Reisner (1936: 138, 248, 270–273) to reconstruct the original sequence of events. Reisner's assistant at Saqqarah, Smith, simply used the dating suggested by the seal fragments found by Quibell when he assigned the tomb to the early third Dynasty. In a circular way, this dating was shored up by the late second Dynasty 'topographical' dates given by Reisner and Smith to the group of mastabas immediately to the east, and the later third and fourth Dynasty dates given to the group of mastabas to the west of the tomb of Hesy – conforming, it seemed, to the general westward development of the lines of tombs at Saqqarah from the 'front line' of first Dynasty mastabas.

In turn, when Smith (1946) came to deal with the tomb of Hesy in his history of painting and sculpture, he treated it as having a unity of design. He saw all of its decorations as contemporary with one another, even though they belong to different

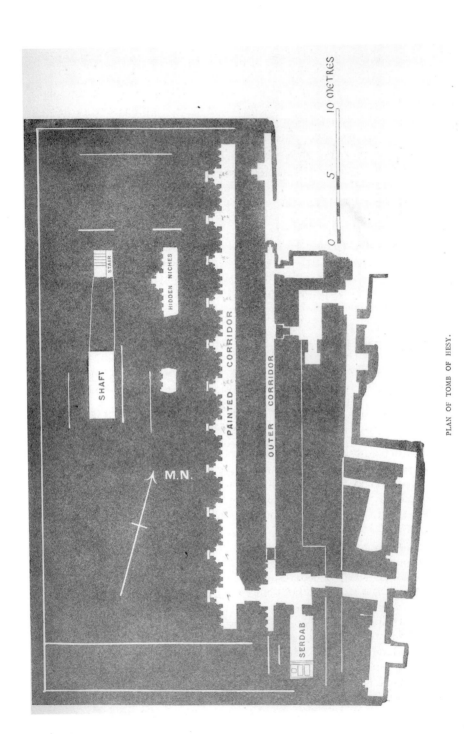

PLAN OF TOMB OF HESY.

Figure 3:1   Plan of the Tomb of Hesy (2403) in the Archaic necropolis, Saqqarah (Quibell 1913: pl. I).

phases of construction of the tomb identifiable in Quibell's plan. The whole configuration of the 11 wooden reliefs, different sets of paintings, some sculptures, and architectural elaboration posed a huge challenge for Smith when he tried to give them all a single stylistic periodization, 'early Archaic', correlated with the single absolute date given by the seal (reign of Djoser).

Probably only a re-excavation of what remains of the tomb of Hesy could settle many of the problems of its architectural history. However, in one plausible reconstruction of the vicissitudes represented on Quibell's plans *Hesy I*, "the older nucleus mastaba" (Reisner 1936: 271), would have been a considerably smaller building than the structure represented on Quibell's plan. It probably started life as a mastaba with a niched 'palace façade' on the eastern face (cf. Emery 1949, 1954, 1958). In its early tradition, the 'palace façade' was used on all four walls of the tomb. In noting the antiquity of this design employed in the 'Covington Tomb' at Giza, Petrie (1907: 7) implied its archaism (cf. Weill 1961: 311–321). In preserving an unbroken palace façade on the east, Hesy's tomb might have impressed a contemporary observer as architecturally archaic if not archaistic in some respects. Indeed, the tomb had an absolute duration that permitted such revision or renovation of its significance as 'younger' structures were built up around and in relation to it. The niches were described by Quibell as "hidden niches" in the mass of the mastaba because they were entirely enclosed in the building. He indicated that the northernmost niche was the last one in the series. Presumably at the southern end of the series one could have found the entrance to the interior corridor within which this niched façade formed the western wall.[4] It is not clear, however, whether this corridor and entrance system was actually constructed, since in *Hesy II* the whole mass and area of the mastaba was well-nigh doubled. The "hidden niches" and the incipient or completed interior corridor to which they belonged were totally absorbed and enclosed within the enlarged mastaba. Its new eastern face was (re)located more than 6 m eastwards of the eastern wall of the now 'hidden' niches.

Quibell's plan (Figure 3:1) suggests that the northern and southern faces of Hesy I were built 2–4 m behind the northern and southern faces of Hesy II. It is clear that there could have been no less than eight and possibly nine deep niches in the palace-façade wall of Hesy I, whether exterior or interior. Within these niches, the owner and builders of the tomb presumably intended depictions of Hesy to be displayed, possibly with wood flooring for the niche and a system of roofing and installing a wooden panel like that used by the artists and builders of Hesy II. It is hard to imagine that the owner and the builders and artists of Hesy II – probably including some of the artisans, if not the very same artisans, who worked on Hesy I – would have abandoned any reliefs made for Hesy I, especially if Hesy I, as seems likely, smoothly became Hesy II. Moreover, it is easy to imagine that the enlargement of Hesy I into Hesy II occurred while the reliefs and other tomb furnishings were being produced and that Hesy II thus required the manufacture of more reliefs than initially envisaged to complete its additional niches. Whether the 11 reliefs were made 'all at once' for Hesy II or included up to nine reliefs made 'earlier' for Hesy I, and whether Hesy I was quickly enlarged into Hesy II in a unitary project of construction or modified later in the lifetime of the owner, the reliefs display variation amongst themselves – as Smith, among others, noticed correctly. These variations are consistent with the possibility that the reliefs (like the tomb itself) had an internal cultural temporality. One should be cautious, then, in treating them as a set – although Egyptological literature has done so – even though they formed a sequence when they were installed architecturally as a group.

In Hesy II, 11 wooden reliefs were installed in the 'palace-façade' niches in the western wall of an interior corridor. Opposite them on the eastern wall of the corridor, registers of painting were laid down (Quibell 1913: pls. 10–23). Four offering stands in front of matting were painted in the short northern wall of the interior corridor (Quibell 1913: pl. 16), and an offering list next to the entrance on the southern end. This was probably done at the same time as the main registers were completed. However, the reliefs and the paintings facing one another in the 'painted corridor' need not be entirely contemporary (in both absolute chronological and culture-temporal terms) if some of the reliefs were 'inherited' from Hesy I – while the paintings could not have been made until Hesy II was almost completed. Perhaps eight or nine reliefs were planned and perhaps produced for Hesy I followed by the planning and production of the paintings for Hesy II. Smith noted that the reliefs as a group and the paintings conceived as a single large composition do not display the same configurative features, such as the formal proportioning and the spacing of the hieroglyphs. Probably the reliefs and paintings had different designers.

Above the door of the southern entrance to the 'painted corridor' in Hesy II there appears to have been some kind of sculptural decoration. Quibell (1913: 4) found a battered limestone hawk "of the familiar archaic type" in the fill of the southern entrance to the corridor. As this object (which he did not publish) was said to be quite weathered, we can infer that the eastern façade of Hesy II formed the *exterior* eastern façade of the mastaba for some time – perhaps many years. In turn this façade was later enclosed by the two-niched western wall of what Quibell called the "outer corridor" of the tomb of Hesy, i.e. *Hesy III*. This new corridor was constructed by enlarging the mastaba yet again. This structure was not entirely satisfactory, it would seem, because its northern segment, where ordinarily the northern niche would be sited, was already occupied by an earlier mastaba (QS 2406).

At the southern end of the eastern addition in Hesy III, a *serdab* was built south of a passage-chamber leading back to the (former) southern entrance of Hesy II in turn feeding back to the southernmost niche of its 'painted corridor'. Three bases found in it suggest that two larger statues of the tomb owner might have been complemented by a third smaller (and subsidiary?) figure. Whether this tomb owner in Hesy III was the Hesy apparently buried in Hesy II, and whose likenesses adorn the 'palace façade' niches of his enlarged mastaba, possibly taken from an earlier siting (i.e. Hesy I), is unknown. The statues in the *serdab* of Hesy III must have been made later than the reliefs – also depicting him? – that had stood for some time in the painted corridor of Hesy II. Quibell (1913: 12) found "fragments of one or of two human skeletons" in the burial chamber, and formed the casual impression that one body was female; the bones were not successfully retrieved. Even if the Hesy of Hesy III was the builder and owner of Hesy I/II, he built his tomb and completed its depictive furnishings over a period of many years.

Although the statues do not survive, evidence for the absolute date of Hesy III derives from the paintings – exceedingly partial and damaged – discovered in the outer corridor (Quibell 1913: pls. 7[2], 15[4–6]). As Smith (1946: xi–xv, 155, 268–270) noted, they appear to derive from a 'swamp scene' such as we find in the tomb decoration of the Old Kingdom. In their technique, construction and style they show sophisticated stippling and other effects that are (also) characteristic of Old Kingdom painting. For Smith, they provided important and surprising evidence of the "earlier" appearance of this iconography and style – perhaps betokening a "lost" ancestral painting tradition of "Old Kingdom" type in the preceding Archaic culture (cf. Harpur 1987: 177, 2001: 55, for a more temperate view). Smith's opinion of the 'swamp scene' was entirely predicated on taking Hesy III to be part of a unitary project of construction and decoration of a mastaba that included Hesy I and Hesy II. Probably, however, the statues in the *serdab* and the paintings in the outer corridor of Hesy III post-dated Hesy I/II.[5]

Replicatory relations in the reliefs of Hesy

Mariette retrieved five reliefs (CG 1426–30) from the southern niches of the 'painted corridor' in Hesy II. The sixth surviving panel (Q) was retrieved *in situ* in the northernmost (11th) niche by Quibell. In a provocative analysis, Wood (1978) tried to reconstruct the location of each of the reliefs in its particular niche partly on the basis of distinguishing between the 'active' and 'passive' (and/or 'more active' and 'more passive') poses of the six depicted figures of Hesy. She proposed that the one depiction of Hesy seated (1426; Figures 3:2, 3:3) must have been placed in the southernmost (first) niche. She proposed to place the best-preserved panel of Hesy standing (1427; Figure 3:4) in the second niche, next to the relief of Hesy seated (1426) thought to begin the sequence of panels from the point of entrance opposite its southernmost niche. But really we know only that the 11th panel (Q) belonged to the northernmost niche. On the basis of some obvious visual features of the panels, it seems more likely that 1428 (Figure 3:5) (not 1427) stood in the second niche next to 1426 – if 1426 *was* installed in the first niche.[6]

In fact, the group of six surviving panels divides into two sets. In one set (1427 (Figure 3:4), 1429 (Figure 3:6), 1430 (Figure 3:7), and Q (Figure 3:8)), the best-preserved panel is the much-reproduced figure of Hesy gripping both his staff and his scribe's kit in his left hand, held out as if in front of him (1427 (Figure 3:4)) – though the construction means to show him with left arm (it is quite clearly unflexed) carrying the implements loosely or lightly swinging at his side, an attitude that can be contrasted with another panel in the set (1429) in which Hesy strides with the staff, grasped in his left hand, planted firmly before or in front of him (here the left arm is shown strongly flexed). The four panels in the set are distinguished from the other set (i.e. 1426 and 1428) in two ways. First, all of them have been divided into a section of hieroglyphs on the top third and a section presenting the figure on the bottom two-thirds of the panels. These sections are not quite metrically – but do appear optically to be – in the geometrical ratio 1:2. Second, the top sections on all four of the panels give exactly the same titles of the owner, Hesy, shown below (Kahl *et al.* 1995: 88–101, 104–111).[7] The top sections of hieroglyphs remain slightly raised above the more deeply sunk bottom sections containing the figure; the bottom section is twice as deep as the top section relative to the most forward plane of the panel itself, which in all six of the surviving reliefs 'frames' the field of depiction. It would have been possible to separate top from

Figure 3:2   Relief of Hesy seated
(CG1426), mid or late third Dynasty
(Quibell 1913: pl. XXXI).

Figure 3:3   Detail of seated Hesy figure (Figure 3:2; CG1426) (Visual Resources Collection, University of California at Berkeley) (Quibell 1913: pl. XXIX).

bottom sections in other ways – for example, by carving a 'register line' in relief. Presumably, then, the device of separating top from bottom by placing them at different levels – the former higher than and 'in front of' the latter – must have some kind of function or significance.

Figure 3:4   Relief of Hesy standing (CG1427)
(Quibell 1913: pl. XXIX, 2).

Figure 3:5   Relief of Hesy standing (CG1428)
(Quibell 1913: pl. XXIX, 1).

Figure 3:6   Relief of Hesy standing (CG1429)
(Quibell 1913: pl. XXIX, 3).

Figure 3:7   Relief of Hesy standing (CG1430)
(Quibell 1913: pl. XXIX, 4).

Figure 3:8   Relief of Hesy (Q)
standing (found by Quibell *in situ*
(Quibell 1913: pl. VII)).

When the panels were painted and installed in their painted niches,[8] roofed and floored with wood, it is possible that the raised top section of the panels would have appeared more prominent – 'closer' to the viewer – and the bottom section of the panel would have appeared 'retracted' or 'further' from the viewer, as if showing what is underneath the inscription inside the panel or 'behind' the doorway of the niche. The viewer would have had practically to crouch down and peer into the bottom of the niche in order to make out the depicted figures on the panels: the top of their heads was only about 65 cm from the floor (Reisner 1936: 271–272, fig. 166, 288–289; Wood 1978: 15).[9] Still, even if this position was required to view all of the panels, only four of the surviving panels display the segmentation that might have contributed to the effect. Perhaps its principal function was compositional; it contributed to the clarity of the distinction between hieroglyphs and depicted figures and between the name and titles of Hesy and the enumeration of his funerary offerings. Such distinction (and the interrelations it sustained) has always been associated with the conventionalization of the canonical Egyptian style, beginning in the early dynastic period (see Baines 1989a; Fischer 1986). The fact that we *do not* find the segmentation on two of the panels of Hesy is perhaps more puzzling than the fact that we *do* find it on four of them.

The second set of panels (1426 (Figure 3:2) and 1428 (Figure 3:5)) differs in both respects from the first. No division of the section of hieroglyphs from the section depicting the figure has been made by raising the top section above the bottom section or in any other way. Hesy's titles, above the figure, smoothly abut the enumeration of offerings in front of the figure with no separation visually defined between them. Indeed, the beautifully formed hieroglyphs on the panels (especially 1426) seem to be spaced precisely in order to create and to fill a unitary field extending from top to bottom and from side to side of the entire sunk portion of the relief raised within it. The virtually geometrical ratio of sections in the first set of panels consequently does not appear in the second. In 1426, showing Hesy seated, a geometrical halving of the panel can be located in the space just above Hesy's head and just below his titles – but the viewer does not sense it as strongly as the proportioning of the sections of the panel in the other set. In 1428, although the height of the figure is approximately two-thirds the height of the entire carved section of the panel, because of the crowded spacing of the hieroglyphs and picture this relation is not as visible as it is in the first set of reliefs. Finally, each of the two panels in the second set presents an individual configuration of titles. In 1426, which provides considerably more room for hieroglyphic inscription than any other panel, four titles not found on any other panel, including 1428, are given, and although 1426 includes the four other titles also given on 1428, they occur in a different order. 1426 is the only panel in the surviving six panels to give the short form of Hesy's name. Although 1428 presents four titles also given on all the panels in the first set of panels, it gives them in a different order, and it omits one of the titles given by them (and by 1426).

It would be tempting to suppose that the two sets of panels refer to two different states of social being of the tomb owner. But despite differences in the attributes and postures of Hesy in the four panels of the first set, they all give him exactly the same titles; and despite the different titles given to Hesy in the second set, one of the panels (1428) is continuous with the first set in depicting Hesy in his official identity. All of the panels put great emphasis – both in text and in picture – on the social identity of Hesy as "master of scribes". To date no interpretation has succeeded in showing how the five panels of Hesy standing – each particularized or individualized in terms of postural attitudes, wig, and perhaps facial expression – might reflect five personal, public, and/or official identities of the tomb owner. The difference between the five depictions of Hesy standing and the one depiction of Hesy seated is chiefly due to the special nature and history of the table scene and its role in the tomb architecture and the funerary cult.

It would also be tempting to suppose that the first set of reliefs was made by one sculptor and the second set by another. But we see one and the same great master at work in both sets – although in only *one* relief in each set, namely, 1426 and 1427.[10] These two reliefs admittedly are the best preserved, but overall they also display the highest quality; they are distinguished by the excellence of the spacing of the extremely slender and finely cut hieroglyphs, not matched in any other panel, and by the virtuoso presentation of difficult and unique constructions of the human figure.

In several places the two reliefs (1426 (Figure 3:2) and 1427 (Figure 3:4)) display particular ways of drawing and carving which seem to betray an individualized – if not a personal – pictorial decision making in the arena of the formation of graphic conventions, of stylization. These decisions were replicated in other panels *not* attributable to this sculptor (e.g. 1428). For just that reason, however, these details cannot be seen as habitual and unintended, nonconventional mannerisms. Hence they cannot be regarded as *Grundformen*, as criteria for an attribution to an individual artist at a particular stage in his artistic development. Instead, they constitute criteria for a stylistic distinction between these two reliefs and the other reliefs in both sets which nonetheless permits the two reliefs to belong to two different phases of an individual artist's development – just as the existence of two distinguishable sets of reliefs might suggest. It is just this kind of evidence, rather than the evidence of general stylistic convention or the evidence of individual stylistic mannerism, which is needed to understand depictive temporalities in culture. In 1426 and 1427, the two slightly raised interior circles in the scribe's palette of inkpaints – in 1426 (Figure 3:3), the palette is slung over Hesy's right shoulder, and in 1427, it is carried in his left hand – have been lightly but carefully and firmly bisected by a single incised line.[11] This detail is not found in 1429 and 1430. It does appear in 1428, but here the half-circles have been carved in relief – the upper half raised well above the lower half, thus using a different technique. It also appears in the carving of the palette hieroglyph (Sign List Y4) in Hesy's title "master of scribes"; in 1426 and 1428, the segmentation appears, but in 1429 and 1430 it does not. In the master sculptor's 1427, the segmentation also fails to appear in the hieroglyph. It is almost as if the segmented palette in Hesy's left hand has been intended to depict the 'real thing' carried by Hesy. Although the figuration categorically signifies his status, 1427 (Figure 3:4) represents a moment of conflict between convention and mannerism. In carving the *hieroglyph*, the sculptor 'forgets' that he could and that he would (and that he has or that he will) segment the circles in depicting the *object* – or he 'resists' doing so – for the segmentation appears in *both* hieroglyph and depiction in 1426. Alternatively, the segmentation of the circles in the hieroglyph in 1426 was a kind of personalized drawing of the hieroglyph. Either way, the sculptor of 1428 – almost certainly an apprentice or junior of the master sculptor of 1426 and 1427 – replicated his master in this individualization, but he did so in his own way: he carved a segmentation of both depicted object and hieroglyph in relief. By contrast, the sculptors of 1429 and 1430 did not notice or at least did not in any way replicate this detail.

All in all, then, in the replicatory vicissitudes of this detail we seem to see the master sculptor – in both sets of reliefs – playing out a specific quirk or perturbation in his stylization of convention (helping us to identify and to some extent to understand him), a process or performance picked up by one 'follower' (helping us to identify and to some extent understand him *as* a follower) and distributed between two distinguishable sets of reliefs (helping us to identify and understand them *as* distinguished) made by sculptors, including artisans, different from both the carver of 1426 and 1427 and the carver of 1428 (helping us to identify and understand them *as* different). The two sets of reliefs were likely produced by two different teams of artists under the supervision, and modelling the style, of the same master sculptor whose own style, although identifiable, displays internal distinction or development and disjunction between the sets, as do the largely replicatory styles of the junior sculptors.

A replicatory temporality of this kind can readily be interpreted in terms of an actual chronological distinction between the sets of reliefs – such as the possibility that as many as nine reliefs were conceived for Hesy I followed by the production of at least two 'new' reliefs for Hesy II, the enlarged tomb. It need not be that any 'new' reliefs were actually made *later* than the existing reliefs, just as it is not necessary to suppose that Hesy I substantially predated Hesy II. It is sufficient to suppose that they were *younger*, even if the production process was continuous and coherent. If these sets should be distinguished as earlier-older and later-younger, then the detail of the segmented inkpots might have been introduced into (or dropped out of) the replicatory sequence. Perhaps it characterized the master's way of depicting Hesy's palette in 1427, but by the time he made 1426 – whatever the absolute lag of time in question, from a single day to many years – it had become his way of drawing Hesy's or perhaps any scribe's palette, whether in depiction or hieroglyph. Although the segmented palette seems to be the same motif on 1427 and 1426, it has quite distinct formal, stylistic, and culture-temporal significances on each panel. In turn, the drawing was depicted by the follower in 1428. And his conventionalization might well have been different from the conventionalization achieved in 1426 (Figures 3:2, 3:3). Whereas the master sculptor of 1426 might have been unaware of the fact that he had devised a personal convention – a manner – for depicting the scribe's palette, the junior sculptor carefully and perhaps deliberately followed him in replicating it, adopting it as *the* way (his master's way) of drawing the form, whereas his master deployed it as *one* way of drawing the form. What seems to be the same motif reveals itself to have distinct formal constitutions and distinct stylistic determinations. Such replicatory temporality inherently relays – absorbs, constructs, and projects – particular real cultural temporalities. (They can also be identified amongst the three surviving panels in the first set of panels seemingly made by less-skilled junior sculptors, i.e. 1429, 1430, and Q.) Replicatory phenomena cannot simply be reduced to a 'mistake' in depiction or writing, as complex replications (of many different particular kinds) have sometimes been described in Egyptological art studies. In the case of Hesy, if the sculptor of 1426 erroneously segmented the hieroglyph which he 'knew' (e.g. in 1427) should remain unsegmented, why did the sculptor of 1428 replicate the 'error'? If there were different contemporary ways of drawing the palette, one segmented and the other unsegmented, neither way of drawing it was a 'mistake'. Why, then, was there a pattern of replication – a distribution of the different ways of drawing? There may well be mistakes in Egyptian depiction – but for the art historian they have culture-temporal and other determinations that need to be investigated.

Cultural temporality in the reliefs of Hesy

The relief of Hesy seated before his offering table (1426) can be grouped with 1428 as one of two sets in the sequence of 11 reliefs in Hesy II and it may be attributed to the same master sculptor as 1427. 1426 and 1427 have long been recognized to be 'key monuments' in our grasp of canonical Egyptian depiction. Raymond Weill (1908: 482) noted nearly a century ago that the reliefs of Hesy seem to manifest a "very pure and very correct Egyptianism" (*égyptienisme*). In ancient Egyptian depiction 'Egyptianism' was undoubtedly the most important cultural temporality of them all. It was enshrined in the most basic constructive and configurative techniques and conventions of the canonical tradition (Davis 1989: 192–224). The 'Egyptianist' or 'Egyptianizing' reliefs of Hesy have seemed to be *both* traditional, certainly classical though perhaps archaically so, *and* modern – to be conventional *and* innovative.

The wooden relief panels of Hesy – especially the first set of reliefs showing Hesy standing in his official capacity – can be associated in technique, style, and iconography with contemporary reliefs of the Horus Neterykhet (and other more shadowy rulers of the time) at Saqqarah and elsewhere.[12] In turn these depictions inherited the early dynastic tradition of the iconography of rulership that had itself revised an ancient, ramified, and heterogeneous late prehistoric depictive culture (Baines 1990a; Davis 1992; Sourouzian 1995a; Wilkinson 2000b: 27–28). Probably the sculptors of Hesy found their training and patronage largely in the royal (Djoserian) projects of the early third Dynasty.

The entire sequence of Hesy's reliefs must, of course, be closely related to the niche-stone slab-stelae and tablets or 'primitive niche stones' retrieved from mastabas at Saqqarah or thought to belong to them. The earliest of these artefacts apparently date to the end of the second Dynasty (Bolshakov 1997: 30–34; Sourouzian 1998).[13] On morphological and epigraphic grounds, other slab-stelae have been dated to the third

Dynasty. Nonetheless, their culture-temporal period (though not necessarily their absolute dates) must be 'archaic' relative to the modernizations of the reliefs of Hesy and certain other tomb owners at Saqqarah.[14] The tradition probably went back to tall and narrow stone stelae used in the first Dynasty (Davis 1989: 166–167; Emery 1958: 13, 30–31, pl. 39) and, in turn, these stelae probably bear some relation to the round-topped stone stelae from royal funerary establishments at Abydos in the first Dynasty (Petrie 1900–1901).

The relief panel of Hesy seated at his offering table (1426) would seem to have a traditional, even archaic, flavour insofar as the table scene – elsewhere at Saqqarah it had already been presented on the more square fields of the earlier niche stones (Quibell 1923: pl. 18 (nos. 1, 2)) – has been squeezed by the sculptor of 1426 and 1427 into a tall, narrow format. It is probably safe to assume that monuments in this format were still visible at Saqqarah when the builders and sculptors of Hesy began their work; perhaps the narrow wooden panels of Hesy reminded viewers of the much earlier private and royal funerary monuments. Of course, the sculptor of 1426 had no real choice. Even if the panel had been made later than the others, and even if it can be said to be 'younger' (whatever its absolute date or its relative date in the group), it still had to conform to the architectural morphology of all the panels. Like them, then, it would look modern in relation to tall narrow prototypes of the first Dynasty. But it might also look even more contemporary ('younger') than the other panels. It could be seen to mediate a 'newish' iconography intensively developed at that time and originating in that format only a generation or two earlier (namely, the table scene on slab-stelae) into a different depictive setting (the tall stelae), in turn associated with its own and considerably older traditions (namely, the early dynastic royal and private stelae) – thus modernizing that tradition. In addition, it added a more recent iconography to a series of standing figures which replicated one of the most ancient iconographies of late prehistoric, early, and Archaic Egyptian depiction. Compared to a niche-stone slab-stela that might be dated a generation earlier (Smith 1946: pl. 32), the table scene presented on 1426 would appear both old *and* new – a contemporary version of a modern image that gave it a traditional configuration and at the same time modernized that very tradition precisely by producing this highly contemporary handling of a classicized image.

In later generations, the table scene achieved its 'classic' formulation in relation to the entire Archaic tradition.[15] But this classicization did not simply reproduce and standardize the now-'older' depictions of Archaic artistic culture, including the once-'young' relief of Hesy at his offering table. It produced numerous palpable modernizations of its own. For example, it introduced a revision of the configuration of the deceased's legs and feet shown as if obscuring the forward leg of his or her chair or low seat – a configurative preference, if not a general convention, in Hesy's 1426 and elsewhere in Archaic artistic culture that could now (in later classicist artistic culture) retrospectively seem to be archaic.

As Cherpion (1989: 41) has recalled, the seat with obscured front leg can be found throughout Old Kingdom depiction. Therefore, as she says, it cannot be a 'dating criterion' precisely because it is not specific enough either in an absolute or in a relative chronology. But precisely because the seat with its front leg *un*obscured was clearly a later and perhaps understood to be 'younger' motif relative to that 'ancient' convention, we must still consider how it helped to establish the cultural temporality of any depiction in which it was used – as an archaic survival, an archaistic revival, a persisting older-classical form, etc. On Hesy's 1426 (Figures 3:2, 3:3) the sculptor included the configuration of the deceased's legs obscuring the seat as an earlier and older configuration in the overall depictive context of a later and younger modernization of the general iconography of the table scene. The remarkable configuration of Hesy's arms, hands and accoutrements in 1426 would have been seen as much as a replication of the image of Hesy presented in 1427 (Figure 3:4) (possibly an earlier and certainly an older depiction by the same master – but equally modern in its context in the tomb of Hesy) as they would have replicated the established pose of the deceased seated at his or her offering table. If 1426 was the first relief in the sequence of 11 that a viewer encountered, as Wood (1978) has argued, then 1427 (wherever it was located) retrospectively constituted 1426 as replicatory: in inspecting the whole series, a viewer would discover that the unusual configuration of Hesy seated, in 1426, could be explained by the prominence of Hesy's identity as "master of scribes" asserted in the whole sequence of reliefs, and especially in the configuration of 1427. If 1426 was located elsewhere – for example, in a niche approximately opposite the burial chamber – then it would have been easy for a viewer to see how it absorbed the configurations of the reliefs of Hesy standing as well as the traditional motif of the deceased seated at his funerary table.

For these reasons, we might question whether the configuration of the deceased's legs obscuring the seat really indexes an 'archaic' style, as has often been claimed in Egyptological art studies. In Hesy's relief it could serve as a way of attaching a later and younger depiction to an earlier and older tradition, perhaps as a means of highlighting the overall creative modernism or contemporaneity of the depiction. Although some early stelae from Saqqarah and Helwan carefully distinguish the deceased's two legs from the forward leg of the seat, the configuration of the obscured leg – well-nigh universal in other early niche-stones, slab-stelae, and panels, including Hesy's 1426 – was not (or not only) an 'archaic' device in terms of style-periodization or the duration of motifs and conventions. Even in its 'archaic' date-context it was also (or instead) an index of traditionalism in the culture-temporal sense. The configurative convention was not terribly old at the time it was replicated by Hesy. As it was broadly accepted in the iconography of the table scene at the time, it can be seen as a typical classicism of the early Archaic style-period. Later classicists of the Old Kingdom would transmute it into an archaism when they perforce revised it by 'de-obscuring' the forward legs of the deceased's seat in some (but not all) replications of the table scene. If they were still accessible, most of the earlier reliefs would now retrospectively appear to be 'older' in their classicism if they displayed the earlier configurative detail. And to replicate the earlier, older motif in the later context would therefore appear to be archaistic if the contemporary 'de-obscured' seat was considered to be the norm.

Once broached, relations of cultural temporality tend to ramify extensively. In 1426 Hesy's sculptor might have been *anticipating* retrospective interpretations of his configurative choices within the tradition projected from his own work. Even if he used certain traditional and classic forms, the modernism of his configuration tended to produce them *as* traditionalisms and classicisms: the sculptor has juxtaposed them in the same configuration with extraordinary, even unique, contemporary configurative choices, especially in the postural attitudes of the figures.[16] Once brought to awareness in this way, henceforth they could be treated *as* traditionalisms that could become 'archaic' in relation to the 'classic' and/or the 'modern' reproductions, reformulations and revisions. This outdating of oneself constitutes one of the basic procedures of modernism on its way toward reconstituting itself as classicism, on its way toward giving itself – despite its origin in contemporaneity – an internal history of tradition and constant renovation. Herein it can configure and publicly claim the normative status of its continuous contemporaneity. One of the most 'archaic' motifs deployed on 1426 (Figure 3:2) – the configuration of the deceased's legs obscuring his seat – would largely turn out to be in the service of its modernism. And a motif which appears within the 'datings' of style- and motif-periodization to require a definitively archaic date would turn out to have a modernizing cultural temporality.

The intentionality of cultural temporality in depiction

We can be sure that the sculptor of Hesy 1426 – however we interpret his own awareness of the cultural temporality of his work – did not replicate an 'archaic' configurative convention simply because he was an Archaic artist living and working in the Archaic style- and motif-period. He replicated the configurative convention as a matter of self-aware intention and careful construction – not an unintentional habit in a particular phase of his development. Thus, although we can use the convention to 'attribute' the cultural temporality of the relief, we cannot use it to 'attribute' its artistic authorship.

Just under the arch of Hesy's forward (right) foot, the sculptor included the bottom band of the hoof on the bull's leg of the seat: the bull's leg *behind* the deceased's foot (Figure 3:3). This small oblong bit of wood beneath Hesy's foot could be taken simply to be a bit of the panel 'left over' in the little gap below the arch of the foot. But in other cases in other Archaic reliefs, the deceased's foot has been shown either fully flat to the ground along its whole length or slightly arched, usually without any infill below it. Whatever appears 'below' the foot of Hesy must have tended to acquire – if it did not originate in – some figurative significance. A viewer might be tempted to see the oblong as the heel of Hesy's back (left) foot. But this would contribute to an impression that Hesy's back left foot has swelled out of all proportion (or had a club-foot conformation) rather than show that it has been set down slightly 'in front of', or slightly advanced in relation to, his front right foot. (In Hesy 1426, the sculptor might have been trying to show that the two feet are actually 'side by side'.) Such a grossly swollen foot already appeared on a second Dynasty stela (Smith 1958: 28, pl. 13) where the sculptor has tried to show the back (right) heel beneath the deceased's front (left) arch; he struggled to configure this area of the depiction by cutting back the forward leg of the seat and cutting down the deceased's right foot in order to distinguish and properly scale the forms. We can appreciate why Hesy's sculptor instead used the 'archaic' configuration of obscured seat leg even as he tried to modernize it spatially. His attempt to produce a 'correct' spatialization of the scene in the terms of his broader constructive technique spread through the scene from the shins and ankles of Hesy all the way to the bottom of the offering table a few inches 'in front of' him. The sculptor

Figure 3:9   Relief of Abneb seated at his funerary table, mid-third Dynasty (Rijksmuseum van Oudheden, Leiden).

clearly tried to tuck the toes of Hesy's two feet 'between' the divided legs or stands of the offering table. Its left (or 'back') leg comes down to the ground 'behind' Hesy's left (or back) foot, and its right (or 'front') leg comes down to the ground just 'in front of' Hesy's front (or right) foot. The construction cannot fully clarify what this depicts: it is difficult to understand exactly how the table stands up on two legs divided in this way. Probably we should associate this perturbation with *avant-gardism* of depiction.

Despite all his care, however, Hesy's sculptor could not escape awkwardness and ambiguity, even in his own new configurative and compositional terms. Later, for example in the stelae of Wepemnofret (Smith 1946: pl. 32[b]) or Nefertiabet (Ziegler 1990: 187–189), all three elements – the fully revealed right front bull's-leg of the seat, the gap under the arch of the deceased's right foot, and the heel of the deceased's left foot visible beneath (behind) it – were depicted. The truly 'archaic' feature of the earlier depictions, including Hesy's, was not that they showed the front bull's-leg of the seat to be totally obscured (in 1426 it was not) but that they presented the deceased's legs just above the ankle to be equally wide, as if they intended the back left leg to be advanced fully in front of the forward right leg instead of remaining partly or even wholly hidden by it, as the overlapping of right foot with left foot would require. In the case of Hesy 1426, this archaic aspect of his configurative work 'dates' him to an archaic style- and motif-period – and this constituted a kind of inertial drag on his contemporaneity and therefore on his own modernization of archaic-classical configuration even as he mastered and renovated or revised it. At the time, however, this aspect of his culture-temporal identity could not have been known to him as such – otherwise he would have revised it, as he tried to do when he included the hoof of the seat below the arch of Hesy's foot. The configuration of the deceased's legs above the ankles could not have been archaic *for him*. It was a contradiction in his configurative practice that not only exemplified his cultural period; it also expressed his cultural *age* – his attempt, successful or not, to come to terms with his period and to replicate it in an appropriately traditional and appropriately modern form. Here we can see something like the 'decorum' that Baines (1990, 1994) has taken to be the fundamental motive organization of Egyptian depiction. However, as this example suggests, 'decorum' can only have content or significance for the consciousness of its practitioners in relation to conventional configurations partly outside any perspective which the participants might have had.

Much the same can be said about the notorious right hand and thumb of Hesy seated (Smith 1946: 274–289). In the most general sense, Hesy's 'wrong thumb' in 1426 (Figures 3:2, 3:3) – as in many Archaic depictions and in the stabilization of this 'error' conventionalized in later canonical works – tried to make the best of an impossible configurative situation in the terms of canonical construction. Hesy's right hand thumb should be 'on top' of his hand. But in that position, to make it at all visible one would have to draw it either sticking up or at least curving up, even if the thumb were held tight against the other fingers in the clasped or gripping position. In some Archaic stelae (and in later works that might be regarded as primitive, slipshod, erroneous, or regressive, though probably not archaistic), we do see this 'out-curving' thumb – positioned, however, on the wrong (bottom) side of the fingers, as if the thumb were on the right side of the right hand (seen from the back) rather than the left side. But in the table scene, the deceased reaches out to the table in order to cup his or her hand around a half loaf of bread. Indeed, if the hand were quite fully cupped, the thumb would touch the ends of the fingers or wrap around or into the fingers. Hesy's sculptor tried to suggest this not only by *up*-curving the thumb on the 'wrong' side of the hand but also by *folding* the hand and fingers: Hesy's fingers seem to go upward and then downward to make an upside-down V which tried to render the bending of the finger joints and/or the prominence of the tendons in this action. (Hesy's sculptor took care to distinguish the 'bent' thumb of the cupped right hand from the gripping clasp, with out-stuck thumb, of the *left* hand: two little wrinkles below the nail on the left thumb in 1426 show the folds of skin at the joint when the thumb is held straight.) Hesy's sculptor 'knew' a good solution to the depictive problem of the hand that showed the thumb as if located at the bottom of the palm of the hand and the fingers at the top because he showed it successfully on the *left* hand of the standing figure in 1427 (Figure 3:4). But in the configuration of the table scene, an iconography inserted into the iconography of the standing figure adopted on all the other reliefs, he could not represent it; he could not fully reconcile the contradiction and perturbation of conventions with which he was confronted in this one particular situation of depiction.

Egyptian art has frequently been characterized as depicting 'what the artist knows rather than what he sees' – or, to use Smith's (1946: xiii) formulation, "to represent things as [the artist] knew them to be, not in aspects which may have appeared to him transitory". But the example of Hesy's thumb in 1426 and countless other examples show why this invidious misleading contrast with post-medieval Western depiction (e.g. Schäfer 1928) must be beside the point. It is very doubtful that the ancient Egyptians 'knew' the thumb to be on the right side of the left hand (palm up) and the left side of the right hand (palm up). Hesy's sculptor certainly *saw* how the thumb and hand actually work in a certain action, and he certainly *knew* their ordinary anatomical relationship, which he rendered perfectly well elsewhere. But here he did not represent or figure it. This was not simply an error or an oversight but instead a motivated replicatory precipitate of the cultural temporality of his configurative work. Hesy's sculptor addressed a configurative problem that he had recognized to be latent but not yet made fully manifest in the contemporary iconography of the table scene. He did not attain a fully satisfactory solution. Nevertheless, the subsequent canonical stabilization of the 'wrong thumb' as a routine convention would have been unthinkable without his demonstration that fingers which are 'too long' are even less desirable than a thumb 'in the wrong place'. Modernization cannot occur in the way and at the pace it does without such *avant-gardism*.

Smith pointed to general features of the depiction of Hesy seated at the offering table which for him associated the relief with works which he regarded to be chronologically later. The 'sharp-edged' (Smith 1946: 149–153, 1958: 28) cutting of the outline of Hesy's figure in 1426, dated by Smith to the first phase of Archaic artistic culture, reminded him of the 'high reliefs on stone' of his third phase of Archaic artistic culture, the 'transition' from the third to the fourth Dynasty (e.g. Arnold and Ziegler 1999: 189–190; Borchardt 1937: 44–47; Harpur 2001; Murray 1905: 2–4; Smith 1942: 518–520; Ziegler 1990: 96–101). In these reliefs, the 'archaic' tendency continued to present the deceased's lower legs just above his or her ankles as equally wide. But in the very same area of the depictive configuration, these reliefs were also culturally younger. If they did not quite 'de-obscure' the forward legs of the seat (perhaps the artists did not consider it as an object that had been obscured in the first place), they did 'un-obscure' it more fully than Hesy's 1426. Again, this is not necessarily a matter of a later date; these table scenes, though culturally younger, can still be seen to be productions contemporary or overlapping with 1426, though it partly 'archaises'.

Hesy's sculptor of 1426, subjected to the inertial drag of existing tradition, also attached or re-attached himself *to* tradition by replicating earlier and older configurative selections in the context of his contemporaneity and modernism, even his *avant-gardism*. If he was attempting to establish his works as original, and to project his modernism for the cultural future in such a way that it could become classical, then in a sense he succeeded. The younger reliefs in other mastabas – whether or not they were *later* than his own – seemed to present the requisite classicism after his modernism, for they stabilized as convention what had emerged in exploration and experiment in Hesy's reliefs. Perhaps, indeed, the enlargement of Hesy I into Hesy II was partly motivated by an effort to 'keep up with the Joneses' – i.e. with the construction of the large 'younger' mastabas behind Hesy's own. In this context, Hesy's sculptor might have had every reason to produce constructions and configurations that were *both* traditional and even archaic *and* fully contemporary though classically correct. His contemporaneity had a fluctuating or disjunctive significance as it related to the reliefs of the king – here Hesy's production was that of a follower – and as it related to the reliefs of younger men, where Hesy's production established him as a leader and innovator both in his own 'self-out-dating' and in their 'out-dating' of him.

Figure 3:10   Relief of Kha-bauw-sokar seated at his funerary table, mid–late third Dynasty (Murray 1905: 4–5).

If the mastabas of Hesy and Kha-bauw-sokar (Murray 1905: 2–4; Borchardt 1937: 44–47) were culturally overlapped (the former was 'older' to the latter's 'younger' in replicatory relations), the same master sculptor of Hesy's 1426 (and 1427) might have been at work on the reliefs of Kha-bauw-sokar. Smith (1946: 138–140) observed the possibility when he noted the strong similarity between certain aspects of the face of Hesy in 1426 and the face of Kha-bauw-sokar (Figure 3:10) in *all* his renditions in his chapel, citing in particular the deep naso-labial fold and furrow. These mark what has often been said to be an 'older' Hesy, but in Kha-bauw-sokar's reliefs, they probably 'idealize' the depiction of the patron's actual age (whatever it was) at the time of production (Cherpion 1999: 104; Terrace and Fischer 1970: 38). Both private patrons might have been imitating the king's depiction: the naso-labial furrow can be found on the great statue of Djoser (Harpur 2001: 297 n. 34). Smith was not sure whether the furrow was a 'portrait' characterization of Hesy precisely because it appears on Kha-bauw-sokar as well. But Hesy really might have looked rather like the older man of 1426 at the time the relief was made – and the sculptor of Kha-bauw-sokar's reliefs, whether or not he was also Hesy's sculptor, might readily have adopted this configuration in recognition and imitation of the 'modern classicism' of the work, especially if it connoted regal grandeur. Of course, if the naso-labial furrow constituted a real *Grundform*, then we *must* attribute Hesy's 1426 and Kha-bauw-sokar's reliefs (and possibly the great statues of Djoser?) to the same sculptor.

The naso-labial furrow had its own replicatory relations in the sequence of Hesy's reliefs. It did not appear in Hesy 1427, a relief which has been attributed here to the master sculptor of 1426. As suggested already, however, 1427 may belong to a different set of reliefs and a different cultural phase and probably (but not necessarily) to a different chronological period of the depictive career of the sculptor of 1426. And the naso-labial furrow *does* appear in 1428, which here has not been attributed to the same master sculptor of 1426 and 1427. Still, as noted already, there is reason to suppose that the sculptors of 1426, 1427 and 1428 enjoyed close interaction – as master and junior, apprentice, or follower – in the culture-temporal phase (whatever its date and duration) that encompasses these depictions. Despite their difference of authorship, 1426/1427 and 1428 can be distinguished as culturally contemporary works by different artists in terms of replicatory relations and cultural temporalities.

Notes

1 For the doctrine of *Nachleben* or "survival", see Didi-Huberman 1998; Rampley 2000; Warburg 1999. The most perspicacious treatment of revivals – in part contrasted with survivals – remains Panofsky's (1939, 1944, and 1960). For discussion of concepts of replicatory histories of depiction and style, see Davis 1996.

2 Ascription of intentionality – an action performed by the agent at the time of the ascribed intention in a self-reflexive fashion under the agent's direct sentient control – can be enormously constraining on analysis. Most stylistic phenomena cannot possibly be intentional. It remains an open question how to handle style which we *do* discover to have been intentional (Davis 1996: 95–198).

3 In all, then, six panels were retrieved and are now exhibited at the Cairo Museum; recently (1999–2000), CG 1428 was exhibited in Paris, New York and Toronto (Arnold and Ziegler 1999: 88, no. 17). In general, colour photographs tend to erase features of contour, modelling and interior detail. Here and throughout I use Smith's orthography for the transliteration of Egyptian proper names in order to facilitate the reader's consultation of his discussions – still the most penetrating discussions of early dynastic, Archaic and early Old Kingdom depiction to have been published within the conventional Egyptological paradigm.

4 Quibell's plan suggests that the 'hidden niches' belonged to an inner corridor of the tomb. However, Hesy I may have begun life as a mastaba with an *exterior* eastern 'palace façade', transformed under construction into a mastaba with an interior corridor having a western 'palace façade' wall. Quibell believed that the 'hidden niches' were constructed precisely in order to be 'hidden' – with some kind of "magical" function (Quibell 1913: 3) – but this interpretation is unsatisfactory.

5 The eastern chambers and façades of the tomb continued to be modified. They came to include two small integral mastabas (QS 2411, 2412) which were reached, like the mastaba of Hesy I/II/III whose eastern façade they walled up, by way of a long corridor which threaded past QS 2406 and gave access at the other end to the interior corridor of the large mastaba (QS 2407) to the east (dated by Reisner (1936: 305) to the end of the second Dynasty).

6 Because Mariette's numbering of 1426 (= Mariette's no. 5) suggested to Reisner (1936: 273) that it came from the fifth niche from the south, he located it there – approximately opposite the burial. However, Wood (1978: 9–10) pointed out that Mariette's numbers probably did not reflect the location of the panels as found *in situ*. The construction history of the tomb allows for 1426 to have been intended for the chief offering niche of a panelled mastaba (i.e. Hesy I). In Hesy II, however, the mastaba had already become a two-niched mastaba with interior palace-façade corridor. In this architectural configuration, as Wood (1978: 10) noted, it would have been appropriate to put the panel of the deceased seated at his offering table in the first niche – i.e. inside the embrasure of the southern entrance-niche complementing the newly constructed northern niche (see Reisner 1936: 271). As Wood noted (1978: 11), 1426 (or whichever panel stood in the southernmost niche) was the only panel that could be seen by a viewer standing in the entrance to the inner corridor. Wood (1978: 10) presumes that the reliefs were "formally and iconographically unified". However, even though they were installed as a group, and must have been experienced in a sequence, they need not have been made as a single set.

7 Although the titles are the same in all four reliefs, the short offering lists included in front of the figure in two of the four, 1430 and Q, are not the same as each other nor the same as the short lists included in front of the figure in 1426 and 1428. Further, the hieroglyphs in Q face away from the deceased, as it were a de-reversal of the reversal of the signs probably intended on the other panels to emphasize that Hesy is the beneficiary of the offerings (Terrace and Fischer 1970: 37). Partly for this reason, Wood (1978: 14–16, 19) suggested that Q depicts Hesy *making* offerings to a personage she reconstructed from the single foot preserved in the northernmost section of the painting on the eastern wall of the 'painted corridor' – namely, she proposed, the king (for her the Horus Neterykhet named on the seal). Although Hesy in Q might be an offering maker (see Fischer 1973) and although Hesy's tomb is unique in many ways, this iconography would have been an extraordinary invention. More likely, the de-reversal of hieroglyphs in Q simply accepts that one could begin 'reading' the inscriptions from the northern end of the sequence of

reliefs as well as from the southern end. The foot in the painting on the opposite wall would then belong to a depiction of Hesy himself.

8   Wood (1978: 12) suggested that a long tight garment with a leopard-skin pattern was worn by Hesy in 1426. The modelling of Hesy's bones, muscles and flesh suggests that the uncovered parts of his body were not painted – the natural wood supplied the colouration. Reisner (1936: 290–292) describes the decorative scheme of the niched west wall (Quibell 1913: pls. 8, 9) and its relation to the painted depiction of offerings and equipment collected for the funeral, depicted on the east wall.

9   A diagram published by Baines and Malek (1980: 63; Friedman 1995: 16, fig. 10b) does not really represent the viewer's experience ('the actor's perspective'?), although their reconstruction does suggest the strong sense of 'looking down' on the image. The configuration would have been neck-wrenching, and surely incompatible with the use of offering stands in the niches – completely blocking any view of the figures on the panels. Quibell (1913: 4–5) implied that the 11th panel was built into the niche and that impressions of the panels were left in the bricks of the niche.

10   Wood (1978: 11) presumed a single artist who designed the series, but she observed variations in the quality of the six surviving figures, and suggested (Wood 1978: 11–13) that some of them were made by two or more 'workshop' artists. However, she considered all the hieroglyphs on all the panels to be "uniformly well made" (Wood 1978: 12), which would imply that the pictures and the hieroglyphs were drawn or at least carved by different hands. However, the hieroglyphs are not uniformly well made; the hieroglyphs in 1428 are chunkier and clumsier than, and not as well spaced as, the hieroglyphs in 1426.

11   Drioton (1942; republished by Terrace and Fischer 1970: 33) incorrectly renders the position of the implements in Hesy's left hand and fails to include the segmentation of the basins visible on the original panel.

12   For the stela of the Horus Qahedjet acquired by the Louvre in 1968, see Ziegler 1990: 54–57. The fragments from a shrine at Heliopolis seem to be securely dated to the reign of Djoser (Smith 1946: 133–137, figs. 48–43). The blocks from the temple of Hathor at Gebelen, probably from the end of the second Dynasty (Davis 1989: 169, Alexanian 1998: 13), could be given to the third Dynasty (Smith 1946: 137) if one sees their style as 'archaic'. In culture-temporal terms, these depictions could constitute an example of 'archaizing' in the early Archaic period.

13   See especially the stelae of Gem-n-sesher (Scharff 1932; Barta 1963: 14–26), Princess Sehenefer (Barta 1963: 16–18; Quibell 1923: pls. 26, 27; Smith 1946: pl. 32), another *zꜣt nswt* (Barta 1963: 22; Smith 1958: pl. 14), and the two stelae found in tomb contexts, though not in their original installations, by Quibell (1923: pl. 28 (1, 2)) at Saqqarah.

14   See especially the stelae of Imet (Barta 1963: 26–27; Smith 1958: pl. 13), Weser-neb-nt (Barta 1963: 27–28; Moret 1919; Ziegler 1990: 157–163), Teti-ankh-ni (Barta 1963: 31; Weill 1908: 225–230), Abneb (Holwerda *et al.* 1905–1908, I: pl. 23; Weill 1908: 219–225) (Figure 3:9) and Zefa-nesuwt (Von Bissing 1914: I, pl. 14). The stone stela of Sa-mery "in the old style", found within a brick enclosure on the eastern side of Tomb R88A (also dated to the third Dynasty) at Reqaqneh (Garstang 1904: 45, 58, pl. 28[a]; Weill 1908: 210–212) presents special problems. Weill took it to be "a first attempt" at the depictive configuration realized in the panels of Hesy (and see Weill 1908: 403–406 for comments on aspects of archaic survival at Reqaqneh). Although this work might be contemporary with the tomb of Hesy, or a generation or so later, for Smith it did not offer useful comparison with it because of its supposedly 'provincial' character (Smith 1946: 142).

15   Good examples include the stela of Isi now in Copenhagen (Koefoed-Petersen 1956: 24–25, no. 17) and the stela of Nefer from Tomb G2110 at Giza now in the Museo Barracco (Careddu 1985: 3–4, pl. 1), thought to date to the reign of Khephren (Smith 1946: 163).

16   The postural attitudes of Hesy on 1426 and 1427 were almost certainly unique – for they seem to have been generated largely within the replicatory relations of the sequence of reliefs. In all kinds of ways 1426 and 1427 replicate each other as much as they replicate any general motif types.

CHAPTER 4

LOOKING BACK INTO THE FUTURE: THE MIDDLE KINGDOM AS A BRIDGE TO THE PAST

Dietrich Wildung

(translated by Fiona Handley)

For anyone embarking on the study of Egyptology, learning Middle Egyptian – the script and language of the Middle Kingdom (2040–1640 BC) – is the key admitting them to the world of the Ancient Egyptians. The beginner is unlikely to be aware that they are in the very best of company while they are learning this language: in the company of all those young Ancient Egyptians who were learning to read and write between 2000 BC and the period of the Roman emperors. The language of the twelfth Dynasty was regarded as the 'classical' variety of Egyptian until the end of ancient Egyptian history (Junge 1985; Loprieno 1995: 5–8). While the spoken language developed further in a dynamic way, evolving into Late Egyptian (1300–700 BC), demotic (700 BC–400 AD) and finally into Coptic (400–1400 AD), Middle Egyptian remained *l'égyptien de tradition* for religious texts for 2,000 years. This is why there were two languages being used for long periods of Egyptian history, when, alongside the everyday language, the Egyptian of the early second millennium BC lives on as the artificial language of the past.

Instruction in schools given in this language, which as early as ca. 1300 BC was no longer the living one, made use of literary texts written in Middle Egyptian in subsequent periods (Schenkel 1990: 7–10). In this way the works of literature from the Middle Kingdom period became 'classics', which were copied again and again in the schools of the New Kingdom and therefore – mainly in short passages of text – have been handed down in numerous copies. The 'Tale of Sinuhe' is not only known to us from two complete manuscripts of the Middle Kingdom (today in Berlin – Morenz Chapter 6: Figure 6:1, this volume), but also from large numbers of ostraca, which were written 500 years later in Deir el-Medina (Morenz Chapter 6: Figure 6:2; Simpson 1984) by those learning to write, who were taught that the language and style of that distant age was a model: the script used was admittedly the hieratic of the New Kingdom and the orthography was partly brought into line with the spellings of Late Egyptian (Herrmann 1957).

Not only was the language of the Middle Kingdom regarded as a model, but so also were certain kings' names from this period. 'Kheperkara', the throne-name of Sesostris I (1971–1929 BC) was assumed 1,500 years later by Nectanebo I (380–362 BC) and this name, resonant with venerable ancient tradition, is encountered once more in distant Meroe in northern Sudan, where, at the time of Christ, the Meroitic king Natakamani, who can readily be compared with Ramesses II in his activities as commissioner of buildings, assumed the throne-name 'Kheperkara' (Eide *et al.* 1998).

Apart from the 'classical' language of Middle Egyptian, the art of the Middle Kingdom also exerted a particularly strong influence on subsequent periods. The sculpture, reliefs and painting of the twelfth Dynasty provide the models on which the academic training of Egyptian artists was focused up until the time of the Ptolemies (Wildung 1984: 9–14). Two examples can be used to illustrate how difficult it is to distinguish between an original from the Middle Kingdom and a classicistic work from a later age: a statue of a king now in Berlin (Figure 4:1), on which the name

Figure 4:1
Kneeling figure of
King Sesostris I,
twelfth Dynasty (ca.
1971–1929 BC),
Berlin Ägyptisches
Museum 1205; ht. 45
cm (© Dietrich
Wildung).

'Kheperkara' is inscribed, was published (Erman 1899: 247) as a depiction of Nectanebo I (380–362). One generation later, however, due to the availability of a significantly broader range of comparative material and a developed methodology, there is no doubt that this figure should be dated to the time of Sesostris I (1971–1929) (Evers 1929: pl. 45). A standard work on the literature of Ancient Egypt (Brunner-Traut 1978) uses, as an illustration of a love song, a 'Middle Kingdom' stela in Turin (Figure 4:2), whose archaizing style definitely calls to mind an original of the twelfth Dynasty (1991–1786), but which, on the basis of the personal name of the owner, Harbes, belongs to the early twenty-sixth Dynasty (beginning 664 BC) (Bothmer 1960b: 28).

Figure 4:2 Limestone stela of Harbes. Twenty-sixth Dynasty (ca. 660 BC); ht. ca. 60 cm (© Museo Egizio di Torino).

The timeless importance of the works of art from the Middle Kingdom can also be gleaned from the fact that the kings of the nineteenth Dynasty (1292–1190 BC) – in particular Ramesses II and his son Merenptah – re-used numerous statues of the pharaohs of the Middle Kingdom (Sourouzian 1988, 1995b; Figure 4:3) by re-installing

Figure 4:3   Middle Kingdom royal statues (ca. 1900 BC) re-used by Ramesses II (ca. 1250 BC), re-erected by the kings of the Third Intermediate Period (ca. 1000–900 BC) at Tanis; ht. 200 cm (© Dietrich Wildung).

them in their temples. Moreover, the names of the former rulers would often be left untouched. So what we have here is not the usurping of former works – the appropriation of such works as the memory of the original owners is fading – but, on the contrary, a deliberate link to a great age of the national past, a reverential use of history in order to legitimize a king's own rule by looking back to exemplary figures from the history of the nation. A statue in Berlin (Figure 4:4a, b) of a figure at prayer from the time of Amenemhet III (1818–1772 BC), on which the name of the king is clearly visible on the belt fastener, has the cartouche of Merenptah (1213–1204 BC) inscribed on the supporting pillar at its back (Erman 1899: 80–81, fig. 14). The mane-bearing sphinxes of Amenemhet III (Figure 4:5) were re-used first by the Hyksos ruler Apophis (ca. 1550 BC), then by Ramesses II and Merenptah and finally by Psusennes I (1050–1000 BC; Wildung 1984: 198–200, fig. 174).

This 're-use' of Middle Kingdom works is also found in sculptures depicting figures other than kings: Maya, architect of Memphis during the reign of Ramesses II, placed his inscriptions on a squatting figure of the Middle Kingdom (Cairo JE 67878; Ziegler and Tiradritti 2002: 439, no. 128), and the most famous architect of the New Kingdom, Amenophis son of Hapu, who worked for King Amenophis III, uses a figure of the late twelfth Dynasty for a portrait depicting him as an old man (Figure 4:6; Schoske 1987: 22–24; Sourouzian 1991). An Amun-priest in Karnak from the twenty-second Dynasty (ca. 870 BC), Djed-Djehuti-iu-ef-ankh, makes a sitting figure from ca. 1800 BC (Cairo CG 42207) 'up-to-date' through the use of his inscriptions, and he writes on a kneeling figure from the era of the Ramessides (Cairo 42178) that he has 'updated' (literally, 'renewed') it (Wildung 1978: nos. 22, 55).

This resurrection of earlier works of art during the period of the New Kingdom continued as the artists of the Late Period came to terms with the works of the Middle Kingdom. Montemhet, mayor of Thebes ca. 650 BC, takes the statue type of Khertihotep from the late twelfth Dynasty (ca. 1800 BC) as a model for his seated figure (Figure 4:7) as regards its formal structure and iconography: the later copy only differs from the model in its cool, academic style (Wildung 2000: 166–167, 172–173). In cases where inscriptions do not provide unequivocal evidence, a confident differentiation between the Middle Kingdom original and the classicistic imitation of the Late Period is sometimes hardly possible. A quartzite head in Munich (Figure 4:8), first published as a work of the Middle Kingdom (Scharff 1939), was later classified as a work of the Saite Period (Müller 1975), while the most recent research re-dates it once more to the Middle Kingdom.

So what underlies this role of the Middle Kingdom as the 'Classical' era of Egypt's language, literature and art? The early part of this era did not suggest that the Middle Kingdom was to become a point of reference for future generations and centuries. The princely lineage of the eleventh Dynasty, which was to lead Egypt after the end of the Old Kingdom around 2050 BC to a new heyday, came from Thebes; namely from a region which in the third millennium BC had not yet played a major role as regards either politics or culture. Upper Egypt at that time was a remote province separated from Memphis in the far north by many days' journey. Despite the political and economic control exercised over it by the central government, life in this part of Egypt was developing in accordance with local traditions (Wildung 1984: 24–25).

Figure 4:4a, b   Granite statue of Amenemhet III at prayer, twelfth Dynasty (ca. 1840–1800 BC), re-used by King Merenptah (1213–1204 BC). Berlin Ägyptisches Museum 1121; ht. 200 cm (© Dietrich Wildung).

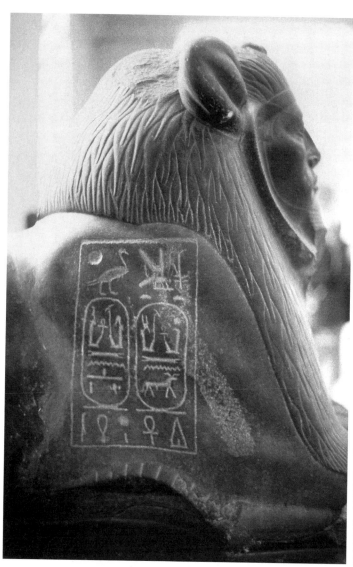

Figure 4:5
Granite sphinx of
Amenemhet III,
twelfth Dynasty
(ca. 1810 BC),
from Tanis. Re-
used by Hyksos
rulers (ca. 1550
BC), Ramesside
kings (ca. 1290–
1215 BC) and in
the Third
Intermediate
Period (ca. 1050–
1000 BC). Cairo
Egyptian Museum
Cat. Gén. 1243;
length 220 cm (©
Dietrich Wildung).

The visible sign of the special position enjoyed by Upper Egypt in the Old Kingdom is its artistic autonomy. The few tombs of the Old Kingdom in Thebes and Edfu supplied with reliefs, in particular the walls in the rock-cut tombs of the Qubbet el-Hawa in Aswan, anticipate later developments in the loose arrangement of the composition of their figures, in the coarse proportions and stiff movements of the bodies and in the Nubian aura of the facial type characteristics, which were only to evolve into a striking provincial style all of their own in the First Intermediate Period. The most important examples of this style are provided by the tombs of Iti in Gebelen (Donadoni Roveri 1988a) and of Ankhtifi in Mo'alla (Figure 4:9 col. pl.; Vandier 1950).

Figure 4:6   Granite squatting figure of Amenophis-son-of-Hapu, eighteenth Dynasty (ca. 1360 BC), from Karnak. Re-inscribed statue of the late twelfth Dynasty (ca. 1820 BC). Cairo Egyptian Museum Cat. Gén. 42 127; ht. 142 cm (© Dietrich Wildung).

Figure 4:7   Quartzite seated figure of Khertihotep, from Assiut, twelfth Dynasty (ca. 1800 BC), Berlin Ägyptisches Museum 15700; ht. 77 cm; and granite seated figure of Montemhet, from Thebes, temple of Karnak, twenty-sixth Dynasty (ca. 650 BC). Berlin Ägyptisches Museum 17271; ht. 49 cm (© Dietrich Wildung).

Figure 4:8   Quartzite head, twelfth Dynasty (ca. 1800 BC), sometimes thought to be twenty-sixth Dynasty (ca. 650–600 BC). Munich, Staatliches Museum Ägyptischer Kunst ÄS 1622; ht. 38 cm (© Dietrich Wildung).

Even the royal art of the Old Kingdom follows paths that are different from those found in the workshops of the royal residence at Memphis. The copper statues of Pepi I from the temple of Hierakonpolis (Cairo JE 33034, 33035)[1] embody both in the proportions of their over-long legs and their atypically wide strides and also in their facial features, with full lips and slightly protruding eyes, a human type which clearly differs from the well-proportioned and idealized physiognomy of royal portraits in the capital Memphis (Vandier 1958: pls. I–VII). As early as the first Dynasty (ca. 3000 BC), these long-legged royal figures are to be found in Upper Egypt – on the Narmer palette from Hierakonpolis (Cairo CG 14716; O'Connor Chapter 9: Figure 9:3, this volume) and on a relief from Gebelen (Museo Egizio, Turin Suppl. 12341; Donadoni Roveri 1988b).

What marks out these human portraits is an original ethnic type, which over millennia remained characteristic of the Nubian-Sudanese Nile Valley (and see Ashton Chapter 10; O'Connor Chapter 9, both this volume). It is to be found in the royal figures of the Kushite twenty-fifth Dynasty, on the Napatan stelae and in the Meroitic temple reliefs (Wildung 1997).

All these specific features of Upper Egyptian art, which in the Old Kingdom are only documented in isolated instances (Wildung 1999) due to its remote location in

Upper Egypt, moved into the foreground after the emergence of Thebes as the leading political power around 2100 BC, and came to constitute the new style for royal art. The Antef and Montuhotep kings of the eleventh Dynasty embody this local style in the bas-reliefs at Schatt er-Rigal (Winlock 1947: fig. 12), in the temple reliefs of el-Tôd (Wildung 1984: figs 47–51), the Osiris statues at Armant (Mond and Myers 1940: pls. 15–17) and the reliefs of the temples recently reconstructed on Elephantine Island, a style which was the clear opposite of the art in Memphis, where the great tradition of the Old Kingdom lived on and was eventually to degenerate into a lifeless style with puppet-like figures.

This provincial style – elevated to the status of official state art – finds its most representative expression in the tomb complex of Montuhotep II in Thebes West (Arnold 1974a, 1974b, 1981). The seated figures (Figure 4:10) and pillar-statues of the

Figure 4:10
Sandstone seated
figure of King
Montuhotep II, from
Thebes, forecourt
of the mortuary
temple, eleventh
Dynasty (ca. 2030
BC); ht. ca. 140 cm
(© Dietrich
Wildung).

king dressed in the heb-sed robe, found in the forecourt of the temple (Arnold 1979), are of massive proportions. They have the 'Nubian' facial type and pronounced body volume, which appears to well up from the interior of the figures through to the surface. This style finds monumental expression in the painted seated figure of Montuhotep II (Figure 4:11), which was found in the so-called Bab el-Hosan, a mock-grave under the temple grounds. In the reliefs at the mortuary temple (Arnold 1974b), stylistic characteristics of the royal portrait are to be found even in the depictions of the subsidiary wives, both in cultic shrines (Figure 4:12) and on limestone sarcophagi and pictures on the inside of the latter (Naville 1907, 1910).

Figure 4:11 Sandstone painted seated figure of King Montuhotep II, from Thebes, mortuary temple at Deir el-Bahri, eleventh Dynasty (ca. 2030 BC). Cairo, Egyptian Museum JE 36195; ht. 183 cm (© Dietrich Wildung).

Figure 4:12   Limestone relief of subsidiary wife of King Montuhotep II, from Thebes, Deir el-Bahri, eleventh Dynasty (ca. 2030 BC). Munich, Staatliches Museum Ägyptischer Kunst ÄS 1621; ht. 37 cm (© Dietrich Wildung).

The architectonic conception of the Montuhotep II tomb complex is no less original than the style distinguishing sculpture, reliefs and painting (Arnold 1974a). A new form of royal tomb had taken the place of the pyramid tombs of the kings of the Old Kingdom in the Memphite necropolises from Abu Roash in the north down as far as Meidum in the south. This new form evolved from the rock tombs of the Theban princes of the First Intermediate Period (Arnold 1994: 217). The actual tomb is sunk deep into the rock and is inclined sharply down towards the west. In this way it constitutes the architectonic translation of the Osirian picture of the hereafter: it forms the path and the space, along which and within which the dead king will be transformed into Osiris. A courtyard and a massive central building are situated in front of this underground part of the tomb. The central building is raised on a podium, reached by a central ramp. A structural parallel for this architectural form is provided somewhat later, at the beginning of the twelfth Dynasty, in the White Chapel of Sesostris I (Lacau and Chevrier 1956–1969) with its ramps, which lead up onto a platform. The later architecture of the Nubian-Sudanese Nile Valley suggests that the platform-temple may have represented an architectural shape which had its roots in the south. From the Temple of Amenophis III in Soleb to the Meroitic temples in Naga and Musawwarat es-Sufra there are numerous instances of this architectural type (Wildung 1996), which is far from common in Egypt.

The transfer of the royal residence from Upper-Egyptian Thebes to Memphis during the reign of the first king of the twelfth Dynasty – Amenemhet I – demonstrates the regained unity of Egypt and the link to the historical continuity with the third millennium. Thebes, however, with its temple of the new god of the state – Amun-Ra – in Karnak, which had been founded during the reign of the eleventh Dynasty, remained the religious centre of Egypt (Wildung 1984: 59–70). The endeavour to turn to a picture of the hereafter defined by Osiris, as reflected in the royal tomb of Montuhotep II in Western Thebes, is also mirrored in the increasing importance of Abydos, the main centre for the worship of Osiris. Hundreds of chapels were erected along the Procession Street (Simpson 1974), leading west out of the Nile Valley into the desert, where the oldest kings of Egypt were buried ca. 3000–2800 BC. These tombs, more than 1,000 years old, which have been interpreted as the burial-place of the god Osiris, became a very popular place of pilgrimage where, it can be assumed from the enormous amounts of pottery, there was a good deal of cult activity (Dreyer *et al.* 1998). In the south of Abydos, a false tomb for Sesostris III was laid out and a whole settlement was built for attendant priests (Arnold 1994: 12–13). The architectonic principle underlying this tomb structure, which leads deep into the mountain towards the west, and in front of which a cult complex was built on a platform, was derived directly from the Montuhotep tomb complex in Thebes. The structure of the systems of underground chambers anticipates the plan of the royal tombs of the New Kingdom in the Valley of the Kings.

The actual royal tomb of Sesostris III, however, lies in a place where the kings of the Old Kingdom were buried – in the Memphite necropolis – and it is in the traditional shape of the pyramids. Already the first king of the new dynasty, Amenemhet I (1991–1971/1962 BC), abandoned the Theban form of the rock-cut tomb when the royal residence was moved from Thebes to Memphis. He had a pyramid built near Lisht and, in so doing, unequivocally declared his firm belief in the past. Albeit a king of Upper Egyptian, and indeed half Nubian descent (in an ancient text, the Prophecies of Neferti, it is written: "Son of a woman of the bow-land, child of Upper Egypt" (Lichtheim 1973)), he allied himself with the traditions of the kings of the Old Kingdom and the First Intermediate Period. The political decision to move the royal residence testifies to the power of tradition, banishes any idea of the 'New', and allows what had been ousted to come into its own again.

This revertion to the traditions of the Old Kingdom remained however a superficial one, a façade. Underneath the carefully erected stone cover for the outer walls of the pyramid there was only a loose in-fill of stones instead of the massive stone structures used at the beginning of the twelfth Dynasty which, after Sesostris II, was replaced by mud brick. This brick core defines today the image of the pyramids of the Middle Kingdom in Dahshur, Illahun and Hawara. What is concealed underneath the traditional pyramid shape, as found first in the pyramid of Sesostris II in Illahun, is a complex system of chambers and corridors, which cannot satisfactorily be explained simply as a safety measure. What is far more likely is that these were seen as chambers of the Underworld, which show the deceased king the way to the Sun between evening and morning (Hornung 1982a: 36, 1991: 210–211). This spatial arrangement would be in accordance with the new vision of the hereafter during the Middle Kingdom as found in the false tomb of Sesostris III in Abydos (Arnold 1994: 12–13) and then later in the New Kingdom in the Valley of the Kings (Hornung 1982b; Robinson 2003: 157–158). In Middle Kingdom pyramids, Memphite tradition as an exterior style is combined with an interior incorporating Theban innovation, which is out of sight, concealed inside the structures.

Inside the pyramid of Amenemhet I, numerous relief-bearing blocks were found (Goedicke 1971) in a temple which had been erected during the reign of Kheops, the builder of the Great Pyramid of Giza. There is little doubt that blocks with relief depictions and inscriptions from the time of the builder of the largest of the pyramids were re-used so as to integrate the legacy of the past with the present and literally to turn this material, pregnant with historical meaning, into the very essence of the way in which the ruler presented himself. If it had only been a question of making use of pre-prepared building materials, there were other old buildings available nearer to Lisht.

The choice of sites for building these pyramids indicates first of all independence from the architectonic omnipresence of the past. Lisht, with the royal tombs of Amenemhet I and Sesostris I, lies far to the south of the pyramids of the Old Kingdom. For his pyramid, Sesostris II chose a place which deliberately involved entering new territory – Illahun at the entrance to the Fayum Oasis, which had been opened up by the pharaohs of the twelfth Dynasty. Only Sesostris III and Amenemhet III had pyramids built for them within sight of the two pyramids of Snofru, the first ruler of the fourth Dynasty (ca. 2600 BC). He was seen by posterity as the king who founded the Old Kingdom, almost as a culture hero (Wildung 1969: 105–152). For Snofru, who had been elevated to a status that was almost divine, statues were erected in the Middle Kingdom, which were set up in the courtyard, thus in the public part of the temple excavated by Akhmed Fakhry (1961), which stands on the approach to Snofru's Bent Pyramid at Dahshur. The texts on these statues are addressed to the temple visitors, calling upon them to pray and promising them benevolence from the venerable Snofru.

Snofru is encountered in a similar capacity in almost 20 instances in Serabit el-Khadim, a mining area in the Sinai peninsula, where it is written (Wildung 1969: 133): "among the very many leaders of expeditions, who came after Snofru, there was not a single one who would have done what I did." This reference to the age of Snofru evokes that mythical primeval time which is referred to in other texts (Kákosy 1964) as the "Time of the Gods" or the "Time of Ra". There is a perfectly pragmatic explanation for the choice of Snofru as representative of that primeval time: he appears in the great rock relief at Wadi Magharah as the victorious hero, who slays the enemies of Egypt.

The veneration of Snofru in Dahshur in the Middle Kingdom can be compared with the cult of long-deceased kings of other pyramids of the Old Kingdom (Wildung 1969). Indirect testimony to this can be found in an unexpected place – Karnak. A seated figure of Djoser (Berlin 7702), dedicated by Sesostris II , and a figure of Ni-user-Ra and one of Sahu-Ra dedicated by Sesostris I (Wildung 1969: 59 ff), were erected in the Temple of Amun-Ra. They testify to a filial cult dedicated to these rulers of the distant past in Egypt's new religious centre, to which they lend legitimacy and which they tie into the history of the country. Direct references to priesthoods of the Middle Kingdom in honour of the old kings are found in connection with Schepseskaf, Nefer-ir-ka-Ra, Djed-ka-Ra, Teti and Pepi II.

These appear, however, to have been locally restricted cults, served by only a small number of people, since the general picture of the monuments of the past in the Middle Kingdom is one characterized by decay and destruction. In the 'Harp-player's Song' (P. Harris 500, VI, 1.4–8), which can be traced back to the textual models of the Middle Kingdom (Lichtheim 1973: 196), it is written:

> The Gods who were before rest in their pyramids.
> Blessed nobles too are buried in their tombs
> (yet) those who built tombs,
> their places are gone.
> What has become of them?
> I have heard the teachings of Imhotep and Hor-djedef,
> whose sayings are recited whole.
> What of their places?
> Their walls have crumbled,
> their places are gone,
> as though they had never been.

The 'Conversation of the Man Weary of Life with his Ba' (P. Berlin 3024, 1.60–64; Lichtheim 1973: 163–169) re-echoes this negative picture:

> Those who built in granite, who erected halls in excellent tombs of excellent construction – when the builders have become gods, their offering-stones are desolate, as if they were the dead who died on the riverbank for lack of a survivor.

The 'present' of the Middle Kingdom was not seen as the fruit of the traditions from the past of the Old Kingdom. It created new traditions, which would be the norm for the next two millennia (Wildung 2000: 166 ff). When old times were cited, these were references to the past which had an artificial ring about them, literary fictions. The P. Westcar (Berlin 3033), written at the end of the Middle Kingdom, uses a background story, which unfolds in the time of Kheops and tells wondrous tales from the time of Kings Djoser, Nebka and Snofru and allows King Khephren to appear as a prince (Lichtheim 1973: 215–222).

The 'actual' literature of the Middle Kingdom finds expression in philosophical and political writings. The 'Prophecy of Neferti' (P. Hermitage 1116B), the 'Complaints of Kha-kheper-ra-seneb' (BM 5645), the 'Admonition of Ipuwer' (P. Leiden 344 recto), and the 'Conversation of the Man Weary of Life with his Ba' (see above) reflect the present, the endeavour to critically evaluate their own situation and peer into the future free of any illusions (Posener 1956). The 'Teaching for Merykara' (P. Hermitage 1116A, P. Moscow 4658, P. Carlsberg 6), the 'Teaching of Amenemhet' (P. Millingen) and the 'Tale of Sinuhe' (P. Berlin 3022, 10499) are texts concerned with *realpolitik*, authentic historic texts, with which, in the non-royal sphere, one might compare the numerous inscriptions on stelae and tombs containing individual biographies (Loprieno Chapter 8, this volume). The autonomy of the individual took the place of the collective bliss of the Old Kingdom, which had offered security in an omnipotent and omnipresent state.

The art of the Middle Kingdom reflects this change of mentality. The Theban royal portrait of the eleventh Dynasty, marked by the Upper Egyptian origin of the rulers, continued with its individualizing style uninterrupted into the twelfth Dynasty (Wildung 2000: 52–59). Sesostris I, who emerges as a striking personality in his statues from Karnak (Figure 4:13), is represented in the pillar-statues and seated figures from

Figure 4:13 Osiride pillar statue of King Sesostris I, from the temple of Karnak at Thebes, twelfth Dynasty (ca. 1950 BC). Luxor Museum; ht. 158 cm (© Dietrich Wildung).

his pyramid-complex in Lisht (Figure 4:14; Wildung 1984: 78–83) as an imitation of the rulers of the Old Kingdom, who could possibly be compared with the works of the Saite period, given the academic stiffness of the bodies and the renunciation of individuality in facial features. Like the return to the pyramids of the Old Kingdom, when the shape of the royal tomb was selected, so the art of the royal workshops in Memphis at the beginning of the twelfth Dynasty referred back to the legacy of the Old Kingdom from Memphis.

Once the new dynasty had declared itself in favour of tradition after the transfer from Thebes to Memphis and had proven its loyalty to the national past, it then straightaway found its own path in literature and art. Looking back to the past had smoothed the way forward into the future.

Note

1 Since their excellent restoration carried out by Chr. Eckmann from the Römisch-Germanisches Zentralmuseum in Mainz they can now be appreciated for the first time in all their extraordinary technical and stylistic glory.

Figure 4:14   Limestone standing figure of King Sesostris I, from the pyramid-complex at Lisht, twelfth Dynasty (ca. 1950 BC). Cairo, Egyptian Museum Cat. Gén. 411; ht. 194 cm (© Dietrich Wildung).

CHAPTER 5

ARCHAISM AND INNOVATION IN ART FROM THE NEW KINGDOM TO THE TWENTY-SIXTH DYNASTY

Robert Morkot

Introduction

Egyptian artists at all periods derived inspiration from the past. Usually termed 'archaism', this phenomenon has been regarded as a particular characteristic of the 'Late' Period, beginning in the twenty-fifth Dynasty. The stylistic influences and possible political motivations have been discussed by William Stevenson Smith (1958, cf. 1981), Bernard Bothmer (1960b: xxxvii–viii), Helmut Brunner (1970), Edna Russmann (1974), Cyril Aldred (1980), Richard Fazzini (1972), and Peter der Manuelian (1983, 1994) amongst others. Some writers have taken a negative attitude to the phenomenon of 'archaism'. Whilst acknowledging that technically much of Late Period sculpture and relief is of superb quality, they claim that it lacks the vitality, imagination and innovation of earlier periods. These attitudes reflect a more generalized antipathy to the Late Period and its culture that is found in much of the older Egyptological literature, and which is now, to some extent, disappearing. Archaism as a cultural feature was not limited to the visual arts, but permeated literature and official inscriptions as well. Whilst this chapter focuses on the use of the past in the visual arts, this broader context should not be forgotten.

It is more difficult to discuss 'archaism', or the use of the past, in the arts of New Kingdom Egypt than those of the twenty-fifth and twenty-sixth Dynasties because of the nature of the surviving evidence. Therefore, the discussion here begins with the rich evidence of the twenty-fifth and twenty-sixth Dynasties, before considering innovation and the past in the New Kingdom.

It is not always easy to determine whether an 'art work' is based on models of a much earlier period, or whether it is part of a continuing, if undocumented, tradition. The clearest and most obvious instance is when scenes from temples and tombs of earlier periods have been directly copied. This type of direct copying is particularly well documented from the Theban region in monuments of the late twenty-fifth and early twenty-sixth Dynasties. The large funerary complexes of the Theban high officials contain direct copies of Middle and New Kingdom tomb and temple scenes, sometimes translating painting into relief sculpture. It was these individual examples, along with the more general stylistic features of statuary, that drew the attention of Egyptologists to archaism. The phenomenon was not confined to Thebes, although the surviving evidence is richer from that city. Particularly good examples of direct use of much earlier models can be found in the scenes in the temple built by the twenty-fifth Dynasty pharaoh Taharqo at Kawa in Sudan, deriving from late Old Kingdom temples at Memphis. Also pointing to Memphis as significant in the development of style at this time are the reliefs in the third Dynasty Step Pyramid complex of Djoser at Saqqarah, which are covered by copyists' grids of the Late Period.

Kushite art

The Libyan, Kushite and Saite periods all looked back to the earlier high points of Egyptian art, but it is in the relief sculpture and statues produced in the Theban workshops of the late twenty-fifth and early twenty-sixth Dynasties that the use of earlier models can be most clearly demonstrated. During the reigns of Taharqo (690–664 BC), Tanwetamani (664–656 BC) and into that of Psammetichos I, Thebes enjoyed her last great period of prosperity. The city had suffered from political upheavals and probably civil war, in the late Libyan period, before being seized by the Kushite king Kashta about 740 BC (Morkot 2000: 158–166). Kushite rule seems to have brought political stability, and wealth captured from northern Egypt was given to the temple of Amun-Ra by Piye, following his defeat of the Saite prince Tefnakht. Archaism is found in the royal titularies of this phase. At his accession in Nubia, Piye adopted the throne name of Tuthmosis III, Menkheperra, and modelled the rest of his titulary on that of the same king as it could be found on a stela in the temple at Gebel Barkal (Morkot 2000: 169–170). Piye later changed his throne name to Usermaetre, which had been used by Ramesses II, amongst others, and was also prominent at Gebel Barkal. The accession of Shabaqo saw a significant change. Although the king's throne name, Neferkara, had been used by Ramesses IX, it was also that of the sixth Dynasty pharaoh, Pepi II, and Shabaqo's choice of the simple formulation Sebaq-tawy for his Horus, Nebty and Golden Horus names was also typical of the Old Kingdom. With the extension of Kushite rule over the whole of Egypt, building work, albeit on a modest scale, was resumed in the temple complexes of Thebes (Morkot 2000: 217–222, 226–228). When Taharqo ascended the throne in 690 BC, Thebes was an important centre of Kushite power in Egypt and had enjoyed a prolonged period of peace. Egypt's principal rival, Assyria, was preoccupied with affairs in Babylonia, leaving Taharqo free to renew Egyptian influence with the old trading partners in Phoenicia. The first decade of Taharqo's reign appears to have been peaceful, and certainly saw the initiation of large-scale building works throughout Egypt and the Kushite homeland (Morkot 2000: 229–258). One of the most significant of these was the temple built for Amun-Ra at Gem-aten (the modern site of Kawa), in the Dongola Reach of northern Sudan. One of several temples of very similar plan and scale built by Taharqo in Nubia, the construction and endowment of the Kawa temple is recorded in several official inscriptions (Macadam 1955).

Kawa

The Kawa temple, begun in Taharqo's fifth year, follows the 'classic' temple plan of pylon entrance, courtyard, columned hall and sanctuaries, with a throne hall typical of Kushite temples (Morkot 2000: 253–254). Although the temple plan is typical of the later New Kingdom, other architectural and sculptural elements are based on Old Kingdom prototypes. In the court and columned hall, date palm columns are used instead of the more typical papyrus bundle columns (Macadam 1955: pl. LX c.). These date palm columns are modelled on those in the fifth Dynasty pyramid temple of Sahura (ca. 2458–2445 BC) at Abusir in the northern part of the Memphite necropolis. The reliefs on the court side of the pylon (Macadam 1955: pls. IX, XLIX) are also adapted from the temple of Sahura. They depict Taharqo as a sphinx trampling a Libyan chief under foot, witnessed by the chief's wife and sons (Figure 5:1; O'Connor Chapter 9: 177–178, this volume). The original scene (Figure 5:2) in Sahura's temple showed the pharaoh in human form, not as a sphinx. Closer to Sahura's own time, the reliefs were copied, in slightly altered form, in the temples of Neuserra at Abusir and Pepi II at Saqqarah (Figure 5:3) (Leclant 1980). Although there are some adaptations in the Taharqo version, the names of the wife and sons of the defeated Libyan chief at Kawa are the same as those in the temple of Sahura, confirming that it served as the direct model (Figure 5:2). The Kawa building inscriptions state that Taharqo sent architects and builders from Memphis to work on the temple, and clearly they had 'pattern books' with copies of scenes. A more generalized inspiration from the fifth Dynasty may be detected in the form of figures. Baines and Riggs (2001: 112 n. 41) note the use of motifs from Abusir in a building of the reign of Ahmose II (Amasis) in the mid-twenty-sixth Dynasty.

The Kawa temple, completed in Taharqo's tenth year, shows quite clearly the royal patronage for such 'archaism' and the searching out and use of Old, Middle and New Kingdom models. Statues from the Kawa temple are modelled on New Kingdom works. The processional way was lined with granite rams, which may be recycled eighteenth Dynasty sculptures (Kozloff and Bryan 1992: 221–222, no. 31). If not, they are certainly modelled upon the rams that similarly flanked the processional way to Amenophis III's temple at Soleb. There had been a large number of statues at Soleb, but most of these had been removed by Piye to adorn the temple of Amun-Ra at Gebel Barkal. A foundation inscription of Taharqo in his temple at Sanam also refers to the transport of statues, in this case from the island of Sai, site of another New Kingdom temple. The re-use of statuary on a large scale is likely to have served as an inspiration to the creators of new works at the time, even if they did not model their own works directly on them.

Of the surviving contemporary sculptures from Kawa, one is a small statue of Taharqo as a lion (British Museum EA1770; Macadam 1955: pl. LXXIV; Russmann 1974: 18, 50, no. 18, fig. 12). This image, in which the king's face emerges from the lion's mane and ruff, has prototypes in both the Middle and New Kingdoms. Similar, but large-scale and elaborately detailed, granite images of Amenemhet III (with inscriptions added for a Hyksos ruler, Merenptah of the nineteenth Dynasty, and twenty-first Dynasty Psibkhanno) stood in the temple of Tanis (Aldred 1980: 127, fig. 86), and a pair of smaller simpler, limestone lions of Hatshepsut at Deir el-Bahri (Aldred 1980: 154, fig. 115). The scale and simplicity of forms of the Taharqo image suggests that the Hatshepsut lions, or one similar, served as a prototype. A second example of this type, unprovenanced (but probably from Egypt rather than Nubia) and uninscribed, but certainly Kushite, is in Turin (Russmann 1974: 55, no. 33).

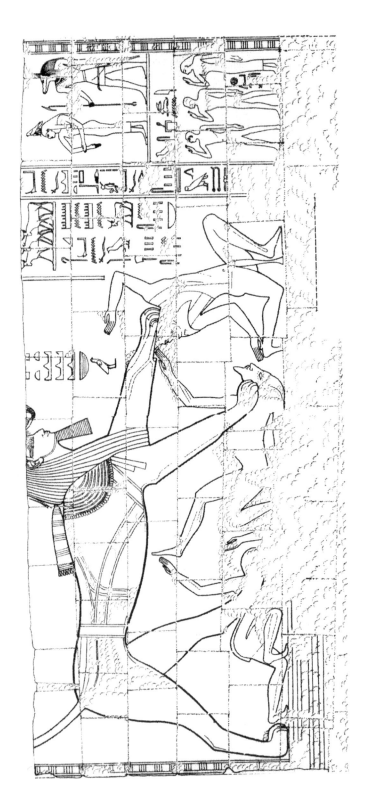

Figure 5:1 Pharaoh Taharqo as a sphinx trampling Libyans, on the pylon of the Kawa temple (ca. 685 BC) (after Macadam 1955: pl. ix, 8). Note that, in relation to Figure 5:2, the deities have been moved to a register above the family, the clothing has been modified and the position of the hieroglyphs have been changed.

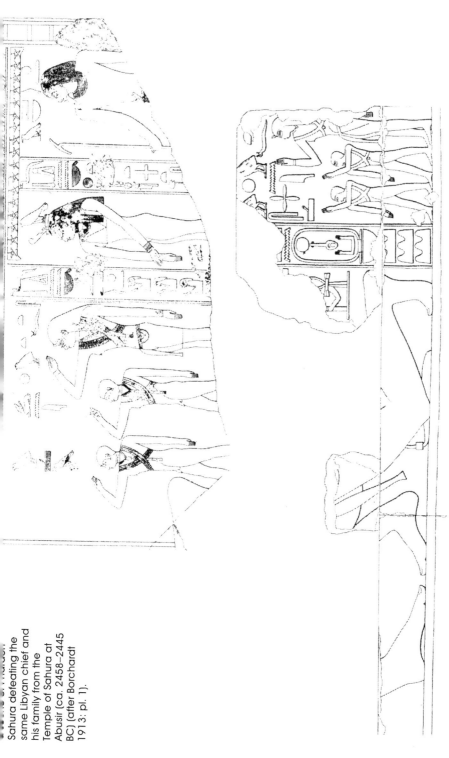

Sahura defeating the same Libyan chief and his family from the Temple of Sahura at Abusir (ca. 2458–2445 BC) (after Borchardt 1913: pl. 1).

Figure 5:3   Slightly altered version from a sixth Dynasty pyramid temple of Pepi II at Saqqarah (ca. 2200 BC). Note the reversed direction of the kneeling Libyan chief (after Jequier 1940: pl. 9).

Another, fragmentary, statue from Kawa also appears to be reviving an old statue type. In gray granite, it depicts a striding Taharqo carrying an offering table (Copenhagen, NCG 1706; Macadam 1955: pl. LXXIII; Russmann 1974: 49, no. 14). Taharqo, slightly unusually for a Kushite statue (although not for relief sculpture), wears the Nemes headcloth. This type of offering statue is familiar from the eighteenth Dynasty, but not well documented for the period following, so this image at Kawa may be another example of a revival, although an exact model cannot be cited. The shendyt-kilt is, as in most Kushite statuary, short, following the style found from the Old Kingdom to the mid-eighteenth Dynasty, and has the wide pleats found on statues of Old Kingdom and twelfth Dynasty date.

The Kushites in Egypt

The accession of Taharqo came some decades after the initial Kushite invasions of Egypt and the creation of the classic Kushite royal image. The facial features of Kushite royal iconography, generally rounded head and columnar neck are distinctive, and largely innovative. The musculature of the torso and legs is often likened to Old Kingdom works (Russmann 1974: 23–24), but is also found on relief sculpture of the eleventh Dynasty (e.g. Aldred 1980: 114, fig. 72) and of the twelfth Dynasty, notably the reign of Sesostris I (e.g. Aldred 1980: 121, fig. 81). If an Old Kingdom influence on the creation of the Kushite style is accepted, it would suggest that Memphite rather than Theban workshops were instrumental in its development, although the same features appear on works from Upper Egypt of the eleventh and early twelfth Dynasties. The issue is further obscured by the undoubted Memphite influences on those Middle Kingdom works produced in the Theban region, but many of those Theban monuments with strong Old Kingdom influences, such as the White Chapel of Sesostris I, had long been dismantled and buried within later structures.

The earliest surviving large-scale work by a Kushite king was the rebuilding and enlarging of the temple of Amun-Ra at Gebel Barkal by Piye. The poor state of preservation of the reliefs in the halls added by Piye makes a stylistic analysis rather difficult, although they do show some characteristics of the twenty-fifth Dynasty style, such as the columnar neck. Piye's control of the Theban region would immediately suggest that he had employed Theban artists, but his alliances with the rulers of Hermopolis and Heracleopolis, and his victory over the dynasts of Lower Egypt, at least allow the possibility of Memphite artists travelling south. What does survive in the Barkal temple reflects the events narrated in the king's great inscription. These are the first battle scenes to have been created since the reign of Ramesses III, and the surviving fragments do not indicate use of earlier models, but invention. The horses (Dunham 1970: pl. L) and their accompanying grooms appear to have no prototypes in Ramesside reliefs.

The style and iconography of the Kushite royal image was probably established in Piye's reign, although relief images of the king are badly preserved, and no statuary survives. The Kushite kings soon revived a long tradition of large-scale royal standing statues in stone. There are heads, and parts of bodies, of several small statues of Shabaqo which have the distinctive new iconography, but the only large-scale statue certainly inscribed for the king is a recycled New Kingdom work (Aldred 1980: 214, fig. 176; Russmann 1974: fig. 4). A headless seated statue of Shabaqo (Curto 1985: 25–30, no. 5, pl. VI) could be argued to have Old Kingdom features on a small scale, and the reliefs on the granite shrine dedicated by the king at Esna (Myśliwiec 1988) have the emphasized musculature of arms and legs that is characteristic of archaizing images. A granite head from Memphis probably represents Shebitqo (Cairo CG 1291; Russmann 1974: 53, no. 29, fig. 7), and suggests that new large-scale works were being created, whilst a broken seated statue with the king's names, also from Memphis, is more likely to be an old piece recarved (Cairo CG 655; Russmann 1974: 47, no. 6).

Even if the Kushite royal image was developed under the influence of Old Kingdom and Memphite models, the colossal black granite statue of Taharqo, of which only the head survives (Cairo CG 560; Aldred 1980: 214, fig. 178; Russmann 1974: 47, no. 9, figs. 8–9; Smith 1981: 402–403, figs. 396–397), and the comparable, if smaller, standing statues of the king from Karnak (Cairo CG 42202, JE 39403–04; Leclant 1954: 103, pls. LXIV–V; Russmann 1974: 48, nos. 11–13), are all Theban products. Taharqo also had identical images set up at Gebel Barkal (Dunham 1970: pls. VII–VIII), where they begin a sequence of statues continued by his successors (Dunham 1970: pls. IX–XVI). Kushite royal statues in Memphis suffered a more dramatic fate than those in Thebes. No doubt because of their distinctive iconography, many were completely destroyed, but two statue bases with Taharqo's names were excavated in the palace of Esarhaddon at Nineveh, looted, very probably, from the city (Russmann 1974: 47, nos. 7–8).

The use of models of Old or Middle Kingdom date is clearly visible in relief sculpture, particularly of large-scale hieroglyphic texts, from Memphis. Very little of twenty-fifth Dynasty date has yet been recovered, presumably because the monuments were mostly dismantled by their Saite successors. However, one surviving block (Berlandini 1984–1985), carrying part of a double crown, the Horus name of Shabaqo and parts of two columns of text, and another carrying a cartouche of Shabaqo (Wildung 1996: 174, no. 166) are distinctly archaizing. The detailing of the crown and the style of the large hieroglyphs and rope frame are similar to works of the Old Kingdom and the twelfth Dynasty, and also reminiscent of one of the major archaizing monuments at Memphis, the gate from the so-called Palace of Apries (Figure 5:4; Petrie 1909b). Indeed, when it was excavated, the gate was suggested to be of early twelfth Dynasty date. Although the gate is well preserved, the spaces for the name of the ruler are blank. As with the archaizing monuments of Shabaqo from Memphis, the style of the hieroglyphs and layout of the royal titles is similar to work of the Old Kingdom and twelfth Dynasty, as is the overall design and execution. It is the facial features of the pharaoh that point to this being a twenty-sixth Dynasty archaizing monument.

The inspiration of Djoser

Of particular significance in any attempt to understand the 'archaizing' process are the reliefs depicting Djoser in the subterranean rooms of the Step Pyramid complex (Firth and Quibell 1935: pls. 15–17, 40–42, 44). These scenes depict the king in various rites associated with the sed-festival. Two of the scenes are covered by a grid square for copying (Firth and Quibell 1935: pls. 15–16) and the proportions are those of the

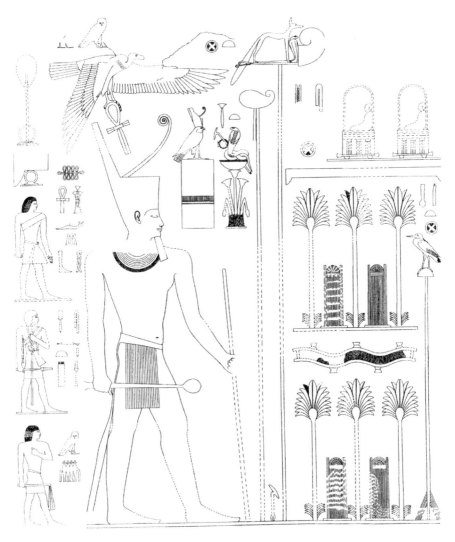

Figure 5:4 Sculptured gateway from the palace Apries at Memphis (ca 589–570) originally attributed to the reign of Sesostris I of the twelfth Dynasty (ca. 1250). The composition of the texts are Old Kingdom/twelfth Dynasty, but the features of the unnamed pharaoh are certainly twenty-sixth Dynasty.

'Saite Canon', which we now know was already in use in the twenty-fifth Dynasty. Baines and Riggs (2001: 111–113) discuss the access to the Step Pyramid and possible Late Period restorations, and the use of the statue of Djoser in the serdab as a model (direct or indirect) for a statue of probably thirtieth Dynasty date (but see Ashton Chapter 12: 223, this volume). This image, as with so many 'archaizing' monuments, is not a direct copy, but adapts elements from its prototype. Baines and Riggs (2001: pl. XV, 2–4) also illustrate the bronze base of a votive statuette from north Saqqarah that has hieroglyphic texts modelled on titularies from the Step Pyramid complex.

It has been quite widely suggested that 'archaizing tendencies' started just before the twenty-fifth Dynasty, and in Lower Egypt (see Fazzini 1972: 64, 65, and n. 74). The crucial period seems to be that phase during which the Kushites under Kashta and Piye took control of Thebes, and Tefnakht and Bakenranef attempted to reunite Egypt under Saite rule. The earliest known pieces to include features that appear undoubtedly to be 'archaizing' are two faience plaques carrying the name of a king, Iuput. Iuput is certainly to be identified with the ruler of Tent-remu, one of the four 'uraeus-wearing' pharaohs named in the inscription recording Piye's conflict with Tefnakht of Sais (Morkot 2000: 191).

The two plaques depicting Iuput were probably parts of a wooden shrine. One is now in Brooklyn (Aldred 1980: 213, fig. 174; Fazzini 1972: 65, fig. 36) and the other in Edinburgh (Aldred 1980). They were once thought, on tenuous evidence, to have come from Karnak, but Anthony Leahy (1992: 237 n. 88) presents more cogent reasons for a northern origin. The Brooklyn plaque is simple, carrying only an image of the king walking, flanked by cartouches (Figure 5:5). The Edinburgh plaque shows the king as the newborn sun god emerging from an open lotus flower. The figure on the Brooklyn plaque has the broad shoulders and narrow waist, and detailed musculature of the legs, typical of classic Kushite images from the time of Shabaqo onwards. But it also has the rather low waist and shortish legs more typical of relief sculptures of the reign of Taharqo. Precise dating of the Iuput plaques within the context of the twenty-fifth Dynasty is impossible: the king is named in the inscription of Piye, and a stela of his twenty-first year is known, so it is conceivable that he continued to reign alongside Shabaqo, and even Taharqo (cf. Leahy 1992: 236). However, the low waist in relation to broad shoulders and a long torso can be found on the stela of Piye's principal opponent, Tefnakht, and on a faience vase of Tefnakht's successor in Sais, Bakenranef. These features may therefore have been a Lower Egyptian development, ultimately used by Taharqo's sculptors. Although, as Fazzini (1972: 65) has noted, the royal costume has parallels in the Libyan Period, it is almost identical to that worn by Djoser in the Saqqarah reliefs (Firth and Quibell 1935: pls. 17, 40, 41): Iuput has no beard, and wears a different crown, but the similarities between the figures are strong. What is also perhaps significant is that Djoser's figures have the same broad shoulders, with narrow, low waist, and muscled legs: but these features also appear on relief sculpture of the eleventh and early twelfth Dynasties. Whether or not Iuput's figure was modelled on those of Djoser, other reliefs that do appear to have been influenced by, if not based directly on, the Djoser reliefs were excavated at Tanis (Montet 1952, 1966).

In clearing the Sacred Lake there, Montet recovered a large number of architectural blocks carrying relief sculpture. These formed parts of monuments of a number of different pharaohs. One group can be identified as parts of a gateway of a ruler named Gemenef-khonsu-bak. In this case the facial features, with heavy beard, preserved on one block are very similar to those of Djoser's reliefs. Indeed, Montet (1952) initially ascribed the archaizing blocks to a hitherto unknown pharaoh of the Old Kingdom. There must have been other influences on the artists responsible for the archaizing works at Tanis and Memphis, since Djoser used only a Horus name, and the full titulary with two cartouche names, as with the block from Shabaqo's Memphite chapel, must have followed later Old Kingdom or Middle Kingdom models. Again there is skilful adaptation and blending of models, rather than stale

Figure 5:5   Glazed plaque of the late Libyan pharaoh Iuput (twenty-fifth Dynasty, ca. 750 BC), whose proportions, musculature and garment have close parallels with the work of the Kushite pharaoh Taharqo (see Figure 5:1), and also Old Kingdom prototypes.

reproduction. Unfortunately, it is almost impossible to date the reign of Gemenef-khonsu-bak with any precision, although the king's throne name, Shepseskara, is strikingly close to that of Tefnakht, Shepsesra, and other blocks from Tanis which name Tefnakht's successor, Wahkara Bakenranef. Although the evidence is limited, there does seem to be a move to 'archaism' at the time of the Kushite invasions and Saite expansion. The relatively few works that can confidently be attributed to the period immediately preceding, such as the gateway of Sheshonq III at Tanis, continue the style of the earlier Libyan period.

The role of Thebes

There are few monuments in Thebes that can be dated to the period immediately preceding the twenty-fifth Dynasty. Some were certainly dismantled, such as a structure of Osorkon III and Takelot III, its blocks re-used by Taharqo (Morkot 2000: 244). The most significant standing monument is the chapel of Osiris Heqa-Djet at Karnak, constructed by Osorkon III and Takelot III with the God's Wife of Amun-Ra Shepenwepet I. The earliest surviving Kushite works in the city were a structure of Shabaqo (Parker, Leclant and Goyon 1979), dismantled by Taharqo, gateways in the temple of Ptah, and reliefs added to the temple of Luxor. More decorated blocks from dismantled structures have recently been recovered from the foundations of the temple of Amun-Ra at Medinet Habu, and from beneath the first court in the temple at Edfu. The relief decoration on the blocks from Edfu and Medinet Habu is similar. They certainly predate the reign of Taharqo, and can perhaps be ascribed to Shebitqo. Shebitqo also built a chapel by the Sacred Lake at Karnak, and, with the God's Wife Amenirdis I, added a hall to the chapel of Osiris Heqa-Djet. Although this evidence is rather sparse, and made more difficult to assess by later re-use, certain stylistic features emerge. The early Kushite works show a fully-formed Kushite style in use for images of the king, but this appears alongside a continuing late Libyan tradition, and the beginning of a more strongly Memphite archaizing influence. This Old Kingdom influence appears in the depiction of female figures (either goddess or God's Wife) on the Medinet Habu blocks, perhaps attributable to the reign of Shebitqo. Although the evidence is limited, it may be that a Memphite-derived archaizing style was introduced in the reign of Shabaqo or Shebitqo: there was probably a period during which different styles coexisted. An even more pronounced archaizing style is found in the reign of Taharqo, in the reliefs of the chapel of Amenirdis I at Medinet Habu.

Certainly the reign of Taharqo saw the most extensive building work at Thebes for some considerable time, and this appears to have been allied with religious practices (Parker, Leclant and Goyon 1979: 80–86) and the rites that connected the temples on the east (Karnak and Luxor) and west (Deir el-Bahri and Medinet Habu) banks of the river. The temple built by Hatshepsut at Deir el-Bahri is particularly significant in the 'archaizing' of the twenty-fifth and early twenty-sixth Dynasties at Thebes. The temple formed the focus for one of the most important of Theban festivals, the Feast of the Valley, when the image of Amun-Ra was taken from Karnak temple to visit the west bank temples of the kings and to reside there overnight. The flat plain in front of the temple, crossed by the great processional way leading from the edge of the cultivation to the enclosure, was now chosen by the Theban noble families as a site for their tombs. These tombs, many on a large scale, were carved beneath the plain, with mud-brick pylons and enclosure walls above ground. Some of the larger tombs had a separate stairway and entrance opening onto the processional way itself, enabling the statues of the deceased to participate in the festival. It is not surprising, then, that scenes within Hatshepsut's temple were copied into those tombs. One of the largest and most important Theban tombs is that of the leading Theban official Montuemhat, who served as Fourth Prophet of Amun-Ra, Mayor of Thebes and Governor of Upper Egypt. Montuemhat's political career is very well known (Leclant 1961), and he served during the crisis years of the end of Taharqo's reign, playing a significant role in the transition from Kushite to Saite power in year nine of Tanwetamani and

Psammetichos I (656 BC). Montuemhat came from a powerful old Theban family, and married, as his third wife, a Kushite princess. The tomb of Montuemhat has scenes showing offering bearers carrying oils, and scenes of the slaughter of cattle, which are directly copied from the Southern Hall of Offerings on the upper terrace of Hatshepsut's temple (Manuelian 1994: 28–51). The offering bearers also appear in the tombs of Basa, Ibi and Pabasa, all of which are dated to the reign of Psammetichos I. Offering lists from Hatshepsut's temple were copied in the nearby tomb of the vizier Nesipeqashuty. This tomb has relief decoration that has parallels in both Old and New Kingdom scenes (Aldred 1980: 224, fig. 187; Smith 1981: 410, fig. 403). Despite the proximity of all these tombs to their ultimate source in the Deir el-Bahri temple, the use of pattern books is a possibility, as Manuelian (1994: 51–58) suggests.

Montuemhat's tomb is also important in that its reliefs incorporate a number of other 'vignettes' copied from Theban tombs of the New Kingdom. The most celebrated of these derive from the tomb of Menna, who lived in the mid-eighteenth Dynasty (perhaps reign of Tuthmosis IV). Menna's tomb-chapel has, typically for the Theban region, scenes painted on plaster. The vignettes have been extracted from their original context and translated into relief sculpture. A fragment of the relief, now in Brooklyn, has a register line with, above, a girl extracting a thorn from another girl's foot, and below, a woman nursing a child (Brooklyn Museum 48.74; Manuelian 1994: 18, fig. 1, doc. 9, 19; Smith 1981: 412, fig. 405; Figure 5:6). In the tomb of Menna, these two vignettes appear in different places. There is also adaptation, including an additional tree (and alteration of the shape of the trees to conform to the space) (Figure 5:7). A second fragment, now in Chicago, depicts two girl gleaners quarrelling (Oriental Institute 18828; Manuelian 1994: 20 figs. 2, 21, doc. 10). Montuemhat's artists also copied a group from the tomb of Rekhmira, vizier to Tuthmosis III, but again translated painting into relief sculpture, and reversed the group to suit its new context (Manuelian 1994: 21, fig. 3, doc. 11, 22). Stylistically too, the figures in Montuemhat's tomb differ slightly, having the proportions of Old Kingdom reliefs.

Manuelian draws attention to the continued use of Theban tombs as a source of individual vignettes and figures into the middle of the twenty-sixth Dynasty. He also points out that the oft-cited copying in the tomb of Ibi of scenes in the tomb of another Ibi of sixth Dynasty date at Deir el-Gebrawi is not as significant as had been assumed (Manuelian 1994: 24–28, doc. 13). Certainly, there is a strong correspondence between scenes in the two tombs, but now that the slightly earlier scenes in Montumehat's tomb are being uncovered, it is apparent that scenes from the Deir el-Gebrawi tomb were copied there first. This emphasizes the likelihood that pattern books were being used at Thebes. In this context it should be noted that relatively few Saite (or Kushite) period tombs in the Memphite region have been published, and it is therefore not known whether there might be quotations from the same sources there.

Montuemhat held a key role in the religious and political life of Thebes, and this is reflected in the large number of surviving statues that depict him. One particularly fine standing example combines the idealized youthful body with a mature face (Cairo CG 42236; Aldred 1980: 220, fig. 184; Smith 1981: fig. 407). The musculature of the body and legs has been compared with Middle Kingdom statues (Smith 1981: 414–415), although the whole image is very similar to statues of Taharqo from the same Theban workshop. Montuemhat's ringleted wig follows mid-eighteenth Dynasty

Figure 5:6   Relief sculpture of a woman and child from the tomb of Montuemhat (ca. 675 BC). Above is a girl removing a thorn from another girl's foot (after a drawing by Peter de Manuelian).

traditions. Differing interpretations of the influences for Montuemhat's statues highlights the difficulties, but also the clever ways in which the sculptors have selected and adapted their models. Aldred (1980: 220) describes Montuemhat as "an antiquarian and a sensitive connoisseur of the art of the past" which attributes the choices to the patron rather than the sculptor, and to the individual rather than to a wider cultural climate. This is another problem in discussing 'archaism': we do not have the evidence of where the stimulus begins. In the revival of classical traditions in Britain in the 18th century, the role of artists such as Piranesi and Robert Adam would be at least as significant as the role of the patrons for whom they worked, and the effect of both groups – artist and patron – on the more general formulation of taste.

Figure 5:7   Painting from the tomb of Menna at Thebes of a woman and child (mid-eighteenth Dynasty, ca. 1400 BC).

Montuemhat's inscriptions inform us of his role in 'restoring' monuments (perhaps following the Assyrian attack on the city in 663 BC), and he must have had a direct role in the production of the workshops. The Theban workshop of the reign of Taharqo produced many fine statues, including a large number in black grano-diorite. In addition to the statues of Montuemhat himself, these include the over-life-size statue of Taharqo of which only the head survives; three standing statues of Taharqo; a statue of the God's Wife of Amun-Ra, Amenirdis I dedicated by Shepenwepet II; statues and two sphinxes of Shepenwepet II; a broken statue, perhaps of a God's Wife, now in Sydney (Morkot 2003); a statue of Nesishutefnut, son of Taharqo; two large rearing cobra statues; the head of a statue of Amun-Ra found in the Mut temple at Karnak; and perhaps a divine image (recently recognized in Southampton Museum). Some of these statues also have the incised 'lip-line' that is a characteristic of fine sculptures of several periods, notably the Old Kingdom and the reign of Amenophis III.

This Theban workshop was 'archaizing', in that it used elements from earlier periods, but it was also innovative. Of certain Theban inspiration are the statues of the God's Wives of Amun-Ra, Amenirdis I and Shepenwepet II. The iconography of these statues derives from images of New Kingdom queens (Morkot 2003). Of particular note, the proportions of the figures are conventionally Egyptian, again harking back to the eighteenth Dynasty, and contrast with some relief depictions of Amenirdis I (in the chapel of Osiris Heqa-Djet at Karnak) which show her with the large hips and thighs used for other Kushite royal women. Indeed, in the tomb-chapel of Amenirdis I at Medinet Habu, both Amenirdis I and Shepenwepet I are depicted with the very slim body and proportions found in the early eighteenth Dynasty, if not modelled on forms of the Middle or even Old Kingdom. Clearly a distinction developed in portrayals of the God's Wives that selected a classically Egyptian iconography, which is at variance with the emphasis on the Kushite physical features and iconography of the kings. The black granite sphinxes of Shepenwepet II (Wildung 1996: 174–175, no. 168) wear the curled wig of the goddess Hathor and again look back to sculptures of royal women of the twelfth Dynasty, perhaps filtered through early eighteenth Dynasty models: such as a female sphinx shown amongst the statues produced in the Theban workshop of Tuthmosis III in the tomb of Rekhmira (Davies 1943: pl. 37).

Unfortunately, no statues or reliefs depicting Kushite royal women other than the God's Wives survive in the Theban region. The majority (most badly preserved) are to be found in the temples at Kawa, Sanam and Gebel Barkal, with some stelae from Abydos (Morkot 2000: 159, fig. 72). A statue base in the precinct of the goddess Mut in south Karnak probably belongs to an image of Taharqo's mother, Queen Abar. All that survives of the statue is a pair of feet, but the overall appearance of the base suggests a very close similarity with a statue from Gebel Barkal, inscribed for Queen Amanimalol (Dunham 1970: pls. XVII–XVIII; Wildung 1996: 222–223, no. 231). The unpolished nature of the Barkal statue raises the suspicion that it might have been an unfinished work of Taharqo's reign. As the king's own images were being produced in both Theban and Kushite workshops, it would be surprising if there were not similar statues of the royal women.

Relatively few statues of gods have so far been attributed to the twenty-fifth Dynasty. The black granite head of Amun-Ra from the temple of the goddess Mut

(Christie's 1991: 36–38, no. 99) is conventional in its iconography, but clearly related to royal depictions. The statue in Southampton Museum (Wardley and Davies 1999) is striking and unusual. The identity of the god is unclear, as there are no inscriptions, although Amun-Ra in one his manifestations as a creator-god seems likely (perhaps Pa-uty-tawy). In this image the most striking feature is the torso, with very broad shoulders, narrow waist and hips and pronounced musculature, reminiscent of Old Kingdom statues.

The Theban evidence from the twenty-fifth Dynasty shows an increase in the use of 'archaism' in the later decades. However, there is considerably more evidence from the reign of Taharqo than from his predecessors, and from the later Libyan period. The evidence from Memphis, and other sites in Lower Egypt, is both less in quantity and often more difficult to date precisely, but a case has been made for 'archaism' as a Lower Egyptian, perhaps specifically Memphite, development under the influence of the Saite rulers of the twenty-fourth Dynasty. Whether any political motivation lies behind it is far more difficult to assess.

Memphis and the Delta

There does seem to be strong evidence to suggest that archaism was developing in Lower Egypt, probably focused on Memphis, in the years coincident with the Kushite invasion of Upper Egypt. The best surviving earlier Libyan period work from the Theban region is painting on coffins, papyri and stelae, which has considerable elegance of line and develops from the late Ramesside style. There is, in contrast, hardly any surviving relief sculpture and statuary from twenty-first Dynasty Thebes. There are problems in attempting to draw any general conclusion based on the surviving monuments, since large-scale building works were concentrated in the Delta, notably at Tanis and Bubastis (and perhaps Sais) and the material from Lower Egypt tends to be different in nature (due to preservation) from that of Upper Egypt. What survives at Tanis incorporates huge quantities of recycled Ramesside stonework, and very little original contemporary sculpture. The material from the royal burials is difficult to assess fully, as there are certainly re-used pieces alongside new production.

Royal statuary in stone is quite rare in the Libyan period. This may be an accident of survival, since there are significant numbers of private statues from Thebes of twenty-second and twenty-third Dynasty date. The earliest major royal statue to survive is the upper part of an image of Osorkon I found at Byblos, and carrying an inscription added at the command of the town's ruler (Paris, Louvre AO 9502; *Tanis* 1987: 166–167). The statue is distinctly in the late Ramesside tradition, and the way in which the cartouche is deeply carved onto the chest raises questions about whether this could actually have been a recycled Ramesside piece.

If not recycled, the statue of Osorkon I allows us to closely date the change in style, since the next royal statues were made for his grandson, Osorkon II. A large statue of Osorkon II, kneeling and inclining forward, presenting an offering table, survives in two pieces. Before it was recognized by Bothmer (1960) as belonging to the body in Cairo (*Tanis* 1987: 108), the head (Philadelphia; Aldred 1980: 209, fig. 171) had been ascribed to the reign of Hatshepsut. The overall appearance is certainly of that period, and the mouth is distinctly Tuthmoside. A second, much smaller scale, statue of Osorkon II is also Tuthmoside in its style and detailing, leading Aldred (1980: 210) to say, "in such details as the design of the belt, the uraeus and ear-lobes, it follows a mid-Eighteenth Dynasty prototype, and gives rise to the unworthy suspicion that it may have been usurped". The eighteenth Dynasty certainly served as the inspiration for the artists of Osorkon II in the design and decoration of the granite gateway in the temple at Bubastis. The 'Festival Hall' (or 'Bubastite Portal') erected by Osorkon II owes much to a cycle of reliefs recording the sed-festival of Amenophis III. The surviving cycle of Amenophis III reliefs is preserved in the temple of Soleb in northern Sudan, but those of Osorkon II doubtless derive from an archival documentary source. Certainly the festival was recorded in Amenophis III's other temples constructed at the time, in both Thebes and Memphis. Kitchen (1973: 321) drew attention to the identical wording of the decree of tax-exemption to the city of Thebes found in the Bubastite reliefs and at Soleb. Osorkon II's reliefs are in a style that is also found on granite blocks of a monument of Osorkon I, also in the temple at Bubastis (*Tanis* 1987: 168–169, no. 44), that show eighteenth Dynasty influence, more Tuthmoside than Amenophis III.

The relationship between the content, if not style, of Osorkon II's reliefs and those of Amenophis III is particularly clear in the inclusion of the royal consort, Karomama, just as Queen Tiye accompanies Amenophis III at Soleb. The image of Karomama on the relief blocks does not, however, follow the example of eighteenth Dynasty female figures, and certainly not those of Queen Tiye in the Soleb temple. Karomama has large breasts and hips and heavy thighs; and her waist is not as narrow, with emphasis on a slightly swelling stomach. Karomama's iconography also differs from Tiye's: she wears the solar disk (but not the cow's horns of Hathor) in addition to the falcon plumes and modius, a sheath dress, rather than the more elaborate garment of Tiye, and she does not have the long sash. Significantly, she does not resemble the (slightly later) bronze statue of her namesake, the God's Wife of Amun-Ra, Karomama, but is closer in form to a group of bronzes depicting priestesses of the later Libyan period. This again suggests that there may have been stylistic differences between Upper and Lower Egypt, the south continuing a more conservative and classical style, with innovations and an interest in reviving older models in the workshops with major royal patronage in the north. The importance of Old and Middle Kingdom tombs as sources for scenes in Theban tombs of the late twenty-fifth Dynasty has already been noted, but they may also have served as models for artists earlier in the Libyan period. This is suggested by a group of faience 'chalices', which are generally ascribed to the mid-Libyan period, and were probably manufactured in Middle Egypt, in the region of Hermopolis (itself an important political centre in the later Libyan period). Both Fazzini (1972: 66–67) and Tait (1963) draw attention to the types of motifs used in the decoration of the vessels, which seem to have their origins in Old and Middle Kingdom tomb scenes of Middle Egypt and Memphis. The artistic role of Hermopolis and Middle Egypt is also raised by the lower part of a statue of a local king of the late Libyan period, Djehuty-em-hat, which was assumed by Wild (1973) to be a re-inscribed twelfth Dynasty royal statue, although the choice of black granite, and the musculature of the legs, is also typical of twenty-fifth Dynasty archaizing statues.

The artisans of the Libyan period undoubtedly excelled in the production of bronzes, and royal images are more common in this material than in stone. A series of splendid large bronze statues of priestesses survives (*Tanis* 1987: 89–90) showing changes in the depiction of women in the later Libyan period. These bronzes form a contrast to the celebrated statue of the God's Wife of Amun-Ra, Karomama, acquired by Champollion from Thebes (Paris, Louvre N500; *Tanis* 1987: 177–180, no. 48). The statue of Karomama is very much in the Ramesside tradition, and depicts her in an elaborately pleated, tight-fitting garment with pointed sleeves, and vulture wings enveloping her belly and legs. The whole is inlaid with gold and silver wires. By contrast, the later bronzes have unpleated dresses, although they sometimes have incised and inlaid designs. More significantly, the proportions of the female form have changed. The breasts are prominent, and become large in late examples, the hips become broader and the belly more pronounced. One of the finest examples, the large bronze of Takushit (Athens; Aldred 1980: 208, fig. 169; Smith 1981: 391, fig. 385) has large, quite pendulous breasts, with a narrow waist and swelling hips and belly, and is quite similar to later Saite works (such as a stone statue of the God's Wife Ankhnasneferibra – Cairo CG 42205), and even images of Ptolemaic queens. This more voluptuous female figure is found, perhaps for the first time, in the relief sculpture depictions of Queen Karomama on the 'Bubastite Portal' of Osorkon II. It appears in Thebes in reliefs of the God's Wife Shepenwepet I in the chapel of Osiris Heqa-Djet at Karnak, from the joint reign of Osorkon III and Takelot III, and this style continues into the early Kushite period, with depictions of Amenirdis I in the addition to the same chapel.

The problems of New Kingdom archaism

Many of the sorts of problems that hinder full understanding of archaism in the Late Period apply equally to the analysis of uses of the past in New Kingdom art. Again, the best preserved monuments are in the Theban region, and considerably less is known (although this is changing) about the monuments of Memphis and Lower Egypt. Again, there are the same problems of identifying prototypes. At the beginning of the New Kingdom, the classical style of the early Middle Kingdom was copied, based particularly on the style of Nebhepetra Montuhotep II found in his temple at Deir el-Bahri. This is in contrast to the continuance of the late Middle Kingdom style that can be seen throughout the Second Intermediate Period in the small scale survivals of the reign of Sebekemsaef and others. As with the Late Period, it is easier to see a generalized modelling on earlier forms than to identify exact models (which, of course, may no longer exist).

One of the important monuments of the beginning of the eighteenth Dynasty that survives intact is the stela of Ahmose from Abydos (Cairo CG 34002; Aldred 1980: 147–148, fig. 105). This finely executed work has distinct Middle Kingdom stylistic antecedents: the technique is typical of eleventh Dynasty sculpture, and the style is also reminiscent of that period (notably with the reliefs of Montuhotep II from Tod). Recent excavations at Abydos have recovered fragments of the sculptured relief decoration from the temple that Ahmose built there. Even in their fragmentary state, they show the influence of the style of Montuhotep II's reign, notably in his temple at Deir el-Bahri.

At Karnak, much of the Middle Kingdom and early eighteenth Dynasty building was dismantled, either by Tuthmosis I in his extensive rebuilding of the central part of the temple, or by Amenophis III in his westward expansion. Most scholars agree that there was a major structure, perhaps a court, at the junction of the east-west and north-south axes, where Amenophis III built his massive pylon. The blocks from earlier monuments found inside Amenophis III's pylon are assumed to have stood in that court. One of the most admired of these dismantled structures is the 'White Chapel' of Sesostris I. This monument in fine white limestone has elegant relief decoration that is clearly modelled on the style of the Old Kingdom. This is particularly apparent in the style and scale of the hieroglyphic texts in relation to the figures, and in the proportions and appearance of the figures themselves. The reign of Sesostris I saw a revival of the Memphite court style of the late Old Kingdom following the troubled First Intermediate Period years in which less formal 'provincial' centres had dominated production. Parts of a building of Amenophis I were also found, which have almost identical style and dimensions to the White Chapel. It seems certain that Amenophis I's artists replicated Sesostris I's building in the new king's name (Björkman 1971: 58–59, 92–93). This way of 'renewing' a monument, but in the name of the reigning pharaoh, is known from other examples at Karnak also. The 'Alabaster Bark Shrine' of Amenophis I was replaced by Tuthmosis III with an identical monument that was given a very similar name (Björkman 1971: 58). In these instances it may be appropriate to say that Amenophis I was 'archaizing' in his copying of the White Chapel of Sesostris I, but hardly so in Tuthmosis III's replication of a monument barely a hundred years old. Yet the motivation behind these 'uses of the past' may be similar. It seems hardly likely that the solid structure of Amenophis I's bark shrine was no longer usable, and the king was certainly not anathematized, so Tuthmosis III's replacement of the shrine seems to reflect a reverence and admiration for the past, in the form of rulers and monuments, balanced with the idea that the living ruler is more potent. The same question arises with replication of statues. A fine grained black granite statue of Tuthmosis III (Cairo CG 42056; Legrain 1906: 34, pl. XXXII) depicts the king carrying an offering table with pendant garlands of quails, lotus flowers, corn and ducks. The king tramples the Nine Bows beneath his feet, and the adjacent plants of Upper and Lower Egypt indicate the statue's intended orientation. A line of inscription describes the statue as the "*twt*-image of Menkheperra bringing flowers to Amun in Ipet-sut". Although the lower part of the statue alone survives, the type and identical offerings are found on another black granite statue, depicting Amenophis III. The middle section, from knees to neck, of the later statue are preserved, showing the close relationship between the two images, but what reasons inspired Amenophis III's sculptors is impossible to determine. It was images such as these that later served as the models for Taharqo's sculptors.

The influence of the reign of Sesostris I can also be detected in the colossal Osiride statues in the *wadjyt*-hall of Tuthmosis I at Karnak (Smith 1981: 230, fig. 224). Their architectural scale and form (*Louxor* 1985: 14–15, fig. 15, pl. II) is rather different to surviving eleventh Dynasty examples which have more sense of the body beneath the enveloping robe (*Louxor* 1985: 12–13, figs. 12–13). With some slight modifications the same type was used by Hatshepsut on the upper terrace at Deir el-Bahri (Smith 1981: 233, figs. 226–227). Hatshepsut's lions as simplified variants of twelfth Dynasty types have already been noted. The influence of twelfth Dynasty private sculpture on statuary of officials of Hatshepsut and Tuthmosis III has been observed by a number of writers, and there was also a direct modelling of the scribal statues of Amenophis III's advisor, Amenophis son of Hapu (*Louxor* 1985: 45–46, pl. VIII, figs. 68–69) on those of Sesostris I's vizier, Montuhotep (*Louxor* 1985: 16–18, figs. 20–21) as Kozloff and Bryan (1992: 251–252, no. 44) have noted. In this case Amenophis son of Hapu's reference to the past is specific rather than part of a wider phenomenon: this official was responsible for 'antiquarian' researches in association with Amenophis III's heb-sed festival, and the above 'archaism' may have been a further response to such interests.

The reign of Tuthmosis III does not appear to have been 'archaizing', but the pharaoh restored and dismantled the monuments of his predecessors, both immediate and farther distant in time. As Björkman (1971: 95–96) observes, Tuthmosis III emphasizes his legitimacy in renewing monuments and offerings of Sesostris I (at Karnak) and Sesostris III (at Semna), and in the latter instance adding a political justification to his activities in Nubia. Björkman (1971: 68) also draws attention to the suggestion that the (presumed) enthronement hall near the sanctuary at Karnak was modelled on a structure adjacent to the pyramid of Pepi II at Saqqarah. However this may be a case where similarity between surviving structures does not necessarily indicate direct derivation. It would seem more likely that any enthronement hall, even if paralleled in a pyramid complex, would have had its direct model in the temples of Memphis or Heliopolis.

In broad terms we may suggest that the very earliest New Kingdom work sought models and inspiration in the works of the eleventh Dynasty that survived, notably at Deir el-Bahri. A political motivation might be ascribed to this, since both Montuhotep and Ahmose were Theban rulers who reunited Egypt. Innovation, and perhaps Memphite influence, also characterize the early eighteenth Dynasty and forged the characteristic 'Tuthmoside' style. To understand the stylistic influences and developments more fully, much more of the building works of Ahmose and Amenophis I need to be recovered, the latter an especially important builder at Karnak and Deir el-Bahri.

The fragments of decoration from Ahmose's temple at Abydos already suggest that the battle reliefs of Montuhotep II (themselves only preserved in fragments) served as a model. However, given the nature of Ahmose's campaigns, innovation could also be expected. Remarkably, scenes of battle are at the same time one of the most prominent and elusive of genres in Egyptian art. The majority of surviving scenes of battle can be dated to the early Ramesside period, the reigns of Seti I and Ramesses II. There are no large cycles of battle reliefs preserved for the pharaohs who actually were responsible for Egyptian expansion into Nubia and western Asia in the early eighteenth Dynasty (Matthews and Roemer 2003), Amenophis I, Tuthmosis I, and Tuthmosis III. This is perhaps surprising given Tuthmosis III's textual record at Karnak. The explanation perhaps lies in religious decorum, and scenes of battle may have been confined to temples specifically associated with the royal cult. The earliest surviving scenes of battle from the New Kingdom are on the chariot of Tuthmosis IV, from his tomb in the Valley of the Kings. This may already be a 'stereotyped' scene since Tuthmosis IV is not recorded as a major warrior. The changes in military technology, and hence in the nature of battle, in the early New Kingdom would have forced innovations in the depiction of events. The most notable change was the introduction of the chariot, and this enabled artists to give a new prominence to the pharaoh. The few surviving complete battle scenes of the Old and Middle Kingdoms are within the context of private tombs, and do not contain royal images. The very few fragments associated with royal monuments do not appear to include the image of the pharaoh. The classic image of the ruler engaged in military action is the 'smiting scene' which can be traced back to the earliest periods. This shows the isolated image of the pharaoh wielding a mace (later the *khepesh*-sword) over one or more kneeling foes. Even if the pharaohs of the Old and Middle Kingdoms did indeed lead their armies into battle, the nature of the fray did not enable artists to give the pharaoh the appropriate prominence. With the introduction of the chariot, even in a melee (in which artists excelled), the pharaoh could become the dominant figure striking a dramatic pose.

The battle scene does not appear in the non-royal temples of the earlier eighteenth Dynasty. There are battle scenes surviving from a temple of Tutankhamun erected at Karnak, and, ironically, there are more extant examples for this pharaoh than his more military predecessors. These scenes show the fully developed type with a large figure of the pharaoh in his chariot loosing arrows at a fleeing host of enemies. Innovation is also apparent in the battle scenes of the reigns of Seti I and Ramesses II, in that they relate to a specific historical moment. How much they owed to scenes of the reign of, for example, Tuthmosis III, cannot be known.

More generally, the stylistic changes of the New Kingdom (based largely on Theban evidence) show a gradual development from Tuthmosis III to Amenophis III that does not appear to be influenced by archaism. Amenophis III states that there were extensive researches carried out for the celebration of his first heb-sed in his thirtieth regnal year. The organization of the festival appears to have been conducted by Amenophis son of Hapu, who claimed that it was a 'correct' celebration according to ancient sources, although it may actually have included innovations deemed appropriate to the time. The Theban monuments associated with this festival display some Memphite influences, notably in the preference for carved relief sculpture over the more usual painted scenes. Sculpted tombs are not unknown at Thebes, but because of the friable nature of the local limestone, painting on a thick layer of plaster was a more common technique, and led to a specifically Theban style.

The artistic changes of the reign of Akhenaten are usually regarded as radical and innovative, and certainly many features have no obvious precedents. One notable characteristic of the style are the scenes of the natural world, and these may well belong to a tradition that goes back to the Old Kingdom solar temples. The obvious antecedents are to be found in fragmentary reliefs from the temples of the fifth Dynasty at Abusir and Saqqarah, but the great solar sanctuaries of Heliopolis are more likely to have been the direct inspiration. The artists of the reign of Seti I looked back to the Tuthmoside style, rejecting the developments of the generation before their own, yet it can be argued that their successors in the reign of Ramesses II returned to that late eighteenth Dynasty style for inspiration. In their case, the demolition of Akhenaten's temples and re-use of the stonework at Hermopolis may actually have generated an interest in the style. The attenuated figures characteristic of some of Ramesses II's sculptures have their closest parallel in the less extreme statues of Akhenaten.

Conclusions

Baines and Riggs (2001) have shown that reference to earlier work can be identified in monuments of the thirtieth Dynasty and early Ptolemaic period, and they highlight the problems of dating works of those periods precisely. Although, as noted earlier, 'archaism' is often regarded as a characteristic of 'Late' Period art, a greater distinction between early and late Late Period may be necessary. There was undoubtedly an artistic resurgence in the thirtieth Dynasty that laid the foundations for the succeeding Ptolemaic period. This no doubt owed much to the political reunification of Egypt under indigenous rulers, following the period of Persian rule and dynastic rivalries. The re-unification of Egypt indeed seems to be an important political factor in archaism, but it is certainly not the only factor. Reverence for specific monuments, perhaps because of their cultic importance, or perhaps because they were considered particularly beautiful, was another. The restoration of earlier monuments for cultic purposes probably also played a role. The extensive use of motifs from Hatshepsut's temple at Deir el-Bahri might be connected with the revival (or elaboration) of the Feast of the Valley in the twenty-fifth Dynasty. Personal, 'antiquarian' interests may also have played a part. This might be the case with Amenophis son of Hapu, and with Montuemhat. The late Ramesside official Imiseba, who had archival responsibilities at Karnak, had scenes of festival processions copied from major Theban temples in his tomb (Bács 2002).

But we must always remember that we are drawing conclusions, or making assumptions using only a fraction of the material, and with considerable biases in its origin. A significant proportion of our evidence is from the regions of Memphis or Thebes, but we rarely have equal amounts of evidence surviving from both centres from the same periods. The surviving Memphite evidence has been predominantly of Old Kingdom date, and that from Thebes, New Kingdom, although this is now changing with the excavation of many important New Kingdom tombs at Memphis. The almost total lack of evidence for temple decoration at Heliopolis, for example, severely hinders our ability to understand how it may have influenced the art and architecture of solar sanctuaries in the rest of Egypt and Nubia, and must warn us of the considerable bias in our interpretation of Egyptian art. Also in considering 'archaism' or the use of the past, in architecture, statuary and relief sculpture, we must remember that it is rarely a stale reproduction of earlier models, but usually a combination of features both old and contemporary, that often serves as the starting point for a whole new artistic movement.

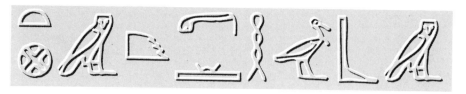

CHAPTER 6

LITERATURE AS A CONSTRUCTION OF THE PAST
IN THE MIDDLE KINGDOM

Ludwig D. Morenz

(translated by Martin Worthington)

One cannot distinguish truth from falsehood.

(P. Westcar, 6,23f)

History and literature

To 'remember', or, more precisely, to assure oneself of one's past and socio-cultural
origins, is a fundamental human need, leading to individual and social identity.
Within the bounds of a given culture, this does not necessarily lead to actual history-
writing, such as we know it from the Hebrew Bible or from Herodotus and
Thucydides (Momigliano 1990). Indeed, in Middle Kingdom Egypt there is no such
history-writing. Nonetheless, reference to a mythically exaggerated or even fictitious
past, both recent and distant, can be found in a variety of different contexts. Huizinga
(1936: 9) defined history as "the intellectual form in which a civilization renders
account to itself of its past" (and see Baines 1989b). Literature can be particularly
fruitful in this regard, where a story explicitly concerns the past, or where a text is set
in illo tempore. Fictionality plays a particular role in this process (Moers 2001: ch. 2, esp.
19–105; Fischer-Elfert Chapter 7, this volume).

   In writing fictitious literary texts, building-blocks and structures were borrowed
from the real world. Of course, fictional texts do not simply reflect the past as it was.
The critical reader has to take into account a myriad of cloudings and refractions.
Historians such as Liverani (1993: 46) in principle counsel scepticism, or at least
caution, regarding surface-historicity. The realization of the existence of secondary
historicity, as distinct from surface historicity, has led Egyptologists to date fictional
texts set in the 'Time of the Regions'[1] to a more recent time (Loprieno 1996a, Chapter
8, this volume). The one remaining plausible, if not certain, candidate for an origin in
the Time of the Regions is the 'Instruction for Merykara' (Morenz 1997). Liverani, on
the other hand, believes that the date of composition of a fictional, would-be historical,
text can be determined from internal evidence. However, a text with no precise
references to any particular period can fit more than one political situation – not least
because different reading strategies can be applied to it and it can be read from

different perspectives; this is particularly true in the absence of a paratext and extratextual information. In the case of fictional Egyptian texts it is often difficult to pinpoint the boundaries of interpretational license inherent in the work and intended by the author (Eco 1990, 1992; Moers 2001). Providing they are not totally absurd, one can view Egyptologists' different ways of reading the same literary texts, such as the story of the 'Shipwrecked Sailor', as indicators of their literariness.

The emergence of belles lettres in the social context of the Middle Kingdom

Belles lettres (mdw nfr.w ts.w stp.w, 'goodly words and choice verses' – as in the 'Prophecy of Neferti' (E 7 ff, repeated in 13)) emerged in Egypt in the Middle Kingdom (Parkinson 1997a: 134–135, 2002), that is, a millennium after the invention of writing, in the fourth millennium. Clearly, however, people would have been telling stories and singing songs much earlier, even if they were not written down. Indeed, at least a few forms of oral poetry are attested indirectly in workmen's songs, which are inscribed in several Old Kingdom tombs (Brunner-Traut 1975); for example, the song of the litter-bearers, which is attested in several Old Kingdom tombs. To these might be added sacred texts which are clearly fashioned poetically, such as the 'Pyramid Texts'; but these presumably served practical purposes as spells and incantations. Furthermore, certain letters can be assumed to have served to entertain. Such exquisite (i.e. 'belles'; i.e. Egyptian nfr) letters, which are best known from the reign of Djed-ka-Ra Asosi (2410–2380 BC), can be interpreted as precursors of the belles lettres of the Middle Kingdom (Morenz 1996: 25–26).

A fundamental technical prerequisite for belles lettres was supplied by a sort of media revolution: in the early second millennium BC an extraordinary expansion in the use of writing becomes discernible in several sectors of Egyptian society (Morenz 1996: 3–5). With this resource, and in the context of the new social cohesion (Morenz 2001: ch. 1), literature was composed which did not just serve immediate practical needs such as divine cult, or the attempt to come to terms with the afterlife, or the demands of daily life. In this complex process and its ramifications, the need to discuss the most disparate matters as well as cultural self-assurance probably played a large part, and early belles lettres can be subsumed under the label 'Problem Literature' (Blumenthal 1996). These texts were conceived aurally, that is, they were intended to be read aloud. In this respect they were closely related to the spoken word. This new type of written word, which was far removed from a primary functional context and was situationally abstract, provided both entertainment ('amusement of the heart', shmh-jb) and intellectual adventure ('search of the heart', hhj n jb).

Texts from texts

The belles lettres of the Egyptian Middle Kingdom can be considered 'Palimpsest Literature' (Genette 1997), that is, literature in which a model textual genre is played with, giving rise to a new, literary, text. Indeed, there are various examples in Middle Egyptian literature in which a written tale is modelled on a more strictly purpose-bound genre:

Hypertext/Parody	Hypotext/Genre used as Model
'Sinuhe'	(funerary) Self-presentation, consisting of various genres
'Shipwrecked Sailor'	Expeditionary report, also Myth Travel-Narrative
'Eloquent Peasant'	Letter or court record with pleas
'Admonition of Ipuwer' and 'Prophecy of Neferti'	Prophetic texts, Lamentations
The so-called 'Herdsman's Tale'	Myth
'Instruction of Amenemhet'	Instruction, Self-presentation and Letters to the Dead

Some of the genres of text listed above as models are not attested in all periods. Thus 'prophetic texts' are not attested directly from the Old and New Kingdoms, but their existence can be inferred. Without them as background, texts such as the 'Prophecy of Neferti' would be inconceivable. Similarly, 'Myth' texts are not directly attested from the Old and Middle Kingdoms, but their existence also can be deduced, since a text such as the 'Herdsman's Tale' (Morenz 1996: ch. 5) would be incomprehensible without them as background. In the case of the 'Instruction of Amenemhet' (see below) the anonymous Egyptian author used the genre label 'Instruction' (sb3.yt) with an especial sense of parody. Here intertextuality was played with consciously (Moers 2001: ch. 2). Of course this did not simply amount to the transference of a given genre into *belles lettres*; rather, for each literary text we must reckon with a complex intertextuality and references to more than one model genre (Parkinson 2002: 17–18).

Since these more or less fictional texts are situationally neutral, the introductory text normally furnishes several keys for reading the text in different ways, thus generating a pact with the reader. Blair (1979: 12) wrote, "The victim (that is, the reader/listener) must agree in advance to participate in trickery (that is, when receiving the text)".

References within texts to historical periods

Occasionally, *belles lettres* texts were authored without deliberate reference to a particular point in time – for instance the 'Shipwrecked Sailor' or the so-called 'Herdsman's Tale'. To follow a suggestion by Baines (1990), this mode of representation could have been consciously intended to remove the story into mythological space by means of the narrative techniques of folklore. On the other hand, in its themes, motifs and language, a text such as the 'Shipwrecked Sailor' clearly belongs to an evolved sphere, employing also particular artistic devices in its language (Collier 1996).

In contrast, the majority of surviving Middle Kingdom literary texts were set in the past. In the process, the authors disguised their fiction as reality, though they probably intended their ideal readers to identify the historical 'costume', and the costume likewise to produce a sense of alienation. In this way the reader was invited to adopt a 'willing suspension of disbelief'.[2] The past lends itself particularly well to generating a milieu in which it could transcend the problematic nature of the present. Together with other alienations, this served to construct a 'tranquil zone' in which to act relatively freely (Morenz 1996: 201, 2000: 53–82; but for the problems in this area, see Moers 2001: 35–38).

More particularly, one can distinguish between settings in the recent, middle and distant past (Morenz 1996: 41). The introduction to the 'Tale of Sinuhe' claims it to be a funerary inscription. It is cast in the form of a funerary self-presentation (a so-called 'autobiography') by way of parody, and is set in the very recent past. Even if the manuscripts (e.g. Figure 6:1) derive from a somewhat later time, a dating of the text to the reign of Sesostris I or to a time shortly after it is at least very plausible; hence, from the point of view of the author and his contemporary readers/listeners, Sinuhe the literary figure belonged to the immediately preceding generation. This allows the tale wider freedom. Though the interpretation of the 'Tale of Sinuhe' should not be reduced simply to seeing it as propaganda literature, the author's 'present time' does play a clear role in the text: to represent the situation under Sesostris I as reflected in the life of a high court official. At the same time, the tale of Sinuhe was handed down through the centuries, being copied numerous times even in New Kingdom schools, and became a sort of classic (Figure 6:2). Culturally speaking, then, the text remained relevant in Egypt a long time after it was written; so the past in this text must have remained of interest to its readers (Parkinson 2002: 54).

It was with especial sense of parody that the anonymous author used the genre label 'Instruction' (sb3.yt) for the 'Instruction of Amenemhet', for here is a text of a different type from the usual instructions. According to the introduction, Amenemhet is already dead and speaks from the afterlife (Burkard 1999: 153–173), and one might think of this unusual situation in terms of an intertextual inversion of the setting of the 'Letters to the Dead'. If it was authored in the reign of Sesostris I (this being its most likely date, even though the oldest manuscripts date only from the New Kingdom), then the speaker's extraordinary situation places this text too in the recent past (Burkard 1999: 164–165).

Scholarly consensus is that the tale of the 'Eloquent Peasant' dates from the Middle Kingdom (Parkinson 1991), while, as the king's name Nebkaura shows, the petitions are set in the Heracleopolitan period. The dating is not given at the beginning of the text, but only after the first petition (B1, 102–104) – and, even then, apparently in passing, and certainly as if it were a matter of lesser interest (this is expressed by the introductory particle *jst rf*: Depuydt 1993):

> This peasant, namely, spoke these words
> in the reign of the dual king Nebkaura, true of voice.

In texts with ambitions of historicity, a dating formula normally appeared at the beginning, so the dating here being treated as a matter of lesser interest can be regarded as an indicator of literariness. Something similar is also true of texts which do not refer to a particular point in time, such as the 'Shipwrecked Sailor', or the so-called 'Herdsman's Tale', which are, as it were, set *in illo tempore*. Depending on context – for tales are fundamentally concerned with the past, even when, as in the

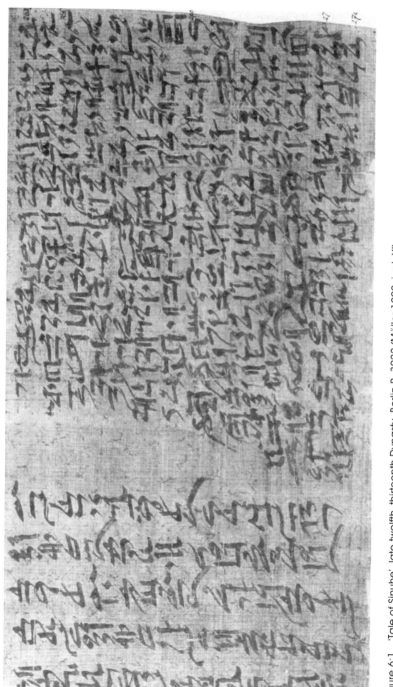

Figure 6:1 'Tale of Sinuhe', late twelfth–thirteenth Dynasty, Berlin P. 3022 (Möller 1909, i: pl. XI).

Figure 6:2 'Tale of Sinuhe', New Kingdom 'school' copy. Ostracon. Left = verso; right = recto.
© Ashmolean Museum, Oxford; ht. 88.5 cm (Barns 1952: frontispiece).

case of the 'Prophecy of Neferti', they are fictionally set in the future – *rk*, 'epoch, time' could refer to a past epoch, though it was also used in dates and self-presentations for the present or immediate past. The 'Eloquent Peasant' does not need a precise indication of when it took place, but it does require a loose historical embedding. The Heracleopolitan Nebkaura was portrayed as a truly good king. By contrast with P. Westcar's 'Tales of Wonder' or the 'Prophecy of Neferti', in the 'Eloquent Peasant' the entertaining features are not made quite so explicitly into a theme. Thus, Nebkaura is a good king, but not such an amusing one as Snofru (Parkinson 2000a). By contrast, Simpson (1991) saw in this a text directed against the king by the elite. Within the textual framework of the 'Eloquent Peasant' and the 'Prophecy of Neferti' (see below), pharaoh appears in each case as a legitimating background figure:

Snofru (in 'Neferti')	Nebkaura (in 'Eloquent Peasant')
wants to be entertained with good words	wants to be entertained with good words
writes words down himself	has words written down
prototypical listener and writer	prototypical listener/reader
interested in a rhetorically gifted outsider	interested in a rhetorically gifted outsider

Such fictionalized narrative settings are typical of this sort of framed narrative, and only very indirectly say anything about the concrete historical figures. 'Neferti' does not actually have a frame as such, but only an introduction and a concluding formula, which is stylized quite differently. In both instances (either by writing it down himself, or having someone else do it), a king from the past acts as the text's patron. By contrast with the famous Snofru (Graefe 1990), little is known about the historical Nebkaura, at least to modern Egyptology. For this reason, the variation between two of the manuscripts is interesting: while B1, 104 actually has *Nb-k3.w-rˤ*, R 17,1 has *Nb-k3-rˤ*. This suggests that there was a certain vacillation even for the Egyptian copyists. However, an abbreviated writing of the same kind, *k3* for *k3.w*, is occasionally attested in royal names. Scribal carelessness certainly cannot be ruled out (but see Morenz forthcoming). That Nebkaura (Khety) shows himself to be a good king through his far-sighted provision for the peasant's family might be relevant to the text's origin in the Heracleopolitan region. A tradition, probably Theban, portraying Khety as evil was highlighted by Vernus (1991). Perhaps the author deliberately selected a king about whom, already in his own day, little was known. This raises the question of why, of all possible periods, the text had to be set in the Heracleopolitan period. Was the portrayal and criticism of officials as bad as *Nmtj-nht* only possible in the past, even granted a good king and high steward? Was, in the view of later times, the accumulation of power by local officials specially typical of the 'Time of the Regions'? Was social criticism tactfully shifted to a past time regarded as troubled?

A more remote distant past is to be found in the setting of the fictional 'Prophecy of Neferti' and in P. Westcar's 'Tales of Wonders' (Parkinson 2002: 47). Historical royal names do appear in these texts, but they can be understood, at least to some extent, as serving to give the text a flavour of historicity and as being proto-mythical. The framing action in the 'Prophecy of Neferti' was shifted back into the past to the time of Snofru, that is, several centuries before the author's present time. Whether the text was composed in the twelfth Dynasty or later, in the Second Intermediate Period (Morenz 1996: 107–110), Snofru's day was already long past, and in this, the author's time, concrete historical memory was being re-cast as proto-myth. Despite these differences in the past, the tale of the 'Eloquent Peasant' and the fictional 'Prophecy' do share significant similarities in the function of the king who is made literary in the framing narrative (see above).

In P. Westcar's 'Tale of Wonders', the days of Old Kingdom kings – Djoser, Snofru, Kheops, and the first three kings of the fifth Dynasty – are brought to life in several sub-tales. The fictional dating to the time of Kheops is clearly contradicted by the information that the sandbanks lay dry because of low water (P. Westcar 9, 15; for the date see Schott 1950: 918). This offers an approximate clue to the text's date. The framing narrative places the tales at the court of Kheops. At least in part, the stories refer to each other in their content, and their import grows by degrees until the Hor-Djedef/Djedi story, which is the highpoint in terms of drama and meaning. The most space in the text as a whole is taken up with the fictional present under Kheops. Piquantly, speaking about the past is made into a theme in the text itself. The literarized figure Prince Hor-Djedef compares the princes' stories with reality:

Story: [So far we have only heard] tidings of the dead.
Reality: One cannot distinguish (rḫ) truth from falsehood. [But] in your time, your own
...
(Surely) he is not known (rḫ), [yet an expert (rḫ-jḫ.t) lives *here and now*][3]

(P. Westcar 6,23–25)

The opposition Story-Reality is to be found even in a historic-novelettish tale. This testifies to a conscious use of the past as a back-cloth. By way of comparison, one might *en passant* consider Hesiod's Theogony (V.27), where the Muses announce to the poet that they know how to tell the truth, and "lies which are similar to truth".

The construction of a (mytho-)historical Dark Age in literature

Most or all of the so-called Lamentation Literature – especially 'Admonitions', 'Kha-kheper-ra-seneb', the 'Conversation of the Man Weary of Life with his Ba', and the 'Prophecy of Neferti' – is actually not the product of a "complaining class" (Lepenies 1992). For antiquity, the Prophets in the Hebrew Bible can more or less be defined as a 'lamenting class', though certain beginnings of this are certainly to be found in Ancient Egypt, for instance in certain features of the figure Djedi (Morenz 1996: 117–119), who is clearly a literary construct, in a certain sense a literary idealization, who nevertheless reflects social realities.[4] With the 'Admonitions', for instance, the following correlations between literature and history can be suggested:

'Time of the Regions'	Direct, strong influence
Middle Kingdom	retrospective viewing of the 'Time of the Regions' as a dark period, an age of extremes

Second Intermediate Period	retrospective viewing of the 'Time of the Regions' as an analogous period
New Kingdom	literary text of the past

Further possibilities remain open; thus, there may well have been multiple editions (Fecht 1972). Despite its evident concerns, scholars no longer really consider this text to be direct evidence for the 'Time of the Regions'. A further consideration is that instances of internal unrest, against which the king advances victoriously, are to the fore in the royal texts of the twelfth Dynasty, being especially well attested in the inscription of Sesostris I in the temple at Tod (Barbotin and Clère 1991). Even so, one must assume that the events and processes of the 'Time of the Regions' were inscribed onto collective memory and appear in words, culturally transformed, in certain passages of the 'Problem Literature'.

In the 'Admonitions', the more or less historical past is constructed as a gloomy backdrop which contrasts with both ideal time and the present (Morenz 1999). For a long time, and for different reasons which were never really made explicit, interpretation of history from the perspective of posterity (Günther 1993) was also followed by modern Egyptology. One of the main contributing factors was the vividness of descriptions in literary sources, which were often believed to be contemporary works. In addition, there were interpretational strategies oriented towards complexity and monumental art. Further, the relatively few genuine monuments of the period offering evidence superficially appeared to be of a lesser quality. For example, the lexeme *ḫpr*, 'transform, happen' – plays an important part in the following passage of complaint poetry, from 'Kha-kheper-ra-seneb' 10–11 (text after Parkinson 1997b), where the end reverts back to the beginning, even lexically:

Introduction: Myself and *ḫpr.wt*
I am thinking of the transformations,
the matters which have occurred right through the land.
Transformations do occur:

World gets worse and worse
It is not like last year (/the past)
One year is more difficult than the other.[a]
The land transforms itself, so that my distress unfolds:
People act with dispeacement![b]

Explanation in three parts

Order and 'plans of the gods'
(a) Maat is given to the outside:
       jsf.t is in the interior of the 'palace'.[c]
       The plans of the gods[d] are disturbed,
       Their care is scorned.

Sickness, death befalling the land
(b) The land is mortally sick,
       Mourners' laments are in every place.
       City and land are up in cries of pain,
       All are under the evil to the same extent.[e]

Not even the dead can rest
(c) Aura – one turns one's back against it,
     The Lords of Silence[f] are troubled (/attacked).

Effect of the *ḥpr.t*
The morning comes every day:
One's face shivers over what has happened.

[a] Here one can presume a pun: *sf – snw=s*.
[b] Here *ḥtp.w* is employed euphemistically, so that the description of a world turned on its
     head is accompanied by a twisting of words, cf. similarly Parkinson 1997b: 67. There also
     seems to be a pun with *ḥd* in the foregoing, parallel verse; thus poetic tension is also
     generated by the word-pair *ḥd-ḥtp.w*.
[c] Cf. the passage (de Buck 1935–1961, VI: 278d–e): "They spoke, that they wanted to confuse
     Maat, that they wanted to set up Isfet at the palace" (see below). The interior of the palace
     stands for the centre of culture.
[d] Reference ought be made to the intratextual reference to "Plans (*sḥr.w*) of the gods" – *sḥr.w*
     nṯr.tq sḥr.w ḥpr ḥ.t tʒ – "the matters (*sḥr.w*), which have arisen throughout the land", and to
     'Prophecy of Neferti', E 68f; comparison in Moers: 2001: 146.
[e] Pun *jʿnw – jwnw* at the end of each verse.
[f] I.e. the dead and tradition.

This poetic lament describes a period of anti-*ḥtp* (cf. the euphemism *ḥtp.w*,
'dispeacing'). This artistically composed and clearly stylized passage has no direct
reference to a particular historical time, and is perhaps supposed to read as if it is
timeless. At the same time it is part of a discourse which we presume to have been
occasioned and shaped in the first place by the *ḥpr.wt* after the Old Kingdom. To this
discursive universe belongs for instance Adm. 2,3: "Everyone says: 'We did not know
(at all) what is happening (*ḥpr.wt*) right through the land.'"

In Egyptian, the root *ḥpr* (Buchberger 1993) is one of the words which mean little
in their own right, and derive their precise meaning from context. When used to
denote a departure from a condition thought of as good, and not a development
towards something good, however, the abstract noun *ḥpr.wt* usually bears negative
connotations in the social and political sphere. This is similarly true of *jy.t*, 'that which
comes' = injustice, disaster (S. Morenz 1996). Both these words seem, at least according
to extant sources, to have been coined in the milieu of 'high culture' in the 'Time of the
Regions'. Considerations of conceptual history (such as made so fruitfully for modern
history by Koselleck 1979) must coexist in the case of Ancient Egypt, with the high risk
of distortion by the accident of preservation. With extreme caution, one can connect
the act of giving a negative meaning to roots which were in themselves colourless,
such as *ḥpr* and *jy.t*, with the situation in the 'Time of the Regions'. One supposes that
in these troubled times the belief in a naive existential security, which is still to be
found in the elite's monumental inscriptions, was lost; that perhaps the rules about
what could and could not be said, altered.[5]

In contrast to the retrospective view, ancient Egyptian contemporary estimate of
changes was, to say the least, not unanimously negative; it even seems markedly
positive from the point of view of those in the ascendant: cf. the self-representations of
this period, in which an overall positive picture of the author's own region is painted,
and the *other* regions stand out as places of chaos. Nonetheless, later Egyptians
elaborated a powerful historical account of the aftermath of the 'Time of the Regions'
(for similar traditions, see S. Morenz 1971, 1972). This approach has lasted right into

modern Egyptology (e.g. Brunner-Traut 1986: 43), and treats the sum of experiences in the light of ranges of expectations (for the terminology, see Koselleck 1979: 349–375; Ricoeur 1997: 343–344). One can recognize the topical element in certain motifs of the Problem Literature thanks to a contrasting picture painted in the accession hymns of Merenptah and Ramesses IV. With the beginning of the new king's reign, run the texts, the exiles returned home, the hungry were sated, the thirsty were given something to drink, those quarrelling became ready to make peace, or, more generally, injustice was banished and Maat restored (Parkinson 2002: 58–60; in particular, see Tutankhamun's 'Restoration Stela' (Sethe 1906–1957: 2,025–2,032; cf. Schlögel 1985: 85–88).

In mytho-historical 'Problem Literature', the dark age was represented as being rooted in the divine plan for history (*shr ntr*: Morenz 1999: 124 n. 74); this is particularly clear at Adm. x + I, 7 ff (Morenz 1999: 120–124). It is possible to link such a plan of history with the notion that, in principle, history was knowable to the initiate (*rh-jh.wt*). Thus the literary figure Neferti asks the protomythical, literarized Snofru: "As something that has happened, or as something that is still going to happen?" (E 14). The prophetic genre of text probably derives from this notion of the possibility of knowing history. In these texts – especially the 'Admonitions' and the 'Prophecy of Neferti' – the distant past seems good, the fictional literary present bad, yet the future is expected to be good once more (Morenz 1999: 120–124). In the literary present constructed as a negative, opposite world, the "man of yesterday" (*z n sf*, Adm. 2,2) is lacking. In turn, this metaphor is characterized by great and immediately clear vividness. The author reveals himself to be such a man of yesterday, and presumes the same of his reader. This becomes apparent in Adm. 10,12–11,10(?), even though, because of serious damage, how this microtext ended cannot be established for certain. The series of appeals to the reader is always introduced by *sh3w*: "bear in mind!" The injurious present is invoked, with an implicit request for it to improve:

> Truly, the (former and intrinsic) nobles are (now) in lamentations (*nhw.t*),
> the (former and intrinsic) beggars are (now) in joy (*ršw.t*).
> Every city (says): 'Let us drive off the strong ones among us!'

(Adm. 2,7 ff)

In respect of their content and form (particularly the once-now pattern), the 'Admonitions' are strikingly close to the Sumerian city laments (Quack 1997), and, from Egypt itself, to the laments for the dead. The land versus city distinction can be explained by the structurally different frames of reference of Egypt and Sumer. In the 'Lamentation over the Destruction of Sumer and Ur', the decline of the land and its (capital) city is bewailed first, while that of the cities follows. Just so, the 'Admonitions' do treat of the decline of Egypt in general, but are particularly concerned with that of the palace (*hnw*; see chiefly Adm. 7,4, 7,6, and 10,6–10,12).

Michalowski (1989) explains the 'Lamentation over the Destruction of Sumer and Ur' as a piece of propaganda, a legitimation of the shift in power from the Dynasty of Ur to that of Isin. If one wished to adapt this explanatory model to the 'Admonitions', one could think first of all of the shift from Memphis to Heracleopolis, or alternatively of the new foundation of the capital Lisht under Amenemhet I; but this is not actually necessary. One might also consider that the social situations in the Isin-Larsa period and the 'Time of the Regions' were somewhat similar, in as much as an empire disappeared (the Third Dynasty of Ur and the Old Kingdom respectively), and the localities acquired greater significance. In contrast to more strongly individual laments (such as 'Conversation of the Man Weary of Life with his Ba' and 'Kha-kheper-ra-seneb'), the 'Admonitions' and the 'Prophecy of Neferti' lament the decline of Egypt as a country. One can imagine the 'Prophecy of Neferti', at any rate, with its announcement of the arrival of Ameny, the saviour king, being recited on the day of the coronation (and perhaps being repeated on a yearly basis). It could even have been composed for such a special occasion and then, gradually, have lost its concrete links with it. Perhaps one can distinguish further within the group of texts that, by reason of their 'Fictionality' and 'Dictionality' (Genette 1993: 21–29), could be termed *belles lettres* and works of art respectively.

The 'Admonitions'' description of an awful time, of the world turned on its head, may be directed at the 'Time of the Regions', transformed into proto-myth as a period of dissolution of order. It is probably the text's function to maintain consciousness of the world's ongoing situation of peril, using the catastrophe as an example. One can speculate that, linked to contemporary and subsequent interpretations and re-interpretations, the experiences in the 'Time of the Regions' led to a perception of existence which lacked the self-understanding of the Old Kingdom. This peril-conscious perception, which is also expressed in a few literary texts, may have contributed to the authoritarian character of the Middle Kingdom state. The tension between historical fact and worldview related fiction remains, in a sense, unresolvable, at least for modern readers.

Two detailed examples of reference to the past

Literature as oral tradition which has trickled into writing: Adm. 10,6–10,12

Though the only manuscript of the litany preserved in Adm. 10,6–10,12 (Morenz 2001: ch. 4b) is badly damaged, it can be reconstructed after the pattern of a destruction-litany from the 'Book of Caverns':

> Vanquished are the enemies of (that) lordly residence + epithet
> + reverse formulation (presumably referring to the epithet).

This pattern appears six consecutive times. The epithet after *špss*, 'lordly', which qualifies the residence is apparently always formed with an exocentric compound. Next to what were probably different nouns, we get the adjectives *sbk*, 'excellent', in the first two sections, and *ꜥšꜣ*, 'much, many' in the third and sixth sections. One can also posit the latter for the fourth and fifth sections. Altogether, one can render the entire section Adm. 10,6–10,12 as follows:

> Destroyed are *the enemies* of the <lordly?> residence, (once) excellent in councilors:
> ... .[a]
> > If the (chief) mayor[b] himself goes out, he has no escort.

Destroye[d] are *the enemies* of the lordly residence, (once)] excellent in ... :
...

... .

[Destroyed are *the enemies*] of the lordly residence, (once) excellent in laws:
...

... .

[Destroyed are *the enemies* of the] lordly residence, (once) rich in ...:
...

... .

[Destroyed] are *the enemies* of the lordly [residence, once rich in ...:
...

... .

[Destroyed are *the enemies* of the] lordly residence, (once) rich in offices:
Truly ...

... .

a In terms of content, one is reminded of Adm. 7,9: "See, the land's civil servants are scattered throughout the land." Here the double meaning of *t}* lends the text tension; *knb.tw n.t t}* designates the central administration in its entirety, which is responsible for the whole land, whereas in the following it is the scattering of single officials which is lamented.

b Bearing in mind that the titles *jm-r} nw.t* and *t}tj* were often combined with each other (Ward 1982: nos. 223–225), the title is likely to refer to a high official, probably the Vizier. When no other city – e.g. Abydos (Ward 1982: no. 221) – is mentioned, *nw.t* in the title *jmj-r} nw.t* in the Middle Kingdom refers (at least for the most part) to the capital.

This reconstruction relies on the assumptions that the strophes were composed with strict regularity, and that the once-now pattern of lament (Schenkel 1984) which is so common in the 'Admonitions' is implicit in the text. But, to judge by the lengths of the *lacunae*, the strophes differed from each other in varying degrees. Our understanding of the text is further contingent upon the interpretation of *hftj.w* as a euphemism (as originally suggested by Vernus 1990: 204 n. 207; and then in more detail by Quack 1993). The context suggests rather that something is being lamented over and not demanded. Nonetheless, the possibility cannot be ruled out that the six strophes are making a demand: "Destroy the enemies of the lordly residence ...!"[6]

If the interpretation favoured here, i.e. that of a euphemistic turn of phrase, is correct, then it would be evidence of an unwillingness to speak of the 'traumatic' destruction of the residence directly. In terms of its content, the first verse of the liturgical pattern would then mean: "Destroyed/vanquished is (that) lordly residence." Passages such as Adm. 7,6–7 also treat the theme of the destruction of the residence:

See, the residence is fearful from the lack of a lord,
Insurrection is breaking out unchecked.

The residence, *hnw*, is at once portrayed as enjoying special significance and being a symbol of the stratification of Egyptian society, whose destruction is being particularly lamented by the author of the 'Admonitions', who is conservative in his values. *hd.w*, which stands at the beginning of each strophe of the litany, can be understood as a passive participle, as for instance in Adm. 10,2 (cf. also the – admittedly very badly damaged – instances Adm. 9,8 and 9,11). Similarly, and still with reference to Egypt, *ḥḏ* is used in the small, poetically impressive lament in the 'Prophecy of Neferti', E 24:[7]

> Destroyed is the land: *t3*
>
>> No one worries about it,
>>
>> No one speaks,
>>
>> No one sheds tears.
>
> What is the land?   *t3*

The *now* section of the 'Admonitions' litany, which was probably largely made up of verse couplets, and describes present misery, may, as in the last preserved strophe, have been introduced by *jw.ms* in the others too. The old, bygone, lordliness of the residence (*ḥnw*) was contrasted with the loss of justice and cult in the here-and-now. The strongest thematic connection is with the 'Lamentation over the Destruction of Administration and Law' (Morenz 1996: ch. 3). Thus the six strophes display the *topos* of the residence as guarantor of justice and centre of culture, and invoke it as an indicator of decline. The once-now contrast implicitly contains an appeal to improve the present in accordance with the normative ideal (of the past).

The element of appeal becomes particularly clear when the normative past is recalled in the groups of verses introduced by *sḥ3.w*, 'remember!' (Adm. 10,12–11,10(?)). How this series of spells ended cannot be determined with certainty because the papyrus is damaged. Westendorf (1986) explained the once-now-once pattern as reflecting the fundamental Egyptian view of the life-cycle; yet the chief intention of Egyptian 'Lamentation Literature' – alongside the 'Admonitions', one should think in particular of the 'Prophecy of Neferti' (Blumenthal 1982; Helck 1970) – lies in contrasting a good world and a bad, in describing the endangering of Maat, and making the good world the object of public desire (Parkinson 2002: ch. 3). This good world appears as a horizon, and, as such, as a task for humankind. The fictional literary present appears to this 'Problem Literature' – or, more precisely, 'Lamentation Literature' – as a bad time, while the good time existed in the past, just as it stood as a task for the future. In this type of representation, anchoring the text (mytho-)historically is 'merely' an example of the fundamental thought's realization in fact (Morenz 1999). Thus allusion was made to the 'Time of the Regions' in literary texts such as the 'Eloquent Peasant' (Morenz 2000, and see above). The set of experiences is appealed to in order to create the set of memories. Moreover, in the Problem Literature a range of expectations is presented and legitimized. In the process, within the framework of Middle Kingdom culture, these texts operate as affirmants of the 'state'. Hence one can at least suspect that, politically and culturally, historical memory was instrumentalized (Assmann 1999b: 13–14). This hypothesis assumes that literary genres can be understood as cultural institutions (Raible 1980). However, such a concrete interpretation is derived exclusively from within the text itself, and little is known about the text's addressees and their way of reading it.

It is quite likely that the destruction lament in the 'Admonitions' refers to the destruction of Memphis at the end of the Old Kingdom. Thus, this fully independent micro-text can be understood as a sort of oral tradition or at least a literarily formed piece of historical recollection which has trickled into writing, but it is clearly a text with literary forms and ambitions – certainly not a historical report in the narrower sense. Indeed, even recently this passage has been understood as an almost concrete historical report (Gundlach 1992).

Historical references in sacred texts as an attempt at coming to terms with the past and as part of the discourse about the Kingdom

Occasionally, certain historical reminiscences ended up in sacred texts, not only in temple reliefs of the New Kingdom or Ptolemaic period – one thinks in particular of reflexes of foreign governments (e.g. Velde 1967) – but already in the 'Coffin Texts'.

Spell 656 of the Coffin Texts appears to be a notable textual encapsulation of the rivalry, known from several sources, which Thebes felt against Heracleopolis about dominion over Egypt. In this passage, an ideologically minute picture from the Theban point of view is transformed into something mythological. So far, the spell is only attested from the Theban grave (TT 319) of *Nfr.w* (a wife of Montuhotep II), and so was chronologically very close to this rivalry and the struggle for power in Egypt and prestige in rule. The relevant extract from the spell (*CT VI*, 277q–278f) runs:

> O Ra:
>
> Those enemies of Osiris spoke,
>
> that they rob (*nhm*) the white crown (*ḥd.t*),[a] the greatness of your[b] head, the
>
> *ȝtf*-crown, which is on the top of your[c] head.
>
> They spoke, that they wanted to destroy[d] (*ḥd.t*) the heads,[e]
>
> that they wanted to confuse (*ẖnn*) the p[eople][f] before (you).[g]
>
> They spoke, that they wanted to confuse (*ẖnn*) Maat,
>
> that they wanted to se[t up][h] *jzf.t* at the palace.[i]
>
> O Ra, concede that the word[j] of the Osiris NN is right.

a   The motif of stealing the crowns is so far attested extremely rarely, and only for the Ptolemaic period. On the cosmic symbolism of the crowns in this passage see Goebs forthcoming; this suggests that the motif is less likely to refer to conventional mythology than to a particular historical event.

b   This pronoun refers to Ra, so that the threat to his rule can be made clear to him. As an alternative, one could conceive of an exchange of pronouns and have it refer to Osiris instead of Ra. Such exchanges of pronouns are attested frequently in Egyptian texts and, importantly, in the 'Pyramid Texts' and 'Coffin Texts' in particular.

c   This pronoun again refers to Ra.

d   Here there is clearly a pun with the white crown *ḥd.t*, mentioned two verses earlier.

e   'Heads' surely stand for 'rulers' here, cf. the expression *tpj.w ȝ.wj* on the Gebelen relief (Kairo 24/5/28/5); see Morenz 2001: ch. IIIa.3. From a historical point of view, one might suspect that there is a reference to bellicose disputes within Egypt here (Morenz 2001: ch. IVd).

f   One could well restore *r[mt]* which would pair up nicely with *tp.w*, 'heads'.

g   Euphemistic omission of the divine name – here of Ra not Osiris – as is more frequently attested for *m bȝh*.

h   One could well restore *s[ʿḥʿ]*.

i   Cf. the verse couplet in the 'Lament of Kha-kheper-ra-seneb', see above. What is described there as an actual bad condition is here only depicted as the enemies' intention. We are dealing with different textual genres, authored from diverging perspectives and with different intentions.

j   For this sign-form, typical of the time, see Morenz 1998a: 197–198.

Quite probably this passage reflects rivalry about the kingship transformed onto another, quite different, plane; the rivalry can quite probably be connected with the 'Time of the Regions' and the Thebans' fight for royal rule. What especially argues for this is the recurring reference to the white crown, symbol of Upper Egyptian kingship. It remains questionable how far the crowns' cosmic symbolism is intended in this passage, for the 'political' dimension seems more important. In this context it is worth highlighting that the text does not speak of a single enemy of Osiris, but of an entire group: this could refer to several potentates (similarly, the phrase *tpj.w t3.wy* on Montuhotep's temple relief at Gebelen qualifies the Theban potentates' opponents within Egypt; Morenz 2001: III a.3). However, elsewhere in this spell, it is a "devourer of Millions" (*ʕm-ḥḥ*), a "donkey" (*ʕ3*) which is spoken of as "chief adversary" (de Buck 1935–1961: 276l and 277k). This mythological identification clearly has negative, Seth-like connotations here, while elsewhere in the Coffin Texts (de Buck 1961: 46n and 347f) the Devourer of Millions clearly has positive connotations. It is precisely in the case of a being with an aggressive name that such ambivalence might be expected. On the mythological plane, one can discern a reference to Seth in these characterizations, while in historical terms one might suspect that the Heracleopolitan ruler is behind them. One can probably explain the whole of spell 656 as a Theban product.[8]

The actions of the rivals, who rob (*nḥm*), destroy (*ḥd.t*) and confuse (*ḫnn*), are presented as a disturbance of Maat. Thus *ḥty* (probably a representative of the Heracleopolitans) is slandered in a verbal challenge in the Theban self-presentation of *h3rj*, of the eleventh Dynasty, as a Seth-like "producer of thunderstorms in the region". Correspondingly, and analogous to the self-presentation of *h3rj*, one can connect the reference to Horus in de Buck 1935–1961: 277f with the Theban Horus-king, thereby reprocessing mythology as history (Morenz 1998b: 12–15).

This interpretation also fits the mention of Ra as an arbitrator between Osiris and his enemies, and indeed starting with Antef III, Theban kings did refer to Ra explicitly in their titulature. In the royal ideology of the later eleventh (Theban) Dynasty, Ra was constructed as guarantor of the dynasty's kingship. Thereby those in the ascendant were, for the purposes of legitimating their historically recent kingship, set into an ancient tradition (Morenz 2001). This becomes clear, for instance, in the later name-forms of Montuhotep II, Nebhepetra (Morenz 2001: IIIa). This was written with the *ḥp.t* – steering tool in an earlier phase, and subsequently with the *ḥp.t* – rudder.[9]

> Truly, the Ship of the South has failed, the cities are hacked to pieces.
> Upper Egypt has become a dried country.

Also, in the 'Prophecy of Neferti', it is said of the saviour king Ameny:

> The one who circles round the fields is in his power,
> the rudder is moving (E 60f).

In this sacred text a large part is played by an involvement with recent history, and hence by the legitimation of the present. It stands in what we suppose to have been, in the eleventh Dynasty, a very intensely conducted discourse about kingship, of which only a few fragments are preserved – especially from the time of Montuhotep II.[10] This formed a fundamental background to *belles lettres* in the Middle Kingdom.

Notes

1   This new historiographical concept should dispel the impression of a 'dark age', evoked by the usual phrase 'First Intermediate Period' (Morenz 2001: ch. 1).

2   Coleridge (1817: ii, 2), in distinguishing the aims of his own poetry from those of Wordsworth's in their joint project 'Lyrical Ballads', stated: "it was agreed, that my endeavours should be directed to persons and characters supernatural, or at least romantic; yet so as to transfer from our inward nature a human interest and a semblance of truth sufficient to procure for these shadows of imagination that willing suspension of disbelief for the moment, which constitutes poetic faith."

3   Despite the serious damage, the sense seems clear. The root rh, 'know', seems to be the strophe's catchword, being repeated at least two times in this brief passage. Hence, the break at the end can be restored with some confidence as rh-$jh.t$. This epithet excellently fits the same Djedi who is hereby introduced into the narrative (Morenz 1996: ch. 4).

4   For the significance of literary sources for historical sociology, a passing reference is appropriate to the works of Lepenies. Lamentation Literature does not actually seem pessimistic, but rather affirmative of culture and the 'State', despite the fact that recourse is had to a mytho-historical disaster, to use as a contrasting backdrop (Morenz 1996). These texts were presumably written by 'men of good knowledge' (Menschen guten Wissens, staatskonforme Funktionselite – Lepenies 1992) and probably originate from the state-conforming functional elite, the opposite of a 'complaining class'. Decline or even the loss of yesterday (*sf*; cf. for instance the paronomastic phrasing Adm. 11,2 *nn z n sf* – the "Man of Yesterday does not exist"), i.e. a break with tradition (*sšm.w n t3*, "instructions of the land", Adm. 15,1; Morenz 1999) was considered in Ancient Egypt to be a basic evil against culture, and not all discussion of it can be directly and immediately anchored in history.

5   Levi-Strauss (1970) and Eliade (1959) assume that as a rule humans find change – i.e. history – difficult to bear, and for that reason they develop certain social manners which generate a feeling of constancy. Behavioural scientists (e.g. Lorenz 1977: ch. 10, esp. 248–250) indicate that concrete changes in animals and humans are generally perceived to be unsettling or downright dangerous.

6   On reading the first draft of this chapter, Roland Enmarch and Richard Parkinson professed themselves to be attracted to this interpretation. A definitive decision is at present hardly possible; nonetheless, it ought be pointed out that the use of euphemisms as realizations of particular linguistic taboos were quite normal in speech (cf. Schorch 2000).

7   And see the 'Eloquent Peasant', B 1, 228 ff (R. Parkinson, pers. comm.).

8   For the creation of texts in Thebes under the influence of a particular historical situation, one can also refer to the continuation of spell 183 of the 'Coffin Texts', which so far is only attested for the eleventh Dynasty Theban *r-ḥtp* (Morenz 2001: ch. 5b). This is argued for both by the content and by the fact that the spell is only attested in connection with the wife of Montuhotep II, "the unifier of the kingdom".

9   For the symbolic meaning of the *ḥp.t*-steering tool, see the text in Fischer 1964: 112–118, no. 45. Both referred back metaphorically to steering the land as done by Ra. For the nature of the metaphor, see Adm. 11,11.

10 A monograph discussing the presentation of Montuhotep II is currently in preparation by the author.

Acknowledgments

My warm thanks are due to Roland Enmarch, Frank Feder and Richard Parkinson for reading and commenting upon early drafts. Roland Enmarch reminded me of the inscription of Sesostris I in the temple at Tod.

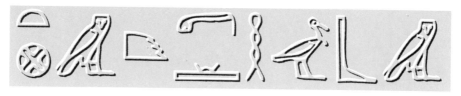

CHAPTER 7

REPRESENTATIONS OF THE PAST IN NEW KINGDOM LITERATURE

Hans-W. Fischer-Elfert

Introduction

The historical period covered by this chapter is the New Kingdom, that is, the centuries from around 1550–1100 BC or the eighteenth to twentieth Dynasties. The term 'literature' is here taken in a rather narrow sense to include texts of educational purport, narrative and lyrical fiction, and entertainment. Also, it is assumed that these texts possessed aesthetic value for their ancient Egyptian recipients, who could evaluate and appreciate their content and style. Members of the literate elite, 'scribes' (*zḥȝ /sš*) or 'wise men; savants' (*rḫ.w(-jḥ.t)*), constitute the social stratum responsible for the reproduction of the so-called classical works of literature, as well as for the creation of new compositions. Furthermore, there does not seem to be the slightest evidence for freelance and economically independent intellectuals; on the contrary, some of the 'authors' are known to have been predominantly involved in their everyday life with administration, on either a small or larger scale.

From a literary point of view the New Kingdom may be divided into two stages/ phases: (1) the pre-Amarna period; and (2) the post-Amarna period (Baines 1996a). This division seems to be justified on several grounds. Linguistically, in pre-Amarna times, educational, narrative and lyrical texts were still couched in the language of Classical Egyptian, albeit of a rather advanced stage. By contrast, in the wake of Akhenaten's theological and linguistic revolution, literary texts without any forerunner in the early eighteenth Dynasty tend to be composed in a special register of Late Egyptian that reflects the language spoken at that time (Junge 1984, 1999: 19– 22). This particular idiom has come to be known as 'literary Late Egyptian' (or as 'Medio-Neuägyptisch'), a style that still retains many of the old verbal and syntactical forms of Middle Egyptian but also includes elements of the vernacular of its day.

In addition to the linguistic division, the pre-Amarna period is remarkably lacking in genuinely new compositions that can be dated with any reasonable degree of certainty to the eighteenth Dynasty and that have no morphological ancestor in the Middle Kingdom or the Second Intermediate Period. This may be fortuitous, but it stands in marked contrast to the time after Amarna which coincides roughly with the Ramesside period or the second half of the New Kingdom. During the nineteenth and twentieth Dynasties, literary activity seems practically to explode on a scale hitherto unknown. This impression, however, may be in part the result of the accident of archaeological discovery. It is especially the Theban, and, to a lesser extent, the Memphite region, that yields most of the available evidence. Moreover, within the confines of the Theban area it is almost exclusively the workmen's village of Deir el-Medina, with both its many individual finds as well as its complete archives, that forms our picture.

This chapter concentrates on scribal reflections of their own literary past in Ramesside times. The non-existence of generic terms for cultural phenomena like 'history', 'theology', 'mythology' and 'literature' does not imply that there were no such phenomena or concepts in the minds of the literate elite. On the analogy of Assmann's (1984) differentiation between 'implicit' and 'explicit' theology, Ramesside literary production can be seen as twofold, that is, as consisting of a reproductive and a productive stream of tradition. It is precisely within the productive stream that a more or less well-defined concept of 'explicit literature', or in Egyptian simply 'writings' (*zḫ.w*), is developed and moral values are discussed for the first time in Egyptian history. With regard to genres, we only find 'instructions' (*sbȝy.t*) and 'discourses' or 'laments' (*md.t/ḥn*) that are attributed to individual 'authors' of the past. Tales like those of 'Sinuhe' or the 'Eloquent Peasant' do not seem to have been connected to any single authentic or 'historical' narrator. In contrast, laments like 'Kha-kheper-ra-seneb' or 'Ipuwer' have no literary successors, whereas narrative texts in literary Late Egyptian constitute the bulk of the available evidence from Ramesside times down into the Late Period. Laments may have been integrated into the genre of hymns and prayers to different gods that was beginning to proliferate at this time – a trend that could not have begun any later than the pre-Amarna period, as texts on ostraca written in a very personal tone demonstrate (Posener 1975; see also Guksch 1994).

Thus, we can observe another aspect of intra-cultural intertextuality that goes far beyond the already ancient custom of quoting old or synchronous texts implicitly or explicitly.[1] The quotation of ancient texts was not simply limited to the accuracy of quotation, word for word, but extended to displaying at the same time a reasonable degree of understanding of their content and an awareness of their co-text or intra-textual context (see below the allusion to Djedefhor in P. Anastasi I). This can only be fully appreciated when it is accepted that there was an inner-circle practice of critical discourse about what one was reading and writing or reproducing and creating.

Representations of the literary past

The corpus of transmitted classics in the New Kingdom

The available evidence suggests that Ramesside scribes must have felt the need for literary self-evaluation. A more or less fixed corpus of Middle Kingdom texts had been established as a set of classics (Assmann 1991: 303–310; critique by Baines 1996a: 170–171) that were copied in schools and in private.

According to Egyptologists' typological – and partially even the Egyptian – classification of these texts as 'instructions', 'tales' and 'laments/discourses', the sheer number of reproductions of examples of ancient 'teachings' in New Kingdom times is striking. Hundreds of mostly partial copies of 'The Teaching of Djedefhor', 'The Teaching of Amenemhet I for his son Sesostris I', 'The Teaching of Khety' or the so-called 'Satire of the Trades', 'The Teaching of a Man for his Son', and 'The Loyalist Teaching' have been found in different parts of Egypt, whereas 'Ptahhotep' is, by contrast, poorly represented. This is all the stranger since it was some of the lines from this text that entered a long-term tradition that can be traced down to Coptic monastic literature such as the 'Apophthegmata Patrum' (Behlmer 1996: 576). The 'Instruction of Amenemhet', for example, was found not only in Deir el-Medina, but also in Memphis, Lisht, Amarna (for Lisht and Amarna see Quirke 1996: 393, fig. 1; Parkinson 2000b) and Elephantine (Fischer-Elfert 2002a). Until recently the 'Teaching for Merykara' was totally undocumented from the Deir el-Medina material of the Ramesside period, but Quack (1990) has now identified a small piece in the Posener/Gasse-Catalogue of literary hieratic ostraca from that site. This meagre evidence hardly suffices to prove that this text was a literary favourite, and why it was placed second or third in the scribal curriculum is not known. In view of the 774 literary fragments published by Posener (1938–1980) and Gasse (1990), one single exemplar of 'Merykara' is not sufficient to show that this text was a scribal classic. The same is also true for the 'Discourse of Kha-kheper-ra-seneb', which is only attested in two copies from the eighteenth Dynasty; the Deir el-Medina apprentice-scribes do not appear to have taken any notice of it (McDowell 2000: 223; Parkinson 1997b). Similarly, for the 'Instruction for Kagemni'. 'The Loyalist Teaching', 'The Prophecies of Neferti', 'The Letter of Kemyt' and 'The Story of Sinuhe' are all well documented, with the 'Letter of Kemyt' substantially outnumbering the others (Fischer-Elfert 2002b).

Although new evidence can of course always change a picture, currently it remains an open question as to why certain texts of Middle Kingdom origin did not enter the stream of tradition until at least the New Kingdom. This holds true for 'The Shipwrecked Sailor', 'The Eloquent Peasant', 'Conversation of the Man Weary of Life with his Ba', 'The Teaching for Kagemni' and other fragmentary compositions. It should be borne in mind, however, that the 'Sailor' as well as the 'Peasant' cannot have been completely unknown in Deir el-Medina, since the draughtsman Menena (who was active in the reigns of Ramesses III–V/VI) felt obliged to quote portions of these texts when admonishing his wayward son Mery-Sekhmet in his instructional letter, written on a large ostracon (Guglielmi 1983; cf. Baines 1996a: 170; Guglielmi: 1984: 352–353, 361; Loprieno 1996a: 47, 1996b: 523).[2] There is no way of knowing how Menena – who was not a scribe – came into contact with these ancient tales, leaving open the possibility that some of these passages may have become fossilized over time as stock phrases. He may even have belonged to that group of semi-educated persons well versed in matters of literature and writing that the author Hori, the military scribe who wrote the genuinely Ramesside 'Satirical Letter of P. Anastasi I', had in mind when he scolded his fictional addressee(s) for quoting 'The Teaching of Djedefhor' in a rather unbecoming and boastful display of his/their putative literary erudition (Fischer-Elfert 1986: 95–97):

You have come, provided with great secrets,
and have quoted to me a verse of Hordedef.

> You do not know whether it is good or bad,
> which stanza is before it, which after it.

(trans. Parkinson 2002: 52)

Thus, there is every reason to believe that there was a certain degree of fondness for ancient literature in Ramesside times on the part of even the less well-educated scribes who belonged to the military administration. Furthermore, this went hand in hand with a tendency to boast of their knowledge, regardless of how extensive their literary awareness actually was.

Hori's critique could have been just as easily directed against an entire literary genre: in this particular case the so-called 'Harper's Songs', in which one of the central themes is *carpe diem*. On P. Harris 500 (BM EA 10060, rt. VI 2-VII 3), on a wall of the tomb of the royal butler Pa-iten-em-heb (Leiden K.6; time of Horemheb; Gessler-Löhr 1989) as well as in the tomb of the scribe of the necropolis Amen-pa-Hapi (TT 355; temp. Ram. IV) is found the following passage (nineteenth Dynasty; Gardiner 1932: ix):

> The gods who were before rest in their tombs,
> blessed nobles too are buried in their tombs.
> (Yet) those who built tombs,
> their places are gone,
> what has become of them?
> I have heard the words of Imhotep and Hardedef,
> whose sayings are recited whole.

(trans. Lichtheim 1973: 196; cf. Osing 1992: 12; Wildung 1977b: 21–25)

Although nothing seems to be preserved of the instructions of Imhotep, in contrast to the instructions of Djedefhor/Hardedef, it is possible that a previously unidentified literary ostracon may one day turn out to belong to 'his' text.

What may be revealed by Hori's general attack on the way in which some Ramesside scribes felt obliged to demonstrate their greater or lesser acquaintance with ancient literature is the conception that these venerable works were meant to be known in full and not to be misused as quarries for popular sayings mined deliberately from the past. The classics of the time were to be memorized completely and comprehended thoroughly before being cited.

With the exception of 'The Admonitions of Ipuwer' (or 'Ipuser'), the date of composition of which is still open to debate but which may have a late Middle Kingdom origin (Parkinson 2002: 204–216),[3] the evidence suggests that no other lament or discourse of this type was in vogue after Amarna (Assmann 1999a: no. 147). Classical literature, if there was ever any concept of what exactly made a 'writing' 'literary', consisted in Ramesside times only of teachings and tales. The first genre was called *sbȝy.t*, a generic term for a speech from a father to his son, with reference to either a biological or a metaphorical relationship. The content of the texts of this genre centres around the proper way of speaking and acting in a variety of situations, and is intended for the 'son' and successor in office. No specific term has been identified for the other genre, but tales of this kind may have been subsumed under such a general label as *md.t*, 'speech; word(s)' (Parkinson 1991b: 111, nos. xii, xiii). Tales like 'Sinuhe' or the 'Eloquent Peasant', in contrast to teachings, never begin with this term. We do not know how such texts were referred or alluded to: perhaps by complete verses or sentences (Guglielmi 1983: 159(z)).

Literary heroes as objects of veneration and the 'magical' aspect of Egyptian literature

'Instructions' were written or, in Egyptian terms, "made" (*jrj*). Three documents are presented and discussed here – two are written on papyrus and the third on fragments of a tomb wall in Saqqarah. With the exception of a magical spell on a previously unpublished papyrus in Athens (Fischer-Elfert 2002), which is accompanied by vignettes depicting some of the illustrious scribes of the past (Figure 7:1), the other two sources have been well known (Fischer 1976: 63–66; Fischer-Elfert and Hoffmann forthcoming; Parkinson 1991b: 97–99; Wildung 1977b: 25–29).

Egyptologists generally agree that names like Ptahhotep, Amenemhet or Khety are to be regarded as pseudepigraphical attributions void of any historical authenticity. Or, in Parkinson's (1991b: 97) words: "All available indications suggest that the 'authors' of Teachings and other wisdom discourses were as fictional as the protagonists of the tales" (see Vernus 1995 on the cult at the Saqqarah mastaba of Ptahhotep (D 64)). This may be true for Middle Kingdom literature as a whole and may also simultaneously mark a distinctive contrast to the literary production of Ramesside times. Thus, there seems little reason to doubt the non-fictionality of such 'teachers' as Ani, scribe of the mortuary temple of Queen Nefertari (Quack 1994), and Amenemope, scribe and overseer of fields in the Abydos nome (Laisney forthcoming). The other authors were also men of flesh and blood, active officials in the administration of Deir el-Medina just like Menena, Amennakhte and Hori, from whom come instructional texts couched in a very personal tone.

One observable consequence of the individual authorship of these texts is the emphasis placed on the personal past of the author and the sense that the instructions were written for a specific, individual recipient. This can be observed, for example, in the instructional texts of Menena, Amennakhte and Hori, alongside linguistically modernized citations of older literary texts (Morenz 1998b: 78). In this way, the instructional genre begins to acquire a more and more personal tone that is intensified by the author's strong critique of his own, as well as his biological(!) son's, faults. The *actual* lapse of time between when the son misbehaved and when the father reacted may in fact have been very brief.

In the case of these texts, the need for composing a didactic treatise seems to have been necessitated and provoked by the listener's neglect of the principles and social norms of the day. This may also explain why very personal texts like those of Amennakhte and Menena do not seem to have entered into the literary mainstream of future generations. At the same time it may have been the very same personal tone that provided the impetus for the authors of these texts to quote older works from the time of the Middle Kingdom. This quoting of older, more personal texts would certainly have enforced and substantiated their claim to be qualified 'educators' of their own sons and would-be followers in office. Of course it may be mere chance that the texts that quoted themselves did not reach the status of

Figure 7:1   Vignette on a papyrus in Athens (National Library, Athens, P. Nr 1826) depicting some illustrious scribes of the past (© Dr Klaus-Valtin von Eickstedt).

classical works of Middle Kingdom literature (see also Grimal 1981: 64 n. 153; 285 [1.3]).[4]

Ramesside writers did not seem to feel compelled to boast of the literary qualities of their own texts, and rarely did so (Derchain 1999: 28–29; Fischer 1976: 78 n. 65).[5] On the contrary, they show every sign of having suffered from a severe inferiority complex with regard to their ancient predecessors. This impression can be substantiated by a remarkable text in which the literary production of the day was denigrated. It is also precisely this text that sets the standard by which texts are to be judged as canonical, even though it is the 'authors' and not the texts themselves that are canonized. The source under consideration is P. Chester Beatty IV (BM EA 10684), a text dating to the transition from the nineteenth to the twentieth Dynasty, which contains a famous chapter about "those learned scribes from the time of the successors of the gods" (vs. 2,5–6; Gardiner 1935, I: 37–41, II: pls. 18–22). The verso of this papyrus begins with maxims about how to behave properly in various situations and different social circumstances, much of which have been lost in the lacunae.[6] Here the personal god ($ntr=k$) is described as the 'builder' (kd) of the official's career and personality. Friendliness to people in need is rewarded with the respect of god and men. A long treatise on the value of writing books follows (vs. 2, 5–3, 11).

> (2,5) **If you do but this,** you are versed in writings.
> As to those learned scribes,
> of the time that came after the gods,
> they who foretold the future,
> their names have become everlasting,
> while they departed, having finished their lives,
> and all their kin are forgotten.
>
> **They did not make for themselves** tombs of copper,
> with stelae of metal from heaven.
> They knew how to leave heirs,
> children [of theirs] to pronounce their names;
> they made heirs for themselves of books ($zh.w$),
> of instructions ($sb3y.t$) they had composed.
>
> **They gave themselves** [the scroll as lector]-priest,
> the writing-board as loving son.
> Instructions [$sb3y.t$] are their tombs,
> the reed pen is their child,
> the stone-surface their wife.
> People great and small
> are given them as children,
> for the scribe, he is their leader.
>
> **Their portals and mansions** have crumbled,
> their ka-servants are [gone];
> their tombstones are covered with soil,
> their graves are forgotten.
> Their name is pronounced over their books ($šfd.w$),
> which they made during their lifetime;
> good is the memory of their makers,
> it is for ever and all time!

Be a scribe, take it to (your) heart,
that your name become (3,1) as theirs.
Better is a book (šfd) than a graven stela,
than a solid tomb-enclosure.
They (i.e. the books) act as chapels and tombs
in the heart of him who speaks their name;
Surely useful in the graveyard
is a name in people's mouth!

Man decays, his corpse is dust,
all his kin have perished;
But a book (zẖ) makes him remembered
through the mouth of its reciter.
Better is a book (šfd) than a well-built house,
than tomb-chapels in the west;
Better than a solid mansion,
than a stela (3,5) in the temple!

(Lichtheim 1976: 176–177)

This long-winded praise of writing as a means of gaining access to the collective memory of society is intended as a mere introduction to the main concern of the speaker, a eulogy to eight famous writers who are said in the text to have flourished directly after the time of creation ("of the time that came after the gods"):

Is there one here like Djedefhor/Hardedef?
Is there another like Imhotep?
None of our contemporaries is like Neferti,
or Khety, the most prominent among them.
I let you know the name of Ptah-em-djehuty,
of Kha-kheper-ra-seneb.
Is there another like Ptahhotep,
or the equal of Kaires?

Those sages who foretold the future,
what came from their mouth occurred;
It is found as <their> pronouncement,
it is written in their books.
The children of others are given to them
to be heirs as their own children.
They may be hidden,
but their magical power applies (3,10) to everyone,
who reads/which can be read in their instructions (sbȝy.t).
They are gone, forgotten their names
but books made them remembered.

This text provides a list of eight poets from the past, arranged in the following chronological order:

1–2	Old Kingdom
3–4	Middle Kingdom
5–6	Middle Kingdom

1–2	Old Kingdom
7–8	Old Kingdom

Djedefhor and Imhotep belong to the fourth and third Dynasties respectively, but their historical sequence has for unknown reasons been reversed (Fischer 1976: 63–64 on Berlin 23673; Peden 2001: 59, 68, 102 on chronologically falsely attributed monuments in graffiti). In any case, they are the first to be mentioned in the text. Neferti and Khety date to the twelfth Dynasty, as is evidenced by their prophecy and teaching. At the end of the instructions on P. Chester Beatty IV, Khety is credited explicitly with having composed 'The Teaching of Amenemhet I for his son Sesostris I' (vs. 6,13–14). The fact that he is credited with the 'authorship' of two teachings may be the reason for his qualification as "their most prominent one" (*pȝy=sn-tpy*). Ptah-em-djehuty cannot be otherwise identified, but Kha-kheper-ra-seneb is clearly the same person that is to be connected with the famous lament on the British Museum writing board EA 5645 and an eighteenth Dynasty ostracon in Cairo. Both men must belong to the twelfth Dynasty. The list closes with another duo from the Old Kingdom, with Kaires perhaps being the 'author' of 'The Teaching for Kagemni'. It is difficult to determine whether the writer of P. Chester Beatty IV was aware of the fact that Ptahhotep, or whoever the author was (I or II: Vernus 1997), is to be dated to the fifth and Kaires to the sixth Dynasty.

The ensemble, when seen as a whole, forms a real literary 'ogdoad'. The number eight might be fortuitous, but if not, this enumeration could have been modelled on a theological(!) forerunner in the form of the Hermopolitan cosmogony. The number eight in any case recalls the name of one of the cult centres of the divine scribe Thoth: *Ḫmn.w* – '(The city) of the Eight'.

The type of text with which these scribes are primarily connected is called *sbȝy.t* – 'instruction', 'teaching'. These instructions were intended to be looked up in or as 'writings' or 'books' (*zḫ.w* and *šfd.w*) to serve as a sort of legacy to posterity. On the other hand, even though Neferti's and Kha-kheper-ra-seneb's texts do not begin with a generic term like *sbȝy.t*, but instead temporally with the words "Once upon a time when the Majesty of Snofru … was a beneficient king" and "A collection of words" respectively, the speaker of the Chester Beatty IV instruction seems to subsume these compositions implicitly under one heading: *md.t*. But the sentence "those who foretold the future/what was to come" in vs. 2,6 (cf. also 3,7–8) certainly refers to sages like Neferti whose final prediction of the epiphany of a royal saviour figure in the person of Amenemhet I reaches its fulfilment. Thus, the quotation of a complete verse may evoke its derivation from a prophetic text in the reader's/listener's mind who has no generic term for what we call a 'prophecy'.

It is remarkable that the speaker of this eulogy stresses the devastating state of the ancient sages' tombs in a manner that invites comparison with the lament in the harper's song of, for example, Pa-iten-em-hab and its *carpe diem* motif: "Their walls have crumbled, their places are gone (etc.)." In contrast to this, 'books' are not subject to decay but linger on for a long time after their writers have passed away.[7] The fragility of collective memory is not contingent upon the respective hardness or softness of the inscribed materials. It is only its contents and 'truth' that matter. The passage implies that the original manuscript may crumble to dust or become worm eaten, but shortly after its composition the text is supposed to enter into the process of being reproduced in the form of physical copies, which are called 'heirs' (*jwꜥ.wt*; vs. 2,8) in the text. The material 'hardware', or durability of the ancient tombs – which are at least in theory impervious to temporal decay – is contrasted with the intellectual 'software' that is to be entrusted to the highly delicate fibres of papyrus. The tombs of the ancient writers that also include the names of these writers are subject to *nḥḥ* – or cyclical eternity, mentioned twice in the text; whereas the contents of their writings are understood to belong to *ḏt* – eternity (see Uphill Chapter 2, this volume).[8] This distribution is all the more remarkable since Imhotep was venerated, among other reasons, because Djoser, his master, was the first to 'open the stone' (*wp-jnr*) which in reality it was the task of Imhotep as his leading architect to achieve (Wildung 1969: 72).

The P. Chester Beatty IV paean concludes with a statement of an aspect of the sages that has been neglected up until now, and that leads directly into the sphere of magic and the powers of the dead:

> They may be hidden,
> but their magical power (*ḥkꜣ*) applies to everyone,
> which can be read/who reads in their instructions (*sbꜣy.t*) (vs. 3,9–10).

This raises the question of whether they all had the ability to practise *ḥkꜣ* simply by virtue of being scribes, viziers and/or priests, like for example Kha-kheper-ra-seneb who was just a simple *wꜥb*-priest of Heliopolis. Alternatively, it is possible that their capability was accredited to them only after they had died, as they became local saints, like Ptahhotep at Saqqarah. It may have been their ontological status as both an *ꜣḥ-jḳr* – "able spirit" and a *sr-ꜥꜣ* – "famous official" that opened up the potential.

The notion of 'magic' was a fundamental criterion of ancient literature in Ramesside times, even when this aspect may not be in accord with our own ideas about literary theory. Indeed, the quality of incorporating and transmitting *ḥkꜣ* to the recipients of the texts is essential, and should even be considered an explicit parameter for identifying a text as 'literary'. It was also this very quality that enabled the writers of the time to "foretell what was to come" (vs. 3,7–8) in a manner which must have been admirable to their Ramesside contemporaries.

This supposition can be substantiated by another source[9] attesting to the veneration of the ancient poets, from the transition from the nineteenth to the twentieth Dynasty; it is almost certainly from Deir el-Medina. Incorporated into a huge composition designed to ward off nightmares and the spirits of the dead is a short spell accompanied by a series of 22 crudely painted anthropomorphic figures, each one of them identified by a name written in front of it. This text adds an absolutely new facet to the reception of the literary past and its protagonists in the late New Kingdom. The spell reads:

> To let you know the names of those able spirits (*ꜣḥ.w-jḳr.w*) and eminent officials (*sr.w-ꜥꜣ.w*):
> When they (i.e. their names) are placed at the neck of a mouse/rat,
> no tomcat can catch it.
> When they are placed at the neck of a bull,
> it cannot be slaughtered.

When they are placed at the neck of NN, born to NN,
no male spirit of the dead,
no female spirit of the dead can befall him.

(P. Athens Nat. Libr. no. 1826 rt. 10,3–6)

Next follows the depiction of 22 individuals, the first 10 of them standing, the rest squatting. Each one has his name written in front of him, and the first row starts with Imhotep and Djedefhor. Since these captions are written in an extremely cursive form, many of them still defy decipherment, but some may nevertheless be read without problems. No. 7 is called Djadja-em-ankh, perhaps to be identified with that famous sorcerer in P. Westcar who is able to "place one side of (a) lake's water upon the other and (to return) the waters of the lake to their place". But the Djadja-em-ankh of P. Athens could just as well be one of the Old Kingdom officials whose tomb is located in Saqqarah (PM III 483: Tepemankh I, fifth or sixth Dynasty). No. 8 is called *Nfr* and may be identical with Neferti, whose prophecy of the advent of King Amenemhet I was copied frequently in the Ramesside age. No. 9 of the sitting figures reads *ḥry*, and can be emended only to *ḥty*, an intermediary spelling of *ḥrty* found in P. Chester Beatty IV vs. 3,6, the "most prominent" of all ancient writers. No. 11 reads *Nfr-sšm-Pt<ḥ?>*, which, like no. 7 of the first row, is another typical Old Kingdom name.

Regardless of the identity of the remainder of the figures on this phalanx of "great/eminent officials" (*sr.w-ꜥꜣ.w*), the importance of this new attestation of, for example, Imhotep and Djedefhor derives from their protective qualities that can be mobilized against roaming night-spirits. This operation is based on their status as an *ꜣh-jḳr* – an 'able spirit' who can turn his knowledge of magic against the evil *mwt.w* or 'damned dead' (Hornung 1968: 35; their role was substantially underestimated by Assmann 2001: 17) to keep them in check. To do so, "their names are to be placed at the neck" of a living person, especially while asleep. This application can be explained only by supposing a small amulet of linen or a strip of papyrus inscribed with the name of one or more of these tutelary spirits. Archaeologically, this practice still remains to be confirmed.[10]

If one considers the P. Chester Beatty IV passage in the light of the Athens spell, the former is now allowed a more concrete understanding. "Their magical power applies to everyone" betrays a very pragmatic use of the ancient sages, if only of their names. But their names are mere vehicles for their products. Their works of art are not only esteemed as the acme of poetic artistry, since their *ḥkꜣ*-potency also makes them suitable for coping with everyday problems in the world of the living as well. Since *ḥkꜣ* is nowhere attested as a force that comes into existence only after the death of a human being, it can only be assumed that this 'magical power' must have been attributed to these scribes already during their lifetime. As mentioned before, this aspect of their personality is not dependent on the exact position that they held in society. Composing a 'book of instructions' or 'foretelling the future' seems to presuppose possession of that particular creativity which Egyptian theologians called *ḥkꜣ* (Koenig 1994: 273–305). We may now surmise that Egyptian literature in general possessed this *ḥkꜣ* quality, without which there would not have been any Egyptian literature at all. Thus, magic, medicine, theology and the fine arts, or 'how to do things with words (*md.t*)', are all dependent on the proper investigation and operation of *ḥkꜣ*. But *ḥkꜣ* does not amount to anything more than a 'creative power' that can also be turned into its negative counterpart. This *ḥkȝ* must also have evoked a certain 'admiring response' on the part of the recipients of ancient literature.

These two texts are much more closely related to one another than P. Chester Beatty IV is to the so-called 'Fragment Daressy', which was known prior to the Athens spell and has up to now been the only comparison with the eulogy. The *tertium comparationis* is *ḥkȝ*, which cannot be detected at first sight when looking at the two wall fragments of the hitherto anonymous Saqqarah tomb of the nineteenth Dynasty (Fischer 1976: 63–67). This tomb is the third source attesting to the worship of sages like Imhotep, Kaires, and Khety. The two extant limestone pieces join directly and display the remains of three registers worked in sunk relief (good facsimile in Wildung 1984: 14; for the Saqqarah tradition of these lists see Redford 1986a: 21–27; Figure 7:2). The upper register is only partially preserved and shows a row of sitting kings, whose names have been lost. In the middle register there follow, from right to left, x+5 viziers and eight Memphite high-priests of Ptah, each of them in mummy form. Here are the two viziers, Imhotep and Kaires. The third register is preceded by a narrow horizontal band of inscription only, where Ipuser or Ipuwer as 'overseer of singers' occurs. It is he who is generally supposed to be identical with the 'author' or speaker of the Admonitions (P. Leiden I 344 rt.). Register 3 lists x+5 minor priests, one of them called Sa-Khety, who is possibly to be identified with the "most prominent" scribe Khety of P. Chester Beatty IV. But the title Khety bears in his own teaching (*zj n-ȝr.t* – 'man of the boarding-school(?)') does not fit well with *ḥry-wḏb* on the Saqqarah wall. This equation must therefore be made with caution. Next follow eight chief embalmers. The other known person of the past is the lector-priest Kha-kheper-ra-seneb whose title *ḥry-ḥȝb* ascribes a leading position to him within the priestly hierarchy not displayed on the BM writing board.

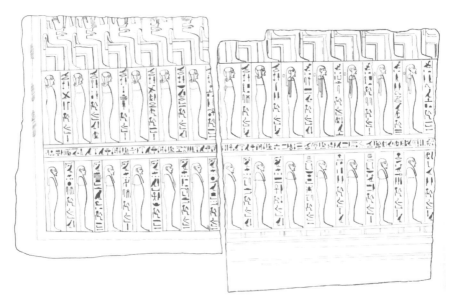

Figure 7:2   A limestone relief from Saqqarah attesting to the workshop of various sages (after Wildung 1984: fig. 72).

It can certainly be assumed that an even greater number of famous historical figures were depicted and named on the lost right-hand part of the wall.[11] Such a wall would fit well with the tomb having been that of Kha-em-waset, son of Ramesses II and himself a high-priest of Memphis – although this is a matter for speculation.

It must remain extremely doubtful whether the tomb owner's reason for depicting ancestors like Imhotep and Ipuwer was motivated by the fact that these individuals were regarded as being the first writers that "came after the time of the gods". Regardless of the actual reason, it is clear that he did not put their names on the wall out of admiration for their 'teachings' and 'laments'. Apart from the row of kings in the top register, all the other non-royal persons give the impression of having found their way into this tomb because of the professional attachment the tomb owner, who might well have been a priest himself, felt towards them. Thus, the individuals did not enter into this 'hall of fame' because of their 'literary' glory alone.

Reflections on the beauty of ancient monuments in visitors' graffiti and their relationship to literature

Whereas the encomium of ancient writers in P. Chester Beatty IV deplores the bad state of preservation of the tombs of even men like Imhotep and Djedefhor, visitors' graffiti in, for example, the pyramid-complex of Djoser praise its heaven-like appearance. These commemorations attest to the certain accessibility of at least parts of this huge assembly of monuments, pointing to the fact that there must have been designated areas inside that were open to the public in New Kingdom times. One of these areas must have been the court to the east of the pyramid proper, with its row of chapels, since it was mostly here that scribes during their journeys scribbled their graffiti in hieratic upon the walls (Firth and Quibell 1935: 78–79). One typical inscription found in the North Chapel, dating to the eighteenth Dynasty, and written by the scribe Ahmose, son of Iyptah, reads:

> The scribe Ahmose came to see the Temple of Djoser. He found it as if heaven were within it, Ra rising in it. Then he said: 'Let loaves and oxen and fowl and good and pure things fall to the Ka of the justified Djoser: may heaven rain fresh myrrh, may it drip incense!'

> By the scribe of the school (*zẖ n-ꜥ.t-sbꜣ*) Sethemhab, and the young scribe (*zẖ-šrj*) Ahmose.

(Wildung, 1977b: 66 Dok. XVI.70.a; 'staff of school' mentioned in Dok. XVI.70.b)

There is no explicit clue in the texts themselves as to the actual state of preservation of the Step Pyramid and its annexes (Peden 2001: 98).[12] Thus it is impossible to say how 'fictional' these comments are or if they reflect nothing but wishful thinking.[13]

P. Chester Beatty IV and the harper's song 'from the time of King Antef' stress that all the sepulchres of the ancient writers had crumbled to dust. It is possible to interpret this lament as a general commentary about the decay of private funerary cultic installations, but there is nevertheless good evidence to the contrary. This evidence, however, concerns not the tombs of Imhotep, Khety or Kha-kheper-ra-seneb, which are still not known, but those of Middle Kingdom nobles of, for example, the Theban and the Oryx nomes. Hieratic inscriptions of eighteenth and nineteenth Dynasty date commemorate pilgrimages to the tombs of Amenemhet and Khnumhotep of Beni Hasan (BH 2 and 3) or Senet/Antefoker (TT 60) at Thebes, all of which are early twelfth Dynasty in date. It is therefore not possible that they could have fallen into complete ruin by the time of the New Kingdom. The depiction of Sesostris I on the south wall of the passage of TT 60 can be presumed to have been the very impetus for the visits.[14] Also, in the case of BH 2 and 3 the toponym 'Temple of Menat-Khufu' could certainly have been misinterpreted by the Ramesside pilgrims as a representation of a temple of King Kheops in this nome (note Peden 2001: 102; Wildung's caveat 1969: 172–173).

It follows from the archaeological record that the negative assessment of P. Chester Beatty IV is to be read as a literary fiction. The overall reality might have been, at least in many cases, completely different. The marked discrepancy between ruined tombs and the eternal memory of their former inhabitants might be an indication of the speaker's awareness of the fact that either these ancient writers never existed, or that the texts of historical figures such as Imhotep and Djedefhor were only attributed to them after their deaths. The Ramesside attitude towards its own literary past would therefore have been not too different from the current Egyptological point of view.

Wildung (1969: 69–72) has shown that the authors of these inscriptions should not be viewed as 'tourists', but as 'pious pilgrims' looking to profit from the mortuary cult of ancient kings, as, for example, that of Djoser, by using him as a medium between the world of the living and that of the gods. Thus, their interest in the 'temple (complex)' (ḥw.t-nṯr) would not have been historically motivated.

Although many of the graffiti are formulaic with phrases recurring over and over again, some display a more individualistic tone by drawing on the educational genre (sb3y.t). In a dedication to the scribe Tjay, son of Wah, the speaker whose name is lost advises the addressee (temp. Ramesses II; Wildung 1969: 68 Dok. XVI.70.k): "Don't make yourself submissive/don't tilt (m-jr-gs3=k), as long as you are upon earth!" The same word gs3 occurs in P. Chester Beatty IV vs. 2,3 with regard to a third person: "(If an orphan petition you, one who is weak and persecuted by another) who would make him submissive, flee to him ..." This passage is located only two lines prior to the beginning of the disquisition on the immortality of writers (see above). Both chapters belong to one and the same composition.

As certain examples seem to suggest, writing graffiti was obviously a topic taught in school. A small ostracon from the tomb of Senenmut (TT 71) preserves only the very first words of a typical representative of this genre (Megally 1981: 240; see also McDowell 1993: 29–30): "Did come the scribe Djeserka in order to see ..." The object of his interest is not mentioned, but it certainly was a tomb in the vicinity of Senenmut's.

Another illustration of the interaction between literature and visitors' graffiti is supplied by seven texts from the mortuary temple of Tuthmosis III in Deir el-Bahri. No. 15, for example, according to the edition of Marciniak (1974: e.g. 74–75, pls. XV–XVI, 1973: 109–112; Sadek 1984: 83 – overlooked by Peden 2001), incorporates a slightly modified quotation from maxim 21 of the 'Instruction of Ptahhotep', which is concerned with the proper treatment of one's own wife. Ptahhotep gives the following advice: "Fill her (i.e. your wife's) body, clothe her back (*s3̉=s*)!" ('Teaching of Ptahhotep' P 327). The Theban graffiti from the second half of the twentieth Dynasty are devoted to Hathor, Lady of Deir el-Bahri. The dedicators implore her: "to fill his (i.e. the speaker's) body and to clothe his back (*3̉.t̉=f*)!" This plea is a clear adaptation of an ancient maxim, whose exact literary provenance must have been unknown to those who quoted it. Although textually not very substantial, the modified quotation from 'Ptahhotep' and its incorporation into a prayer on a temple wall testifies to a certain awareness of moral maxims from the past that could also be transposed and adapted to completely new contexts.

Graffiti not infrequently appear in clusters. This practice enables the writers to read older or contemporary specimens of this genre and sometimes leads to scribal competition, or even to denigrating the scribblings of one's own professional ancestor, as seen, for example, in the graffito: "like the work of a woman who has no mind/style."[5]

This sort of dedication text can to a certain extent be regarded as a welcome complement to the 'praise of cities' (*laus urbis*), preserved on papyrus. There is an important difference, however: visitors' graffiti were first and foremost inspired by the *ancienneté* of sacred sites of the past. The hymns to centres like Thebes, Memphis or Piramesse were mainly inspired by the fact that they were simply good places to live in.[15]

There is thus an obvious contrast between the eulogy of sacred edifices of antiquity in graffiti on the one hand, and their actual state of preservation in the New Kingdom and their characterization as having fallen into ruin in P. Chester Beatty IV on the other. A simple explanation would be to insist on the radically different degree of sacrality attributed to the two media of communication at that time (Vernus 1989). A personal, although highly stylized, commemoration on the walls of an extremely sacred monument such as a temple or tomb, especially on the premises of a royal mortuary complex, would certainly not have been permitted, especially if the text assumed a critical tone towards its ruinous condition and called attention to the fact that its cult had been extinguished. Such a phrasing would have seriously violated the rules of decorum, at least as far as private persons as speakers are concerned. This rule seems not to have applied to kings or future pharaohs, or at least members of the inner circle of the royal family. An illustrative example of this privilege is the famous 'Sphinx' or 'Dream Stela' of Tuthmosis IV (Sethe 1906–1957: 1,543, 7–8). In this particular case, however, it is the 'object' of the past itself or its god Harmakhis-Ra-Atum that calls for restoration. This spares the prince from having to utter any complaint in the first place. This may reflect a deeply rooted fear of verbalizing the elusive character of history and culture's former grandeur, and especially of its monumental manifestations. Critical remarks about the ruined state of private individuals' tombs, regardless of whether these tombs belonged to cultural and literary heroes such as Imhotep or Djedefhor, or to less important scribes, may, however, have been acceptable on an impermanent and fragile papyrus and would therefore not have been regarded as threatening to the monuments depicted in these texts (Peden 2001: 120 ff).

Representations of the 'historical' past

Interest in kings of the past must certainly have been selective, since not all of the royal ancestors found their way into the literary tradition. New Kingdom literature includes Pepi II of the sixth Dynasty, Amenemhet II of the twelfth Dynasty, Tuthmosis III, Amenophis II and Ramesses II of the eighteenth and nineteenth Dynasties. Tales of – mostly military – bravery and glory were told about the last three kings. It is also clear, however, that some private individuals were also allowed to receive the interest of story-tellers. Three examples were generals, and therefore members of the military stratum. This may be a reflection of their status within society.[16]

Aside from the Second Intermediate Period P. Westcar (Berlin P. 3033) with its tales of wonder at the court of the kings Snofru and Khufu, the second most ancient king of the Old Kingdom mentioned in New Kingdom literature is Pepi II of the sixth Dynasty. According to fragments of the eighteenth and perhaps twenty-fifth Dynasties, he is said to have had homosexual relations with one of his generals (Parkinson 1991b: 117, no. xxvi, 1995, 2002: 296–297; van Dijk 1994). He gets tracked by a so-called "pleader of Memphis", who wants to publicize his observations, but every time he attempts to do so he is prevented from telling his story by a band of noisy musicians. Pepi II is portrayed as "doing everything he wishes to do to him" (the general), and this wording is reminiscent of the 'Myth of Divine Birth' as, for example, transmitted by Hatshepsut in Deir el-Bahri. If any 'mythologizing' reading of the text is to be allowed, this particular king may have been chosen because he had occupied the throne for 90(?) years, making him the king who had reigned the longest up until the time of the composition of this text. Furthermore, there are some indications that it dates to almost the same period as P. Westcar.

Two Moscow papyri from the eighteenth Dynasty preserve fragments of two episodes from the reign of Amenemhet II of the twelfth Dynasty. Their date of composition may well go back to the Middle Kingdom. In any case, it is at least certain that the texts occupy an "intermediate [position] between Middle Kingdom *belles lettres* and texts of the Ramesside Period" (Baines 1996a: 161; Caminos 1956: 1–39, pls. i–vii, pls. viii–xvi; Parkinson 2002: 311–312). Their stories of the 'Pleasures of Fishing and Fowling' and the 'Sporting King' are currently unique examples.

The Hyksos period is reflected in a story on P. Sallier I dating to the nineteenth Dynasty, but the story itself may be slightly older (Wente 1973). It centres around the foreign 'ruler' of the fifteenth Dynasty called Apopi, and his Egyptian colleague in office, the so-called 'great one of the southern city' (= Thebes) Seqenenre Ta'a of the seventeenth Dynasty. In his Delta residence, Avaris, Apopi feels deeply offended by the noise of a herd of hippos located somewhere in the east of Thebes, which prevents him from sleeping during the day and at night. He asks Seqenenre to put a stop to this annoyance. He also advises him to send tribute to the Delta, to which Seqenenre agrees. After the Theban vassal has declared that he will comply, the text stops and we do not know what and how much is missing. There are some features of the text that call for an ironic reading. Apopi, certainly because of his semitic origin, is portrayed as being unable to write a letter in Egyptian by himself, since he is forced to have his scribes and 'wise men' do the job for him. Seqenenre, on the other hand, does not match the prototype of a determined Egyptian pharaoh. After having decided to comply with Apopi's request, he informs his entourage of his decision. Instead of breaking into servile applause as expected after an order from pharaoh, his courtiers remain absolutely mute for "a long moment". Their reaction turns the episode into a mockery of the standard so-called *Königsnovelle* (literally 'king's novel').

This tale is in all probability correctly supposed to be a work of fiction, devoid of any historical facts. How could it have been possible to get annoyed in Avaris by animals as far away as Thebes? Moreover, since both rulers get their just deserts, it is extremely unlikely that the text was composed merely to deride and make fun of the Hyksos.

A very fragmentary papyrus in Turin (Botti 1955)[17] relates an episode during one of Tuthmosis III's Syrian adventures. The central column preserves part of a speech of a man called Paser addressed to his king Menkheperra (Tuthmosis III) in which he tries to assure his master of the assistance of Amun-Ra. The king himself then seems to praise his divine helper, with Month of Hermonthis on his right arm, Month of et-Tod on his left and Month of Thebes "exterminating (the foes) in front of the king Menkheperra". The column ends with something about the asses of the prince of Syria being "smashed down".[18] There is no clue as to which Syria campaign is being referred to but, indeed, it may be that this is a completely invented story, influenced or inspired by the annals on the walls of the Karnak temple, or possibly by day-book accounts, perhaps still preserved at the time of composition. In any case, this story might well mark the beginning of a long-lasting tradition of Tuthmosis III in literary discourse (Quirke 1996: 273(3); Redford 1986b: 545).

There is some evidence from the Ramesside period that the same protagonist could appear in a series of stories or in a narrative cycle. This is manifest in demotic literature, but the practice may already have been in use by the time of Tuthmosis III. It is from within such a narrative context that a second story derives, dated to the time of this prototypical royal warrior. The first three columns of P. Harris 500 recto (BM EA 10060) contain the end of what Gardiner (1932: xii) called "The Taking of Joppa" managed by a general called Djehuty. This military official is a well-documented historical individual who is known outside the fictional texts, as shown, for example, by his famous gold and silver cups in the Metropolitan Museum of Art in New York and the Louvre (Lilyquist 1988). This story with its stratagem of conquering a Palestinian town during one of Tuthmosis' Near Eastern campaigns by smuggling 200 soldiers hidden in baskets into the town presents the king as passive. At the end Tuthmosis III is shown as the recipient of Djehuty's victory, when he sends a message to his lord in Egypt. In the story, the king is represented by means of his 'baton', which serves as a sort of royal mascot during the expedition.

The next king in historical order is Tuthmosis III's own son Amenophis II, who was a famous warrior like his father. He marched north as far as Takhsi and Kadesh in his third year, and followed this by two further campaigns in years 7 and 9. He is referred to in a literary context by the very beginning of the so-called 'Astarte Story' preserved on P. Bibl. Nat. 202, which joins a fragment in the Amherst collection (Coulon and Collombert 2000; Gardiner 1932: no. vii, date Horemheb). The overall story is that of tribute claimed by the Sea(-god) Yam, his desire for the goddess Astarte and the fight of various gods against this monster. It can be situated 'historically' in year 5 of Amenophis II, and is said to be an account of his feats while he was still a young lad. The main intent of the text, however, seems to have been the commemoration of the king's installation of the cult of Seth-Ba'al in Egypt (Coulon and Collombert 2000: 222–223). From the standpoint of 'hard' historical facts, Bietak (1989) has demonstrated that Ba'al's introduction to Egypt took place in the time of the Hyksos king Nehesi. The text has a strong propagandistic appeal in its presentation of the king as a god-like warrior. As its original 'publication' remains unknown and the extant papyrus may well be a later copy, it is not possible to tell if this text has its origins in an official – although literary in style – proclamation instigated by Pharaoh Amenophis II himself during his reign. As far as it is comprehensible, the main plot of the narrative is situated in a mythical, or at the very least distant, past. Due to the extremely fragmentary state of the text, the exact temporal relation between the king's 'youth' and the action of the gods is hard to ascertain.

Conclusions

Reflections of the past in New Kingdom literature consist mainly of the names of private individuals who were held responsible for creating cultural values entrusted to 'writings' and 'bookrolls'. Their compositions were destined to be transmitted in written, not in oral form, to the end that "the words/phrases of Imhotep and Djedefhor are in everybody's mouth" (Antef song). Instructions and laments/discourses, and perhaps even tales, were thought to have originated in a mythical past or in "the time of the successors of the gods" (P. Chester Beatty IV). Their *ancienneté* made them standard reference tools for posterity. From the literary 'ogdoad' only the very first two members can be verified in the historical and archaeological record: Imhotep and Djedefhor. By Ramesside times at the latest these sages had become the object of a collective ancestor cult in scribal circles. Ancient writings like the instructions of 'Ptahhotep' or the laments of 'Kha-kheper-ra-seneb' were invested with a 'magical' component and effect (ḥkꜣ). Their 'authors'' names were instrumentalized in everyday magic against nocturnal terrors (P. Athens). Thus, according to the Ramesside definition, 'literature' was understood to be imbued with magic.

Kings of the past and (perhaps in their wake) generals feature mainly as actors in tales of their military feats or failures. In contrast to, for example, the pharaoh Sisobek in the Late Period story of P. Vandier, whose name might be a pseudonym, all of them are historical personalities of flesh and blood.

Notes

1   For this differentiation compare Merykara's (P. 127/8) implicit quotation of Djedefhor (II2) or vice versa, and, on the other hand, Khety's (IId–e) explicit quotation of the end of 'Kemyt' (§ XVII).

2   The very first words of the 'Eloquent Peasant' (*sj-pw wnn.w-N rn=f* "(Once upon a time) there was a man called N" recur at the start of the autobiographical self-dedication of Simut-Kyky to his personal goddess Mut, thus transcending the narrow boundaries of a well-established genre and bringing it more into line with tales of the literary past.

3   Thirteenth Dynasty or later, the manuscript of P. Leiden I 344 dating paleographically to the nineteenth Dynasty.

4   The quotation from the 'Shipwrecked Sailor' (ll. 69–70) in Piye's victory stela may serve as an exception to this rule. The 'Eloquent Peasant' is not found beyond the New Kingdom.

5   A famous but still unpublished exception to this rule is to be found in an eighteenth Dynasty graffito at the Step Pyramid at Saqqarah left by an annoyed scribe scribbling his impression of the intellectual quality of his predecessors on one of its walls. Their inscriptions are to him "like the work of a woman who has no mind/style" (*s.t-mj-bȝk* [*n*]-*s.t-ḥjm.t jw-nn-sḥr=s*); Fischer 1976: 78.

6   It is at exactly this point that the huge ostracon with the complete text of Amennakhte's teaching found by the Swiss mission of the University of Basel in 2002 next to the tomb of Ramesses X invalidates Posener's (1955: 71–72) suggestion that P. Chester Beatty IV verso x+1 ff forms the continuation to BM EA 41541 (T. Schneider, pers. comm.).

7   There is a splendid parallel to the whole Chester Beatty IV-excursus in Thomas Carlyle's 'Sartor Resartus' (first published in *Frazer's Magazine*, London 1833/34; see Carlyle 2000: 129).

8   Scribal scribbling on tombs and temple walls creates a completely different, much more positive picture of the durability of tangible monuments. This fact is all the more surprising in light of the fact that many of these locations must have more or less 'crumbled to dust' by the time their visitors had arrived to comment upon them.

9   The National Library of Athens preserves a huge papyrus roll of about 3.6m in length covered on its recto and on parts of its verso with a compendium of more than 20 magical spells, most of them attested for the first time. Its date is almost the same as that of P. Chester Beatty IV.

10 Dietrich Wildung kindly refers me to a figurine of Imhotep (Wildung and Schoske 1985: 122, no. 103) that to judge from a hole at the back would have been worn at the neck.

11 The horizontal line between registers 2 and 3 mentions another Imhotep, this time bearing the title "royal scribe (and) lector-priest" in the *pr-nfr*.

12 But see Wildung (1977b: 65–66) who observes that some of the graffiti are placed no more than half a metre above ground. This fact speaks strongly in favour of a still functioning cultic maintenance of the buildings in question.

13 A visitor's graffito from year 30 of Amenophis III mentioning the "very great pyramid" is reported to have existed in the mortuary temple of Meidum (Peden 2001: 118). The evidence speaks in favour of its still having been largely intact.

14 Peden (2001: 68–69) does not discuss this possible motivation. However, we can assume that visitors were well acquainted with the eighteenth Dynasty custom of depicting the reigning king in one's own tomb. Middle Kingdom precedents are few: TT 60, an even earlier example, TT 311, and possibly TT 386 from the time of Nebhepetre Montuhotep II. Pilgrims may have wondered why it took until the reign of Tuthmosis III to resume this iconographic motif (Radwan 1969).

15 An absolute contrast to the uncritical *laus urbis* in the corpus of the 'Late Egyptian Miscellanies' is to be found in a complaint of an official abroad (Gardiner 1937: 48–49, with a quotation(?) from Khety's 'Satire on the Trades' (P. Sall. II, 6) in P. Anast. IV 12,7).

16 General Mery-Ra is referred to for the first time in a fragmentary story on P. DeM 39 and is certainly identical with one of the protagonists in the Late Period P. Vandier (Kammerzell 1995).

17 According to a letter on its verso containing the cartouche of Ramesses II, the recto cannot be much older. In any case it must be a copy made long after Tuthmosis' death, which on palaeographical grounds can be dated to the twentieth Dynasty.

18 On rt. 2,1 somebody is "found like a bird pinioned in the hand of a fowler" which recalls Ramesside P. Anast. III 7,8–8,1 in a description of "The sorry plight of the soldier in summer-time". Rt. 2,3–4 recalls 'The Poem of the Battle of Kadesh' (P. 128–30; Moftah 1985: 165–170; Spalinger 1986: 154–158).

Acknowledgments

My sincerest thanks go to Paul Anthony Delnero (Leipzig) for correcting my English and for asking good questions.

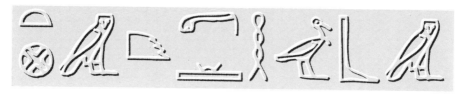

CHAPTER 8

VIEWS OF THE PAST IN EGYPT DURING THE FIRST MILLENNIUM BC

Antonio Loprieno

History versus historiography

Among the civilizations of the ancient world, Egypt stands out as a culture with a keen sense of its exceptional historical depth: references to past people or events abound both in visual and in written records, and we can generally say that in many aspects of their social life Egyptians looked at their history as a source of political or intellectual legitimation (Baines and Yoffee 1998: 212–225). Whether in the sense of modelling one's present actions upon the memory of the past (Vernus 1995: 35–54) or in the sense of stressing one's own achievements against the background of tradition (Vernus 1995: 54–121), one can argue that Ancient Egypt conforms to the cultural historical generalization that literate cultures tend to ascribe canonical status to individuals or events perpetuated in a fixed written record (Assmann 1992: 93–97). Yet, classical Egypt did not know a genuine discourse of history (Assmann 1996: 15–38), a 'historiography' written by individual authors comparable to Herodotus or Thucydides who project to the study of the past their own intellectual agenda (Hunter 1982: 3–13; Schadewaldt 1982: 113–119, 275–283): much like the transmission of literary works, the knowledge of the past was an important component of the elites' cultural identity, but the study of the historical and literary past privileged timeless paradigms of political function or intellectual prestige over contextualized, concrete examples of individual achievement. This is why, for example, Egyptian annals, king lists or priestly genealogies consist of chronologically organized but semantically repetitive sequences of names and deeds (von Beckerath 1997: 13–31; Redford 1986a: 1–96), or the names of classical literary authors tend to function as pseudepigraphic referents (Loprieno 1996a: 225–226).

While most scholars would probably agree with this generalization when applied to the earlier periods of Egyptian history, the first millennium BC provides a more complex picture that obliges us to revisit common assumptions on Ancient Egypt's cultural traits. During the Third Intermediate Period, from the 11th to the eighth century (Taylor 2000: 330–368), the Late Period, until 332 BC (Lloyd 2000a: 369–394), and the hellenistic age, under Ptolemaic (Lloyd 2000b: 395–421) and Roman rule (Peacock 2000: 422–445), we can observe a variety of different streams in Egypt's approaches to the past, which also resulted in an intense dialogue between Egypt and other civilizations of the Mediterranean world, such as Israel and Greece. This study shows that a historiography in the sense of a more critical dialectic with the past than was the case in earlier centuries developed during the first part of the first millennium BC and appeared as a feature of Egyptian civilization from the eighth and the seventh centuries BC, eventually reaching its peak in hellenistic times (Loprieno 2001: 89–128).

History of events versus history of memories

It is rather difficult to obtain a coherent view of Egyptian approaches to the past, because Egyptian reflections on history are not transmitted by a well-defined textual corpus (Eyre 1996: 415–433). The texts that display the closest connection with historical writing in the Western sense, i.e. the so-called "annals" (*gn.wt*), are originally expansions of the 'year's name' (von Beckerath 1997: 13–19, 203–205; Redford 1986a: 65–96): they identify a specific regnal year by one or more noteworthy episodes. Moreover, every historiography is inherently ideological, but because of the ties that the Egyptian tradition recognized between the cosmic order, the timeless organization of the universe, and the political order, its worldly administration (Assmann 1990b: 201–236), the link between historiography and ideology is in Egypt even more explicit than in other intellectual traditions. As articulated in the eighteenth Dynasty text known as the 'King as Sun-priest' (Assmann 1970: 58–65), the cosmic function of the king to *shtp ntr.w*, "appease the gods" is wholly parallel to his political function to *wdꜥ rmt.w*, "judge mankind", as well as to his funerary function to *rdj.t pr.t-ḥrw n ꜣḥ.w*, "give offerings to the dead". In trying to isolate a specific discourse of historiography, Egyptologists are confronted with the same set of problems they encounter, for example, in trying to establish the conventions of 'literary' as opposed to 'religious' discourse (Derchain 1996: 353–360; Eyre 2002: 31–35).

One way to circumvent this problem, and one that proves particularly fecund in the study of the Egyptian world during the first millennium BC, is to devote a certain attention to what one might call a history of 'memories' rather than of 'events' ("mnemohistory" in Assmann 1997: 1–22), i.e. to the study of the reading of past episodes in later traditions rather than to the way these episodes are described in official annals or celebrational texts. In this way, the results of traditional historiography are enhanced by the study of what one might call the *semiotic traces* of the past in specific cultural settings. Besides the overt statements of celebrational texts, therefore, we should also take into account the covert attitudes less formal texts display *vis à vis* past events and their protagonists. This procedure has recently been applied to the echoes of two titanic, if typologically very different, figures in the history of the Mediterranean world, the Hebrew prophet Moses and the Egyptian king Akhenaten (Assmann 1997: 23–54), or to the images of Egypt among Greek intellectuals from Aeschylus to Alexander the Great (Vasunia 2001: 1–32). In classical Egypt, the most explicit form of 'mnemohistorical' treatment of the past is the reference to episodes or individuals framed within a narrative context, whether this be for literary or for pragmatic purposes: one could mention the so-called historical sections in the 'Teaching of Merykara' from the Middle Kingdom (Quack 1992: 89–97) or in P. Harris I from the Ramesside era (Grandet 1994: 333–342), or the reception of

Snofru (Graefe 1990) and Kheops (Derchain 1986) in the entertainment literature of the late Middle Kingdom.

The fundamental danger we should avoid, however, is that of underestimating the importance of less literate periods, such as, for example, the first half of the first millennium BC, in the creation of later Egyptian perceptions of history. In other words, the richness of the textual records of the New Kingdom might prompt scholars to overlook the importance of the intellectual developments of the Third Intermediate Period, the Iron Age in the terminology of Near Eastern archaeology, during which Mediterranean cultures, including Egypt, show a quantitative and qualitative decline of the diverse written documentation that had characterized the Late Bronze Age. This is sometimes seen as the result of a historical catastrophe that led to the so-called 'Dark Age' (Drews 1993). But it was precisely during this period of contraction of literacy, comparable to the "death and resurrection of written culture" (Martin 1994: 116–181) in early medieval Europe, that traditional views of history founded upon the archive (Quirke 1996) – as they are displayed, for example, by the priestly genealogy of Ankhefensakhmet of the twenty-second Dynasty (ca. 735 BC), where the origins of a family of Memphite priests are dated back to the kings of eleventh Dynasty (von Beckerath 1997: 29; Borchardt 1935: 96–111) – were complemented by a rich oral tradition on figures or episodes of the Bronze Age. Much in the same perspective and under comparable historical circumstances, the memory of events in the Syro-Palestinian world of the 13th and 12th centuries was 'canonized' in written form in the Pentateuch during the first part of the first millennium (Finkelstein and Silberman 2001: 27–96), and peoples and names of the Mycenaean age are maintained through the Dark Age down to Homer's epic account of the Trojan War in the eighth century (Latacz 2001).

A break between past and present

I argue in favour of a multi-layered reading of the development of critical historical consciousness during the first millennium BC. I label this reading 'multilayered' because its development displays an anachronistic overlapping of episodes often rooted in different historical experiences. During the eighth and seventh centuries, this development leads to the awareness of a break in precisely that solidarity between *past* and *present* which had been the most important feature of traditional Egyptian views of the past. Early dynastic annals, for example, present a sequential record of the state's achievements that is also meant to confer legitimacy upon the reigning king, as already shown by the first Dynasty ivory labels from Abydos (Wilkinson 1999: 109–150); in Middle Kingdom literature, for example in the tales of P. Westcar, a correct succession of Old Kingdom kings provides the frame for literary entertainment (Parkinson 2002: 182–187); in New Kingdom king lists, such as those in Abydos, Saqqarah or Thebes (von Beckerath 1997: 23–28), the chronological sequence of clearly identified names of past kings is placed at the service of the present king's power display. The very *topos* of surpassing past achievements (Vernus 1995: 60–110) conforms in fact to this ideological model, because the present is always presented as following in the past's footsteps, i.e. as adhering to the existing interpretative paradigm. In the Late Period, this type of *reproductive* historical knowledge is challenged, and to a certain extent superseded, by a less sequential view of the past in which periods and individuals often acquire mythical traits: the past is remembered, retrieved and also *productively* reconstructed in a variety of texts ranging from literary to religious, with a frequent juxtaposition of figures and times. While a gradual loss of information about the past is to be expected even in societies with a high level of literacy, the survival of a tradition of archival copies of older (broadly speaking) historical texts as late as the Roman period (e.g. Osing and Rosati 1998: 55–84) seems to indicate that fuzzier Late Period readings of history are not simply the objective mirror of a less detailed knowledge, but also the sign of a subjective change in intellectual attitudes.

I start with the knowledge of New Kingdom events and people as displayed in later Egyptian sources, and examine their connections with contemporary approaches to history in other cultures of the Near East and of the Mediterranean world. In searching for the memories of these antecedents, we also partially deal with the problem of how these memories relate to the archaeological horizon or the philological evidence we derive from contemporary sources. The treatment of stories set in the Late Bronze Age provides useful insights into the underlying understanding of the role of the past in later periods. It is important to stress that during the first millennium BC, the temporal setting of most 'reconstructed' history is precisely the long-gone Bronze Age; a Bronze Age, however, that through the primarily oral transmission of the centuries of the Iron Age experienced a profound interpretative reassessment. 'Reconstructed' history does not by any means signal a rejection of the historicity of the reported events. Rather, the term underscores the encyclopaedic relevance of this history (or of these stories) within their respective traditions, i.e. the fact that in this history (or in these stories) is crystallized a particular form of reception of the past which corresponds to the intellectual agenda of first millennium societies. 'Reconstructed' history thus equals 'mythical' as opposed to 'archival' history, the history of a past that has acquired symbolic cultural relevance for the present, but that cannot be easily segmented in a sequential way; a point *in illo tempore* that linguists might call a 'perfective' aspect.

Manetho of Sebennytos

Manetho of Sebennytos was a third century BC Egyptian priest who wrote a history of Egypt in Greek, the *Aigyptiaka* (Waddell 1940), that still constitutes a basis for modern Egyptological reconstruction and division of Egyptian history, for example its breakdown into 30 dynasties (von Beckerath 1997: 35–40; Redford 1986a: 231–332). Manetho is an important witness to the Egyptian understanding of history under Ptolemaic rule; he was a product of the same cultural milieu that developed under the rulership of Ptolemaios II Philadelphos (281–246) and saw the renewal of an interest in the 'national histories' of the different ethnic groups that formed the multicultural society of Ptolemaic Egypt (Johnson 1992). A counterpart to Manetho's *Aigyptiaka* on the Jewish side is the Greek translation of the Bible, i.e. the so-called 'Septuagint', which in this perspective functioned as the national history of the Jews (Kasher 1985: 4–6). But rather than the fact that he writes in Greek, which makes him no less an Egyptian author than the Septuagint is a Jewish text, when analyzing Manetho's contribution to Egyptian historiography we should consider the fact that he is known to us not directly, but through the somewhat later reception of two different types of readers: on the one hand, through the Jewish historian Flavius Josephus (first century AD) in his apologetic treatise *Contra Apionem* (Clementz 1993: 77–204; Niese 1889); on the other hand, through later Church historians, particularly Julius Africanus and Eusebius (von Beckerath 1997: 35–40).

In general, one can say that Josephus chooses to comment on the portions of Manetho's text which in his opinion are especially important for Jewish national history and identity, whereas Christian commentators are also interested in matching Manetho's text with the biblical account and in providing, as it were, the first apologetic version of a continuous history of salvation that already began with the book of Genesis. All these factors have somewhat reduced the attractiveness of his writings for modern studies on Egyptian history, but not his relevance for our understanding of Egyptian society in later times. In fact, the caveats that are necessary in order to establish what happened in factual history prove to be a blessing if we decide to look at the 'semiotic' aspect of Egyptian perceptions of history, at the traces it left in later reception. The reading of Manetho's text in Christian times is a sign of the vitality of a *productive* local historiographical tradition which complements the *reproductive* approach displayed, for example, by the Saite copies of the First Intermediate Period autobiographical texts from Asyut (Manuelian 1994: 1–58). They are a response, as we shall see, to two different Egyptian types of codified historical memory from the Late Period to Late Antiquity.

An Egyptian account of the Israelites' Exodus

There are two Manethonian narratives transmitted by Josephus, *Contra Apionem*, which are relevant here. The first, fragment 42 (Waddell 1940: 77–85), refers to the time immediately following the Middle Kingdom, in absolute chronology the 17th century BC. Manetho (through Josephus) tells us that during the reign of a Pharaoh Tutimaios, for unknown reasons, "a blast of God" smote Egypt: invaders of obscure race invaded the country, burning cities, destroying temples and enslaving people. They appointed as their king a certain Salitis, who established himself in Memphis and administered the whole of Egypt. He placed his army in the region of the eastern Delta, for he feared an attack by the Assyrians, and founded in the Sethroite nome a city by the name of Avaris, which at that time already enjoyed an ancient religious fame. He fortified this city, where he used to spend the summer, and established an army of 240,000 soldiers to protect its borders. After a reign of 19 years, Salitis died and was followed by another king whose name was Bnon and who reigned for 44 years. After him came Apachnan, who reigned for 36 years and seven months, followed by Apophis for 61 years and Iannas for 50 years and one month. Finally came Assis, who reigned 49 years and two months. These were the first six kings of this race, called "Hyksos", which means "shepherd kings" for *hyk* in the sacred language (i.e. the one written in hieroglyphs) means "king" and *sos* in the popular language (i.e. the one written in demotic) means "shepherd". Josephus adds that in a different version of Manetho's text the expression *hyk* does not mean "king" but that *hyk* or *hak* rather indicate the concept of 'prisoner'; the term, therefore, would mean 'captive shepherds', and Josephus seems to prefer this interpretation of the compound.

This text provides a number of details on important aspects of the complex Egyptian perceptions of history during hellenistic times. First of all, we should observe what we defined as the 'multilayered' structure of the narrative in terms of historical strata: while the story itself takes place at the transition between the Middle and the Late Bronze Age, anachronistic elements such as the reference to the Assyrian empire or the extremely high numbers of soldiers clearly derive from the Iron Age experience (Gnirs 1999a: 83–87). Second, in the name of the first Hyksos king Salitis (or Saites) we can probably recognize the trace of a double historical memory. One points to a factual Hyksos name, perhaps that of a Sharek also known from the twenty-first Dynasty genealogy of Memphite priests (von Beckerath 1999: 120–121; Schneider 1998a: 46); the other echoes the Semitic predicate *Šallit*, "the powerful one", a form of royal onomastics based on titles that is well documented in late Middle Kingdom Egypt, for example through king *mr-mšᶜ*, "general" of the thirteenth Dynasty, known from the Royal Canon of Turin (Winlock 1947: 96). This name itself probably represents an Egyptian translation of a Semitic title such as *naśi'* (Ryholt 1997: 221–222; Schneider 1998a: 157). I (Loprieno 1998) recently tried to show that a similar phenomenon of cross-cultural translation may be the reason for the name of the mysterious king *nḥsj*, "Nubian", the first king of the fourteenth Dynasty in the Turin Canon, who has been identified with king *ᶜȝ-zḥ-rᶜw* and who established the cult of Seth in Avaris, celebrated during Ramesside times in the so-called 400 years Stela (Murnane 1995b: 194–197; Stadelmann 1965: 46–60). This king *nḥsj* may in fact have nothing to do with Nubia, which would be difficult to justify in that position in that place at that time, but rather represents a cultural translation of a Semitic *yamin* or *ben-yamin* "he of the right hand", i.e. the happy one: through the channel of the geographic correspondence between "right hand" and "Southerner" in Semitic, a hitherto unknown positive connotation also came to be associated with the Egyptian version of *ben-yamin*, i.e. *nḥsj* "Southerner". Thus, beyond a knowledge of the historical Hyksos themselves, Manetho's account documents the cultural memory of a Semitic presence in Egypt at the end of the Middle Bronze Age, already abundantly known from textual sources (Luft 1993: 291–297; Schneider 1987: 255–282), archaeological excavations (Bietak 1996: 14–21), and tomb paintings (Kamrin 1999: 93–96) and recently supported by the extraordinary discovery of a Semitic alphabetic writing dated to the Middle Bronze Age in the Theban desert region of Wadi el-Hôl (Wimmer and Wimmer-Dweikat 2001: 107–112).

It is important to stress that the period of the Hyksos is also the time of Egyptian history when Christian readers of Manetho date the patriarch Joseph. Eusebius says that "it was in their time that Joseph was named king of Egypt" (Waddell 1940: 95–97). While the objective reasons for this equation are to be sought in the desire to adapt Egyptian history to the biblical narrative and to present it as part of a global history of salvation, we should nonetheless stress that the names of some of the Hyksos rulers are indeed reminiscent of the narrative of the Patriarchs, for example <*yᶜqb-hr*>=/*yᶜqb-hd* "the god Haddu protects" (Schneider 1998a: 126–131), in which appears the name "Jacob". While the epic of the patriarchs, written during the first part of the first millennium BC, might keep a genuine memory of the history of Palestinian immigration to Egypt during the Middle Bronze Age, Egyptian approaches to the past during hellenistic times display the multi-layered intercultural dialectic we referred to above: first of all, an internal dialectic of Egyptian historiography itself; secondly, a Jewish-Egyptian intellectual dialogue rooted in the cultural horizon provided by the Ptolemaic rule but whose origins go back to the Jewish colonies in Memphis (Schipper 1999: 242–246) and especially in Elephantine, established at the latest during the first Persian rule in the fifth century (Silverman 1981: 294–300); and finally, a Greek-Egyptian dialectic that begins with Hecataeus of Miletus in the sixth century and continues through Late Antiquity (Burstein 1996: 593–604).

The memory of the Hyksos represents, therefore, the backbone of the perceptions of Egyptian national history during hellenistic times, thus expanding on the ideological reading of this historical episode already established in the twenty-eighth Dynasty in the Speos Artemidos inscriptions of Hatshepsut (Gardiner 1946: 47–48) and in entertainment literature from the nineteenth Dynasty (Goedicke 1986). During the latter part of Egyptian history, however, the Hyksos rule began to be read in an *international* perspective: Manetho (through Josephus) associates these Hyksos invaders explicitly with the ancestors of the Jews, with whose culture and writing he was certainly very familiar, as we observed when discussing the parallels between Manetho and the translation of the Septuagint within the frame of the early Ptolemaic interest in the history of the different components of the Egyptian population (Hölbl 1994: 64–66). He tells us (Waddell 1940: 85–91) that these shepherd kings and their successors controlled Egypt for 511 years, after which the kings of Thebes and of the rest of Egypt rebelled against them and eventually succeeded in driving them out of Egypt under a King Misphragmuthosis, who confined them to the city of Avaris and its surroundings. Misphragmuthosis' son Thummosis tried to conquer the city with an army of 480,000 soldiers, but failed and asked the shepherds to leave Egypt and go wherever they wanted. At these conditions, 240,000 people left Egypt, dwelled for a while in the desert and then entered Syria. There, representing a constant threat to the Assyrian power, they built in the country known as Judaea a city large enough to host all these people, and they called it Jerusalem.

This passage is also extraordinarily significant. First of all, we should observe the difference between the Ancient Egyptians' reading of history and the modern Egyptologists' reconstruction of the same events. Apparently, a local Egyptian tradition considered a King Misphragmuthosis, in whose name we can most probably recognize a corrupted version of *mn-ḫpr-rʿw ḏḥwtj-ms*, Menkheperre-Tuthmosis, i.e. Tuthmosis III, the protagonist of the victory against the Shepherd kings, viewing his successor Thummosis, possibly his grandson Tuthmosis IV, as the ruler in whose reign they finally left Egypt. It is important to appreciate that this local Egyptian tradition is by no means only late, since it is documented by the Speos Artemidos inscription in which Hatshepsut, Tuthmosis III' predecessor, claims to have repelled the Asiatic foreigners, using an expression, *shr.n=j bw.t ntr.w*, "I dispelled the Gods' abomination" (Gardiner 1946: 48), comparable to Manetho's "blast of god"; mass deportations, moreover, are indeed documented for the time of Amenophis II and Tuthmosis IV (Bryan 1991: 332–347; Manuelian 1987: 47–83). More importantly, this tradition is also sustained by a wealth of documentary indications that it was during Tuthmosis III's reign that Egypt reached a complete unification, also visible in the archaeological record (Raue 1999: 109–116). This myth of Tuthmosis III as repeller of the Asiatics is presumably also at the root of the literary fame of this sovereign in works ranging from the Ramesside Taking of Joppa (Goedicke 1968) to the hellenistic demotic 'Tale of Setne Khamwase', where a Pharaoh *mnḫ-pȝ-rˁ zȝ-jmn*, Menekhpre-Siamun, an obvious reinterpretation of the original *mn-ḫpr-rˁw*, Menkheperre, appears as the protagonist of the story of a competition between Egyptian and Nubian sorcerers (Tait 1996: 184; Hoffmann 2000: 212). We should also observe that already in the third century Manetho established an explicit historical connection between the mythical Hyksos of his own tradition and contemporary Jewish narratives of the emergence of their national identity. That is why, apologetically, Josephus considers this story as good news for the Jews, since their antiquity is ostensibly documented by an 'objective' Egyptian source.

From events to causal links

In this cultural milieu, both on the Egyptian and on the Jewish side, historiography is not primarily the reconstruction of *events*, but rather the construction of *causal links*, of interpretative bridges that would have been inconceivable in the time the events are dated to. This mythical reading of the past, however, does not go without a price, which is a loss of interest for what had been the cornerstone of Egyptian views of political history, namely the emphasis on the sequence of rulers that had characterized Egyptian annals from the Palermo Stone (Wilkinson 2000a) to Ramesside king lists. In these lists, the historical sequence and the personal identity of the rulers are the only object of celebrational attention. Manetho's text, on the contrary, displays a more complex approach: while the five kings following Salitis are indeed organized according to the ancient model (Schneider 1998a: 50–75), the mythical reading of specific kings such as Salitis or Misphragmuthosis tends to decontextualize them, as it were, and to replace clearly identifiable rulers with composite figures that represent the merger of various historical kings.

Thus, for Egyptian historiography in the third century BC, a traumatic experience in the cultural history of the country is on the one hand firmly rooted in factual history as conveyed by archaeological evidence, on the other hand linked with the ideology of the national triumph over a 'foreign' occupation, of dispelling an intruder from the country. This is the Egyptian cultural *topos* symmetrical to the 'departure' from a foreign country as presented in the biblical myth of the Exodus from Egypt, which also responds to the need to read earlier national history in terms of causal links. It is important to emphasize that the Egyptian historian saw the emancipation from foreign invasion linked to the emergence of a new political entity, which he identified with Judaea and its capital Jerusalem. In fact, Manetho's Christian interpreters, such as Theophilus, bishop of Antioch in the second century AD, who compiled a version of Manetho based on Josephus' account, as well as the later compilers Africanus and Eusebius, identify Moses as the leader who led the Shepherds out of Egypt (Waddell 1940: 107–115). This is certainly the result of an apologetic reworking of the original Manethonian account which, according to Josephus in *Contra Apionem* (Waddell 1940: 119–131), says something different, namely that a 'pseudepigraphic' King Amenophis, who reigned 518 years after the expulsion of the Shepherds, developed (as had one of his predecessors named Hor) a desire to see the gods. In this case, Josephus considers Manetho's account unreliable since the narrative, as we shall see, can be interpreted as highly critical toward the Jews. In order to reach his goal of seeing the gods, this Amenophis, a late successor of two brothers named Sethos, also called Aigyptos, and Hermaios, who acquired the name Danaos, and of Sethos' eldest son Ramses, received from his counsellor Amenophis son of Paapis, a semidivine figure, the advice to rid the country of lepers and other polluted individuals. The king followed the advice, gathered the 80,000 Egyptian people affected by a polluting disease, among whom there were also some priests, and segregated them to work in the eastern mines. The wise Amenophis, fearing the god's wrath upon him for the inhumane treatment to which the outcasts were subjected, wrote a prophecy according to which the lepers would eventually ally themselves with some enemies of Egypt and control the country for 13 years, and committed suicide. After many years of severe constraints, the lepers asked the king to be allowed to move to the city of Avaris, the traditional centre of worship of the god Typhon, uninhabited since the Hyksos had left it. In Avaris, the lepers prepared the rebellion: they appointed as their leader a Heliopolitan priest by the name of Osarseph, who introduced a series of purity laws such as the obligation to sacrifice and eat from the meat of animals that in Egypt were sacred or taboo, or the prohibition on engaging in sexual intercourse outside the confederation, and sent an embassy to the Hyksos in Jerusalem asking them to become their ally. When 200,000 Hyksos came to Avaris, King Amenophis remembered his homonym's prophecy, hid all the sacred animals and divine images, sent his son Sethos (also called Ramesses after his grandfather Rapses) to a safe place and organized an army of 300,000 soldiers to march against Avaris. But before attacking the city, he became fearful of the gods and retired to Memphis. From there, accompanied by the sacred bull Apis, he flew to Ethiopia with his army. The Ethiopian king had become an Egyptian vassal in recognition of a favour he had received from Egypt and gladly hosted the Egyptian king and his army for the prophesied period, placing an army at the border to protect them. These were the most terrible 13 years in the history of Egypt, for the lepers proved much more savage than even the Hyksos had been: they burned towns and villages, ransacked temples and destroyed divine images, roasting sacred animals and obliging priests to go around naked. During this period Osarseph, whose name derived from the god Osiris, worshipped in Heliopolis and changed his name to Moses.

The Egyptological exegesis is unanimous in recognizing in this story the memory of another historical catastrophe which marked Egyptian cultural memory down to the hellenistic age: the religious revolution of Akhenaten (Assmann 1997: 23–54; Schneider 1998a: 30–44). Many features of the narrative seem to confirm this link: the king's name Amenophis and his desire to "see the gods" would indicate a memory of Akhenaten, although the prosopographic reference to Amenophis son of Hapu, a historical vizier from the time immediately preceding the Amarna age who enjoyed a broad later reception (Wildung 1977b: 201–297), points to a possible merger of the figure of Akhenaten with that of his father Amenophis III. Moreover, the very choice of 'leprosy' as a moral disease *par excellence* in the ancient world (Stol 1987–1988: 22–31; Westendorf 1999: 311–312) would suggests a translation of religious taboos onto the physical sphere (Assmann 1996: 440–446). Through a procedure of historical levelling, however, the two negative episodes of the history of the Late Bronze Age, i.e. the foreign invasion and the religious revolution, came to be perceived as causally linked: the "Lepers" who destroy the Egyptian encyclopaedia are the nemesis of the

"Shepherds": the prototypical 'internal' enemies, the religious outcasts, become in Manetho's narrative the allies of the prototypical 'external' enemies. This passage marks the beginning of the discourse on "Moses the Egyptian" (and, conversely, on "Akhenaten the Hebrew") that has accompanied the development of western cultural imaginary ever since (Assmann 1997: 29–38).

But this story also presents clear anachronisms that betray its roots in the historical experience of the Iron Age, such as once again the very high numbers of soldiers in the Egyptian and Hyksos armies, which would have been inconceivable in the New Kingdom, and the references to the Assyrian military power and especially to Ethiopia and its king, who hosts the fleeing Egyptian army and who saves the country from domestic as well as external impurity. These references point to the memory of historical episodes not of the Late Bronze Age, but of the eighth and seventh centuries BC. As in the previous Manethonian passages, here too we are in the presence of names whose etymology is often difficult to reconstruct, such as Osarseph, the lepers' leader, whose name is probably the result of the confluence of a 'mythical' and of a 'prosopographic' antecedent: a trace, acknowledged by Manetho himself, of the name of the Egyptian god Osiris-Sepa, but perhaps also of the throne name $Wsr-ḫpr-r^c$ carried by the Hyksos ruler Khamudi (Schneider 1998a: 97–98). This story also presents 'etiological' names such as *Aiguptos*, the Greek name of Egypt, for King Sethos and *Danaos* for his brother Hermaios, in which we recognize eponymous references to one of the Greek myths of cultural foundation (Parada 1993: 7, 59) that bear witness to the cultural dialectic between Egypt and Greece and the desire to establish Egyptian history within the context of a Mediterranean, international perspective.

This text also emphasizes the importance of purity, both in the ritual and in the physical sense. Egypt's evil foes are people struck by leprosy, the impure disease *par excellence*, and rebel against all the priestly rules of purity that characterized rather the Late Period, the time in which the story was transmitted, than the Late Bronze Age, the period of the story's setting. In fact, during the first millennium BC Egyptian religion underwent a transition from the theological orthodoxy that had been crystallized in the New Kingdom to a focus on what might be called a personal *orthopraxy*, that is, proper religious practice. If we want to look for the initial signs of this evolution that also affected the royal sphere – we need only think of the text of the famous Stela of Piye (Grimal 1981: 132), where the Ethiopian king derives his legitimacy from the re-establishment of pristine ritual purity and seals the sanctuary of Heliopolis to prevent future rulers from entering it – we will find at the end of the Ramesside era an unusual 'negative confession' by King Ramesses IV on a stela from Abydos, in which the king, within the context of a hymn to Osiris, emphasizes his personal adherence to religious prescriptions (Peden 1994: 94–100). $W^cb.w$, "priests", i.e. the pure people, are the protagonists and the readers of the literature of the Late Period, in which individual orthopractical piety replaces the traditional, more theologically inclined approach to personal religiosity (Loprieno 2001: 33–44).

A binary approach to history

The result of analysis thus far is that during the later first millennium BC, Egyptian and Jewish cultural memory identified two episodes of their respective Bronze Age past that had played a paramount role in shaping their national history and in which the destiny of the two countries was seen as being tied. In the Egyptian perception, these two past episodes were the invasion of the Shepherds and their expulsion to Syria 511 years later under a King Tuthmosis, and the rule of the Lepers and of their Shepherd allies during 13 years of terror in the time of a King Amenophis, followed by their extermination thanks to Ethiopian help. In the Jewish view, these two events were the Exodus from Egypt with the subsequent organization of Jewish law by Moses and the eventual emergence of Israel as a political Israel with Jerusalem as capital.

Manetho displays a binary approach to history. On the one hand, his is a history of cultural memories, with an emphasis on narrative and folkloric accounts, such as the passages we considered above. We call it a 'mythical' history, or, in linguistic terminology, a history in the _perfective_ aspect. Second, a history of sequential kings such as Salitis' followers on the Hyksos throne, with an emphasis on didactic lists, on vertical successions of people and deeds that lead – without interruption – from the past to the present. Let us call it a history of events, or, as linguists would call it, a history in the _perfect_ tense. It is an opposition that might superficially be interpreted as one between 'legendary', i.e. mostly oral, versus 'documentary', i.e. primarily written history, but which in fact runs much deeper. It is a dual approach to history that finds its roots in the perception of a cultural break between the 'past' and the 'present'.

Manetho was not the first historiographer to treat Egyptian history in this dual manner. His text exhibits close similarities to many portions of Herodotus' (484–425 BC) Egyptian _logos_, written two centuries earlier (Hunter 1982: 50–92; Tait Chapter 1: 6–9, this volume; Vasunia 2001: 75–109). Certainly under the direction of Egyptian informants, the historian from Halikarnassos offers an earlier account of the history of Egypt based on the same materials later codified by Manetho: sources as diverse as king lists, local Egyptian legends, and traditional priestly accounts (Lloyd 1975: 77–140). A striking feature in Herodotus' presentation of Egyptian history, however, is that it divides into two typologically quite different halves: the first half (II.99–141) goes from Min, the first king, to Sethos, the priest of Hephaistos. Its tone and approach to history are in all respects similar to Manetho's account of the Shepherds' or the Lepers' reign: more interested in the narrative of extraordinary events than in their chronology. All royal figures are legendary, 'mythical' kings, in whose feats can be recognized here and there historical episodes known from contemporary sources, but who always appear filtered by a form of cultural reception. These are the kings of the 'past'. The second half (II.147–182) goes from the Dodecarchs to Amasis, i.e. it covers the period from the time immediately preceding the twenty-sixth Dynasty (the 12 Dodecarchs probably representing the historical memory of the fragmentation of the country during the Libyan and the Ethiopian rule) to Amasis, the last important king of this same dynasty, that after the battle of Pelusium in 525 was superseded by Persian rule (von Beckerath 1997: 84–93). Here, all royal figures are 'real': they are linked to very specific political events and are impeccably organized from a chronological point of view. These are the kings of the 'present'.

We should not be misled by an interpretation of this dichotomy as only due to the fact that the twenty-sixth Dynasty was for Herodotus more recent and thus the information more readily available (Hunter 1982: 87–92). Certainly, the author himself claims that the presence of Greek informants for the latter period of history provided him with a more reliable background of information, and we also know that the Persian rule, under which Herodotus visited Egypt, maintained a programme of continuity with the Saite dynasty (Baines 1996b: 83–92; Lloyd 1982: 166–180; Tait 2003: 29, 31). Herodotus, however, writes between one and two centuries *post eventum* – no negligible time-span to be covered by informants, reliable as they may be. What is more important, it seems to me, is that Herodotus' account contains no *linear* development from a more legendary past to a more documented present. On the contrary, the last kings of the 'past' are not less mythical than the first: Sethos and Anysis are not less surrounded by fiction than Min or Nitocris. The break between the former and the latter sequence of Egyptian kings in Herodotus' *logos*, therefore, is not factual or chronological, but rather cultural and ideological. It is motivated by the perception of a loss of solidarity between the past and the present that emerges between the twenty-fifth and twenty-sixth Dynasties and determines the Egyptian views of the past in the following centuries.

Historical consciousness in later literature

The renewal of literary production between the end of the eighth and the beginning of the seventh century, which follows three centuries of almost complete silence and is accompanied by an archaizing retrieval of the past (Manuelian 1994) also at the artistic level (Smith and Simpson 1998: 232–251), is probably the most evident sign of the new historical consciousness that developed in this period and was originally marked by a centralistic reform of the administration (Spalinger 1978: 12–36; Gnirs 1999b: 647–654), as evidenced, for example, by the political relevance acquired by the office of the Divine Consort of Amun (Graefe 1981: 108–112). During the reign of Shabako, the centrifugal effects of fragmentation were further neutralized through the integration of the Libyan feudal families into the political system (Onasch 1994: 7–11).

The literature that emerges from this renewal displays a variety of new features, both in the nature of the texts and in the treatment of past historical figures. While the knowledge of classical literature is extremely marginal (Jasnow 1999: 193–210; Verhoeven 1999: 255–265), which is itself an ostensible sign of a break with the past, new tendencies appear in narrative literature, in particular the development of the imaginary realm, of fictive countries or figures often localized in a fantastic region or in an unreachable past (Hoffmann 2000: 195–225), with blurred royal names typologically identical to the 'kings of the past' in Herodotus' account: just as Herodotus' Sesostris represents a *mélange* of the factual Sesostris I and III of the twelfth Dynasty, his Phero is etymologically an unidentifiable 'pharaoh', and his Rhampsinitos evokes a *rˁw-msj-sw zȝ-nj.t* who never existed, King Sisobek of P. Vandier is struck by a disease that had already plagued his predecessor Djedkara of the fifth Dynasty. The king's name *zȝ-sbk* could also be analyzed as "the son of Shabako", i.e. the Ethiopian king Shebitko, whose inthronization name was precisely Djedkara (Fischer-Elfert 1987: 5–21). A royal tale on P. Berlin 23071 verso, that probably constitutes the narrative frame of the 'Book of Temple' (Burkard 1990; Quack 1999: 267–278), mentions the famous Kheops, but also a second Dynasty king Neferkasokar who is indeed known to Ramesside royal lists (von Beckerath 1999: 45), but not to contemporary historical sources or archaeological horizons. The same tendency continues in demotic literature: in the first tale of Setne Khamwase (Griffith 1900), a prince Naneferkaptah is the son of a Pharaoh Mernebptah, presumably from an original Merenptah (Hoffmann 2000: 209); in the second tale of the same cycle appears a king *mnḫ-p3-r῾w z3-jmn*, Menekhpre-Siamun, a mythical Tuthmosis III that might also be 'concealed' behind Manetho's Misphragmuthosis.

Similarly, pseudepigraphic monumental texts often present past kings with fuzzy names at the service of the political needs of the present: the text of the so-called Bentresh Stela shows a pharaoh whose name is part Ramesses II and part Tuthmosis IV (Broze 1989: 16–17), but behind whom is easily recognizable the Persian Darius as 'renewer' of Egyptian temple piety (Morschauser 1988: 203–223; Burkard 1994: 35–57). The Famine Stela from the time of Ptolemy V Epiphanes confronts us with a Pharaoh Djoser who could have never actually consulted a lector-priest in the temple of his own contemporary Imhotep, but who provides a model of appropriate royal behaviour in the eyes of the clergy of the god Khnum at Elephantine, on whose behalf the text was composed and who was undergoing serious economic difficulties (Wildung 1969: 85–91; Hölbl 1994: 148–149). On the other hand, the kings of the twenty-sixth Dynasty, i.e. the kings of the 'present', are identified in later Egyptian literature as perfectly as they were in Herodotus' *logos*: the mummy of Psammetichos I is the object of attention by the young priest who is the protagonist of the narrative in P. Berlin 13588 (Smith 1991: 101–109), Apries is the pharaoh of the wisdom text in P. Brooklyn 47.218.135 (Jasnow 1992), Amasis offers an example of his reputation as drunkard in the tale on the verso of the 'Demotic Chronicle' (Hoffmann 2000: 197–199; Spiegelberg 1914: 26–28).

Besides the renewal of literary activity, another intellectual phenomenon that marks the revolution of the eighth and seventh centuries is the emphasis that the texts of this period, whether literary or not, place on the renaissance of the 'temple' as the centre of intellectual activity, of the importance of the 'book'. They underscore royal piety by dwelling on the king's building activities; in Herodotus' account, kings are frequently introduced by listing the temples they built or restored, and the prototype of the genre is probably the mythological tale on the Naos of el-Arish, where the narrative on the divine succession of Shu, Geb and Osiris mirrors the debate on royal legitimacy which plagued the kings of the twenty-ninth to thirtieth Dynasties, Achoris, Nectanebo I and Nectanebo II, by stressing their ritual piety (Schneider 1998b: 240–242). The same applies to the protagonists of the literary texts: the tale of P. Vandier emphasizes the performance of temple duties by King Sisobek, and the second tale of Setne Khamwase presents King Menekhpre-Siamun as continuously dedicating offerings and buildings to the great temples of Egypt.

Significant evidence also comes from the so-called 'Monument of Memphite Theology' of King Shabako of the twenty-fifth Dynasty (701–695 BC), which claims to be the copy of an ancient document "eaten up by worms" (Breasted 1901; Krauss 1999). The *topos* of discovering and copying an ancient text is found in a variety of documents of the Late Period, from P. II from Tanis (Griffith and Petrie 1889: XIV) to the so-called 'Book of Temple', a manual for the organization of temple worship framed into a narrative, fictionally set in the time of King Kheops of the fourth Dynasty, about the discovery "in a chamber in ruins" of a royal decree of King

Neferkasokar by the 'competent' prince Djedefhor (Quack 1999), to biographical inscriptions such as those of Petosiris, where the tomb owner stresses his merits as reorganizer of temple activity (Lefebvre 1923–24: 102, 1924: 36). The same attitude to the writings of the past underlies of course the discovery of the book of Deuteronomy under Josiah in II Kings 22:2–13, a similarity to which we shall return.

History of the past versus chronicle of the present

At first sight, Shabako, Djedefhor or Petosiris' piety towards ancient writings and temples may remind us of the archaeological restoration works performed by prince Khamwase during the nineteenth Dynasty (Allen 1999; Gomaà 1973). But there is a fundamental difference between the 'monumental' (or 'classical') approach of the New Kingdom and the 'antiquarian' (or 'canonical') approach of the Late Period. In the first case, which on the philological level corresponds to the praise of past authors contained in P. Chester Beatty IV (Loprieno 1996a: 227–231) and on the iconographic level to the ideology of the Fragment Daressy from a Memphite tomb, where the owner presents himself as the heir of the intellectuals who came before him (Wildung 1977b: 25–29), the past is a classical model to be emulated by the present, which is perceived as being less prestigious. The scribe's rhetorical question, "Where is now someone like Ptahhotep?" corresponds to prince Khamwase's desire to restore the monuments of the Old Kingdom or to the tomb owner's view of himself as the actualizer of ancient achievements. Much along the same conceptual lines, contemporary Ramesside king lists legitimize the present ruler against the background of the chronological sequence of past kings. In the later 'antiquarian' approach, on the contrary, the past is not a productive model to be recuperated, but rather a lost cultural memory to be copied, retrieved, reconstructed: to copy passages from an autobiographical inscription of the First Intermediate Period (Gnirs 1996: 239–240) means to recreate an artificial continuity based on such thin pillars as name identity. The actual present is not any more in monumental continuity with the past, as was the case during the Bronze Age, but rather critically divorced from it.

This approach to the reconstruction of earlier periods of Egyptian history represents Egypt's cultural programme beginning with the Ethiopian dynasty as documented already in the Stela of Piye, with its emphasis on the re-establishment of pristine ritual purity, and the 'Monument of Memphite Theology' of Shabako, a cultural programme which is still alive in the figure of Manetho's Ethiopian king who saves Egypt from the lepers. On the side, we can observe that in some Jewish traditions such as the one documented in Numbers 12:1, Moses' wife Zipporah was considered to be an Ethiopian ("because indeed he took a Kushite woman"). The same tradition is known from the *Exagogê* of Ezechiel the Tragedian, a Jewish author of the second century BC; Zipporah introduces herself to Moses with the words: "This land, o stranger, all bears Libya's name, but tribes of sundry faces live throughout; the dark-skinned Aethiops. Yet there is one who ruler, prince, and sole commander, he rules all this state and judges mortal men: a priest, the father of myself and these" (Kugel 1997: 299).

Finally, an important phenomenon that contributes to the shape of Late Period conceptions of history is the evolution that affects the sphere of writing: traditional

Hieratic is superseded by demotic, with its completely new graphic philosophy accompanied by the loss of a one-to-one correspondence between monumental and cursive sign, and monumental hieroglyphs know a dramatic expansion of the iconic potential of the system (Loprieno 1996b: 524–528). This creates a profound institutional and conceptual gap between (reproductive) 'sacred' writing and (productive) 'popular' writing, between, to use the expressions on the Rosetta Stone (Quirke and Andrews 1989: 6), *zḥꜣ mdw.w-nṯr*, "the writing of god's words" as opposed to *zḥꜣ šꜥy*, "the writing of documents". The developments in the graphic conventions are once again a mirror of the break between a mythical, 'perfective' *history* of the past and a documentary, 'perfect' *chronicle* of the present.

The term 'chronicle' is used purposively on purpose, because it allows us to move from the Egyptian world to the international context. On the Egyptian side, we think of course of the third century BC 'Demotic Chronicle' (Spiegelberg 1914), a text contemporary with Manetho's *Aigyptiaka* in which the recent history of the country from the Persians to the Macedonians is given, as in other oracular texts of the same genre in Greek and Egyptian (Assmann 1996: 418–425; Depauw 1997: 97–99), an eschatological interpretation *post eventum*: Egypt's decadence and foreign domination are due to a series of impure kings, whereas Egypt's future salvation after the Ptolemaic rule will come from Heracleopolis, a city whose association with religious piety was rooted in its pivotal role in the First Intermediate Period and during the Libyan age:

> *Be happy, prophet of Harsaphes.* This means that the prophet of Harsaphes will be happy after the Ionians, for a ruler has risen in Heracleopolis. *May he open the furnaces, I have given him oxen.* This means that the future ruler will open the temples' doors and let again offerings be brought to the gods. Hail to thee, son of the month. *Very good indeed is Heracleopolis.* This means that much good will happen to Heracleopolis in the time to be.
>
> (Spiegelberg 1914: 10, 16)

An international perspective on history

It seems that the same dichotomy discussed in the Egyptian approach to history can be perceived at precisely the same time (eighth–seventh century BC) in other Mediterranean civilizations: in Greece with the transition from Homer, who is linked to the aristocratic society of Archaic Greece and its myths, such as the Trojan War, and Hesiod, who inaugurates the poetry of mercantile Greece (Latacz 1997: 74–77), and of course in the Bible if we contrast, for example, the mythical 'History of the Past' in the Pentateuch, with narratives inspired by events of the Late Bronze Age, with the deuteronomistic 'History of the Present', which sets out with the discovery of the book of Deuteronomy (II Kings 22:8) under Josiah in the seventh century (Assmann 1992: 215–222) and is followed by the entire history of the monarchic age. On the one hand, we have global mythical narratives; on the other hand, precise historical sequences, as they are presented in the biblical books of Kings or Chronicles of Israel and Judah, a work of the so-called deuteronomistic history (Albertz 1994: 198–206, 231–242; Roemer 2000).

I suggest, therefore, that the codification of Bronze Age experiences in the *Iliad* and the *Odyssey* or of the Israelite cultural memory in the Bible, in spite of very different historical backgrounds, occurred surprisingly at the same time as Egypt was developing a dual approach to the past. The 'discovery' of the book of Deuteronomy, exactly like the discovery of a document eaten up by worms in the case of the Ethiopian king Shabako, is tantamount to the recognition of the break between past and present. That this cultural revolution took place in Egypt and Israel in a surprisingly simultaneous period is also shown by an interesting point of onomastics. If the names of Patriarchs such as Abraham, Isaac, Jacob or Joseph fit very well Amorrite onomastics of the Bronze Age (Schneider 1998a: 43–49), the name acquired in Genesis 41:45 by Joseph in Egypt (Saphnatpaneah, from Egyptian *dd-p3-ntr-jw=f-ʿnh*, "the god has decreed that he will live"), that of his wife (Asenath, from Egyptian *ns-nj.t*, "she belongs to Neith") and of other individuals of the story (e.g. Potiphar, that is *p3-dj-p3-rʿ*, "he whom Ra has given") are not names of the Late Bronze Age, the period for which the events are reconstructed, but rather of the Late Period, precisely of the centuries of the twenty-fifth and twenty-sixth Dynasties that saw the development of an Egyptian discourse on archaism. This epoch may, therefore, turn out to be the era in which the dialectic between Egypt and Israel, a dialectic that, as Manetho shows, came to be viewed as rooted in the most traumatic events in the history of the two civilizations, was independently codified in Egypt and in Judaea: the era in which in Egypt a copy of the Book of the Dead is written on the verso of P. Vandier. In Greece oral traditions derived from the Mycenaean world were given written form, soon emerging as the classical works of Greek literature. The book that gathered the cultural memory of the Israelites began its journey towards becoming the 'Bible', i.e. the religious code of the Jews.

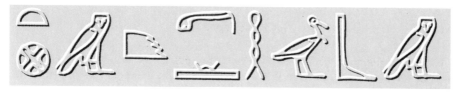

CHAPTER 9

EGYPT'S VIEWS OF 'OTHERS'

Introduction

The ancient Egyptians distinguished sharply between themselves and foreigners, i.e. non-Egyptians. In art – apart from representations of 'the Nine Bows', discussed below – there is no such thing as a generic foreigner. Every representation of a foreigner can be identified, via his or her distinctive skin tone, hair treatment, dress and accoutrements, as the inhabitant of a specific, named region, such as Nubia or various parts of the Levant, the Aegean or Libya. Egyptian texts are also often very specific about foreigners in terms of their land of origin, but do use generic terms for foreign lands and peoples in general. In contrast, the Egyptians were usually identified as the people of *Kmt*, 'the Black Land', meaning the fertile flood plain of the Egyptian Nile Valley.

The two most common generic terms for foreigners were *ḫȝstyw* and 'the Nine Bows' (*psḏt-pḏwt*). The first means 'peoples of the *ḫȝst*', *ḫȝst* being the 'hill country' or 'desert region' (Figure 9:1). The determinative for the word represents a three peaked range of hills over the edge of the green cultivation of the Egyptian Nile Valley (Gardiner 1957: 488, sign N 25). Obviously, in reality foreigners

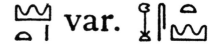

Figure 9:1   Two writings of the word *ḫȝst* 'foreign or desert land' (after Gardiner 1957: 584).

came from a variety of environments, some deserts or hill lands, but others coastal plains, inland valleys and river deltas. The basic contrast, however, is more a symbolic one. The Egyptian Nile Valley's ideal environment (as compared to those of foreign lands) corresponds to the epitome of civilization the Egyptians represented. The harsh, non-ideal environments (hill country, deserts) assigned – often arbitrarily – to foreign peoples corresponded to their essentially uncivilized (from the Egyptian perspective) societies.

'The Nine Bows' (*psḏt-pḏwt*) is written literally with a bow followed by, or placed over, nine vertical signs standing for 'nine' (Gardiner 1957: 566 under *pḏ*). Throughout Egyptian history the term is usually applied to the totality of foreign lands, and finds alternative expression in lists consisting of nine specific, named foreign lands or peoples. This list varies in content, and can even include northern and southern Egypt

(Uphill 1965–1966: 393–420). The bow was apparently regarded as a quintessential foreign weapon (although the Egyptians also made extensive use of it from prehistoric times onwards!). Perhaps the term 'Nine Bows' also relates to the Egyptian word $p\underline{d}$ (which in written form also includes a bow, but of a different type), which means 'stretch, (be) wide' (Gardiner 1957: 566 under $p\underline{d}$) and the numeral 9 could also be read as a triple version of the writing for the plural (a group of three vertical strokes). 'The Nine Bows' might, then, have an alternative or complementary meaning, and refer to the spatially endless, innumerable foreign lands. These characteristics were antithetical to the perfect order of Egypt, the borders of which were finite and the people of which could be counted.

Egyptians and Egypt were therefore sharply distinguished from foreigners and foreign lands in speech and writing, and also in art, but here in more specific ways. It is important to note, however, that Egyptians could take on the negative, symbolically chaotic aspects of foreigners should they, like foreigners, 'rebel' in some way against the established, divinely-ordained order (Maat) of Egyptian society. Criminals were axiomatically chaotic and were punished as cruelly as defeated foreign foes, while the losing side in Egypt's occasional civil wars would have, at least notionally, been ascribed an alien status.

Anyone perusing the much anthologized literature of Ancient Egypt (e.g. Lichtheim 1973, 1976; Parkinson 1997a; Simpson 1973) is likely to be struck by the hostility it expresses towards foreigners, foreign lands and the foreign or the 'other'. Defining Egyptian 'literature' is problematic (Loprieno 1996b, c), but the more traditional and inclusive approach includes royal inscriptions (of a literary or rhetorical character); autobiographies (idealizing, and mostly from mortuary contexts); mortuary spells; didactic literature, or 'instructions'; hymns addressed to deities; and prose or narrative tales.

Substantial reference to the foreign is made in only some of these genres, and then by no means in every example of them. Such reference occurs in many royal inscriptions and some examples of didactic literature (if put in the mouth of a king) and of prose narratives, if the protagonist represents the king in some significant way, as with Sinuhe (Parkinson 1997a) or Wenamun (Lichtheim 1976: 224–232). References to foreigners and foreign lands are rarer in religious hymns, though of substance and significance when they do occur, but are virtually absent from mortuary spells and most idealizing autobiographies.

Within these contexts, the hostility expressed towards foreigners in Egyptian literature seems frequent, consistent and, from a modern perspective, downright disquieting. Extreme examples are provided by royal inscriptions of Pharaoh Amenophis II (1426–1400 BC). In one context, he not only boasts of laying waste to Mitanni (northern Mesopotamia) and the Hittites of Anatolia – great powers of the day (see Warburton 2003) – but also of metaphorically raping the defeated kings of Babylon, Byblos, Alalakh and Arrapkha (both in Syria) who – no less disquieting – are respectively imagined as a "woman, maiden, little girl and crone" (Redford 1992: 230). In another text, and *not* metaphorically, Amenophis II is described as returning to Egypt "joyful of heart" after "he had slain with his own club the seven rulers who had been in the land of Takhsy [in Syria], they being placed head downwards at the prow of His Majesty's ship ... six of these enemies were hanged on the face of the enclosure wall at Thebes, the hands [lopped off earlier] likewise, and the other enemy shipped up to Nubia and hanged upon the enclosure wall of Napata", all in order to "cause to be seen the victorious might of His Majesty" (adapted from Gardiner 1961: 199–200).

Metaphorical brutality towards foreigners is usual in many Egyptian texts, and actual brutality of the kind evinced by Amenophis II may have been relatively common. The relatively rare examples may be indicative of general practices normally masked or restricted in literature and art, by the Egyptians' strong sense of decorum in these contexts (Baines 1991: 137–147). For example, Amenophis may have slain his opponents in the heat of battle (although ceremonial execution is also a possibility), but 190 years later Pharaoh Merenptah (1213–1204 BC) explicitly command-ed that defeated Libyan invaders be "impaled on the south side of Memphis" (adapted from Schulman 1988: 91 n. 123) (Figure 9:2) and other instances of similar brutality can be cited (Schulman 1988: 89–92).

Figure 9:2   Text describing the impaling (note arrowed determinative) of Libyan prisoners ordered by King Merenptah (after Trigger et al. 1992: 238).

Nor was such brutality restricted to the New Kingdom and later periods. On the Narmer Palette (Figure 9:3), one of Egypt's earliest historical (or pseudo-historical) records, bound prisoners are shown as executed and humiliated, their heads cut off and their penises removed (Davies and Friedman 1998; Petrie 1953: pls. J, K). Whether these were foreigners or defeated Egyptian rebels is irrelevant, because both rebellious foreigners and rebellious Egyptians are considered identically lawless, and open to exemplary punishment. In this regard, the severe punishments meted out to Egyptians under Egyptian criminal law should be remembered; death by impalement or burning, mutilation, and permanent servitude, sometimes in extremely harsh and probably fatal conditions (Eyre 1984; Lorton 1976).

On the rhetorical side, and to cite the example of a 'historical text' of Ramesses III (Edgerton and Wilson 1936: 75–87), foreign enemies can be depicted as panic stricken small birds ripped apart by a falcon (pharaoh); wild cattle ensnared, or killed by a lion (pharaoh); grain, that is bundled into sheaves to be reaped (i.e. cut down), or that is threshed so the foreigner becomes "straw, winnowed with the wind behind it". Male foreigners, in their terror and helplessness, can even be transformed into women giving birth (Edgerton and Wilson 1936: 73 n. 23e), an event implying pharaoh had metaphorical sexual access to them (O'Connor forthcoming). Most, perhaps all, of these ideas, even if most vividly expressed in the New Kingdom, are likely very old ones in Egypt; thus, Ramesses III can be verbally described as a griffin or a lion rending his foreign foes (Edgerton and Wilson 1936: 76, 78), and Old Kingdom pharaohs are rendered as such in art (Borchardt 1913: pl. 8; Jequier 1940: pls. 15, 16).

Indeed, art – insofar as the depiction of foreigners is concerned – often seems to parallel the negative attitudes to foreigners expressed in literature, and conveys in explicit or in more subtle implicit forms the imagery applied to foreigners in texts. In the New Kingdom and earlier foreigners are frequently shown as being killed or, more appropriately, massacred in 'battle' (e.g. Smith 1965: figs. 210–221; for earlier examples, Smith 1946: 212, figs. 85, 86), often in a compositional mode that equates

Figure 9:3 The Narmer Palette from Hierakonpolis: slaughtered prisoners are shown in the upper right of the obverse side. The reverse side depicts an emblematic rendering of domination that becomes standard in Egyptian iconography (ht. 63 cm) (Petrie 1953: pls. J, K).

them with hunted wild animals (imagery used directly in texts; see also literature cited in Van Essche-Merchez 1992: 225 n. 1). Moreover, from early historic (or even prehistoric) times down to the Roman period a favourite and much used image shows pharaoh preparing to ceremonially strike a helpless foreign prisoner, or group of prisoners (Hall 1986), a scene that has been interpreted as reflecting actual and frequent executions (e.g. Schulman 1988).

Yet other kinds of texts, particularly those of a mundane administrative or communicative nature, as well as much archaeological and, for that matter, some art-historical data, reveal that the reality of Egyptian contacts with the foreign, and of Egyptian attitudes towards foreigners, was much more complex and varied than some literary and art-historical evidence would suggest. The bestialization, feminization and even demonization of the foreigner was the legitimate expression of one Egyptian sphere of reference. However, in others the Egyptians practised a *realpolitik* in which foreigners were sometimes enemies, sometimes subjects, sometimes allies or trading partners, and treated accordingly; or – in the religious sphere of reference – pictured as inherently valuable, a product of the divine creative process and a loyal subject of the sun god who ruled all cosmos, including Egypt and its king. Moreover Egyptians, like other ancient peoples, seem to have been free of racial prejudice as we understand it today (Snowden 1983; see also La'da 2003). Foreigners, if acculturated to Egyptian norms, seem to have been relatively rapidly assimilated into Egyptian society, perhaps in large numbers.

If we are to make some sense of the variety and complexity displayed by Egypt's 'views of others' we need to look at the interrelationships between three aspects of the Egyptian attitude towards foreigners. These are first, the actuality of Egypt's foreign relationships, what kind of experiences it actually had so far as foreigners and foreign lands are concerned. Second, the ideology that developed with reference to foreigners, the speculative ideas that underlay Egyptian theories about their economic and political relationships with the foreign, outside world. And third, what might be called the theology of foreign relations, how foreigners were conceptualized and valued within the belief system of the Egyptians (see Baines 1996c).

These issues can also illuminate the ways in which Egyptians' experience of the foreign, and the ideas they had about it, impacted substantially on Egyptian art and literature. This is important in itself, but also enables us to some degree to assess the accuracy of depictions of the foreign in both of these contexts.

This chapter is structured around the issues of actuality, ideology and belief. First, I outline what is known of Egypt's foreign relations over the millennia (pitifully little) and characterize the variety seen in those relationships. An important question is whether we can detect substantial change in Egyptian attitudes to some or all foreigners in response to changes in historical circumstances, or in Egyptian thinking in general. Alternatively, such attitudes may well persist over very long periods; efforts to identify significant changes from the New Kingdom (ca. 1550 BC) onwards must be qualified by the much smaller database available from earlier periods. Seemingly novel ideas or imagery about foreigners may turn out, in some cases, to occur earlier. Although change is *a priori* likely, the evidential problems just mentioned make it difficult to establish which specific features are genuinely new.

The year 1000 BC provides a more likely divide in terms of Egyptian attitudes to foreigners because from that time on (with an earlier experience in the Second Intermediate Period: 1630–1520 BC) Egypt experienced increasingly frequent and increasingly longer periods of domination by external, foreign powers – first the Nubians (715–657 BC); then the Assyrians (briefly) and later the Persians (525–404 BC; 343–332 BC), the Ptolemies (Egyptian based but Macedonian Greek in origin; 305–30 BC), and then the Romans (30 BC–395 AD) (see La'da 2003; Warburton and Matthews 2003). This surely must have led to significant change in Egyptian attitudes, but also to the intensification of some long-existing ones. The basic ambiguity is clear: these foreign rulers typically had themselves presented as traditional pharaohs (for the most part), yet their exotic and even alien character, and the peripheral status of Egypt (except under the Ptolemies) must have been evident to the Egyptian elite, and to a substantial proportion at least of the larger, native Egyptian population. Presumably traditional attitudes, ideas and beliefs were affected by these experiences. Moreover, ideological complexity had deepened: foreigners, once emblematic of the chaotic force Egyptian kings restrained and subdued, now – as kings of Egypt themselves – had that same responsibility.

The issue of ideology focuses primarily upon the Egyptian elite, the source of the writings and images that document that ideology insofar as foreigners (like all other major issues) are concerned. The attitudes expressed in this way might have been shared by the population at large, but this is difficult to establish.

Two interrelated factors are especially significant so far as the ideology of foreign relations is concerned. One is Egyptian cosmology in general, their understanding of how the universe, and especially their world, came into being and was thereafter constituted. In this regard, foreigners are especially affected by the notions that cosmos, or cosmic order (Maat) is locked in eternal combat with a chaotic force (Isfet) that ceaselessly tries to absorb and destroy it (Allen 1988); and that cosmos is structured, in terms of both form and process, as a hierarchy, in which foreigners have a well defined and – *vis à vis* Egyptians – subordinate place.

The other factor is the need for the exploitive Egyptian elite to maintain its legitimacy and authority *vis à vis* the population, and at the same time to provide itself with a sense of self-legitimization, continually reinforcing its sense of superiority and its own stability. The elite comprise on the one hand the king and the royal family (itself an extensive, complex and hierarchically organized entity); and on the other the 'nobility', not so much a hereditary elite group (although there are some elements of this) as the governmental, military and priestly bureaucracy of each reign. The 'nobility' itself falls into different socio-economic levels, and each of these comprises elements that were often competitive. There was also a certain implied competition between the theoretically omnipotent ruler and his theoretically completely subservient bureaucracy, a covert tension that sometimes became more obvious. For example, the thirteenth Dynasty (1755–1630 BC) comprises an unusually high number of rulers, typically with unusually short reigns and, according to Quirke (1991: 216), "consists of a series of men from different families, attesting to the oligarchic structure latent within the government of a complex society".

Analysis of ancient Egyptian and Mesopotamian elites and their history can be productively organized, as Baines and Yoffee (1998) have persuasively argued, around the themes of order, wealth and legitimacy. In these regards, foreigners and foreign lands were particularly significant for the Egyptian elite. Literally, they were a significant source of wealth additional to that generated by Egypt internally; and most of that wealth was exploited via the elite, who monopolized much of the results. At the same time, the elite (especially as personified by the king) assumed the leading role in defending Egypt against foreigners, and in extending Egyptian influence, domination or at times direct rule over them. This service to the nation at large was an important source for the legitimacy (and self-legitimization) of the elite and their disproportionate share of power and wealth.

Elites represented themselves as crucial to the maintenance of cosmic order in general, in part through the stability and correct behaviour they brought to the society of their own land. But actual or notional subordination of the foreigner was a welcome extension of that role (and was also particularly susceptible to vivid dramatization in ceremonies, art and literature); the elite's suppression of the foreigner on earth was equivalent to the divine suppression of the efforts of chaotic force to penetrate and destroy cosmic order.

Finally, in Egypt there was no separate secular frame of reference, so it is not easy to distinguish between religious belief on the one hand, and what we might call philosophy, ethics and political theory on the other. Egyptian ideology, for example, is couched in religious terms; the state and the king do not achieve victory on their own, but rather do so because empowered and vitalized to do so by the divine. Thus a great battle of Ramesses II (1279–1213 BC) (Figure 9:4; Warburton 2003: Figure 5:3) is described in relatively mundane, historical terms up to the point that Ramesses finds himself and a small troop cut off from the rest of his army by the enemy Hittites (see Warburton 2003). At this point, Ramesses appeals directly to the imperial god Amun: "I call to you, my father Amun, I am amongst a host of strangers; All countries are arrayed against me, I am alone, there's none with me!" In response, the king reports that "Amun came when I called to him, He gave me his hand and I rejoiced. He called from behind as if nearby" (Lichtheim 1976: 65–66).

Nevertheless, it is possible to single out what might be called more purely religious beliefs from ideology, insofar as foreigners are concerned, and in this religious context foreigners are seen more positively, as depicted in religious hymns and sometimes didactic literature or prose narratives. This attitude, and the often more negatively structured ideology, are reconcilable in Egyptian terms in that all humans, Egyptians as much as foreigners, have free will and hence the potential to act according to Maat, or to rebel against it. Thus, hymns depict the foreigner in lawful mode, accepting of his position in cosmos; while royal panegyrics and similar texts focus on the foreigner entered into lawlessness and anarchy, and the meaning of his subordination by Egypt (Figures 9:5 and 9:6).

Perhaps the most striking visual manifestation of the former concept, that of the 'good' foreigner, is found in certain royal tombs of the New Kingdom. Detailed renditions of the nether world were shown on the walls of royal tombs, and occasionally foreigners typical of the alien lands known to Egyptians were shown as capable, like Egyptians, of making a successful transition into the nether world, and thus experiencing rebirth and eternal sustenance (Figure 9:7 col. pl.). Some suggest that this specific notion was peculiar to the unusual cosmopolitanism of the Egyptian

Figure 9:4   Ramesses II at the battle of Kadesh (Ramesseum) (Wreszinski 1880–1935, 2: pl. 101).

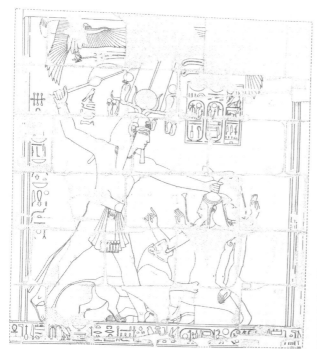

Figure 9:5 Ramesses III in emblematic pose dominates foreign enemies, whom he grasps by the hair: note the king's lion (Medinet Habu) (after Hall 1986: fig. 72).

Figure 9:6 Representations of pharaoh dominating foreign enemies had a long history: this pylon shows a Meroitic king and queen (Lion Temple, Naga, Sudan, Roman period) (after Hall 1986: fig. 88).

elite at that time and that thereafter: "Arrogance and the normal disdain for foreigners resumed" (Hornung 1990: 139, see also pls. 105, 107–109) but the logic underlying the idea is evident in much earlier sources, such as the story of Sinuhe (Parkinson 1997a). Loyal foreign subjects or allies of the Egyptian king were in effect demonstrating their status as obedient subjects of the sun god, and thus implicitly could expect to experience the benefits of all good humans, even if their burial customs were alien, and hence inferior to Egyptian ones.

Thus, the Egyptian concept of 'the other', at least in foreign form, provides considerable insight into the larger Egyptian worldview, and into factors influencing the actuality and the symbolic rendition of hierarchical relations within Egypt itself, as well as between Egypt and foreigners. In some ways, the Egyptians saw themselves, at least potentially, as the 'other' also, a notion involving a variety of nuances. Elite males are potentially rebellious, like foreigners; elite and other women are inherently subordinate (despite the unusual status and legal privileges of elite Egyptian women) like foreigners, and are also potentially rebellious, like the latter. A woman "away from her husband" is a "deep water whose course is unknown", likely to ensnare a man sexually into a "great deadly crime" (Lichtheim 1976: 137).

The issues of actuality, ideology and belief are also deeply involved in efforts to understand the many levels of meaning incorporated into the principal surviving Egyptian sources on foreigners, namely literature (as broadly defined above) and the art of temple, palace and tomb-chapel. These sometimes incorporate specific real-world events directly: and at other times are at least modelled in part on general real-world experiences. But such actuality is typically subordinated to a luxuriant or elaborate presentation of ideological issues in verbal or visual terms. Yet textual or pictorial rhetoric had great meaning for the Egyptians, and is in these contexts deeply informative about their complex reactions to 'the other' and the foreign, and should not, therefore, be dismissed as mere banalities. Less obviously present, in many instances, is the concept of the good foreigner (though this is sometimes quite overt), yet this latter concept is an implied contrast that would have heightened the effect of the rendition of the 'bad' foreigner for the Egyptian reader or viewer.

Ultimately, literary or pictorial representation of 'the foreign' is part of a cosmologically ordered structure involving all the other components of the text or the work of art, and indeed the entire building in which such works were typically displayed. It is within their larger concept of cosmos that, for the Egyptians, the actuality of experience with foreigners finds meaning, and the seemingly opposed notions of the foreigner as 'bad' and 'good' can be reconciled.

Actuality

A number of good introductory texts on the pattern and history of Egypt's foreign relations, insofar as reconstructable, exist (for Nubia, Adams 1977; O'Connor 1993; Trigger 1976; for the Levant and Near East, Redford 1992; for Libyans, Hölscher 1937; Leahy 1990; for the Aegean, Vercoutter 1956; for the Ptolemaic period, see especially Hölbl 2001). The primary structuring factors in those relations were Egypt's own internal dynamics and fluctuations; and the relative contiguity of various foreign lands to Egypt.

Foreign relations were a constant in Egypt's historical experience, but internal political and societal stability was not. The Egyptian political system fluctuated between periods of relatively strong centralization (possibly somewhat exaggerated by historians) and others of breakdown and even anarchy, most typically in the 'intermediate periods' between the Old and Middle, and the Middle and New Kingdoms; and between the New Kingdom and the 'Late' Period (the latter, 715–332 BC). During such intermediate periods the strength of centralized, royal government declined, and the country split into competitive, often conflicting kingdoms, typically a northern and a southern, but in the Third Intermediate Period (1075–715 BC) many more than this.

The historical record indicates that during the periods of centralization Egypt was typically expansive in foreign affairs, with not only extensive trading and, to some degree, diplomatic relationships, but also a capacity to intimidate, and even to occupy and rule for a period, some of the closer foreign lands. During periods of internal disturbance, however, this latter capacity diminished or disappeared (although trading relationships remained important), and Egypt itself became vulnerable to foreign penetration (with foreigners occupying, more or less forcibly, large tracts of Egyptian territory) and even outright invasion, the first such to be documented being the 'Hyksos' invasion (from Canaan, in the southern Levant) and occupation of northern Egypt (1630–1520 BC).

Thus, over time Egyptian historical experience of the foreigner varied in nature and intensity; at times (in the Old, Middle and New Kingdoms) the sense of superiority over the foreigner was supported by that experience, but at other periods the threatening, anarchic and destructive potential of 'the foreign' was strongly impressed upon the Egyptians. As noted earlier, the situation changed substantially after 1000 BC, as Egypt found itself – whether internally united or not – increasingly under pressure from geo-political entities with larger, sometimes much larger resources, and the experience of invasion and long-term occupation became increasingly frequent.

It was inevitable that Egypt's most intense foreign relations were with geographically contiguous lands (separated from each other by large regions of desert, and low or virtually no population), specifically Libya (probably equivalent to modern Cyrenaica), northern Nubia (along the Nile from the first to the fourth cataracts), Punt (on the western shore of the Red Sea, perhaps straddling the modern border between Sudan and Eritrea) (see Meeks 2003; Harvey 2003) and what became historically known as Canaan, essentially the southern Levant (today, Lebanon, Israel and western Jordan). Egypt's relations with all of these, virtually continuous throughout history, were influenced by many factors, but especially by issues of comparative accessibility and desirability.

Libya/Cyrenaica was relatively difficult to reach and control, and its level of desirability not very high; its population was largely nomadic, its chief products animal, and its environment unsuitable for settlement by Egyptians. However, Libyans seem attracted by Egypt from early on, so the Egyptians repeatedly were engaged in repelling infiltration, settlement and – increasingly over time – organized invasion from Libya. Nubia was much more accessible, since like Egypt it lay along the Nile and proffered substantial human, natural and mineral resources, as well as serving as a route to more southerly regions productive of another range of products, long known to and desired by Egyptians. Moreover, environmentally Nubia could support sedentary Egyptian settlement.

Punt (Harvey 2003) was relatively remote, and most conveniently accessible by ship (although land routes, from Nubia, also existed). It produced especially a highly desirable form of incense as well as other materials, and so far as one can tell was largely free of Egyptian intimidation, although trading relationships between the two persisted into Ptolemaic times (when Egypt began to develop permanent bases along the southerly stretch of the Red Sea's African shore) (Meeks 2003: Figure 4:12).

To the north-east, Canaan comprised varied environments, significant human and other resources, and contact with the wider world of the eastern Mediterranean (also directly accessible to Egypt) and the Near East as a whole. Egyptian contacts, and bursts of imperial expansion, were very much shaped by the region's variability: some areas were susceptible to Egyptian control, influence and occupation, others much less so. Between Canaan and Egypt, Sinai – relatively arid and rugged – was important as a land bridge (along the Mediterranean shore) and, in its southern and central areas, for its mineral resources (turquoise and copper).

Texts and archaeology attest to Egypt's relatively intense if varied relationships with all of these lands (some archaeologically much more poorly known (Libya, Punt) than others (Canaan, Nubia)) but much remains to be discovered. Moreover, since these lands are viewed through an Egyptian lens (the chief written sources about all of them *are* Egyptian, except for Canaan in the New Kingdom and later), we tend to underestimate the capacity for substantial state formation in all of them throughout Egypt's Old and Middle Kingdoms. Even the Libyans, by the later second millennium, may have generated a "nomadic state" (O'Connor 1990). These state formation processes would have both influenced the character of Egypt's relations with these lands, and intensified Egypt's security concerns, in terms of Egyptian dominance or influence, or even of foreign intrusion into Egyptian territory.

The basic motivations for Egypt's foreign polices were actual, real-world ones. Contiguous regions contained desirable resources, which Egypt could acquire by trade, intimidation or outright occupation; and they also presented, in varying degrees, security concerns that had to be addressed. Egyptians incorporated their experiences along these lines into their ideological and religious realms, but neither ideology nor religion were the engines of foreign policy. The Egyptians were not seemingly attracted to empire building for its own sake, nor wished to proselytize their particular forms of ideology and religion.

Beyond these immediately contiguous (more or less) lands of Libya, Nubia, Punt and Canaan was a larger but more remote foreign world, the relationship of which with Egypt is harder to define. While contact westward may not have extended much further than Cyrenaica until relatively late times, contacts with more southerly areas of Nubia – always independent of Egypt – were probably more substantial than we realize, and the Egyptians – by the New Kingdom at least – were clearly aware of other regions in the vicinity of Punt. To the north and north-east our knowledge of Egypt's contacts is a little fuller.

In the New Kingdom, Egypt had considerable involvement in the political, economic and military affairs of the northern Levant (roughly, modern Syria) and Anatolia (especially the Hittite empire) (see Warburton 2003). Contacts with northern Mesopotamia were also close, and significant with more remote Mesopotamian entities (Assyria, Babylonia), though not, seemingly, with even more remote powers, e.g. in Iran. Earlier, in the Old and Middle Kingdom, contact seems much less, with very little if any direct contact with Anatolia and Mesopotamia, although some, poorly defined interaction with Syria. As for post-New Kingdom times, Anatolia and the Near East loomed ever larger in Egypt's historical experience, in part due to the expansion of Assyria, then (for Egypt, much more forcibly) Persia into the eastern Mediterranean.

As for the Aegean lands and islands, trading contacts (not necessarily direct ones) with Egypt extended back to the Old Kingdom, and became much closer in the New, with Aegean peoples unquestionably visiting Egypt, and Egyptians (less certainly) entering the Aegean (see Bevan 2003). Later, the Aegean region was important in other ways: Egyptian kings of the Late Period recruited mercenaries or allies from there in their struggle against Persian expansion, and commercial contacts also intensified, especially as Greek colonization grew around the shores of the eastern Mediterranean. Later, under the Ptolemies, links with the Aegean world were naturally even closer.

Thus, Egypt's experience of 'the foreign' was varied, and sometimes significantly changeable, over the long millennia of its history (ca. 3000 BC to the early centuries AD). Foreigners were experienced as allies; as trading partners, in some cases free of Egyptian intimidation, in others (like the Nubians (Figure 9:8)) more forcibly related to Egypt; as subjects, either abroad in Egyptian dominated areas, or in Egypt itself; as 'rebels', resistant to Egyptian control or expansion, or even attacking, invading and sometimes occupying Egypt itself. Finally, foreigners themselves become 'the pharaoh', the quintessential figure in the Egyptian scheme of things so far as human, and to a significant degree divine affairs are concerned.

It is not surprising that this richly varied experience should have produced an equally richly nuanced view of 'the other'.

Ideology

Egyptian ideology about the foreigner is developed along an axis between the poles of the 'good' and the 'bad' foreigner, the former acting according to Maat or divine order (which corresponds to Egypt's interests), the latter acting in opposition to Maat, and hence becoming identifiable as a manifestation of Isfet, of chaotic formlessness which aggressively attempts to abort cosmic process, and annihilate cosmos – the epitome of divine order – itself.

In the real world of historical experience, these two extremes incorporated much variety and flexibility. Foreigners could be coerced subjects, diplomatic and military

Figure 9:8 Depiction of Nubian captives at Abu Simbel (© Lisa Daniel).

allies, or independent trading partners, while yet less rich in population, territory and resources than Egypt. In administrative texts and diplomatic correspondence all these realities would be recognized, manifested and provide the basis for appropriate Egyptian policy. The 'Amarna Letters', cuneiform tablets received by the Egyptian royal court in the 14th century BC are an outstanding, and unusually detailed, revelation of this (Redford 1984). In them, we see Egypt dealing with both remote 'great powers' through correspondence, reciprocal gifts and intermarriage; and even with vassal rulers or other lesser entities in the Levant with a mixture of administrative, economic, and military activity. Throughout Egyptian history, these patterns recurred, on larger or lesser scales according to circumstances, although the other surviving evidence is usually less rich and detailed.

All such categories are positive in terms of Egyptian interests, and the foreign participants involved belong to the 'good' category of foreigners. In the ideological realm, however, the many variations in relationships historically attested or likely to exist become smoothed out in literature and art, so that the foreign peoples and lands involved can be uniformly presented as loyal tributaries and subjects of the Egyptian king.

In the real world, Egypt and foreign entities often clashed militarily, or engaged in long-drawn-out processes of conflict and resistance conveyed through vassal or allied states. Sometimes aggression was initiated by Egypt, sometimes by the foreigner. Resolution might come with Egyptian victory, but often involved some form of agreement or treaty, probably more often and much earlier than we realize. The famous treaties – with Mitanni and the Hittites (see Warburton 2003) – belong to the New Kingdom, but similar formalized understandings probably existed with many entities. Such relationships of course often broke down, or were disrupted by the rise of new foreign powers, and conflict developed again.

Nevertheless, even aggressive relationships were nuanced ones. Egyptian interests or concerns were often not fully met; and sometimes the defeated enemy was relatively well treated in order to foster Egypt's long term interests. A famous example is the New Kingdom Egyptian policy of sometimes reinstating defeated kings as Egyptian vassals, and reinforcing their loyalty by holding their sons hostage at the Egyptian court, where they were educated in Egyptian norms, and inculcated with loyalty to the pharaoh. Ultimately, they would be dispatched to succeed their fathers, and theoretically at least provide a better basis for Egyptian power – the 'bad' is literally transformed into the 'good'. This was a policy applied equally in the Levant, Nubia and – insofar as possible – Libya, and was likely not confined to the New Kingdom.

However, in the literary and art-historical record, these subtleties about the 'bad' foreigner are for the most part blended into a homogeneous picture of the rebellious or resistant foreigner as the witless opponent and doomed victim of Egypt's superiority. The point is most vividly made in the great 'battle' scenes found in New Kingdom temple (and palace) art – and replicated verbally in literature – which are in fact virtually always massacre scenes (there are some noticeable, but rare, partial exceptions). The enemy forces make no resistance, but collapse before the charging Egyptian king (on a superhuman scale, and often virtually alone) sometimes accompanied by rather token Egyptian military forces, and are appropriately slaughtered, or made into prisoners to be dispatched into servitude in Egypt. This general theme runs through Egyptian literature and art in all periods.

Yet even in literature, if less so in art, a more nuanced attitude to the foreigner can be accommodated. Many royal inscriptions take a uniformly hostile stance, but didactic or narrative literature can be more subtle. A famous, and early example is the story of Sinuhe (Parkinson 1997a, 2002: 149–168) in which an expatriate Egyptian spends years living abroad in the Levant, in a self-imposed exile (he fears, incorrectly, punishment from the Egyptian king) yet continues to promote Egyptian interests. The historical accuracy of the picture of the southern Levant in the early 19th century BC is uncertain, but the complex ideological thrust of the tale is evident.

Sinuhe, the exile, becomes the vassal of a foreign ruler, and rules a component of the latter's political system, yet he continues also to represent the interests of the Egyptian king, whose superiority Sinuhe's Levantine overlord clearly recognizes. The 'good' and the 'bad' aspects of the foreigners are both incorporated in the tale; the former range from anonymous tribesmen who succour Sinuhe when he nearly dies of thirst on his flight from Egypt, to Levantine leaders who are all loyal to Egypt, yet are also subtly hierarchized, a reference to historical reality. Some seem potential allies, who need to be cajoled or treated diplomatically, others – perhaps, like Retjenu, closer to Egypt – are more subject to intimidation, and are accordingly equivalent to the Egyptian king's 'hounds'. The 'bad' is present not so much in the form of opponents of the Egyptian king, but Levantine enemies of the latter's Levantine supporters. One of these enemies Sinuhe defeats in hand-to-hand combat, which culminates in a scene of Sinuhe emulating the emblematic pose often presented in Egyptian art of the king overcoming and dominating a single foreign foe (Hall 1986: fig. 26).

While recognizing the complex reality of the foreign *vis à vis* Egypt, however, the 'Tale of Sinuhe' makes it clear that foreignness – foreign language, culture and lifestyle – is inherently inferior to the customs of Egypt, which set in these and all other ways the norms for the entire terrestrial world. When Sinuhe is persuaded to return to Egypt, and is welcomed at the royal court, the king's family makes fun of his alien appearance, the virtues of the Egyptian lifestyle he is about to resume are extolled, and his foreignness is literally scraped off him, as he is barbered, washed and anointed, and the foreign detritus, i.e. dirt, thrown out into the desert.

These concluding images of Sinuhe reflect another important aspect of Egyptian relations with foreigners. Those who can fully accept Egyptian norms and achieve complete acculturation were seemingly relatively easily assimilated into Egyptian society. The historical and archaeological record, incomplete as it is, provides a number of examples, from a wide range of periods (see also La'da 2003).

Art, as noted above, was less susceptible to such a nuanced approach, and presented a more ideologically extreme picture. This has a lot to do with the contexts in which art typically survives, contexts dictating specific approaches to the foreign, rather than the limitations of the Egyptian artists and their elite patrons. Representations on papyri could belong to different spheres of activity and interest, and may have been able to depict more realistic situations. A unique papyrus from Tell el-Amarna (Figure 9:9), for example, shows Libyans attacking and killing an Egyptian (Parkinson and Scholfield 1993), whereas in temple and mortuary art such a situation is never shown, though Egyptians kill other *Egyptians* in scenes of civil wars. The analogy to be drawn here is perhaps the highly restrained depiction of sexuality in temple and mortuary art, and the startlingly graphic nature of the 'erotic papyrus' (12th century BC) of Turin (Omlin 1973).

However, in terms of what exists, 'good foreigners' are rarely depicted, and occur mainly in scenes from elite tomb-chapels of the New Kingdom in which the official owning the tomb is shown supervising the presentation of foreign tribute to the pharaoh (for example, Davies 1926: pls. XIX–XXX, 1943: pls. XVI–XXIII). These scenes are characteristic of Egyptian ideology concerning foreigners in several ways.

Figure 9:9   Libyans attack and presumably kill an Egyptian: a unique scene on a papyrus from Tell el-Amarna (eighteenth Dynasty; after Parkinson and Scholfield 1993: 35).

First, they represent actual ceremonials in which the specific relationships between pharaoh and foreigner, Egypt and the other were dramatized. The king, seated on a dais and under a baldachin, and set in some relatively open and public locale, is approached by long lines of foreigners organized in groups according to their geographical origins (Figure 9:10). They are literally tribute bearers, conveying the materials, artefacts and other items characteristic of their respective lands as gifts or tribute to the king. The scenes convey the fact that the foreigners are 'good' (recognize Egyptian authority) but subordinate, while their prominently exotic character (in terms of dress, ornamentation and physical appearance) signals their inferiority to Egyptians as a whole, represented by the elite individuals clustered around pharaoh. Moreover, real-world differences are elided in favour of a presentation of pharaoh's universal power. Puntites and people of the Aegean, independent trading partners of Egypt, are depicted as tributaries as much as actual Egyptian vassals and subjects from the Levant and Nubia.

That such scenes hardly ever occur in temples (their typical locales are elite tomb-chapels and probably royal palaces) indicates how strongly context affected the ideological representation of the foreigner in Egypt. In temples, the emphasis was placed rather on the negative relationship between Egypt and the foreign. At all periods, emblematic representations of the king seemingly about to execute captured foreign enemies, were popular (Hall 1986; Sliwa 1974); and in the New Kingdom (but also earlier and later) there were more specific scenes or conflict, sometimes developed into episodic cycles depicting successive events in campaigns against foreigners (for developed examples, see Nelson 1930, 1932).

This, of course, highlights the 'bad' foreigner, the rebel identified with Isfet or chaos, and does so for specific reasons connected with the meaning and functions of the Egyptian temple. In addition, the placement of representations of foreigners is also significant. Depictions of foreigners, in both emblematic scenes (the king about to smite prisoners, or presenting them as booty to the deity of the temple; Figure 9:11) and more actualized ones ('battles' and campaigns) are typically displayed on the front façade (pylon) of the temple, around its exterior wall faces, and sometimes on the inner faces of the walls of its courtyard, or courtyards. They are excluded from the inner programme of the roofed, rear-lying part of the temple, which focuses on ritual, king and deity reciprocity, and royal ceremonies, such as the coronation.

In both subject matter and placement, scenes involving foreigners relate in specific ways to the functions and meanings of the temple, and these in turn reinforce and deepen the imagery of the 'bad' foreigner which is the dominant theme.

Temples at one level celebrate the interaction between deities and king so far as foreigners are concerned. Amongst the other powers and attributes deities allot to a king as their delegate (the more pacific ones commemorated in the roofed part of the temple) is the capacity to effortlessly repel the foreigner, and reduce him to subjection. In return, the king acknowledges the divine source of this power, and reciprocates it by presenting prisoners and booty to temple estates and treasuries. Here, the relevance of scenes involving foreigners is fairly obvious, and the more elaborate, episodic versions of royal victories are so placed that they flow towards the pylon, the place of presentation.

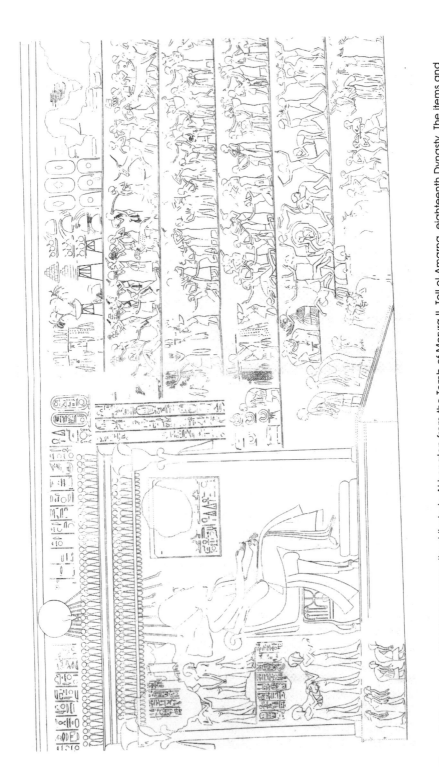

Figure 9:10 A scene of foreigners presenting tribute to Akhenaten from the Tomb of Meryra II, Tell el-Amarna, eighteenth Dynasty. The items and tributaries in the upper four registers are from Nubia (after Davies 1905a: pl. xxxviii).

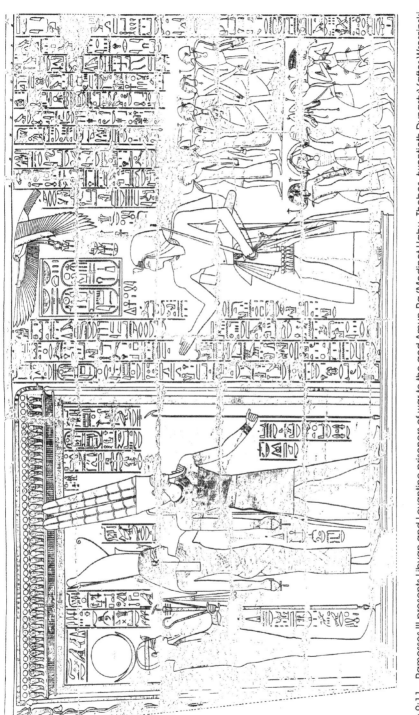

Figure 9:11 Ramesses III presents Libyan and Levantine prisoners of war to the god Amun-Ra (Medinet Habu, Thebes, twentieth Dynasty) (after Wreszinski 1880–1935, 2: pl. 150b).

At another level, the representations of foreign foes relate to the cosmological aspects of Egyptian temples (Baines 1995; Finnestad 1985; O'Connor 1997, 1998b; Van Essche-Merchez 1994). Insofar as the temple is a representation of all cosmos, its ceilings, and much of its wall programme (especially in the roofed area, and the upper parts of courtyard walls and even temple exteriors) represents the celestial realm, the world of the deities. The floor, and (in varying degrees) the lower parts of walls, however, represent the earth, and more specifically the terrestrial realm of humanity, i.e. Egypt and the foreign lands beyond it. This notion receives subdued, minimal attention within the roofed area, but on court walls, and temple façades and exteriors is permitted to expand into much greater visual prominence, especially insofar as representations of foreigners are concerned, particularly in the New Kingdom. Ptolemaic practice is different, for scenes in temples no longer present the great victory cycles of the New Kingdom, although emblematic representations of pharaoh dominating foreign foes still occur occasionally.

Just as the foreign lands are peripheral to Egypt, scenes involving foreigners are literally placed in and on the peripheral zones of the temple. Moreover, by highlighting royal victory, such scenes also became a form of apotropaic protection, vivid renderings of the victory of order over chaos, at the terrestrial level, and hence a powerful protection against the entry of chaotic, negative supernatural force into the temple (especially via gateways and doorways), a matter of perennial concern to Egyptians.

However, the temple also represents the birth of cosmos, rendered via the metaphor of the annual Nile inundation which seems first to engulf, then release – revitalized – the Egyptian landscape; and the daily renewal of cosmos via the metaphor of the solar cycle, the daily reappearance or rebirth of the sun (god), and its equally regular, and regenerative disappearance. The various components of the temple, from rear to front, literally represent – in form and programme – the successive episodes in both processes.

Characteristically, the processes of cosmogony and cosmic renewal are opposed by chaotic force or Isfet, which concentrates its powers upon especially crucial and simultaneously vulnerable points – the 'birth' of the creator, the 'growth' of cosmos, and the first sunrise, that vitalizes it; and the 're-birth' of the sun god, his appropriate 'burial,' and regeneration in the nether world. In this context, the display of hostile yet defeated foreign enemies equates them with the demonic forces that oppose, unsuccessfully, cosmic process; and again, the image of the 'bad' foreigner is more appropriate than that of the 'good' in this context (Figure 9:12; O'Connor and Quirke 2003: 11).

Belief

The fundamental point with regard to religious belief is that the cosmogonic process, as envisaged by the Egyptians (Allen 1988), incorporates everything in cosmos, including foreigners; and that everything in cosmos ultimately is part of the substance of the creator deity. Thus foreigners, like everything else, have positive value, and in this regard are similar or identical to the Egyptians themselves. This idea is a very

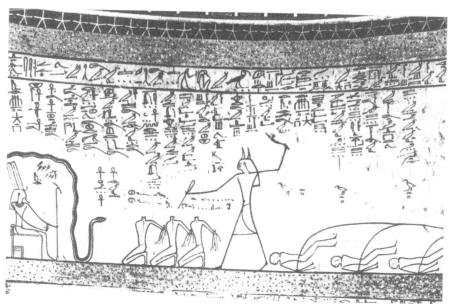

Figure 9:12   Foreigners as demons: in a wall painting from the tomb of Tuthmosis III, bound, decapitated and kneeling demons are shown in the same pose as submissive foreigners (Valley of the Kings, Thebes, eighteenth Dynasty) (after Hall 1986: fig. 91).

ancient one in Egypt, but in surviving documents is expressed in an implicit rather than explicit way until the New Kingdom. At this time, it is a concept referred to in religious hymns especially (particularly those directed towards the sun god or Amun-Ra – a particular form of the sun god – in his capacity as creator and cosmic ruler). In the context of the sun's rising, equivalent to a renewal of the creation, the god is hailed as "the creator of the *rekhyt* (here, humankind in general), who distinguished their races and made them live, who differentiated their skin (colours) one from the other" (translated and adapted from Barucq and Daumas 1980: 195). The ascendant sun god is told that there are "gestures of joy because of you in all foreign lands" (Barucq and Daumas 1980: 198), while of Amun-Ra it is said: "All lands are in awe of you, their inhabitants bow down because of your prestige, for your name is exalted, powerful and strong" (Barucq and Daumas 1980: 28). Further, "every land is tributary [to the sun god] as his subject, for it is the Eye of Re which cannot be resisted" (Barucq and Daumas 1980: 229).

This sense of the inherent value of the foreigner no doubt assisted the assimilation process referred to earlier, but these quotations indicate how the concept elides into that of the foreigner who knows his place, and is a faithful subject, in the first instance of the sun god, but implicitly also of the sun god's son and delegate, the Egyptian king.

However, this does not distinguish the foreigner in any fundamental way from Egyptians, for they too are subjects of sun god and king, and share with foreigners inherent capabilities of conforming to Maat, or relapsing into Isfet. It is not accidental that the prototypical emblems for the king's Egyptian subjects (distinguished from the nobility) are birds, the *rekhyt* or lapwings, which are often shown with their wings twisted one around the other to symbolize their limited capacity for free action, and sometimes even grasped firmly (by their wings) by the king. The message is clear: the Egyptians, like foreigners, have an inherent capacity to rebel, and must be ruled benevolently, and yet restrictively.

This idea had considerable mythological richness in Egypt, for in primeval times humankind had actually rebelled against the sun god, disrupting an initial harmony of the divine, the human and the natural, and almost resulting in humankind's annihilation. In the event, humans were forgiven, but the deities withdrew to the celestial realm, and Egyptian kingship instituted, so as to ensure that Egyptians and foreigners alike followed the paths of Maat (Hornung 1982a: 153–154). Thus, Egyptians who 'rebel' (criminals, or the losing side in a civil war) enter the realm of the chaotic and the lawless, and can be treated with exemplary punishment.

At the same time as religious belief provides the foreigner with positive meaning, it also places him in a subordinate position within cosmos. Cosmos is hierarchically structured; the deities serve the creator and sun god, humankind serves the divine, and in turn the creator makes for humans "plants and flocks, fowl and flesh to feed them" (Parkinson 1997a: 226). Of course, there is internal hierarchization also; within humanity, the king ranks above all, the nobility above the populace, and Egypt as a generality ranks above the foreign.

This is visually rendered in a famous stela of King Amenophis III (1390–1353 BC; for the stela, O'Connor 1998a: 163–167) which lists the monuments the king created in Thebes for Amun-Ra's benefit, and quotes the deity's response to these pious acts, in effect a statement that Amenophis, as an Egyptian king, is assigned full rule over both Egypt and foreign lands. This information is conveyed textually, but visually the stela is a cosmogram. At the top, a winged sundisk represents heaven; below it, scenes of the king and Amun-Ra interacting represent the temple, the transition between heaven and earth. Below these scenes extend 30 horizontal lines of text. The first 25 relate to and evoke Thebes, the royal centre of Egypt in this context. The next two refer to Egypt as a whole, the last four to the full extent of the foreign lands: taken together, these last six lines are equivalent in vertical height to the celestial symbolism at the top of the stela, and in terms of content represent the earth below as opposed to the heavens above.

Thus, the stela presents to us the hierarchy of heaven/the deities; temple and royal city/king; Egypt; and the foreign lands, the latter literally at the bottom of the cosmographic heap. An extended version of such a hierarchy would place foreigners between Egyptians and the natural world, and hence help to explain the ease with which foreigners, when viewed with hostility, can assume the form of animals and birds, and even insects and vegetation.

After the New Kingdom

After 1000 BC the Egyptian experience of the foreign changed in important ways, with a consequent effect upon the attitudes to or views of 'the other'. The exploration of these issues in depth belongs to a discussion of Egypt in the Late Period, and Ptolemaic-Roman times. Here I focus on the Third Intermediate Period. This was a time of political fragmentation and social stress in Egypt (Kitchen 1973; summary discussion O'Connor

1992: 232–252), two aspects of which are relevant here. The first is the emergence of royal families or dynasties, and of a supporting elite, which were of Libyan descent and which, although largely acculturated, nevertheless continued to proclaim their alien dimension by the use of distinctly Libyan personal names and the display of attributes such as an ostrich feather worn in the hair (Baines 1996c: 378–382). Subsequently, Egypt came under the control of a dynasty of Nubian rulers (twenty-fifth Dynasty, 715–657 BC) who ruled both Egypt and Nubia. Despite re-establishing an effectively re-centralized system of governance in Egypt, insofar as it served their interests, these Nubians did not reform the basic fragmentation of Egypt's political structure. The establishment of Nubian power had required substantial fighting in Egypt, during which the Nubian forces were opposed by regional kings of Libyan descent as well as other power holders of similar origin and labelled 'Great Ones of the Ma', a famous Libyan tribe. These kings and others of Libyan origin subsequently served as vassals of the Nubian rulers in the newly re-centralized system.

The Nubians had already achieved a high degree of acculturation prior to their occupation of Egypt, and this intensified thereafter. Nevertheless, they still maintained an alien or exotic dimension, by favouring (like the Libyans) Nubian personal names, and using distinctive attributes, such as a unique double form of the uraeus or cobra on their crowns and headgear. The sensitivity and interest of these Nubian rulers and their advisors insofar as Egyptian history, religion and culture was concerned was quite extraordinary, and produced – amongst much else – a specific work of art that conveys the complexity of ideas about the foreign at this time very well, but which – from a viewpoint external to Egypt – is also richly ironical.

King Taharqo (690–664 BC) had built, at Kawa in Nubia, a temple of canonical Egyptian form (dedicated to a local manifestation of Amun) and provided a programme of texts and scenes not only Egyptian in form, content and style, but actually produced by Egyptian craftsmen sent to Kawa from far away Memphis. Amongst the scenes they produced are several seemingly banal, yet in actuality quite complex and subtly allusive scenes involving foreigners (MacAdam 1955: pls. IX, XI) (Morkot Chapter 5, this volume: Figure 5:1).

On the transverse walls of the temple's courtyard were two sets of scenes bearing a subtle complementary, yet also oppositional relationship. On the east transverse wall the doorway into the roofed area is flanked by two similar scenes of King Taharqo about to smite a group of helpless foreign prisoners; the theme goes back to the Old Kingdom, but was likely strongly evocative of the New, when such scenes where almost axiomatic for temple façades. The foreigners are incompletely preserved, but grasp ostrich feathers, hence were likely all representing Libyans, one of the three traditional groups (Libyans, Nubians, Levantines) more usually assembled together in such scenes.

On the facing west wall, the doorway leading from the exterior through the pylon was flanked by scenes of the king as a sphinx (human headed lion) trampling foreign and specifically Libyan enemies (Morkot Chapter 5, this volume: Figure 5:1). Ancillary scenes show that these two identical scenes are close adaptations of a depiction of victory over Libyans that, while once relating to a specific event, became a standard one in the programme of Old Kingdom royal mortuary temple complexes (MacAdam 1955: 63, 64).

The meanings thus conveyed are complex. An 'Egyptian' pharaoh who is actually a foreigner is shown in traditional representations of pharaoh overcoming foreign rebels. The New Kingdom is contrasted and correlated with the Old, an index to the Nubians' deep interest in the Egyptian past, and to their manifestation of it (some royal names of the twenty-fifth Dynasty rulers were intentionally Old Kingdom in character). And finally, the foreign enemies highlighted are not the typical mélange of types; for obvious reasons Nubians are not included, and more specifically only Libyans are utilized, a reference to the opponents of Libyan descent whom the Nubians had overcome and subordinated in Egypt. Finally, there is also a degree of grim humour, in the comparison of contemporary 'Libyans' with their defeated prototypes of the preceding millennia. Indeed, humour is to be detected in a number of Egyptian references to the foreign, as in the amusement of the royal family at Sinuhe's alien appearance, mentioned above, or in some pictorial treatments of the foreigner in various periods.

Conclusion

The image of the foreigner and the foreign presented by ancient Egyptian sources seems kaleidoscopic, but this is due to the variety of contexts in which foreigners are represented. In reality, the Egyptian view of the foreign was integrated and comprehensive, and based upon a fundamental set of ideas.

The foreign was part of a larger Egyptian concept about what comprised 'the other'. The other consists of everything which, in the experience of the Egyptians, opposes the perfected or ideal dimension of the cosmos, a distinction derived from two opposing but complementary entities, Maat and Isfet. Maat personifies, in the form of a goddess, perfection; Isfet is the antithesis of Maat.

Perfection in both cosmic and human order is the emanation or 'daughter' of the creator god, who brought perfection into being. Isfet is the formlessness, non-being and 'chaos' which existed before creation and, extending to infinity, still surrounds the created cosmos. Maat and Isfet, in this situation, have a confrontational relationship, yet one that is also dynamic and complementary. Maat is actualized life, Isfet is potential life, and the interaction between them is the process which sparks the transition from one to the other, in the form of an eternal cosmic oscillation between the two. Perfection grows from its antithesis, anarchy is transmuted into order; yet Isfet is essential to the eternal regeneration or revitalization that this process involves, yet all the while threatening to overwhelm and abort it through the destructive potential of chaotic force.

For the Egyptians, this complex interaction was played out at every level of cosmos. The deities, led by the sun god as an embodiment of the creator, struggled endlessly (and successfully) to overcome Isfet's destructive forces, which continually sought to abort the solar cycle and so bring perfection to an end. At the same time, Isfet's potential for life, the basis of cosmic order, had to be integrated into the processes which brought about perfection. Every evening, sun god and cosmos sank back into the depths of Isfet, but maintained their perfect order therein to emerge, revitalized, every morning.

The Egyptians not only visualized these processes taking place at the divine level but themselves mimicked and re-enacted them at the human level. At the latter, the demonic, negative force of Isfet took on supernatural form, but also manifested itself as corrupt, criminal or rebellious Egyptians, and as foreigners who were hostile or threatening to Egypt. Here, too, struggle and victory were required so that perfect order, as exemplified by Egyptian society and its environment, could be maintained against the immense negative power exerted by perfection's antithesis. Yet at the same time potentially rebellious but quiescent Egyptians, and culturally alien but submissive foreigners were part of that perfection and were to be celebrated as examples of the transmutation of anarchy into order, potential life into actual life, Isfet into Maat.

The concepts described above are essential to our understanding of two complementary realities: on the one hand, the actual historical experience, insofar as reconstructable, of the Egyptians with foreigners, and on the other, the ways in which the Egyptians interpreted that experience. As reliable a picture as possible of the complex and changing interrelationships between Egypt and foreigners needs to refer to texts and art that focus more on Egyptian perceptions of those interrelationships, rather than on the historical actualities involved. However, these same sources, when compared to those actualities, reveal yet another reality, the power of the concepts Egyptians had about the foreign, especially as a manifestation of a broader entity, 'the other'. Here can be seen actual experience of the foreign being incorporated into concepts fundamental to Egypt's cultural dynamics, to its capacity to be a successful society with its own distinctive vision of its place in the world and in cosmos.

As to the reliability or accuracy of the different types of sources, some are more focused on the actuality of foreign relations and others on the Egyptians' conceptions about those relations, yet virtually no source lacks some value and the distinctions to be made between the different types are nuanced and relative, not absolute. Egyptian art, and literary, rhetorical and religious texts all strongly emphasize the conceptual aspect of foreign relations, yet very often still contain important information about their actuality as well. Other kinds of texts, as well as archaeological evidence, typically provide information which we consider more objective, yet they too reflect Egyptian attitudes to foreigners as well as contacts with them. For example, the more mundane types of texts which we find more accurate or less biased concerning foreign relations include relatively 'matter of fact' 'biographies' of Egyptian officials provided in their mortuary texts; or lists of people with foreign names, and presumably of foreign origin or descent; or land surveys incidentally identifying some land owners or tenants as foreigners. Yet such texts also relate to Egyptian attitudes towards the foreign.

An official boasts, from beyond the grave, "Then (the town of) Avaris (occupied by Canaanites) was despoiled, and I brought spoil from there: one man, three women; total, four persons. His majesty gave them to me as slaves" (Lichtheim 1976: 13). This information is valuable both specifically (an important attack, attested also in other sources) and generally, as to common practice (rewarding victorious Egyptian soldiers with some of the foreign booty they acquire). But this particular event is highlighted in this 'biography' because it is a part of a general, almost standardized litany of individual official achievements, which can be made more specific as to detail, yet always represents the effective deployment of royal power and authority which has been delegated, in different forms, to the king's officials. Lists of foreigners document relations at the specific period (e.g. Redford 1992: 78) yet also reflect the processes whereby foreigners become parts of broader ones transforming anarchic, i.e. alien, energy into orderly practice. Such foreigners are typically slaves or servants, and their occupations are those typical of a specific kind of foreigner, such as domestic service or weaving on the part of Canaanites. As a final example, a late New Kingdom land survey identifies Sherden – an Aegean or east Mediterranean people – amongst many otherwise Egyptian tenants (Gardiner 1961: 297), a valuable direct reference, but one needing to be glossed for full understanding. These Sherden (Heinz 2001: fig. I.17) land holders are part of a more general policy of providing subsistence for military personnel in general and at the same time exemplify the capacity of the orderly to absorb and transform the alien and anarchic.

Archaeological evidence, which we also like to think of as a more objective source of information, also has these conceptual nuances. In a general sense, such data document contact with foreigners, whether by Egyptians in foreign lands or foreigners temporarily or permanently resident in Egypt, e.g. as traders, envoys, soldiers, and the like. Yet, once again, full understanding may require reference to the conceptual also.

Thus, significant archaeological evidence in connection with Nubia includes the actual remains of sophisticated fortresses built within part of that country during the Middle Kingdom to ensure Egyptian domination, a 'practical' end (Taylor 1991: fig. 16). Yet some find the fortresses so disproportionate to an assumed indigenous weakness that they see them as ideological statements as much as functional entities (Adams 1977: 187–188; Kemp 1989: 166–178). Seemingly less tinged by ideology is the archaeological evidence for an increasing (and increasingly formidable) Canaanite presence at the town site of Tell el-Da'aba (ancient Avaris) in the eastern Delta during the Second Intermediate Period (Bietak 1997: 87–140). Yet this must be understood as reflecting a process whereby Egyptian attitudes permitted both a Canaanite presence (initially to serve pharaoh; subsequently to usurp pharaonic power themselves) and an opportunity for the Canaanites to acculturate to a degree and thus facilitate their eventual takeover of a substantial part of the Egyptian state (Redford 1997: 1–45).

As for literary and rhetorical texts, they may more reliably document concepts and attitudes rather than actual contact and interaction; yet they too can often be significant with regard to the latter. Most of the enormously long inscriptions dedicated to the victories of Ramesses III over the Libyans and Sea Peoples (Edgerton and Wilson 1936: 4–93) concern the concepts of the hostile foreigner as a beast, demon and even men transformed into women through terror and panic, as well as the broader theme of Maat triumphing over Isfet. Yet at the same time the reality of the relevant contacts are succinctly described, and some indications of their nature provided. The much earlier story of Sinuhe, mostly set in Canaan, may be a literary fantasy (Parkinson 1997a, 2002: 149–168), yet uses contemporary knowledge of Canaan and its peoples to provide simultaneously authenticity and conceptual relevance.

As for Egyptian art, its emphasis on conceptuality has already been noted above, yet here too there is valuable information about actual circumstances. In both tomb-chapel and temple art significant detail is provided, based on direct observation if also tending towards stereotypicality, about the physical appearance, dress and accoutrements of various foreign peoples. In some cases, Egyptian art is the only source for such information about peoples (Puntites, Libyans) whose indigenous archaeology is as yet undocumented. Moreover, exotic environments are, occasionally, evoked, such as the geography of Punt and contiguous regions (Meeks 2003: Figures 4:1, 4:2 and 4:3) recorded in Hatshepsut's mortuary temple (O'Connor 1982: 935–939; Smith 1965: 137–139) or the vivid detail of a bear (Figure 9:13) seizing a man in the coniferous forests of Lebanon (Smith 1965: 174–175).

The case history of King Akhenaten, the 'heretic' or monotheistic pharaoh, is particularly informative. Once his ideas had fully developed and he had moved to a new and purer royal centre at Tell el-Amarna (ancient Akhetaten), Akhenaten seems to some scholars to have been remote from foreign affairs; the king seems to have "abnegated the responsibility of keeping in touch with the world in which he lived and has delegated that task to subordinates" (Redford 1984: 168). This impression is derived from the Amarna Letters, an archive of foreign correspondence between the king and various major and minor rulers in the Near East. However, the archive itself shows that whatever may be thought of Akhenaten's policies, foreign affairs continued to be a major concern of the royal court. Moreover, the wider range of sources reveals a substantial interest in the foreign at Tell el-Amarna, although again one that is complex in nuance.

The tomb-chapels and the now demolished temples of Tell el-Amarna abounded in inscribed hymns celebrating Akhenaten's new concept of divinity, a single, all-powerful deity manifest in the sundisk or Aten. In these hymns, foreign peoples and lands are – along with Egyptians and Egypt – evoked as examples of Aten's benevolence, a tolerance about 'the other' that has impressed scholars who

Figure 9:13   Egyptian forces attack a Lebanese city. On the left a bear attacks a man in a thickly wooded landscape (Ramesses II, nineteenth Dynasty) (Wreszinski 1880–1935, 2: pl. 67).

nevertheless recognize it as a more extreme form of "a generalizing and universalizing attitude that must be viewed in the context of Egypt's general openness to the world during the New Kingdom" (Assmann 2001: 205). However, positive attitudes to foreigners are typical of religious hymns; what is more significant at Tell el-Amarna is the absence of the rhetorical texts (and accompanying large-scale art) describing the violent overthrow and punishment of foreign foes, material typical of temples rather than tomb-chapels. This should not be read as exemplifying a more pacific or tolerant attitude on the king's part, for in fact the art of the royal palace at Tell el-Amarna celebrates a very traditional triumphalist attitude to foreigners. The exclusion of such themes from temple art has to do with a new concept of decorum associated with a new set of religious ideas, rather than a fundamental change in the Egyptian view of the foreigner.

Archaeologically, the Tell el-Amarna palaces are poorly preserved, but it is clear that their decoration included frequent if emblematic depictions of foreigners as the defeated and now humiliated foes of the pharaoh. Representations of bound prostrate foreigners (Figure 9:14) (and 'the Nine Bows') occur on palace floors (painted on mud plaster, but also carved into stone floor slabs; Pendlebury 1951: 77; Weatherhead 1992) so pharaoh literally trampled them into submission as he walked or was carried through the palace. 'Windows of appearance' (Figure 9:15), in which the king and queen appeared to oversee the appointment or rewarding of officials before a bureaucratic audience (including foreign envoys), were elaborately decorated with boldly scaled depictions of bound foreigners standing on either side of emblems of Egyptian unity and dominion (seen in tomb-chapel scenes, e.g. Davies 1905a: pl. XXXIII; see also Weatherhead 1995: 98–106) and even on the sides of thrones (Figure 9:16). Apparently even the royal barges were decorated with images of the king (and queen) smiting foreigners in traditional mode (Aldred 1988: pls. 40, 41); and there may even have been 'battle' scenes in the palace recording royal victories (implied by bound prisoners guarded by soldiers; Pendlebury 1951: 62, items 203, 204).

Not only palace decoration, but also royal ceremonial celebrated the subordination of the foreigner. At least once, Akhenaten at Tell el-Amarna was the recipient of a seemingly huge ceremony of foreign tribute presentation, which presented a more benevolent view of foreigners, but made clear their subordination to Egypt and their cultural inferiority (Davies 1905a: pl. XXXVII, 1905b: pls. XIII, XV).

Thus, a consideration of a fuller range of sources opens up a nuanced and complex version of Egypt's view at this particular time. Archaeology is also relevant here. Through the eighteenth Dynasty a distinctive series of ceramic vessels foreign in form and fabric had been entering Egypt and diffusing outwards among the population, probably as a result of both trading networks and the redistributive policies of the Egyptian state. This exotic assemblage included distinctive Mycenaean pottery, but it is striking that whereas a huge palatial complex – a 'palace city' – of Akhenaten's father, Amenophis III, contains amongst its hundreds of thousands of sherds virtually no Mycenaean ware, Tell el-Amarna is comparatively rich in it (Cline 1994: 31–36; Merrilles and Winter 1972: 115–125). Why this is so is unknown, but it displays yet another facet of significant interaction with foreign lands under King Akhenaten.

Tell el-Amarna also provides evidence that the Egyptian representation of the foreigner could be more unusual than might be imagined, in the form of a depiction

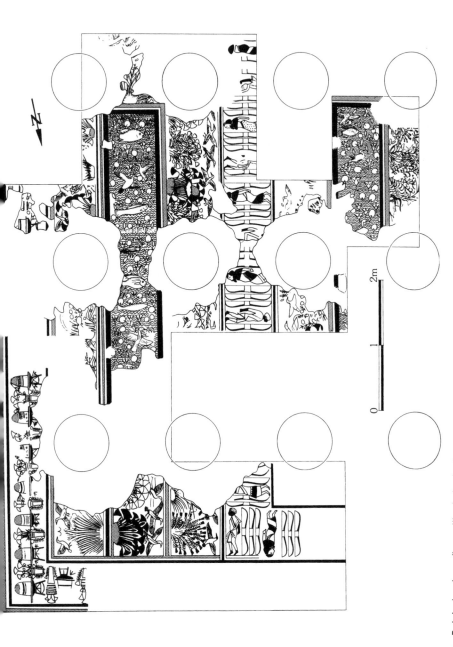

Figure 9:14   Painted palace floor with circles indicating the bases of columns, Tell el-Amarna. The central band shows bound, prostrate foreigners alternating with bows (eighteenth Dynasty) (Weatherhead 1992: 189).

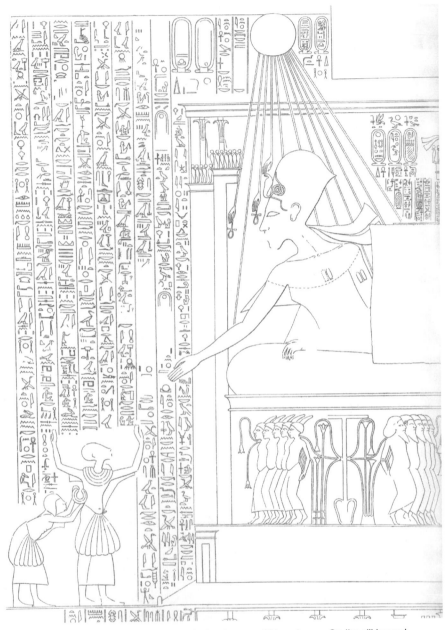

Figure 9:15   Akhenaten appears at a window in one of his palaces. On the sill bound foreigners are depicted (Nubians to the left, Levantines to the right) attached by their necks to a central symbol of Egyptian unity (eighteenth Dynasty) (after Davies 1908: pl. xix (left)).

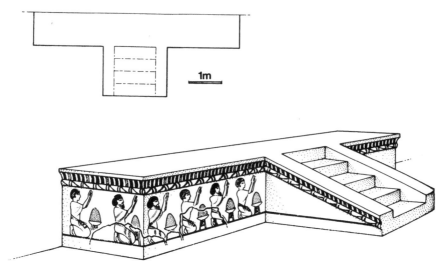

Figure 9:16   Kneeling foreigners painted on the side of the throne dais in a palace at Tell el-Amarna (eighteenth Dynasty) (Weatherhead 1995: 102, fig. 4).

of an Egyptian killed by foreign foes (Figure 9:9; Parkinson and Scholfield 1993). Sketched on papyrus, this theme would be inconceivable in the art of temple or tomb-chapel, where the concept of an always triumphant Egypt was dominant, but its existence suggests that there were other genres of pictorial representation in which such unusual images were permitted. Yet such 'realistic', un-idealistic motifs find an echo in even the highest level of royal literature; in the highly wrought texts describing the clash between Ramesses II and his foes near the Syrian city of Kadesh, the pharaoh is depicted at one point as almost paralyzed with fear as he envisages his possible death or capture during a pitched battle, and it is only the intervention of the god Amun which saves him from the fate depicted graphically on the Tell el-Amarna papyrus (Lichtheim 1976: 65–66).

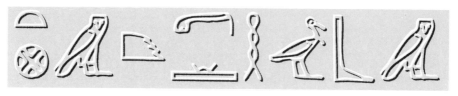

CHAPTER 10

FOREIGNERS AT MEMPHIS? PETRIE'S RACIAL TYPES

Sally-Ann Ashton

... the discovery of the portraits of the foreigners was not even thought of; and only gradually was it realised that we had before us the figures of more than a dozen different races.

(Petrie 1909a: 15)

Petrie goes on to categorize the terracotta heads[1] to include Greek, Egyptian, Persian, Sumerian, Semitic Babylonian, different races of Indians (including "a Tibetan type which is also found in Orissa" and "an Aryan Punjabi type"), Scythian, and Roman (Figures 10:1–10:9 col. pls., respectively; Petrie 1909a: 15–17, pls. XXXV–XLIV). In Petrie 1909b (16–17, pls. XXXIII–XXXIV) several other racial types are added to this list: Iberian, Carian, Hebrew and Kurd (Figures 10:10–10:13 col. pls., respectively), other Greeks, and Mesopotamian races (Figure 10:4 col. pl.); later still, Petrie (1910: 46, pls. XLII–XLVI) illustrated more of the same. In addition, each of the above publications includes several categories of 'unknown' racial types, and although initially Petrie (1909a: 16) believed the terracottas to be Egyptian on account of the Greeks' disdain for barbarians, he later suggested (Petrie 1909b: 16) that a comparison of representations of racial types within Greek art might be useful. This chapter considers both Greek and Egyptian traditions in an attempt to place the terracottas into more coherent groupings.

Petrie's keenness to see these terracotta heads as a single group is hampered by the variety of manufacturing techniques and styles which were used in order to make them. It should also be remembered that nearly all of the examples, with the exception of Petrie's (1909a:17) Scythian riders (e.g. Figure 10:8 col. pl.), which were cast whole, are without their bodies. Certainly in the case of the hellenistic Tanagra types, the heads would have been attached to a body, often slotted into or joined to a separately-made torso. The length of the neck of some of the other solid examples would suggest that this was also the case for some non-Greek types that were collected. So great, it seems, was Petrie's enthusiasm for these 'portraits' that the bodies were not seen to be important. Originally the figures would have been covered in a plaster-based wash and decorated with paint which is now mostly missing. Therefore, what remains as the moulding or modelling would originally have been unseen. As well as the missing decoration and bodies, there is an additional problem: the heads are without a secure archaeological context. Petrie (1910: 46) records, "The terracotta heads were seldom found in the work of this year, as we were not excavating in the foreign quarter from which they come; but I secured all that I could of those found by the natives". Therefore, we do not know the type of context from which the heads came, nor do we know if they were all from a single area. Furthermore, Petrie's interest in the heads meant that some at least might have been found in other areas of the site. The 55 that appear in *Memphis III* (Petrie 1910) would suggest that there were possibly sources other than the "foreign quarter" to which Petrie refers.

The majority of the heads are manufactured from Nile silt clay, although some figures have been made from marl clay (e.g. Figure 10:2 col. pl.) which represent Egyptian-style female figures. The processes of manufacture vary, with some hand-modelled heads with either moulded, incised features or modelled features from added clay. The mould-made pieces divide into two sub-categories of solid and hollow, and the latter are typically manufactured in two halves and joined together. Petrie (1909a: 15) saw these divisions as chronological indicators, suggesting that the earliest terracottas had been manufactured during the period of Persian rule (525–405 BC), and the Greek Archaic period, which he defined as the sixth century BC. However, the hand-modelled head in question (Petrie 1909a: pl. XLII, 56) has little in common with the types of terracotta figurines from Archaic Greece (Higgins 1967: 25–56). Like the statuary from this period, Greek terracottas in the seventh and sixth centuries BC are usually in the form of *kouroi* or *korai* (Tanner 2003: 132–138). More important, they are typically mould-made and hollow. Furthermore, a comparison between Petrie's heads and earlier terracottas from geometric Greece reveals little in common between the two groups; it is therefore unlikely that any of the Memphis heads can be attributed to archaic Greek craftsmen. The third group of mould-made solid terracottas were dated 500–300 BC; finally the moulded hollow figures Petrie dated to the early Ptolemaic period, 300–200 BC. There are, however, solid mould-made terracotta figures from the early Ptolemaic period; the dwarfs and dancers (e.g. Figure 10:14 col. pl.) with exaggerated features often tend to have solid heads and bodies. Hollow versus solid is not, therefore, an accurate chronological indicator.

The terracottas were found in an area described by Petrie (1909a: 15) as the "foreign quarter" which lies close to the Ptah temple (Jeffreys 1985: 19–21). Recent publications, although aware of the flaws in Petrie's methods of categorization, often accept his conclusions regarding this group of material quoting Strabo (XVII.1.32): "The city is both large and populous, it ranks second after Alexandria and its population is a mixed one." The archaeological and epigraphical evidence confirms that several different ethnic groups inhabited the city, even before the Ptolemaic period (Jeffreys 1985:14; Thompson 1988: 82–105). Of the types identified by Petrie there is evidence of Canaanites and later Phoenicians, Ionians (Figure 10:1 col. pl.) and Carians (Figure 10:11 col. pl.) from the sixth century BC; Jewish settlers also came to Egypt at this time, or earlier (Jeremiah 42:13–14) and in the second century BC Idumeans are recorded as a military presence at Memphis. Finally, under the Ptolemies the Greeks, who had also enjoyed a presence in Egypt from the sixth century BC, grew in number, while the other ethnic groups continued to emigrate to Egypt throughout the Ptolemaic period (although many had, by this time, adopted Egyptian traditions – see La'da 2003). Thompson's (1988) distinction between 'settlers' and 'visitors' may represent an important advance in the understanding of this group of material.

Groups within the terracotta representations have been studied since Petrie's publications, and their purpose and identification questioned. Scheurleer (1974), who published similar figures in the Louvre, questioned some of Petrie's identifications and dating. Where Petrie (1909a: 16, pl. XXXVI, 16) identified one particular head (Figure 10:3 col. pl.) as a "Persian Great King", he compares the Paris and Petrie heads to an Achaemenid vase, but concludes that the rosettes on the Memphis head are not the same as those commonly found as decorative elements in Achaemenid art. He goes on to compare a squatting Bes-like figure to the Scythian riders and an Egyptian-style head, which he also dates to the fifth century BC, and concludes that some of the material must be of this date.

Harle (1991, 1992) dismisses the idea that the so-called Indian terracottas (e.g. Figures 10:6 col. pl., 10:7 col. pl.; Petrie 1910: pl. XLII, no. 140) were Indian imports, or that they derived from Indians living in an Indian colony in Egypt. Instead he compares the figures with images of Harpocrates. The features of these figures are similar to dwarfs or actors – perhaps linked to a specific festival – and their date cannot be earlier than the Ptolemaic period, and stylistically they are closest to the Ptolemaic and Roman Harpocrates figures. Dwarfs also wear a similar garlanded headdress when offering a libation at an altar (Philipp 1972: pl. 22, no. 24), which might suggest that the so-called Indians were in fact somehow associated with festivals in the Ptolemaic or Roman periods. Furthermore, the raised left hand can also be found on images of dancing dwarfs, which supports the idea that the Indians may be revellers. Gordon (1939: 37) commented on the introduction of Indians at festivals during the reign of Ptolemy II, which would support the idea that this group served a religious purpose. However, while it is possible that the terracottas were intended to represent a link between India and Dionysos, there is no real evidence to suggest that they are of Indian origin.

This supports Gordon's view that the terracottas are later than Alexander's conquest of Egypt, and this hypothesis is supported by much of the evidence presented in this chapter. Gordon (1939) argued that if there were Indian figures amongst the Memphite terracottas, the closest parallels dated to the first and second centuries AD. He suggested that the Sumerian heads represented Buddhist priests, and explained the other racial portraits as part of the Buddhist custom of modelling heads of the people to whom they preached. The Sumerians can, however, be linked more closely to Egyptian portraiture dating to the first and second centuries AD; the bald head an indication of Egyptian priests at this time, as well as Buddhists.

The heads were assumed by Petrie to have been made by Greek or Egyptian craftsmen as representations of members of the Memphite community; Harle (1991, 1992), however, has suggested that the images may have been the result of foreign settlers in Egypt manufacturing terracottas that were relevant to their own traditions or religious beliefs. This suggestion seems more likely, particularly in view of the variety in manufacturing techniques and styles.

If Petrie's interpretation is accepted, the function of such images needs to be explained. The majority of parallels for the depiction of foreigners in Egyptian art come from relief decorations, or the representation of captives in the round. Perhaps the closest parallel is an execration figurine from Defenneh (Petrie 1888: pl. V; Ritner 1993: 138, fig. 13b); however, the shape of neither its head nor its body resembles any of the examples from Memphis. The clearest indication of a bound captive is the lack of neck because of the position of the hands behind the back, and most of the Memphis examples have necks. Therefore, the terracottas do not easily fit into this genre and are more likely to have served a religious purpose, be it within the household or temple environment (Harle 1991: 56). This would imply that the terracotta heads from Memphis are likely to represent gods, heroes or associated characters and caricatures from festivals. Some of the examples in the Petrie Museum remain enigmatic, but the majority should be allocated a Ptolemaic or Roman date. Furthermore, while the terracotta representations may accord with the multi-cultural environment of Memphis, they were not intended to symbolize the population, but were a direct consequence of the presence of foreigners within the city. That is not, however, to say that they were from the same archaeological context or that they should necessarily be considered as a homogenous group.

If hypothetically some of the group were intended to represent foreigners, it is possible that they were not necessarily those living in Memphis but rather those associated with Egypt at a specific time. If this hypothesis is correct, the date range of the material would be greatly affected. The Persian ruler, discussed by Scheurleer (1974: 84–89), may have been intended to represent a Persian or a Parthian rather than an Achaemenid; and the association between Egypt and its neighbours becomes particularly relevant in the Ptolemaic period. Excavated examples from Athribis (Myśliwiec 1994) have been found in contexts dating to the fourth century BC, suggesting that if they were Persian then they belonged to the second Persian period. There are key points when it would perhaps have been relevant to produce images of foreigners, Marc Antony's 'gifts' to Cleopatra and Egypt perhaps being the most spectacular. Plutarch (*Antony* LIV) records that Cleopatra was declared queen of Libya, Cyrenaica and Coele Syria; Alexander Helios was given Aremenia, Media and Parthia; and Ptolemy Philadelphos was awarded Phoenicia, Syria and Cilicia. He records that the former wore a Median costume at the ceremony and the latter a Macedonian *kausia*. If the terracottas did represent foreigners, they perhaps served a celebratory or commemorative function. The more likely interpretation is that the terracottas represent material commonly associated with Greek and Egyptian traditions.

Greeks

The dating of Greek and Roman terracottas is not as straightforward as is often implied. The recent excavations at Athribis have produced a quantity of stratigraphic material of the Ptolemaic period and other material can be dated from stylistic analysis and comparison with larger sculptural material. The manufacturing processes for terracottas should, in theory, also help to determine date but this is greatly influenced by the tradition to which the terracottas belong. In terms of Greek art, terracotta had been a popular medium from the earliest examples dating to 7000 BC from Crete, through the Bronze Age to the geometric forms of the eighth and seventh centuries BC and the carefully crafted images from the classical and hellenistic periods (Higgins 1967; Uhlenbrock 1990). As previously noted, Greek terracotta figures from the periods relevant to Memphis are mould-made and hollow.

Furthermore, the east Greek terracottas are hollow from as early as the seventh and sixth centuries BC (Higgins 1967: 37; Jarosch 1994). Other forms such as mould-made plaques can also be found in this period (Boardman 1999: 76, fig. 74), however the examples from Memphis have more in common with the Egyptian tradition in that they are solid. The choice to mould certain categories such as the dwarfs and dancers from solid clay may have been influenced by the Egyptian tradition, and could be an important link to our understanding of this particular group and its origins (Himmelmann 1983: 193–194).

It is from the Greek tradition that the first group of securely datable heads come. The so-called Tanagra type of terracotta is well represented in the group, and shows that at least some of the heads date to the Ptolemaic period, more specifically the mid-fourth to third centuries BC (e.g. Figure 10:1 col. pl.; Higgins 1967: 96; Uhlenbrock 1990: 131, no. 22). Although Uhlenbrock states that the wreath, represented on some examples, is unlikely to have served a religious purpose, it *is* associated with religious festivals, as indeed many of the Greek-style terracottas may have been. Furthermore, the presence of Tanagra type terracottas throughout the hellenistic Greek world does not support Petrie's view that such images were intended to represent Greeks abroad, but rather that they served a specific purpose, perhaps related to festivals. In support of this argument it is worth noting that they have been found in both funerary and domestic contexts (Nachtergael 1995: 263). Some of the heads may also have been attached to divine images (as illustrated in Uhlenbrock 1990: 136, no. 24 on a statuette of Nike, dated to the second century BC). Because of the method of manufacture and collection, the contexts have been lost, making the material difficult to interpret.

A second group of hellenistic terracottas supports a Ptolemaic date for some of the heads. The so-called hellenistic grotesques, images of men with distorted and exaggerated features, were, like the Tanagra figurines, found throughout the hellenistic world (Figure 10:14 col. pl.). Schreiber (1885: 380–391) concluded that the 'realistic' style of art had originated in Alexandria, although this hypothesis has met with strong objections since it was first mooted (Himmelmann 1983: 193–198). The origins of this type of terracotta image have been the subject of much debate, although generally it is accepted that they originated in either Alexandria or Asia Minor (Himmelmann 1983: 193). Himmelmann (1983: 203–207) offers a convincing argument in support of an Egyptian origin for this type of figure, some of which are intended to represent actors (Himmelmann 1983: 201). There are also representations of dwarfs, often with exaggerated features (Higgins 1967: 132; Uhlenbrock 1990: 144, 162), although these are often difficult to distinguish, because of their lack of scale due to the absence of bodies in the Petrie Museum examples. Many of the Greek terracottas have parallels from Alexandria (Breccia 1934). Himmelmann (1983) suggests that the origins of the hellenistic 'grotesques' can be found at either Smyrna or Alexandria (Nachtergael 1995: 261–262); the evidence from Memphis, however, suggests that this site should also be included in the equation.[2] To this category can be added terracottas depicting people with medical conditions such as Potts disease or those afflicted with a hunchback (Figure 10:14 col. pl.). Hellenistic bald headed dwarfs and actors are characterized by their Greek modelling, and there is no reason why some of the other examples from Memphis could not have been precursors. Comic actors and dwarfs also commonly appear on Greek vase painting in the fourth century BC, so the Greeks were familiar with such images before the hellenistic period; it is, however, possible that the type was developed in the round by Greek artists in Egypt. There are also depictions of non-Greeks in Greek art, including several of the types identified by Petrie, but they have little in common stylistically or iconographically.

Another striking parallel is that between Petrie's "Semitic Syrians" (Figure 10:15 col. pl.) and the portraits of the Late Ptolemaic rulers (Petrie 1909a: pl. XXVIII, no. 72) as shown by the low beard, large hooked nose and fleshy cheeks. Another (Petrie 1910: pl. XLIII, no. 147) resembles the images of Ptolemy IX (Ashton 2001: 56–57). There are other, less carefully manufactured examples also dating to the Ptolemaic period which have close parallels with a figure in a private collection (Bothmer 1996: 219, fig. 16). Of similarly poor quality is the head of a bearded male wearing an elephant headdress (Figure 10:16 col. pl.), which is possibly a reference to Dionysos or Alexander's Indian campaigns, perhaps linked to the later Ptolemies on account of the beard. Ptolemy II can also be found wearing the elephant cap on a bronze statuette now in the British Museum (EA 38442; Smith 1988: pl. 70, no. 5), on which he also holds the club of Heracles. The modelling supports a Ptolemaic date for the piece, and the depiction of a *kausia* is a common feature during this period.

Other heads are clearly representations of gods, such as Heracles (Petrie 1910: pl. XLIII, no. 146), and in the Roman period Serapis and Harpocrates are popular subjects (Nachtergael 1995: 263). Parallels in the Egyptian tradition can also be found at Memphis, and representations of Dionysos, on which the archaizing curls are clearly visible, although Petrie (1909b:17) believed the former to be the representation of a female.

Egyptian tradition

Scheurleer (1974: 97–98) dated an Egyptian terracotta head in the Louvre to the late fifth to fourth centuries BC, on the basis of Bothmer's (1960: 106) catalogue of Late Egyptian sculpture. Such a date offers several possible parallels for many of Petrie's foreigners, including the image of an Egyptian man from a tomb painting at Siwa (Boardman 1999: 159, fig. 200). The body is executed according to the Egyptian tradition but the man is bearded with a swollen occipital bone at the back of the skull. Interestingly, his son wears a Greek *himation*, but in the case of the Siwan tomb owner and vase-painter Exekias' Amasis, the bodies remain unaltered, drawn according to the usual artistic traditions.

The depiction of Amasis (an Egyptian name) as a Nubian or African by a sixth century BC Athenian vase-painter is a parallel for what Petrie was proposing at Memphis – the recognisable depiction (almost caricature) of a foreigner. Nubians also formed one of the traditional groups of foreigners in the ancient Egyptian repertoire, recognizable by a specific wig and black skin. Hellenistic and Roman artists copied the earlier Greek type of Nubian representation, showing their subjects with tight curls of hair and features that they considered to be typical of this race (Figure 10:21). It is strange, then, that Petrie does not mention the Nubians or Africans amongst his racial types, and the lack of Nubians/Africans amongst the Memphis material presents a flaw in the excavator's treatment of this material. For depictions of this group were precisely what Petrie believed he had found for other races.

Figure 10:21   Front view of head with African features, probably of hellenistic date. Formerly of the 'Major R. G. Gayer-Anderson Pasha' collection, no. 143, donated to the Institute of Archaeology, University College London in 1946 as UCL 1343.

Many of the terracotta heads appear to be misshapen. Some of the hellenistic Greek figures, such as Figure 10:14 (col. pl.), have exaggerated features, where the parietal bone appears extended; others have misshapen skulls by artificial flattening (Petrie 1909a: 16, pl. XXXVIII, no. 28; UC 49911). Similar features can also be found on heads which compare well to Egyptian sculpture during the Late and Ptolemaic periods.

Close parallels for the different shapes of heads can be found on sculpture, which may in turn help with the dating of the Memphite pieces. In fact, so close are many of the Egyptian-style heads to sculpture of this period that they may represent a link between workshops in Memphis during the Ptolemaic period. The majority of closely related examples date to the third century BC, and can also be related to plaster models that Petrie found in the area. The unusually square skulls are found on several examples, including Petrie 1909b: pl. XXXIII, no. 123 and one of Petrie's Sumerians (Figure 10:4 col. pl.; Petrie 1909b: 17). Similar square skulls appear on Egyptian sculpture of the first century AD (Bothmer 1960: 182–184, nos. 140, 141, pls. 132–133), and indeed on many other statues from this period. The bearded type with a full hairstyle can also be paralleled from a sculpture of a man, and on painted linen representations (Bothmer 1960: 173–174, pl. 125); both are closely similar in style to some of the bearded heads from Memphis (dated by Bothmer to 70–30 BC). Swollen parietal bones are also found on a relief representation dated by Bothmer (1960: 109–110, pls. 82–83) to the thirtieth Dynasty, about 350 BC. The slightly squarer appearance of Figure 10:4 (col. pl.) can be found in sculpture dating to the mid-third century BC (Bothmer 1960: 129–130, pl. 95). There are, therefore, enough parallels with sculptural representations of the thirtieth Dynasty, and the Ptolemaic and Roman periods, to conclude that the majority of Petrie's foreigners date to these periods; this accords with the hellenistic Greek-style examples. Furthermore, this re-dating of the Egyptian-style heads supports Gordon's (1939: 35) argument concerning the similarity between some of the Memphis heads and the representations of priests on Pompeiian wall paintings.

The bodies of the heads that have been preserved also support the identification of many of these portraits as images of priests. Figure 10:17 (col. pl.) is unique in that the head and upper torso are preserved. The portrait is one of the smaller examples but still reveals the same slightly squared skull and hand-modelled features. It is important because it shows a *naophoros*, although the shrine itself is now missing; the area where the top was attached to the body is clearly visible and the forearms indicate that the subject held his arms out, holding something. Although the features are crudely modelled, the down-turned mouth may indicate a late Ptolemaic date for this piece. If the artist was carefully copying a sculpture, it would confirm the identity of the heads not as foreigners but as Egyptians. The other bodies wear costumes associated with the Ptolemaic period, one showing a plain garment with a string of amulets around the neck, which can also be paralleled in Ptolemaic representations of priests, and the priesthood commonly wear the serrated shawl at this time, as seen on Figure 10:18 (col. pl.). Figure 10:19 (col. pl.) shows a traditional Egyptian costume worn by officials or priests and supports the idea that these heads were intended to represent Egyptians.

Other bodies are slightly more problematic, in particular those which show a poorly modelled male, preserved from the abdomen to the knees. One (Figure 10:20 col. pl.) wears what appears to be an animal skin around its hips, the markings inferred by the incised lines. The body may represent a priest, albeit poorly executed, or perhaps some association with Dionysos on account of the pattern. The proportions seem to rule out the body being the lower section of a Nubian or pygmy, both of whom were often shown wearing animal skins in the Roman period

The idea that many of the Memphis heads represent priests is further supported by several traditional Egyptian-style representations of women. Figure 10:2 (col. pl.), and others, are very similar to the statue of Heresankh, priestess of the cult of Philoteira, from the Serapieion at Memphis now in the Louvre (Quaegebeur 1983: 118: Musée du Louvre N2456). There are also representations of Ptolemaic queens such as UC 47952 (Walker and Higgs 2001: 65, 39), identified by the *stephane* and cornucopia that the subject holds, and dated to the second century BC on stylistic grounds as well as by the style of the corkscrew wig. Such objects were a reflection of the more general interest and support of the deification and worship of Ptolemaic queens. There are other representations of women, although as Petrie (1909a: 16) noted they are in the minority. Several wear a short wig, most commonly associated with the twenty-sixth Dynasty, the sculpture of which inspired many thirtieth Dynasty representations (Bothmer 1960: 101). The archaizing statue, often referred to as the Dattari statue (Bothmer 1960: 100–102, pl. 76), wears the same type of wig, which supports a thirtieth Dynasty or Ptolemaic date for many of the pieces.

Another statue with archaizing features, such as moulded eye-lines (Petrie 1909b: pl. XXVIII, no. 77), may also have served a religious purpose. This particular head (UC 48155) – with the remains of a beard and what appears to be a crown – seems to have represented the god Osiris; the softly modelled features, however, suggest a thirtieth

Dynasty or Ptolemaic date. It is very similar to the head of the god in the Metropolitan Museum of Art (Josephson 1972: 118.195; 1997b: 8, fig. 8), which is dated to the thirtieth Dynasty, on account of its claimed archaizing twenty-sixth Dynasty features.

As has been seen, therefore, many of Petrie's racial groups are in fact Egyptian dating to the Ptolemaic and Roman periods. There are also attributes associated with the Syrians commonly found on portraits from the late second century BC, and beards continue on sculptures made by Egyptian craftsmen into the Roman period. Representations of Persians could be expected within the group since they controlled Egypt on two occasions in the Late Period, and were a popular theme in the classical and hellenistic periods of Greek art.

The presence of Carians (Figure 10:11 col. pl.) in Memphis is confirmed by inscriptional evidence, which may support Petrie's (1990b: 17) identification of a group of heads wearing cockerel-shaped headdresses. The crested headdresses are, however, not dissimilar to those worn by Ptolemy X on Edfu sealings (Milne 1916; Royal Ontario Museum, Toronto 906.12.97). A similar headdress also features in Persian art.

The similarities between the Scythian riders (Figure 10:8 col. pl.) and Bes have already been noted and the idea that these riders might in fact represent a Roman form of the god cannot be dismissed. A comparison with the more usual first century AD form illustrates that the round shield and short sword were attributes associated with the god. The closest parallel for the modelling can be found outside Egypt on a small figure of a god, now in the Louvre (Ghirshman 1962: 102, fig. 115), where the same flat face with high, rounded cheeks and beard appears; the statuette is dated to the first or second century AD. These heads do not have the characteristic moustache of many of the Roman Parthian figures. In terms of Greek, Roman and Egyptian art, the closest link is to Bes. Gordon (1939: 35) pointed out that the horsemen from Memphis cannot on stylistic grounds be dated to either period of Persian occupation: "Iranian horsemen in a collection of types of all nations would have looked like these any time up to the end of the first century BC, probably later, and the same applies to the Persian officer (Petrie 1909a: 16, pl. XXXVI, no. 18) who is recognizable from quite late frescoes at Pompeii."

Conclusions

This chapter has concentrated on the identifiable material from the Late, Ptolemaic and Roman periods, material that is tied chronologically but not necessarily contextually. Some of the heads are extremely difficult to date on account of their crude execution. For example, some hand-modelled features resemble Middle Kingdom terracottas such as the head of a man on a vase (Petrie 1898: pl. XXI, bottom left). Although poor craftsmanship from any period is difficult to date, this particular head is not dissimilar to the swollen and misshapen heads on the hellenistic figures with exaggerated features. Perhaps this was the work of an unskilled person attempting to reproduce similar figures to those made by his Greek neighbours. Generally, Egyptian craftsmen of the Ptolemaic period are successful in their copies of Greek features or art, as seen clearly on the representations of Ptolemaic rulers with

Greek portrait features. While some of the group are very similar to stone heads of the same period, the production of terracotta figures is a very different form of art and effectively uncontrolled, and of less consequence than stone carving. In any case these heads would have been covered in plaster and paint, and so modelled more carefully than they now appear. On manufacturing grounds, the hellenistic period cannot be ruled out, but nor can it be assigned for certain.

Other examples from Petrie's 'unknown' category show similar modelling and features to others which are better preserved. A head (Petrie 1909b: pl. XXXIV, 30) reveals that some artists were producing poorer quality versions of the exaggerated hellenistic types. This could have important consequences, most significantly for the origins and development of this type of hellenistic genre, which has always been assumed to have been Pergamene or Alexandrian (Himmelmann 1983: 193); the modelling on heads such as that of an old woman from Ras el-Soda in Alexandria (Himmelmann 1983: pl. XI) is not very different from the head described above.

Some of the other figures have different attributes but are similar in terms of technique and style. Several of the heads wearing helmets also have beards: (Petrie 1909b: pl. XXVIII, no. 76, pl. XXXII, no. l12,) while the unusual head categorized by Petrie (1909b: 17; Figure 10:13 col. pl.) as a Kurd is manufactured from a micaceous clay which is distinct from the other examples from the site. It has the same modelling as the heads that can be securely dated to the Ptolemaic period, in particular by the modelling of the eyes. Similarly, the coffee-bean eyes and mouths which appear on several of the heads may be indicative of a certain period or culture, perhaps similar to those excavated by Petrie at Defenneh (Petrie 1888: pl. XXIV, nos. 7 and 8); from a context with seventh century BC east Greek pottery.

Petrie's methods of categorization were based on limited and sometimes misleading information; consequently the idea that the terracottas form a single related group of representations of foreigners living in Memphis must be questioned, as had already been noted by several earlier scholars. They had also remarked that the material largely dated to the Ptolemaic and Roman periods. While certain sub-groups are lacking exact parallels in terms of manufacture and style, they too could fit within such a general chronological framework. In fact, there is nothing to suggest that the various types were related, simply that they were manufactured at around the same time.

Notes

1   Further information, including dimensions of the Memphis material mentioned in this chapter, can be accessed through an online catalogue of the Petrie Museum of Egyptian Archaeology (UCL) at: www.petrie.ucl.ac.uk/search/index.html.
2   In my opinion the term 'Alexandrian' should not be used, since the evidence from Memphis suggests that this site played an important part in the manufacturing and development of this genre of figure.

Acknowledgments

I thank David Jeffreys for his help with the references, Stephen Quirke for the many discussions we have had, and for his helpful comments on the material, Jack Golson for his help with the text, and Chris Lyes for photographic work.

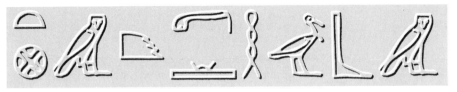

CHAPTER 11

ALL IN THE FAMILY? HEIRLOOMS IN ANCIENT EGYPT

David Jeffreys

The subject of heirlooms seems not to have been very frequently or specifically addressed in the Egyptological literature. Generally speaking, artefacts might be speculatively presumed to be and described in passing as heirlooms if, for example, they have been found in funerary contexts but show signs of use, or if their manufacture or acquisition is thought to be substantially older than the context itself (e.g. Arnold 1999: 310, 446; Baumgartel 1960: 102; Sparks 2003). Similarly, objects that have been broken and mended in antiquity may be classed as heirlooms; conversely many heirlooms or their fragments may have gone undetected in the vast body of archaeological material judged to be residual, such as Old Kingdom ceramics so frequently found in younger (sometimes much younger) contexts, and therefore often ignored or relegated to a lower echelon of information value. In the case of ceramics, as a rule it is only when intact pottery forms present clear evidence of ancient damage and repair, or even 'repair' where there had been no damage, that questions of their purpose, longevity and shared value arise, for example some of the predynastic vessels, especially black-topped and black-burnished Badarian (e.g. Brunton and Caton-Thompson 1928: pls. 12, 13).

The English word 'heirloom', which is perhaps more precise and descriptive than French *meuble de famille* or German *Erbstük*, contains the element 'loom', a tool; the original sense was probably a craft item such as a chisel or knife, passed on, no doubt with the specialist skills and knowledge that its possession implied, to successive generations. From this has developed its present meaning of 'a valuable object that has belonged to a family for several generations' (*COD* 10th edn, 1999: 660). The Egyptian language itself had words for 'heir/ess' (*iwˁt*) and 'inheritance' (*iwˁt*) but no word for 'heirloom', although *iwˁw*, suggestively perhaps, has the meaning 'ring' (Faulkner 1962: 12–13).

In the following discussion I therefore understand a broader sense of the word than others who have taken it to mean a personal memento such as a lock of hair deliberately packaged, as in the tomb of Tutankhamun, discussed below. A consideration of predynastic and dynastic Egyptian heirlooms (and whether they existed at all) therefore prompts reflection on, among other things, gender issues affecting property transfer, the Egyptians' conception of past time, and especially the perception of ancestors in Egyptian society at all levels.

This chapter therefore also adopts a rather different approach from the recent discussion of the archaeological and ethnographic contexts and social significance of heirlooms by Lillios (1999), which links heirlooms with the emergence of societies displaying inherited social differentiation and treats them as markers of hereditary rank or ancestry. Lillios considers case studies from the Americas, south-eastern Asia and Oceania (but not from Africa or the Middle East) and she proposes (Lillios 1999: 252) a set of properties or characteristics for the anthropological and archaeological examples of heirlooms: that (1) "heirlooms will date to an earlier period than other objects in that context"; (2) "heirlooms, within a culture area, are conservative in their general form over time"; (3) "heirlooms, particularly as symbols of authority associated with chiefly succession, are often represented in different raw materials"; (4) "heirlooms are often items of ornamentation, agricultural implements made of highly valued materials, weaponry, textiles, and ceramic or metal vessels used for food production, preparation, or storage."

While such markers of rank undoubtedly existed in the Nile Valley, they were evidently not confined to the elite and some of the best evidence for the social context of heirlooms, often with detailed textual support, comes from one of a small number of middle-echelon settlements of the second millennium BC.

The role of heirlooms and of their cognitive, archaeologically invisible associations raises questions about the ways in which cultural knowledge was transferred in Egyptian society. An implicit modern assumption is that heirlooms carry knowledge or memory of individuals beyond two generations (living memory) through sentimental value and associated verbal explanation and elaboration, although some or all of the factual detail may be lost in the process. Although this may have been the case in Egyptian society, where in general life expectancy was rarely more than 30 years but could be much higher in exceptional cases among the elite (Janssen and Janssen 1996: 60–69, 114, 119–120), the innate functional value of the piece may also have been part of its prestige. It has been noted, for example (Redford 1992: 212), that light arms, which, although often ceremonial, do occur in funerary contexts, are likely to have been part of the range of goods freely obtained in warfare or in other competition. Tallies of weapons are conspicuously absent from, or seem to be of minimal importance in, official booty lists in monumental inscriptions, and given the evident biographical significance of successful military service (e.g. Ahmose, son of Abana or Ahmose, son of Nekhbet) their transfer within a family group will surely have carried added power and prestige. At the elite level, for example, the rapid adoption by the Theban military aristocracy of the chariot as a status symbol, following its introduction during the period of Hyksos (Levantine) control of the northern part of the country, may be a comparable phenomenon. One explanation for the late arrival in Egypt of iron tools and weapons is that the few imports to the Nile Valley travelled only in this way as items of military acquisition, and that widespread and regular access to iron as a nationally imported resource was not something that the weakened Egyptian rulers of the late second millennium BC were able to achieve, even if they had realized its economic potential and social value.

If heirlooms really are a regular and potent characteristic of highly stratified societies, then Egypt, as the world's oldest pristine territorial state with a clearly demarcated social ranking (Wilkinson 2001), could be expected to show signs of a particular attachment to them. On the other hand strong descent groups and a highly centralized, bureaucratized state may have been incompatible with one another (Janssen and Janssen 1996: 36). It is worth considering whether Lillios' criteria for heirloom status hold good for Egypt: that heirlooms predate their taphonomic context; that they are morphologically conservative; and that, whether for ornament, or tools, weapons, clothing and other items, by their nature they will be made of different, prestige raw materials which might or might not be copied in inferior materials for burial.

Meskell (1999: 134) also notes that for Egyptians the act of commemoration was believed to be essential to a successful transition to the afterlife. Funerary cults at all levels of society depended on the perpetuation of a relative's memory and functioned through a system in which the raw material (tomb/grave offerings and equipment in the form of bread, beer, meat and vegetables, textiles, incense), and added value in the form of the craft skills needed for the construction and decoration of the tomb and its accessories (stelae or grave markers, statues, sarcophagi), were provided by the terms of the cult endowment. Cult officiants (close family or household members) shared in the proceeds and might expect to benefit also by being depicted on funerary stelae and perhaps being eventually accommodated in the same burial place. The observation of the cult was thus strengthened and might assure the postmortem future of the entire household.

Heirlooms in Egypt might presumably have been held and transferred over time both by formal conveyance or contract, for which there was evidently a constant provision (e.g. Pestman 1961), and by informal gift or donation. In skilled-craft contexts, apprentices may well have inherited valued tools, especially of metals whose distribution was controlled and regularly audited by the state apparatus (Černý 1973: 159), as well as other materials and equipment, as they assumed a greater role in the family trade. In this sense the extremely detailed 'trial' reliefs of individual hieroglyphic characters, perhaps intended as models for others to follow or as public evidence of competence or excellence, could also be considered as being transmitted from senior to junior partners in a craft apprenticeship. Actual examples or *simulacra* of both specialist and generalized tools do also occur as tomb contents, though their precise nature might be contested, and the question whether the funerary domain is necessarily the best context to test for the transfer of family possessions and individual wealth deserves more discussion (Ucko 1969).

Ritual and magical objects almost certainly circulated in this way, especially perhaps among women for whom certain kinds of inherited object may have had powerful protective properties, especially those relating to dangerous life transitions such as childbirth. One artefact group in particular, the bone and ivory wands or knives usually worked from hippopotamus ivory, which were probably produced and applied during and following birthing ceremonies (Pinch 1994: 130–131), often show a break, which has sometimes been anciently repaired, in the approximate centre of the natural curve of the tusk (Figure 11:1). Whether this damage was due to natural wear, to some violent action during a particular moment in the rite (a pair of 'wands' being used as clappers for example), or to a specific requirement that the wand be ritually broken (to divest the potentially hostile forces depicted of their power to harm), is unclear, as is the reason why they were kept in the family

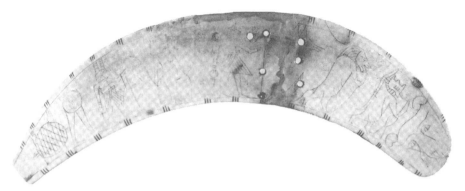

Figure 11:1   Ivory apotropaic wand with repair holes (19th to 18th centuries BC) (Pinch 1994: fig. 38; and see Robinson 2003: Figure 8:6a) (British Museum).

possession when already broken. Significantly, the recently discovered and first recorded archaeological example of a magical birth brick, from Abydos (Wegner 2002), although similarly decorated, shows no such fracture or even particular signs of use wear. Even to describe these artefacts as 'heirlooms' is questionable since there is no firm evidence that they actually passed down from one generation to the next, and – in the case of the wands – their archaeological find context is often doubtful or unknown.

There are other indications that heirlooms might have been a more common phenomenon among women than men: for instance under the legal system property and title passed through, and ancestors were normally traced back further in, the female line of descent rather than in the male (Petrie 1923: 109); familial duty was moreover the duty of the daughter, not the son, although brothers and sons could become responsible for the maintenance of the mortuary cult of their immediate ancestors. Both these factors make it likely that keepsakes and other objects, which were not related to craft skills and were intended to stay in the family group, would be transferred to and kept by women of all ages rather than men.

Work on the subject of the Egyptians' awareness of the past and of past family members, notably at the archaeologically well-known artisan colony of Deir el-Medina (Demarée 1983; McDowell 1992; Whale 1989), suggests that more remote ancestors were not treated as fondly remembered or respected individuals, but were considered impersonal or generalized spirits. Neither of the two major groups of relevant text-bearing artefacts, the funerary and votive stelae and the 'letters' to the dead, seem to refer to ancestral figures beyond two generations, i.e. within the maximum range of living memory in normal circumstances. With no evocative visual markers of the kind we have today in the form of portraiture, photographs, hoarded family ephemera etc., and with the conspicuous absence of personal diaries from the Egyptian documentary record (Gardiner 1973: 18–24), the capacity for direct access to the personal forebears will have been limited to such small-scale monuments and items of personal association.

This seems to deny the evident importance of inscriptions with detailed royal and private genealogies and biographies, such as are found in some tomb schemes (although these are not common at Deir el-Medina itself), but those more formal texts are precisely the kind of composition for which access to local, regional, or even national archives was required, rather than being personally or 'naturally' recalled, and they may have had the quite different aim of establishing the privileged status of the tomb owner, the tomb, and its location through direct association. McDowell (1992) has demonstrated that while knowledge of the past among Egypt's elite might well have been maintained within that social milieu through the scribal monopoly of inscriptions and archives, any informal or folk memory of past kings and their achievements may have been very differently structured and understood.

Rather like personal ancestors, remote kings may have lived on in the popular consciousness as idealized and sometimes even deified figures, but they also feature as players in stories and entertainments in which they assume a far less dignified role: the somewhat enigmatic tale of King Neferkara (Pepi II) and his general Sisene, with its apparent undertones of sleaze and possibly homosexuality, may be an example of this (Manniche 1987: 73). In this story, the king and courtier apparently embark on a night of debauchery (although their escapades are not made explicit), in a way that seems almost to reproduce here, to the detriment of the king, the high-culture literary form of the *Königsnovelle*. Similarly, the vignettes of the Turin 'satirical'/'erotic' papyrus (Figures 11:2, 11:3), which may conceivably have been a story-telling aid, clearly replace the conventional figures of king and courtiers, and even deities, with those of domestic animals – and humans. Cats, mice, birds, donkeys and monkeys wear human clothing and tuck in to funerary repasts, hunt from chariots, and attack and defend walled cities. In the separate, so-called 'erotic' section of the Turin P., which has often been treated as a kind of Egyptian Kama Sutra (e.g. Omlin 1973; Shaw and Nicholson 1995: 93), several of the sexual positions of the men and women shown almost resemble those of the earth and sky deities Geb and Nut (Allen 2003; Layton 2003; Manniche 1987: 108, 112) in which, significantly in the Nile Valley where the 'normal' climatic conditions for the Mediterranean basin are reversed, Geb/earth is male and Nut/sky is female. The mental juxtaposition of the supra-human and the socially relegated human (the women are assumed to be prostitutes and the men shown are the stereotypes of agricultural labourers) may well have had a deliberately satirical, degrading effect, but will also have perpetuated the memory of past times and personalities.

Since heirlooms are essentially family- or kin-based property, the question arises as to what the term 'family' means in the Egyptian context. The constitution of the Egyptian household was, however, probably fairly flexible, with new non-blood members accepted relatively freely, and equally able to leave the group when they desired (Whale 1989). Another point of uncertainty is whether objects transmitted within the family or other local groups acted as a complement to written or orally relayed information, or operated independently. As McDowell (1992) shows, the inhabitants of Deir el-Medina (or some of them at least) had access to local archive documents, such as records of property transfer and wills, as required; ancestor stelae existed to recall the names of former family members. It is not known what incentive existed to distribute material possessions, whether of high or low intrinsic value, to augment the formal record (cf. Redford 1986a: 138).

Figure 11:2   Detail of satirical scenes (after Omlin 1973: pl. XIII).

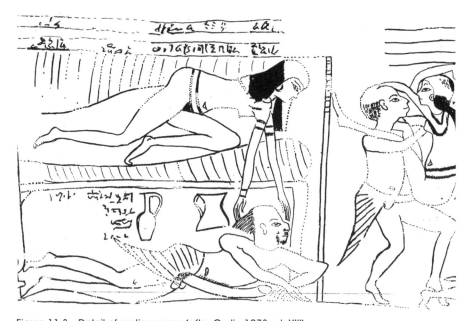

Figure 11:3   Detail of erotic scenes (after Omlin 1973: pl. XIII).

While Lillios makes portability one of the defining characteristics of heirloom status, other categories might equally well be considered heirlooms in the broader sense. Family burials and commemorative architecture, and indeed the physical remains and funerary accessories of the ancestors themselves, may in a certain sense have been bequeathed to succeeding generations. Cases of the re-use of important parts of funerary architecture, or statues modified for later use, are usually explained as being 'usurpation' (a loaded term in any case, implying wrongful acquisition), although Goedicke (1971: 6–7) has suggested that there was an element of respect or even reverence in the process, and the same can surely be assumed to have been true of the Egyptian 'archaizing phenomenon' (Manuelian 1993; and see Davis Chapter 3, Morkot Chapter 5, and Wildung Chapter 4, all this volume). Goedicke's argument concerned architectural fragments from Old Kingdom royal mortuary buildings, removed and incorporated, perhaps deliberately, in the early twelfth Dynasty pyramids at Lisht, possibly in order to legitimate both the choice of burial site in the time-honoured and prestigious Memphite necropolis, and the form of structure (the pyramid) which would recall the glory days of the Old Kingdom. There is another, perhaps more convincing, example of the re-use of a key fragment – an inscribed central lintel block originally from the doorway of an elite but non-royal tomb (Figure 11:4) – integrated and locked into a similar decorative scheme in a different, later private mortuary chapel found at Memphis (Badawi 1956: 161). It would be valuable to know whether there is any kind of family connection in this case, but, since over 400 years separate the two building episodes, this is impossible to establish.

Figure 11:4   The tomb of Shoshenq as re-constructed, showing re-used lintel (after Badawi 1956: pl. IV).

Similarly, there is no reason why human resources – slaves and other retainers – and livestock should not also be considered articles of ownership capable of being passed down from one generation to the next, with their own family associations and perhaps their own craft specialisms. Some categories of slaves in ancient Egypt, who were often drawn from the ranks of settled prisoners of war, were legally considered chattels (though they retained certain civil rights and could expect certain norms of treatment) and might, with or without their offspring, be bought, sold, emancipated or bequeathed (Allam 2001; Bakir 1952: 69–70, 81), although the precise legal conditions of transfer to heirs of the owner, and the heirs' ensuing obligations, are not entirely clear from the documentary evidence (Bakir 1952: 78). An inherited slave may have been valued for particular craft abilities, but also as an exotic, providing a vehicle for information about earlier generations and also about the outside world, both beyond the local context and even beyond the Nile Valley. The prominent appearance of 'Asiatic' (Levantine) names in domestic contexts at the Middle-Kingdom pyramid town of Lahun (Luft 1998: 29–31) suggests that new arrivals in the Nile Valley might have been coerced or invited to settle at this new building project of the royal mortuary cult, but it is not known whether they came attached to existing retinues or were imported as part of a state-organized population movement.

Statues of domestic deities, both formal pieces as well as the particularly intriguing group of anthropoid or 'ancestor' busts with non-specific facial features (Keith-Bennett 1981), might be considered heirlooms in the sense that they were exclusive to particular households and probably travelled with them, although the fact that so many of the anthropoid busts at the main find site, Deir el-Medina, were apparently randomly discarded, although in the immediate vicinity (especially around the temple – Meskell 1999), seems to argue against this. Most of those from recorded contexts, whether from Deir el-Medina or elsewhere, were not in fact found in direct association with house interiors, although they, like the ancestor stelae, were discovered more often in broad association with the settlement area rather than with the neighbouring necropolis (Demarée 1983: 279; Keith-Bennett 1981). The one example (Figure 11:5) recorded from a clearly domestic situation (at Memphis: Giddy 1999: 43) was from a deflated, poorly stratified context. Other domestic votives, such as the pottery bowls and free-standing figurines of a snake deity (Renenutet?) found at settlement sites such as Amarna, Memphis, and elsewhere (Giddy 1999: 13–27; Kemp 1981: 14–16; Redmount 1997: 76–77), may well have been concealed and displayed on certain occasions within households, just as the anthropoid statues, and maybe the ancestor stelae, are thought to have been. However, by their very nature these classes of object are rarely chronologically sensitive enough to establish on their own whether they predate their find context.

Jewellery and amulets worn as body decoration would seem to be an ideal candidate for transmission as heirlooms, operating in the past as they do today. However, such finds are rarely distinctive or recorded well enough to be able to be so identified, except perhaps in the case of amulets such as ring bezels, scarabs and scaraboids, and cartouche-amulets, whose inscriptions show that they were named for a specific ruler. Although notoriously dangerous to use for precise dating purposes, both for the usual stratigraphic/taphonomic reasons and because of the suspicion of 'retrospective' scarabs produced long after the reign they appear to commemorate (especially those with the name of Tuthmosis III), it might be worth

Figure 11:5
Anthropoid or
'ancestor bust'
from Memphis
(Giddy 1999:
pl. 82).

asking if they were not simply heirlooms of greater than usual longevity, and particularly whether certain kings carried greater and longer-lasting prestige value than others.

Shaw's study of named ring bezels from the eighteenth Dynasty city at Amarna, and from the walled artisan village outside the city centre (a community contemporary with, and in many respects similar to, that of Deir el-Medina), suggests that occupation of the village continued well beyond the end of Akhenaten's reign and the abandonment of the rest of the city, but that the village still yielded a high proportion of earlier bezels (Shaw 1984: 130–131). The question of whether these were heirlooms, or were simply abandoned at earlier stages of the village's occupation, is not easily resolved: since the greatest number of bezels are named for Tutankhamun and were also dropped or discarded nearby, some presence at the village at least as late as his reign is indicated. The residual population may, however, have been employed decommissioning and dismantling the site, and to have held little regard for the rulers of the earlier, moribund dynasty. Interestingly, there were very few bezels named for the Aten, perhaps the deified form of Akhenaten's father Amenophis III (Johnson 1996), suggesting that the oldest bezels were not numerous and that the royal cult never took root (or were not encouraged to do so) outside the immediate court circle.

The function of those scarabs specially commissioned by the ruler to record and celebrate key events of his/her reign, and almost certainly bestowed on individuals as a signal of merit or favour in the same way as medals in modern times, brings into question whether the recipients were at least notionally regarded as being admitted to a favoured outer circle of the royal family, and whether this privilege or the memory of it descended with the amulet to later generations. If only better provenanced, the well-known large commemorative scarabs, mostly of the reign of Amenophis III (Figure 11:6), would be a useful test case, since their manufacture would be of a reasonably well-established date, and they are unlikely (because of their size) to have travelled much or to have been discarded trivially or accidentally, and their potential for onward transmission through several generations could be assessed and compared. Unfortunately, however, 174 out of a total of 201 (87 per cent) of the recorded scarabs are poorly pedigreed if at all, or are lost (Blankenberg-van Delden 1969). Of the remainder, eight do come from secure, well-documented and reasonably well-dated contexts in the Nile Valley, of which two are from Amarna and could

therefore be contemporary with, or only slightly older than, their find contexts. Of those remaining that were found as residuals, only two are stratigraphically well-recorded examples from a context that must be substantially later than their manufacture: these steatite 'lion-hunt' scarabs (Blankenberg-van Delden 1969: 194–195) were found in Clarence Fisher's (unpublished) excavation of the Palace of Merenptah at Memphis (Kom el-Qala); this would mean, since the palace was almost certainly founded on a virgin site (Jeffreys 1996; Jeffreys and Giddy 1989: 8), that their deposition must postdate Amenophis III's reign by at least 150 years, or six generations or seven reigns, and that they must therefore have changed hands several times. The state of preservation of one of them shows that it survived this time span intact, though with some evidence of

Figure 11:6 'Lion-hunt' commemorative scarab (provenance unknown) (Blankenberg-van Delden 1969: pl. 11).

Figure 2.1   Scene from the tomb of Seti I depicting figures towing the barque of the sun god with the serpent Mehen coiled round and guarding the god's shrine (© E. P. Uphill).

Figure 4:9   Wall painting on mud plaster from the tomb of Ankhtifi in Mo'alla, First Intermediate Period (ca. 2150 BC); ht. ca. 60 cm (© Dietrich Wildung).

Figure 9.7 Levantines (left), Nubians and Libyans depicted in the tomb of Ramesses II, Valley of the Kings, Thebes (Hornung 1990: 148, pls. 107–109).

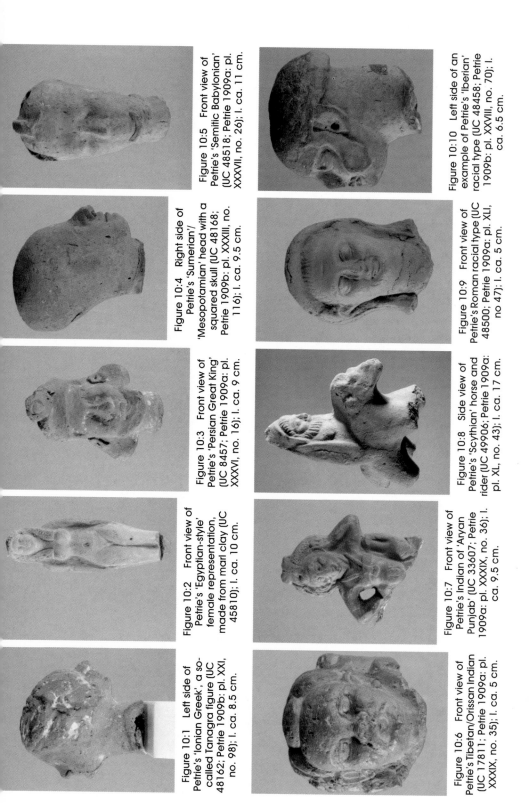

Figure 10:1 Left side of Petrie's 'Ionian Greek', a so-called Tanagra figure (UC 48162; Petrie 1909b: pl. XXI, no. 98); l. ca. 8.5 cm.

Figure 10:2 Front view of Petrie's 'Egyptian-style' female representation, made from marl clay (UC 45810); l. ca. 10 cm.

Figure 10:3 Front view of Petrie's 'Persian Great King' (UC 8457; Petrie 1909a: pl. XXXVI, no. 16); l. ca. 9 cm.

Figure 10:4 Right side of Petrie's 'Sumerian'/ 'Mesopotamian' head with a squared skull (UC 48168; Petrie 1909b: pl. XXXIII, no. 116); l. ca. 9.5 cm.

Figure 10:5 Front view of Petrie's 'Semitic Babylonian' (UC 48518; Petrie 1909a: pl. XXXVII, no. 26); l. ca. 11 cm.

Figure 10:6 Front view of Petrie's 'Tibetan/Orissan Indian (UC 17811; Petrie 1909a: pl. XXXIX, no. 35); l. ca. 5 cm.

Figure 10:7 Front view of Petrie's Indian of 'Aryan Punjab' (UC 33607; Petrie 1909a: pl. XXXIX, no. 36); l. ca. 9.5 cm.

Figure 10:8 Side view of Petrie's 'Scythian' horse and rider (UC 49906; Petrie 1909a: pl. XL, no. 43); l. ca. 17 cm.

Figure 10:9 Front view of Petrie's Roman racial type (UC 48500; Petrie 1909a: pl. XLI, no 47); l. ca. 5 cm.

Figure 10:10 Left side of an example of Petrie's 'Iberian' racial type (UC 48458; Petrie 1909b: pl. XXVIII, no. 70); l. ca. 6.5 cm.

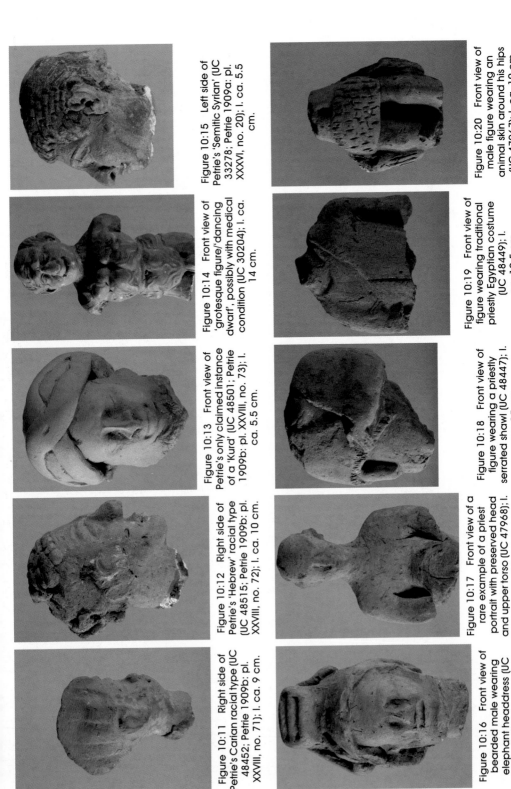

Figure 10:11 Right side of Petrie's Carian racial type (UC 48452; Petrie 1909b: pl. XXVIII, no. 71); l. ca. 9 cm.

Figure 10:12 Right side of Petrie's 'Hebrew' racial type (UC 48515; Petrie 1909b: pl. XXVIII, no. 72); l. ca. 10 cm.

Figure 10:13 Front view of Petrie's only claimed instance of a 'Kurd' (UC 48501; Petrie 1909b: pl. XXVIII, no. 73); l. ca. 5.5 cm.

Figure 10:14 Front view of 'grotesque figure'/'dancing dwarf', possibly with medical condition (UC 30204); l. ca. 14 cm.

Figure 10:15 Left side of Petrie's 'Semitic Syrian' (UC 33278; Petrie 1909a: pl. XXXVI, no. 20); l. ca. 5.5 cm.

Figure 10:16 Front view of bearded male wearing elephant headdress (UC 48177); l. ca. 6 cm.

Figure 10:17 Front view of a rare example of a priest portrait with preserved head and upper torso (UC 47968); l. ca. 10 cm.

Figure 10:18 Front view of figure wearing a priestly serrated shawl (UC 48447); l. ca. 15 cm.

Figure 10:19 Front view of figure wearing traditional priestly Egyptian costume (UC 48449); l. ca. 10.5 cm.

Figure 10:20 Front view of male figure wearing an animal skin around his hips (UC 47967); l. ca. 10 cm.

wear (Blankenberg-van Delden 1969: 114 (C83)). Since Fisher's excavations were unusually well recorded for the time (1916–1923), further research into the precise stratigraphic context may well confirm the identification of this find as an heirloom and provide a social context for it. A small number of these kinds of scarab were also found outside the Nile Valley, some as far away as Gezer and Ras Shamra (Blankenberg-van Delden 1969: 195), perhaps reflecting awards or gifts to royal hostages that were retained as heirlooms on their repatriation.

The relationship that such objects established between ruler and subject could be interpreted as a pious fiction in which the gift (although of little intrinsic worth from a modern point of view, unlike the gold pectorals and other impedimenta with which successful courtiers were also honoured) gained value from its illustrious donor and passed down, not just as an heirloom but as a record of the favoured status that it conferred. The same may well be true of the re-used/re-deposited stelae of the early eighteenth Dynasty found at the same site and at the near-contemporary Ramesside Ptah temple (Petrie 1909a: 7; Schulman 1967), which have usually been regarded more as obsolete temple furniture being ritually buried or otherwise disposed of.

Given the large and omnipresent pantheon of formal and semi-formal deities common to the Nile Valley, it would certainly be premature to try to determine lines of transfer of their more easily portable and transmissible cult objects. Some deities (Taweret, Bes, Bastet, Anubis) were clearly more frequently represented in amulet form because of their association with critical stages in the life cycle (birth, puberty, death) rather than because they were geographically or ethnically distinctive: amulets of different deities might appear together on ornaments such as pectorals and bracelets. The cults of other, maybe more popular, folk heroes such as Imhotep and Amenhotep son of Hapu will certainly have generated portable memorabilia (statues, funerary cones) which might then have been transferred as heirlooms (Wildung 1977a: 90–97). Once again the lack of any consistently recorded context for such objects makes it impossible to assess their rate and scale of distribution or even whether they typically appear in funerary or non-funerary situations.

There has been a continuing if sporadic debate over the years about the extent to which tomb furniture was especially or exclusively manufactured for the funerary industry, or was largely a selection of everyday artefacts pressed into service as grave contents (e.g. Tait 1982: 42). This is an important consideration, as it may allow the possibility of assessing the frequency with which prestige possessions might be taken out of the redistributive wealth loop by being interred. Even this, in the Egyptian context, is a large assumption, since tomb cult officiants (usually family members) may have had legitimate access to the tomb interior and use or disposal of its contents, and even the sarcophagi and physical remains may have been moved more than once. Free access to the tomb interior may have been encouraged or essential, since this was the deceased's main link with posterity (Redford 1986a: 154–156). The well-known example of the royal cache of Deir el-Bahri, in which the mummies of many of the most celebrated pharaohs were re-housed and stored together in an inaccessible part of the Theban cliff, demonstrates that authorized persons were able to enter tombs and to disinter and relocate royal human remains where their safety and security were in doubt. The opportunity that this would certainly have provided for any funerary goods to re-emerge in an everyday context, and be re-interred, perhaps several generations after their first burial, opens up an intriguing if daunting range of possibilities, and such goods may well have alternated between funerary and domestic contexts for hundreds of years.

The famous tomb of Tutankhamun was so obviously and lavishly provided with actual, socially valuable objects that the common view seems to have developed that all, or nearly all, elite and royal tombs were similarly fitted out, at least during major periods of acquisition by the ruling family and its entourage, and that their relatively sparse furnishing as discovered is due to repeated depredations and even systematic tomb robbery. This assumption, however, seems to ignore the possibility that Tutankhamun's tomb was so amply provisioned simply because it was a makeshift solution for the sudden and premature death of the king: there had been no time to decorate it with the usual repertory of relief and/or painted wall scenes of the period, which the piled contents of the tomb (chariots, boats, beds, statues, baskets, bowls) so accurately reproduce, even down to the guardian statues of the king flanking the blocked and sealed entrance to the sarcophagus room. Indeed, the only decorated zone within the tomb is the actual burial chamber, the third in the series and at the same level as the others (there is no burial shaft), which carries rudimentary painted scenes; the other chambers are undecorated, although the antechamber had been gessoed white in preparation for a painted schema (Reeves 1990: 71), either for Tutankhamun or for a different (original?) tomb owner.

Viewed in this light, it is by no means a foregone conclusion that elite/royal tombs were equally equipped, on a regular basis, with such rich assemblages of prestige goods, apart from their sarcophagus and canopic containers. We might compare the numerous tombs of the Middle Kingdom that contain quantities of (often very detailed) models and miniatures, again representing the main range of pious requirements (houses and gardens, breweries, bakeries, cattle inspection scenes, military cohorts, boats with crews and accessories), and again provided in place of wall decoration or actual objects. In many cases this is perhaps because the quality of the local bedrock was considered unsuitable for carrying decorative schemes and inscriptions, since tombs containing such models tend to have extremely rough-hewn and rudimentary wallface treatment. However, there seems to be a more persuasive chronological argument for the phenomenon: even where the rock is or was sufficiently compact and fine-grained for nearby tombs of other periods to have completed wall decoration, Middle Kingdom tombs such as those of Meketra at Thebes or Karenen (?) at Saqqarah still have the models instead (Quibell 1908: 7–14, pl. xii; Winlock 1942: 18–30, fig. 24).

The tomb of Tutankhamun should, then, provide a useful and rare case of the selection of actual private possessions, some of which might well be heirlooms returned to the Theban area from Amarna and removed from circulation at short notice, or taken from a single stockpile of possibly obsolete or surplus prestige goods at the former Theban royal residence. Beyond the self-evident observation that many heirlooms will only have been recognized as such to the user-owner and not to an outsider – then or now – certain finds should nevertheless be identifiable as potential heirlooms from their non-standard nature.

It may be that we have in any case been making an unnecessarily rigid distinction between 'funerary' and 'non-funerary' objects in the Egyptian context, since many items clearly intended for burial, apart from the actual mummified remains, must have been prepared well in advance and probably (in the case of Tutankhamun) even before the tomb itself was ready. Such intended items of tomb furniture may well therefore have been housed within the palace or, on a less exalted level, in the private house. In fact Tutankhamun's tomb seems to present an assortment of funerary-specific artefacts and sequestered 'actual possessions', a feature which is perhaps itself indicative of the hasty and scrambled nature of its preparation. In addition to the multi-layered sarcophagus itself, there are some items that seem to have a definite funerary purpose (a statue of Anubis with fabric shroud, the canopic shrine, and a sawn-off gilded Hathor head, all from the 'Treasury'), but many more that can be shown to have been used prior to death, such as the chariots, the boxed gaming sets, and the sets of thin-walled metal trumpets, each with its use-worn wooden core or form-filler inserted into the bell of the instrument to preserve its shape (Figure 11:7).

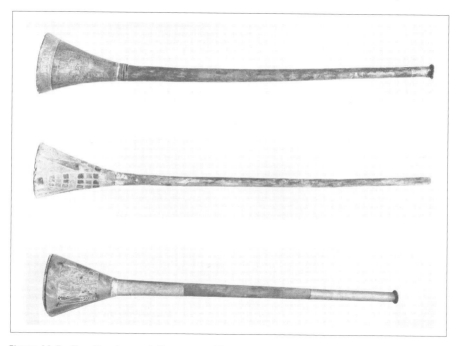

Figure 11:7   The silver trumpet, its core and the copper/bronze trumpet (Griffith Institute, Oxford; Manniche 1976: pl. V).

Some of the stone vessels in the assemblage had again been anciently damaged and repaired (el-Khouli 1993: 4), and the wine amphorae could have been part of a royal cellar laid down five years or more before the king's death, although whether vintage in wine was valued at all or as much in ancient times as it is today is moot (Murray 2000: 598). Among these 'actual' possessions are several which must have been in the family for at least one or two generations, and several of the travertine vessels with palimpsest dedications to the tomb owner were originally inscribed for Tuthmosis III, approximately 150 years or 10 average generations (though only seven dynastic reigns) earlier (Figure 11:8). The finds singled out as 'real' heirlooms, such as

Figure 11:8   Jar from
Tutankhamun's tomb
(Griffith Institute, Oxford).

the examples of a lock of hair of the royal grandmother Tiye and a small unascribed
royal statue, both found within miniature coffins (Reeves 1990: 168–169), clearly have
a special significance from their unusually careful preparation and packaging; others,
such as the two sisters' ivory palettes, though no less acceptable as heirlooms in the
more general sense, were not so treated, possibly because of the difference in status
between the transfer of an ancestral and a sibling possession.

Conclusions

Heirlooms must by definition remain in circulation for at least one generation after
their production. The very nature of heirlooms means that they will themselves
usually be poor internal dating tools: the date of their production depends on their
carrying some clear, chronologically sensitive relative criteria, and on their being
found in securely dated and confidently recognized contexts. As has been seen, even
artefact classes such as scarabs and other objects with royal names, which seem at first

to be ideal for the purpose of dating, carry associated problems and provoke lingering uncertainties.

There is a long-standing perception of the Egyptian internal chronology, with its continuity and its detailed though often complex textual underpinning, as providing a sound basis for cross-cultural temporal references across the Middle East; but this has been eroded in recent years with the arrival and development of absolute dating methods, which are often more successfully applied outside the Nile Valley but are difficult or problematic for the Egyptian material itself. One particular and curious phenomenon, the appearance in Minoan Crete of elite pre- and protodynastic Egyptian stone vessels which are then locally copied or modified (Sparks 2003), might however be taken as evidence of heirlooms transferred over a greater than usual scale of space and time. The difficulty here is to determine how these elite grave goods, presumably buried long before in Egyptian tombs, emerge in such a very different context. One proposal is that they were removed from those tombs close in time to their find context (the Second Intermediate Period?), and traded or otherwise transported overseas. Could they in fact not have been grave contents originally, but heirlooms circulating or kept intact in or re-acquired by households over many generations? Do the Hyksos interludes of non-indigenous rule, or for that matter any other period, represent a time when political conditions allowed and even stimulated the intrusive acquisition of tomb furniture to provide the material for elite gift exchange? On the domestic front too, elite goods of this kind provide a range of likely scenarios, particularly vessels showing signs of repair that seem to indicate an attachment beyond the merely functional; these might be containers found in predynastic graves, or later examples such as those in the tomb of Tutankhamun. In the Egyptian context, examples are overwhelmingly likely to come from cemeteries, though the distinction between funerary and domestic is not a straightforward one, and objects could even have alternated between the two domains.

The archaizing phenomenon in funerary and municipal religious architecture (including sculpture) may likewise reflect both a regard for the past and the survival of actual templates that were accessible and able to be copied or adopted. While no doubt most easily recognized in the monumental context, the respect for and reproduction of former styles in other areas of production is also worth noting: thus, for example, the prestige ceramics made at Kerma during its 'Classic' stage (in Egyptian terms, the Second Intermediate Period) so reminiscent of the burnished wares of the Badarian period.

It seems, then, that heirlooms in the broadest modern sense probably did exist in pharaonic Egypt; they were not confined to the elite but were a potential means of both conferring status and perpetuating the memory of the original owner among all sectors of society. There were, however, a number of other effective mechanisms for the transmission of cultural information, and such objects found their way into the most commonly recorded kind of Egyptian context – tombs – only in extreme or anomalous circumstances. The paucity of domestic sites in the Nile Valley, and the generally poor recording of those that have been found, remains a serious challenge to analysis of the quantity, regularity and character of this kind of property transfer and the cognitive issues associated with it.

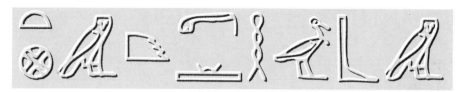

CHAPTER 12

THE PTOLEMAIC ROYAL IMAGE AND THE EGYPTIAN TRADITION

Sally-Ann Ashton

Although Ptolemaic royal sculpture has recently enjoyed an academic revival, there remains confusion and debate over the dating of key portrait types, and often in distinguishing representations of Ptolemaic rulers from those of the thirtieth Dynasty. Whether this uncertainty is a modern phenomenon remains to be explored. This chapter attempts to gather the relevant evidence to investigate the possibility that similarities between the two royal imageries were a deliberate attempt by the later rulers to associate themselves with their predecessors.

One of the most striking similarities to occur in Ptolemaic royal sculpture is that between the portraits of the early Ptolemaic rulers and those of the thirtieth Dynasty kings. So alike are the representations in the round that modern scholars have struggled to distinguish between representations of Nectanebo I and II and those of the early Ptolemaic rulers. Josephson (1997a) attempted to establish chronological indicators for identifying late period and early Ptolemaic royal portrait types, although some of his identifications have been challenged. The fragment of a statue of a Ptolemaic king now in the British Museum (Figure 12:1) was identified as an image of Nectanebo II; more recently, however, it has been identified as Ptolemy II by comparison with an inscribed statue of the ruler, now in the Vatican Museum (Ashton 2001: 20, 84–85).

A similar pattern emerges when the so-called sculptors' models are considered, in that the majority of examples date stylistically to the thirtieth and early Ptolemaic Dynasties (Figure 12:2). Previous studies of this group of material have tended to concentrate on their use as models or ex-votos, rather than attempting to establish a chronological sequence for the many examples (Bianchi 1979; Varga 1960; Young; 1964). Like the finished portraits from statues, it is often difficult to distinguish the Ptolemaic from the thirtieth Dynasty models, which may point to a deliberate policy on the part of the Ptolemaic royal house or their artists. Whilst the portrait features remain essentially unchanged, some scholars believe that it is possible to date individual pieces from the form of uraeus (Josephson 1992).

Although the iconography remains static during the Ptolemaic period at least, technical and stylistic features are prone to change rather suddenly and dramatically. This in itself would not be a problem if the changes were unanimous, but often they

Figure 12:1   Fragment of a statue of a Ptolemaic king, recently identified as Ptolemy II
(© Trustees of the British Museum, EA 941; ht. 61 cm).

are isolated examples with perhaps one small feature that betrays the statue's date.
From the late second and early first centuries BC, these experiments are usually
archaizing. This can be seen clearly on the fragment of a colossal sculpture of a
Ptolemaic queen or goddess from Hadra, Alexandria, that formed part of a dyad with
a male representation which clearly dates to the first century BC and is often
erroneously associated with Marc Antony (Mariemont E49 and Alexandria 11275;
Ashton 2001: 39, 102–03 cat. 42, 30–31, 98–99 cat. 34). The female figure is executed in
a more traditional fashion, and the facial features are more typical of those from the

Figure 12:2   Sculptors' model (© Fitzwilliam Museum, E. GA. 3209.1943; ht. 11 cm).

third century BC rather than the first. Thus, if this statue was considered in isolation, it is likely that it would be assigned to the early Ptolemaic period; a stylistic analysis of the adjoining male ruler, however, indicates that the date of the pair cannot be earlier than the first century BC.

It is clear that the early Ptolemaic sculptors continued to use very similar if not the same portrait models for the Egyptian representations of their rulers, possibly as part of a policy to ensure the association between the last Egyptian dynasty and the new ruling house. It is tempting to view the soft modelling on these pieces as the result of Greek influence, but there is no evidence to suggest that the artists looked outside their own tradition for inspiration. The development of the Egyptian royal portraits during the third century BC is extremely instructive because angular lines replace the soft modelling, as seen on the New Haven bust of a king (Yale University Art Gallery 1.1.1953; Scott 1986: 165–67, no. 94). The reappearance of the softly modelled features on representations of Ptolemies VIII, IX and X suggests that there were models still in circulation or that the sculptors re-used earlier models.

The restricted use of models or ex-votos may well explain the close bond between royal portraits from the Ptolemaic period and those from the thirtieth Dynasty. The one component that these rulers have in common is that they took control of Egypt after foreign occupation; it is an interesting fact that the Macedonian rulers chose to associate themselves with native Egyptian dynasties, a policy that was echoed in their patronage of native temples. Such affiliations effectively dismissed the Persian occupation and severed the psychological link between two foreign dynasties. Was this phenomenon then a deliberate policy or simply a continuation of an artistic convention?

The evidence of early Ptolemaic patronage of Egyptian temples supports the idea that there was an attempt to continue the policies of the thirtieth Dynasty and, for the purposes of this chapter, it is the work on thirtieth Dynasty projects that is of interest. Whilst building at Memphis and the new capital Alexandria was to be expected, there are other more surprising programmes that were undertaken by Ptolemies I and II, with the founder of the dynasty demonstrating his support of the Egyptians by patronizing religious sanctuaries at Therenuthis and Tebtunis (Arnold 1999: 154–157); a new city was also founded in Upper Egypt at Ptolemais Hermiou. Ptolemy I's cartouche appears on architectural blocks at Naucratis where it is suggested by Arnold (1999: 155 n. 57) there may have been a thirtieth Dynasty temple, in support of which are several finds from the Ptolemaic period that are associated with the royal cult (Ashton and Higgs 2001: 52, cat. 15). Naucratis with its colonial Greek past was an interesting choice for the rulers' patronage, and the dedication of Egyptian material at a site where there had been a strong Greek cultural presence offers an interesting insight into royal policy.

The evidence dating to the reign of Ptolemy II suggests that the completion of earlier building programmes was a policy rather than merely a coincidence. Under Ptolemy II there was a consistent scheme of reviving and completing building programmes that had been interrupted by the Persian occupation (Arnold 1999: 158). In the Delta, Isisopolis (Behbeit el-Hagar), Sebennytos, Saft el-Henne and Tanis were all patronized by Nectanebo I and II and later enjoyed Ptolemaic support; this served not only as a link to the previous Egyptian dynasty but also as a display of the Ptolemies' political allegiance. The temple of Amun at Hibis in the Kharga Oasis, which was added to by Darius, also connected the thirtieth and Ptolemaic Dynasties: Nectanebo I had built a kiosk at the front of the temple and later Ptolemy II built a wall around the precinct (Arnold 1999: 113). At Philae, Ptolemy II, with the aid of tax revenues, completed the temple of Isis, which had large thirtieth Dynasty additions, (Arnold 1999: 162 n. 86). Koptos received a new enclosure wall during the reign of Nectanebo I (Arnold 1999: 115) and a new temple and a kiosk under Ptolemy II (Arnold 1999: 160–161), although the site's prominent position may explain its popularity.

The completion of such work is very different from the policies of Ptolemy III, who erected a gateway opposite that of Nectanebo at Karnak rather than working on the completion of an earlier project. Also under Ptolemy III or IV the earlier thirtieth Dynasty temple at the Serapieion, Memphis is disregarded, since the placement of the

Greek-style philosophers' hemicycle effectively blocks the entrance to the earlier building, whilst taking advantage of the end of the dromos of sphinxes, which originally lined the walkway to the temple door as illustrated in the publication of the re-excavation of the site by Lauer and Picard (1955: pl .26).

In the second century BC, the Egyptian artists adopt very obvious foreign features, faithfully reproducing the Greek portrait types rather than showing traits of minor artistic influence. It is almost as if the artists are adopting foreign attributes and simply placing them in an unaltered Egyptian context, very similar to the iconographic attributes that appear on statues of the Ptolemaic queens. Perhaps the most surprising confusion within the study of the Ptolemaic royal image is over the portraits of Nectanebo I and Ptolemy X. The small head of a ruler wearing a blue crown in the Musée du Louvre (E8061) was initially dated to the thirtieth Dynasty but the original identification for the Brooklyn exhibition was questioned in a review, where it was proposed that the portrait represented Ptolemy V rather than Nectanebo I. The debate has since continued, with some scholars supporting the original identification of the piece, whilst others have suggested that the head is a representation of Ptolemy IX or X on account of its similarity to the portraits on seal impressions. A second head, now in the Ägyptische Sammlung, Munich (5339) has suffered a similar fate and scholarship is divided as to whether this represents a late Ptolemy or Nectanebo I; a full bibliography and discussion can be found in Ashton (2001: 86–87).

The inscribed reliefs from the thirtieth Dynasty and Ptolemaic period do little to resolve the confusion, since the distinct profile with a fleshy, hooked nose and rounded cheeks appears on examples from both periods, as is illustrated by the architectural fragments inscribed with the cartouche of Nectanebo I in the British Museum (EA 22) and the Museo Civico di Bologna (1870). The royal images were assigned to the late Ptolemaic period by Josephson (1997a: 13, 1997b: 15–16), who argued that the original slabs were decorated with images of a late Ptolemy, an idea which has important implications, not only with regard to the identity of this group of portraits, but also for the re-use of earlier dynastic material in the Ptolemaic period. In support of his idea is the representation of the priest Pasherenptah on a stela now in the British Museum (EA 886), which dates to the reign of Cleopatra VII (Andrews 2001: 184–185, cat. 192). The same fleshy face and hooked nose were used to represent this private individual, possibly as a response to the Physcon portraits that occur under Ptolemies VIII to X. The inspiration for this new type of corpulent image, particularly in the case of the rulers, was presumably associated with their actual appearance, which in the case of Ptolemy VIII, according to Athenaeus, was obese: "Through indulgence in luxury his body had become corrupted with fat and with a belly of such a size that it would have been hard to measure it with one's arms" (Athenaeus, *Deipnosophistai* XII.549 e). If, however, the representations on the Bologna and British Museum relief decorations were executed at the time of their dedication, the inspiration for such a sudden change in the royal image may have come from the thirtieth Dynasty rulers. Such archaizing appears in other forms on royal statuary of the first century BC, and will be discussed below.

A survey of the temples patronized by Ptolemy VIII, however, offers important information in terms of a later Ptolemaic association with the work of Ptolemy II and the thirtieth Dynasty rulers. This connection might explain the similarity between images of Nectanebo I and the later Ptolemaic rulers, since some thirtieth Dynasty temples remained unfinished until the reign of Ptolemy VIII. This particular ruler built a birth house at Philae and completed the decoration of other parts of the temple (Vassilika 1989: 57–71), where there are considerable areas dating to the reigns of Ptolemy II and the thirtieth Dynasty. Koptos, which had received a new enclosure wall during the reign of Nectanebo I (Arnold 1999: 115) and a new temple under Ptolemy II, was also financed during the reign of Ptolemy VIII, when a monumental gateway was erected (Arnold 1999: 194). His keenness to be associated with thirtieth Dynasty and early Ptolemaic building works is further illustrated by the completion of the projects at Karnak, begun by his ancestors. Similarly, under Ptolemy VI and Ptolemy X work was undertaken at Dendera and during the late Ptolemaic period Memphis received further royal patronage, which built upon early Ptolemaic interest at the site (Thompson 1988: 134–138). Although it is difficult to establish whether such building projects were undertaken on account of royal policy, completion of earlier projects must have linked the rulers to their predecessors. On the other hand such projects could be described as usurping. Nevertheless, they show that the artists may have been working alongside early styles which may in turn have led to the replication of portrait types, which may go some way to explaining the confusion between thirtieth Dynasty and late Ptolemaic images. If the specific evidence from the reign of Ptolemy VIII is considered, it may also be necessary to re-identify heads such as the Louvre ruler or the Munich model as this particular Physcon, rather than Ptolemy IX or X.

For the early rulers this was an obvious way to associate themselves with their pharaonic past; similar occurrences under later Ptolemaic rulers need to be more carefully explained, since by the reign of Ptolemy III the dynasty's own cults were established enough to provide a link which could legitimize the accession and right to rule. The process of completing or working on buildings in particular, which were decorated with earlier artistic styles, did, as illustrated, continue into the first century BC. It is therefore possible that artists could be influenced by earlier styles, particularly if they lacked models for their work, as previously noted in the case of the portraits of Nectanebo I – a late Ptolemy. It is also possible that artists were forced to turn to earlier models or that they chose to do so.

The reversion to earlier portrait types accords with nationalistic papyri of the second century BC, and may be a further indication of a desire for the return of earlier dynasties and the great rulers. The various myths surrounding Sesostris III, Ramesses II and Nectanebo II often present the rulers in association with the conquests of Alexander the Great (Eddy 1961: 281–286). Even in Herodotus' *Histories* (II.102–110) Sesostris III was said to have conquered Asia, on the basis that the ruler was known to have been involved in Asiatic campaigns; it is also of interest that 'Sesostris' became connected with 'Ramesses'. The association with the twelfth Dynasty may also help to explain the emergence of the so-called naturalistic portrait type for private individuals of the fourth and first centuries BC. Similarly, from the fourth century BC Ramesses II was said to have conquered Baktria (Hekataios in Diodorus I.46.8–47 and Strabo XVII.1.46). Perhaps more worryingly were the oracles which prophesied the downfall of the Ptolemaic Dynasty and the return of earlier pharaohs. A later account by

Pseudo-Kallisthenes, of what has been suggested was a third century original (Eddy 1961: 284–285), predicted the return of Nectanebo II.

If the re-use of earlier images and the similarity between those of Ptolemies I and II and the thirtieth Dynasty show an underlying support for earlier Egyptian pharaohs in the Ptolemaic period, the evidence of earlier imports to Ptolemaic sites such as Alexandria may in fact date to the third or second centuries BC. The re-use of portraits of Sesostris III may also explain the resurgence of the so-called realistic portrait type in the fourth and second centuries BC, which would support Bianchi (1988) and the idea that these heads owed nothing to hellenistic influence. Was the practice of cross-cultural borrowing introduced for the first time as a consequence of Ptolemaic rule, or is there earlier evidence of a foreign influence in the history of Egyptian art?

As previously noted, it has been suggested that there was a Greek influence on Egyptian portraiture from as early as the fourth century BC (Josephson 1997a: 11), whereas Bothmer (1996: 215) concluded that hellenistic influence on sculpture in the round did not occur until the third century BC. This influence manifests itself in two ways: first, the softer modelling of the features on images of Nectanebo I and II, and second, the non-idealized private images such as the Boston and Berlin Green Heads. However, the adoption of the so-called naturalistic portrait type needs addressing more thoughtfully, because it is effectively opposite to the softly modelled images, because one type favours hard lines whereas the other is soft, with a more fleshy appearance. The former is documented in the portraiture of the twelfth Dynasty, where Sesostris III adopted a more 'naturalistic' portrait type. Its re-emergence during the fourth century BC may have been a consequence of the political instability and a need to look back to a historical figure to reaffirm Egypt's position. There is a reference in the *Alexander Romance* to the rebirth of Nectanebo in the form of Alexander; this concept was echoed by the similarity of the Egyptian portrait types of the thirtieth and Ptolemaic Dynasties (Eddy 1961: 284–285). It is possible that there was a degree of discontentment in Egypt under the thirtieth Dynasty, since Nectanebo II's rule was not always peaceful, ending in defeat by the Persians. Thus, the reappearance of this type of image is a continuation of a form of archaizing that was also found in the twenty-sixth Dynasty (Bothmer 1960b: 28, no. 24).

The possibility that naturalistic portraiture should appear in both the fourth and first centuries BC accords with the archaizing royal portraits which were manufactured during the reign of Cleopatra VII. This phenomenon has lead to further confusion between early Ptolemaic representations of royal women and those of Cleopatra VII; in between the sculptors seem to have favoured more naturalistic representations for the royal women, which mirrored those of their male consorts. Consequently the dating of sculptures has become problematic. Usually, however, there are features, such as the portraits, which betray the true date of individual pieces, as noted on the Stern head of a late Ptolemy and similarly the statues of Cleopatra VII, with a triple uraeus and distinctive facial features: down-turned mouth, square chin and often inlaid eyes. Finally, the royals or sculptors were able to use Ptolemaic models for their inspiration.

The usurping of statues is another complicated matter, not least because it is often difficult to determine the reasons – whether in honour of, or with indifference to, earlier rulers. In addition to the obelisk from Heliopolis, Arnold (1999: 161) also suggests that a monumental *naos* from Koptos dates to the thirtieth Dynasty but was also usurped by Ptolemy II; however, it seems equally likely that it was produced as well as inscribed during the latter's reign.

Bianchi (1991: 3) suggests that the Ptolemaic artists had a second-hand knowledge of Ramesside monuments though their awareness of those dating to the thirtieth Dynasty. Whilst this may in part be true, the artists working on royal representations seem to have been familiar with material from the New Kingdom, which there is no evidence of artists during the thirtieth Dynasty having used. This statement is particularly true of the iconography adopted by the Ptolemaic royal women, which has much in common with attributes adopted by royal women of the eighteenth and nineteenth Dynasties. This appropriation occurs very early in the Ptolemaic period on the statues of Arsinoe II (275–270 BC), wife of Ptolemy II. Fortunately, the queen's statutes are amongst the few from the Ptolemaic period that are inscribed; thus we know that she appeared with a double rather than single uraeus.

One particular statue which includes this specific iconography, but which is believed to have been a re-working of an eighteenth Dynasty statue of Tiye, may offer an important link between the earlier queens of Egypt and those of the Ptolemaic period; it may also help to explain the reappearance of a specific iconographical feature on images of Arsinoe II. The statue in question is in the Shumei Collection in the Miho Museum, Japan (Figure 12:3). The statue is said in the catalogue entry (Kozloff 1997: 34–35) to be made from granodiorite, although the photographic record would suggest that it was basalt; it measures 159.5 cm in height by 50 cm in width and its provenance is unknown. Kozloff suggests that the statue was deliberately usurped by or for Arsinoe II from an earlier image, representing Tiye (1391–1353 BC) on account of the "assimilation of both queens to the goddess Isis", and the measurement of what is interpreted as the lower line of the collar, which is noted as being exactly the same size as those on representations of Queen Tiye. This same kind of mark, however, can also be found on the Hermitage queen and is more likely, in the Ptolemaic period, to represent the neckline of the dress.

The identifications are supported by the double uraeus that the queen wears, although this particular form of royal insignia can have a variety of meanings, which are discussed fully in a forthcoming paper by the present author. Tiye and Arsinoe are included amongst them, but more careful attention needs to be given to the dating of the piece and the question of its re-use. Stylistically the statue fits well into the Ptolemaic period and there is little to betray its proposed eighteenth Dynasty origins. The shape and execution of the wig are similar to those found on the first century BC images of Cleopatra VII and the diadem appears on the purely Egyptian-style representations, such as the San José queen (Ashton 2001: 102–103, cat. 39). The form of the uraei is very different to either eighteenth Dynasty or Ptolemaic examples, since the cobras are typically more abstract in appearance and without tails. Similarly, the more usual type worn by Tiye have broader bodies than those on the Miho statue. The lily sceptre can also be found on first century BC representations, such as the recently published statue of Cleopatra VII in the Louvre (inv. 13102); it also appears on a representation of a queen with a vulture headdress and double uraeus in the Egyptian Museum, Cairo (CG 678). The sheath-like drapery is not an accurate dating tool, since

Figure 12:3   Statue of Arsinoe II, believed to be a re-working of an eighteenth Dynasty statue of Tiye (© Miho Museum; ht. 159.5 cm).

it continues into the first century BC and is also found on early Ptolemaic representations. The position of the hand is more important; it sits flat against the subject's thigh with elongated fingers, which does not accord with the usual hand positions of first century BC images, namely clutching the drapery or loosely holding an object, but appears in this exact form on statues that are generally dated to the third century BC. Proportionately the statue also fits well into the Ptolemaic period, with soft curves, prominent breasts and a slightly swollen stomach.

The facial features compare well to the early images of Arsinoe II, particularly in respect to the narrow line of the eyebrows and the slightly modelled eye lines (New York MMA 38.10; Ashton 2001: 100–101, cat. 36). Furthermore, the wide, fleshy mouth is also similar to other representations of the queen and the Egyptian-style portraits of her brother and consort, Ptolemy II, most obviously on the sphinxes from the Alexandrian Serapeion. The tripartite wig is not, however, commonly used on the images of Arsinoe II, but is found on statues from the third century BC. Finally, the back pillar is likely to be the deciding factor in dating this piece, since it ends below the wig. This feature is common on both third and first century BC statues but is not usually found on eighteenth Dynasty representations, where the back pillar goes to the top of the head. It is therefore likely that this statue is a Ptolemaic original, representing either Arsinoe II or a goddess. The date of its manufacture is more problematic because the uraei are unique in their style, but the crown, which was added to a modius, is a third century BC feature. Even if the statue is not a usurped eighteenth Dynasty original, it offers an important link between the representations of earlier queens and those of the Ptolemaic period.

Another problematic statue was found at Karnak temple, close to the Roman chapel (Karnak Museum 177). An eighteenth Dynasty date has been suggested for the original statue, which was then inscribed with the cartouche of Cleopatra II (Lauffray 1970: 71, fig. 13; Bianchi 1980: 11) or Cleopatra III (Lauffray 1979: 88–89); however, a comparison with known inscriptions and texts would suggest that the statue is more likely to represent Cleopatra II (compare Gauthier 1916: 317, 322). The representation is preserved from the abdomen to the lower thighs and only the last few characters of the cartouche survive. The hypothesis that the statue was an eighteenth Dynasty original has more recently been questioned (Quaegebeur 1989: 103), and a comparison with the Cairo statue of Arsinoe II (CG 678) supports the idea that this image, like that from the Miho Museum, was an original Ptolemaic composition. Like the Miho statue, the right hand was pressed flat against the thigh and the lack of impression on the left thigh would suggest that the left arm was held across the upper abdomen. The costume, which has been described as the traditional *haik* type (Bianchi 1980: 11), is also found on Ptolemaic statuary (Cairo JE 38582) and the fragment of a triad of Ptolemy II, Arsinoe II and Amun (Quaegebeur 1989: 103 n. 62). Similarly the swollen abdomen and thighs are common features on Ptolemaic sculpture.

Archaizing in the Ptolemaic period, whether it be immediate or drawn from much earlier periods, follows a distinct set of rules and illustrates that artists are capable of copying earlier styles exactly, rather than executing Ptolemaic 'versions' of earlier Egyptian sculpture. This can clearly be seen on the images of rulers with Greek portrait features, where the Egyptian artists are often capable of producing a more finely carved portrait than their models provided. The only exception to this rule occurs during the late second and early first centuries BC, when artists produced versions of Greek portrait types, according to Egyptian canons. It has, however, recently been suggested that British Museum EA 941 (Figure 12:1) is a copy of the seated statue of Djoser from Saqqarah (Baines and Riggs 2001). The two are not stylistically similar, and in fact many of the common features that are listed can also be explained by a comparison with partially carved models, and may equally be the result of the carving techniques of sculptors at this time, namely the removal of thin layers of stone to form the final surface. The posture of the arm across the chest is a feature of statues of Arsinoe II, as illustrated by the Miho queen and also on other statues where the queen's hand remains empty. Finally, the existence of a back pillar on the British Museum statue would suggest that the statue was in striding stance rather than seated. The comparison of EA 941 to the "Vatican sphinxes of Ptolemy II" (Baines and Riggs 2001: 107), which to my knowledge do not exist, would suggest that the authors are not familiar with all of the comparative material from the Ptolemaic repertoire, and whilst it is tempting to link Ptolemaic sculptures to earlier models it is necessary to consider pieces within the wider framework of royal policies and artistic practices. There are no recognized examples of archaizing on the royal representations of the thirtieth Dynasty rulers, but examples from the twenty-fifth and twenty-sixth Dynasties again suggest that artists copied earlier forms exactly.

Whether or not images such as the Miho and Karnak statues were usurped is, in some respects, of less importance than the fact that the artists in the Ptolemaic period were clearly using earlier images as models. The movement of statuary and the re-emergence of earlier styles of representation are testimony to a link with earlier traditions and fashions. The artists and sculptors in the Ptolemaic period found themselves in the position of having to produce new types of imagery to serve the many personalities of their Ptolemaic kings and queens, and it is, in such circumstances, of little surprise to find them looking at earlier rulers and their ancestors' representations. The link with the past also may have served as a political tool, which may explain the similarity between some of the thirtieth Dynasty and late Ptolemaic portraits; the idea that the so-called Physcon portrait type was produced in both periods cannot be dismissed. Similarly, with the so-called naturalistic representations of private individuals, dating should be considered in a wider context and the idea that this type of portrait may have appeared in more than one period also needs to be addressed. There is a danger in assuming that changes in royal or private imagery, and in particular portraiture, during the Ptolemaic period are the result of Greek influence; in many cases, however, the roots of developments can be traced back to earlier Egyptian contexts (Bianchi 1980, 1988; Bothmer 1970: 35–48). It is, however, possible that Greek images inspired the Egyptian artists to reproduce representations which were familiar to their tradition, resulting in a truly but not intentionally bilingual representation.

Acknowledgments

The author would like to thank Dr Stephen Quirke of the Petrie Museum for his helpful comments and discussion on several points in this chapter; Dr Hajime Inagaki of the Miho Museum, Japan for supplying me with information about the back pillar of the statue, and Mr Vivian Davies of the Department of Ancient Egypt and Sudan at the British Museum for permission to use an image of EA 941.

References

Note: references to chapters and books in the *Encounters with Ancient Egypt* series are denoted in bold type.

Adams, W. Y. 1977, *Nubia Corridor to Africa*. London: Allen Lane

Agrawal, D. P., V. Bhalakia and S. Kusumgar 1999, Indian and Other Concepts of Time: A Holistic Framework, in T. Murray (ed.), *Time and Archaeology*, 28–37. London: Routledge

Albertz, R. 1994, *A History of Israelite Religion in the Old Testament Period*. Louisville: Westminster

Aldred, C. 1980, *Egyptian Art in the Days of the Pharaohs 3100–320 BC*. London: Thames and Hudson

Aldred, C. 1988, *Akhenaten: King of Egypt*. London: Thames and Hudson

Alexanian, N. 1998, Die Reliefdekoration des Chasechemui aus dem Sogenannten Fort in Hierakonpolis, in N. Grimal (ed.), *Les Critères de datation stylistiques à l'ancien empire*, 1–30. Cairo: Institut Français d'Archéologie Orientale

Allam, S. 2001, Slaves, in D. B. Redford (ed.), *The Oxford Encyclopedia of Ancient Egypt*, 293–295. Oxford: OUP

Allen, J. P. 1988, *Genesis in Egypt: The Philosophy of Ancient Egyptian Creation Accounts*. New Haven: Yale UP

Allen, J. P. 1999, A Monument of Khaemwaset Honoring Imhotep, in E. Teeter and J. A. Larson (eds), *Gold of Praise. Studies on Ancient Egypt in Honor of Edward F. Wente*, 1–10. Chicago: Oriental Institute

Allen, J. P. 2003, The Egyptian Concept of the World, in D. O'Connor and S. Quirke (eds), *Mysterious Lands*, 23–30. London: UCL Press

Allen, T. G. 1974, *The Book of the Dead, or, Going Forth By Day: Ideas of the Ancient Egyptians Concerning the Hereafter as Expressed in Their Own Terms*. Chicago: University of Chicago Press

Andrews, C. 2001, Catalogue entry 192, in S. Walker and P. Higgs (eds), *Cleopatra of Egypt: From History to Myth*, 184–185. London: British Museum Press

Arnold, D. 1974a, *Der Tempel des Königs Mentuhotep von Deir el-Bahari, I: Architektur und Deutung*. Mainz: von Zabern

Arnold, D. 1974b, *Der Tempel des Königs Mentuhotep von Deir el-Bahari, II: Die Wandreliefs des Sanktuares*. Mainz: von Zabern

Arnold, D. 1979, *The Temple of Mentuhotep at Deir el-Bahari*. New York: Metropolitan Museum of Art

Arnold, D. 1981, *Der Tempel des Königs Mentuhotep von Deir el-Bahari, III: Die Königlichen Beigaben*. Mainz: von Zabern

Arnold, D. 1994, *Lexikon der Ägyptischen Baukunst*. Munich: Artemis

Arnold, D. 1999, *Temples of the Last Pharaohs*. New York: OUP

Arnold, D. and C. Ziegler (eds) 1999, *Egyptian Art in the Age of the Pyramids*. New York: Metropolitan Museum of Art

Ashton, S-A. 2001, *Ptolemaic Royal Sculpture From Egypt. The Interaction Between Greek and Egyptian Traditions*. Oxford: Archaeopress, British Archaeological Reports

Ashton, S-A. and P. Higgs 2001, Identifying the Egyptian-style Ptolemaic Queens, in S. Walker and P. Higgs (eds), *Cleopatra of Egypt: From History to Myth*, 148–153. London: British Museum Press

Assmann, J. 1970, *Der König als Sonnenpriester: ein kosmographischer Begleittext zur kultischen Sonnenhymnik in thebanischen Tempeln und Gräbern*. Gluckstadt: J. J. Augustin

Assmann, J. 1975, *Zeit und Ewigkeit im Alten Ägypten*. Heidelberg: Akademie der Wissenschaften

Assmann, J. 1983, Schrift, Tod und Identität: das Grab als Vorschule der literatur im Alten Ägypten, in A. Assmann, J. Assmann and C. Hardmeier (eds), *Schrift und Gedächtnis*, 64–93. Munich: Wilhelm Fink

Assmann, J. 1984, *Ägypten. Theologie und Frömmigkeit einer Frühen Hochkultur*. Mainz: Kohlhammer

Assmann, J. 1990a, Egyptian Mortuary Liturgies, in S. Israelit-Groll (ed.), *Studies in Egyptology presented to Miriam Lichtheim*, 1–20. Jerusalem: Magnes

Assmann, J. 1990b, *Ma'at. Gerechtigkeit und Unsterblichkeit im Alten Ägypten*. Munich: C. H. Beck

Assmann, J. 1991, *Stein und Zeit. Mensch und Gesellschaft im Alten Ägypten*. Munich: Wilhelm Fink

Assmann, J. 1992, *Das Kulturelle Gedächtnis*. Munich: C. H. Beck

Assmann, J. 1996, *Ägypten. Eine Sinngeschichte*. Munich: Hanser

Assmann, J. 1997, *Moses the Egyptian. The Memory of Egypt in Western Monotheism*. Cambridge, Mass: Harvard UP

Assmann, J. 1999a, *Ägyptische Hymnen und Gebete*. 2nd edition, Freiburg: Universitätsverlag

Assmann, J. 1999b, Literatur zwischen Kult und Politik: Zur Geschichte des Textes vor dem Zeitalter der Literatur, in J. Assmann and E. Blumenthal (eds), *Literatur und Politik im Pharaonischen und Ptolemäischen Ägypten*, 3–22. Cairo: Institut Français d'Archéologie Orientale

Assmann, J. 2001, *The Search for God in Ancient Egypt*. Ithaca: Cornell UP

Aston, D. A. 1999, Dynasty 26, Dynasty 30, or Dynasty 27? In Search of the Funerary Archaeology of the Persian Period, in A. Leahy and J. Tait (eds), *Studies on Ancient Egypt in Honour of H. S. Smith*, 17–22. London: Egypt Exploration Society

Bács, T. 2002, Theban Tomb 65: The Twentieth Dynasty Decoration. *Egyptian Archaeology* 21, 21–24

Badawi, A. 1956, Das Grab des Kronprinzen Scheschonk, Sohnes Osorkon's II und Hohenpriesters von Memphis. *Annales du Service des Antiquités de l'Egypte* 54, 153–177

Baines, J. 1982, Interpreting Sinuhe. *Journal of Egyptian Archaeology* 68, 31–44

Baines, J. 1989a, Communication and Display: The Integration of Early Egyptian Art and Writing. *Antiquity* 63, 471–482

Baines, J. 1989b, Ancient Egyptian Concepts and Uses of the Past, in R. Layton (ed.), *Who Needs the Past? Indigenous Values and Archaeology*, 131–149. London: Unwin Hyman

Baines, J. 1990a, Restricted Knowledge, Hierarchy, and Decorum: Modern Perceptions and Ancient Institutions. *Journal of the American Research Center in Egypt* 27, 1–23

Baines, J. 1990b, Interpreting the Story of the Shipwrecked Sailor. *Journal of Egyptian Archaeology* 76, 55–72

Baines, J. 1991, Society, Morality and Religious Practice, in B. Shafer (ed.), *Religion in Ancient Egypt. Gods, Myths and Personal Practice*, 123–200. Ithaca: Cornell UP

Baines, J. 1994, On the Status and Purposes of Ancient Egyptian Art. *Cambridge Archaeological Journal* 4, 67–94

Baines, J. 1995, Palaces and Temples of Ancient Egypt, in J. Sasson (ed.), *Civilizations of the Ancient Near East* I, 303–317. New York: Charles Scribner's Sons

Baines, J. 1996a, Classicism and Modernism in the Literature of the New Kingdom, in A. Loprieno (ed.), *Ancient Egyptian Literature: History and Forms*, 157–174. Leiden: Brill

Baines, J. 1996b, On the Composition and Inscriptions of the Vatican Statue of Udjahorresne, in P. der Manuelian (ed.), *Studies in Honor of William Kelly Simpson, vol. 1*, 83–92. Boston: Museum of Fine Arts

Baines, J. 1996c, Contextualizing Egyptian Representations of Society and Ethnicity, in J. S. Cooper and G. Schwartz (eds), *The Study of the Ancient Near East in the Twenty-First Century*, 339–384. Winona Lake, IN: Eisenbrauns

Baines, J. 1999, On Wenamun as a Literary Text, in J. Assmann and E. Blumenthal (eds), *Literatur und Politik im Pharaonischen und Ptolemäischen Ägypten*, 209–233. Cairo: Institut Français d'Archéologie Orientale

Baines, J. and J. Malek 1980, *Atlas of Ancient Egypt*. Oxford: Phaidon

Baines, J. and C. Riggs 2001, Archaism and Kingship: A Late Royal Statue and its Early Dynastic Model. *Journal of Egyptian Archaeology* 87, 103–118

Baines, J. and N. Yoffee 1998, Order, Legitimacy and Wealth in Ancient Egypt and Mesopotamia, in G. M. Feinman and J. Marcus (eds), *Archaic States*, 199–260. Santa Fe: School of American Research Press

Bakir, A. M. 1952, *Slavery in Pharaonic Egypt*. Cairo: Institut Français d'Archéologie Orientale

Barbotin, C. and J. J. Clère 1991, L'Inscription de Sésostris Ier à Tôd. *Bulletin de l'Institut Français d'Archéologie Orientale du Caire* 91, 1–32

Barkan, L. 1999, *Unearthing the Past: Archaeology and Aesthetics in the Making of Renaissance Culture*. New Haven: Yale UP

Barns, J. W. B. 1952, *The Ashmolean Ostracon of Sinuhe*. Oxford: Griffith Institute

Barta, W. 1963, *Die Altägyptische Opferliste von der Frühzeit bis zur Griechisch-Römischen Epoche*. Berlin: Bruno Hessling

Barucq, A. and F. Daumas 1980, *Hymnes et prières de l'Egypte ancienne*. Paris: Cerf

Baumgartel, E. J. 1960, *The Cultures of Prehistoric Egypt II*. Oxford: Griffith Institute

Beckerath, J. von 1997, *Chronologie des Pharaonischen Ägypten*. Mainz: von Zabern

Beckerath, J. von 1999, *Handbuch der Ägyptischen Königsnamen*. Mainz: von Zabern

Behlmer, H. 1996, Ancient Egyptian Survivals in Coptic Literature: An Overview, in A. Loprieno (ed.), *Ancient Egyptian Literature: History and Forms*, 567–590. Leiden: Brill

Berlandini, J. 1984–1985, La Mout *Hnt-pr-Pth* sur un fragment Memphite de Chabaka. *Bulletin de la Société d'Égyptologie de Genève* 9–10, 31–40

Bevan, A. 2003, Reconstructing the Role of Egyptian Culture in the Value Regimes of the Bronze Age Aegean: Stone Vessels and their Social Contexts, in R. Matthews and C. Roemer (eds), *Ancient Perspectives on Egypt*, 57–74. London: UCL Press

Bianchi, R. S. 1979, Ex-votos of Dynasty XXVI. *Mitteilungen des Deutschen Archäologischen Instituts, Abteilung Kairo* 35, 15–22

Bianchi, R. S. 1980, Not the Isis Knot. *Bulletin of the Egyptological Seminar* 2, 9–31

Bianchi, R. S. 1988, Pharaonic Art in Ptolemaic Egypt, in R. S. Bianchi (ed.), *Cleopatra's Egypt: Age of the Ptolemies*, 55–80. Brooklyn: Brooklyn Museum

Bianchi, R. S. 1991, Greco-Roman Uses and Abuses of Ramesside Traditions, in E. Bleiberg and R. Freed (eds), *Fragments of a Shattered Visage: Proceedings of the International Symposium of Ramesses the Great*, 1–8. Memphis, TN: Memphis State University

Bietak, M. 1989, Zur Herkunft des Seth von Avaris. *Ägypten und Levante* 1, 9–16

Bietak, M. 1996, *Avaris. The Capital of the Hyksos*. London: British Museum Press

Bietak, M. 1997, Avaris, Capital of the Hyksos Kingdom: New Results of Excavations, in E. Oren (ed.), *The Hyksos: New Historical and Archaeological Perspectives*, 87–140. Philadelphia: University Museum, University of Pennsylvania

Bissing, F. W. B. Von 1914, *Denkmäler Ägyptischer Sculptur*. Munich: Bruckmann

Björkman, G. 1971, *Kings at Karnak. A Study of the Treatment of the Monuments of Royal Predecessors in the Early New Kingdom*. Uppsala: University of Uppsala

Blair, J. G. 1979, *The Confidence Man in Modern Fiction*. London: Vision

Blankenberg-van Delden, C. 1969, *The Large Commemorative Scarabs of Amenhotep III*. Leiden: Brill

Blumenthal, E. 1982, Die Prophezeiung des Neferti. *Zeitschrift für Ägyptische Sprache und Altertumskunde* 109, 1–27

Blumenthal, E. 1996, Die Literarische Verarbeitung der Übergangszeit zwischen Altem und Mittlerem Reich, in A. Loprieno (ed.), *Ancient Egyptian Literature: History and Forms*, 105–135. Leiden: Brill

Boardman, J. 1999, *The Greeks Overseas*. London: Thames and Hudson

Bolshakov, A. O. 1997, *Man and His Double in Egyptian Ideology of the Old Kingdom*. Wiesbaden: Harrassowitz

Borchardt, L. 1913, *Das Grabdenkmal des Königs Sa3hu-Re', II: Die Wandbilder*. Leipzig: Hinrichs

Borchardt, L. 1935, *Die Mittel zur Zeitlichen Festlegung von Punkten der Ägyptischen Geschichte und ihre Anwendung*. Cairo

Borchardt, L. 1937, *Denkmäler des Alten Reiches (ausser den Statuen) im Museum von Kairo, Nr. 1295– 1808, I, Text und Tafeln zu Nr. 1295–1541*. Berlin: Reichsdruckerei

Bothmer, B. V. 1960a, The Philadelphia-Cairo Statue of Osorkon II. *Journal of Egyptian Archaeology* 46, 3–11

Bothmer, B. V. 1960b, *Egyptian Sculpture of the Late Period, 700 BC to AD 100*. Brooklyn: Brooklyn Museum

Bothmer, B. V. 1970, Apotheosis in Late Egyptian Sculpture. *Kêmi* 71, 35–48

Bothmer, B. V. 1996, Hellenistic Elements in Egyptian Sculpture of the Ptolemaic Period, in P. Green (ed.), *Alexandria and Alexandrianism*, 215–230. Malibu: J. Paul Getty Museum

Botti, G. 1955, A Fragment of the Story of a Military Expedition of Tuthmosis III to Syria. *Journal of Egyptian Archaeology* 41, 64–71

Breasted, J. H. 1901, The Philosophy of a Memphite Priest. *Zeitschrift für Ägyptische Sprache und Altertumskunde* 39, 39–54

Breccia, E. 1934, *Terrecotte Figurate Greche e Greco-Egizio del Museo di Alessandria*. Bergamo: Officine dell'Istituto Italiano d'Arti Grafiche

Bresciani, E. 2001, Persia, in D. B. Redford (ed.), *The Oxford Encyclopedia of Ancient Egypt*, 35–37. Oxford: OUP

Broze, M. 1989, *La Princesse de Bakhtan*. Brussels: Fondation Egyptologique Reine Elisabeth

Brunner, H. 1970, Zum Verständnis der Archaisierenden Tendenz in der Ägyptischen Spätzeit. *Saeculum* 21

Brunner-Traut, E. 1975, Arbeitslieder, in W. Helck and E. Otto (eds), *Lexikon der Ägyptologie*, 1, 378–385. Wiesbaden: Harrassowitz

Brunner-Traut, E. 1978, Altägyptische Literatur, in W. Röllig (ed), *Altorientalische Literaturen*, 84. Wiesbaden: Akademische Verlagsgesellschaft Athenaion

Brunner-Traut, E. 1986, Stilwandel, in W. Helck and E. Otto (eds), *Lexikon der Ägyptologie*, 6, 41– 45. Wiesbaden: Harrassowitz

Brunton, G. and G. Caton-Thompson 1928, *The Badarian Civilisation and Predynastic Remains Near Badari*. London: Quaritch

Bryan, B. M. 1991, *The Reign of Thutmose IV*. Baltimore: Johns Hopkins UP

Buchberger, H. 1993, *Transformation und Transformat. Sargtextstudien I*. Wiesbaden: Harrassowitz

Buck, A. de 1935–1961, *The Egyptian Coffin Texts*. Chicago: University of Chicago Press

Buck, A. de 1961, *The Egyptian Coffin Texts VII*. Chicago: University of Chicago Press

Budge, E. A. W. 1913, *The Papyrus Ani: A Reproduction in Facsimile with Hieroglyphic Transcript, Translation and Introduction*. London: Warner

Burkard, G. 1990, Frühgeschichte und Römerzeit: P. Berlin 23071 vso. *Studien zur Altägyptischen Kultur* 17, 107–133

Burkard, G. 1994, Medizin und Politik: Altägyptische Heilkunst am Persischen Königshof. *Studien zur Altägyptischen Kultur* 21, 35–57

Burkard, G. 1999, 'Als Gott Erschienen Spricht Er'. Die Lehre des Amenemhet als Postumes Vermächtnis, in J. Assmann and E. Blumenthal (eds), *Literatur und Politik im Pharaonischen und Ptolemäischen Ägypten*, 153–173. Cairo: Institut Français d'Archéologie Orientale

Burstein, S. M. 1996, Images of Egypt in Greek Historiography, in A. Loprieno (ed.), *Ancient Egyptian Literature: History and Forms*, 591–604. Leiden: Brill

Caminos, R. A. 1977, *A Tale of Woe, from a Hieratic Papyrus in the A. S. Pushkin Museum of Fine Arts in Moscow*. Oxford: Griffith Institute

Caminos, R. A. 1956, *Literary Fragments in the Hieratic Script*. Oxford: Griffith Institute

Careddu, G. 1985, *Museo Barracco di Scultura Antica: la collezione Egizia*. Rome: Istituto Poligrafico e Zecca dello Stato

Carlyle, T. 2000, *Sartor Resartus: The Life and Opinions of Herr Teufelsdröckh in Three Books*. Berkeley: University of California Press

Černý, J. 1973, *A Community of Workmen at Thebes in the Ramesside Period*. Cairo: Institut Français d'Archéologie Orientale

Cheetham, M., M. A. Holly and K. Moxey (eds) 1996, *The Subjects of Art History*. New York: CUP

Cherpion, N. 1989, *Mastabas et hypogées d'ancien empire: le problème de la datation*. Brussels: Connaissance de l'Égypte Ancienne

Cherpion, N. 1999, The Human Figure in Old Kingdom Nonroyal Reliefs, in D. Arnold and C. Ziegler (eds), *Egyptian Art in the Age of the Pyramids*, 103–116. New York: Metropolitan Museum of Art

Christie's Sale Catalogue 1991, Fine Antiquities, 2 December. London: Christie, Manson and Woods Ltd

Clementz, H. 1993, *Flavius Josephus. Kleinere Schriften*. Wiesbaden: Fourier

Cline, E. H. 1994, *Sailing the Wine-Dark Sea: International Trade and the Late Bronze Age Aegean*. Oxford: Tempus Reporartum

Cline, E. H. and D. O'Connor 2003, The Mystery of the 'Sea Peoples', in D. O'Connor and S. Quirke (eds), *Mysterious Lands*, 107–138. London: UCL Press

Coleridge, S. T. 1817, *Biographia Literaria*. London: Rest Fenner

Collier, M. 1996, The Language of Literature: On Grammar and Texture, in A. Loprieno (ed.), *Ancient Egyptian Literature: History and Forms*, 531–553. Leiden: Brill

Concise Oxford Dictionary 1999. 10th edition, Oxford: Clarendon

Cook, J. M. 1983, *The Persian Empire*. London: Dent

Coulon, L. and P. Collombert 2000, Les Dieux contre la mer. Le début du "Papyrus d'Astarte" (pBN 202). *Bulletin d l'Institut Français d'Archéologie Orientale du Caire* 100, 193–242

Cremo, M. A. 1999, Puranic Time and the Archaeological Record, in T. Murray (ed.), *Time and Archaeology*, 38–48. London: Routledge

Crum, W. E. 1939, *A Coptic Dictionary*. Oxford: Clarendon

Curto, S. 1985, *Le Sculture Egizie ed Egittizzanti nelle Villa Torlonia in Roma*. Leiden: Brill

Davies, N. de G. 1905a, *The Rock Tombs of El Amarna Part II. The Tombs of Panehesy and Meryra*. London: Egypt Exploration Fund

Davies, N. de G. 1905b, *The Rock Tombs of El Amarna Part III. The Tombs of Huya and Ahmes*. London: Egypt Exploration Fund

Davies, N. de G. 1926, *The Tomb of Huy*. London: Egypt Exploration Society

Davies, N. de G. 1943, *The Tomb of Rekh-mi-Ré' at Thebes*. New York: Arno

Davies, V. and R. Friedman 1998, The Narmer Palette: A Forgotten Member. *Nekhen News* 10, 22

Davis, W. 1982, Canonical Representation in Egyptian Art. *Anthropology and Aesthetics* 4, 20–46

Davis, W. 1989, *The Canonical Tradition in Ancient Egyptian Art*. New York: CUP

Davis, W. 1992, *Masking the Blow: The Scene of Representation in Late Prehistoric Egyptian Art*. Berkeley: University of California Press

Davis, W. 1996, *Replications: Archaeology, Art History, Psychoanalysis*. University Park, PA: Pennsylvania State UP

Demarée, R. J. 1983, *ȝḫ iḳr n Rᶜ-Stelae: On Ancestor Worship in Ancient Egypt*. Leiden: Nederlands Instituut voor het Nabije Oosten.

Depauw, M. 1997, *A Companion to Demotic Studies*. Brussels: Fondation Eyptologique Reine Elisabeth

Depuydt, L. 1993, Zur Bedeutung der Partikeln *jsk* und *js*. *Göttinger Miszellen* 136, 11–25

Depuydt, L. 1997, *Civil Calendar and Lunar Calendar in Egypt*. Leuven: Peeters

Derchain, P. 1986, Deux notules à propos du Papyrus Westcar. *Göttinger Miszellen* 89, 15–21

Derchain, P. 1996, Théologie et Littérature, in A. Loprieno (ed.), *Ancient Egyptian Literature: History and Forms*, 351–360. Leiden: Brill

Derchain, P. 1999, Femmes. Deux notules. *Bulletin de la Société d'Egyptologie de Genève* 23, 25–29

Didi-Huberman, G. 1998, Viscosités et survivances: l'histoire de l'art à l'épreuve du matériau. *Critique* 611, 137–162

Dijk, J. van 1994, The Nocturnal Wanderings of King Neferkare, in C. Berger and B. Mathieu (eds), *Hommages à Jean Leclant, vol. 4*, 387–393. Cairo: Institut Français d'Archéologie Orientale

Donadoni Roveri, A. M. 1988a, *Ägyptisches Museum Turin. Das Alte Ägypten. Das Alltagsleben*. Turin: Istituto Bancario San Paolo

Donadoni Roveri, A. M. 1988b, *Ägyptisches Museum Turin. Das Alte Ägypten. Die Religiösen Vorstellungen*. Turin: Istituto Bancario San Paolo

Drews, R. 1993, *The End of the Bronze Age. Changes in Warfare and the Catastrophe ca. 1200 BC*. Princeton: Princeton UP

Dreyer, G., U. Hartung, T. Hikade, E. C. Köhler, V. Müller and F. Pumpenmeier 1998, Umm el-Qaab: Nachuntersuchungen im Frühzeitlichen Königsfriedhof 9/10 Vorbericht. *Mitteilungen des Deutschen Archäologischen Instituts, Abteilung Kairo* 54, 77–167

Drioton, E. 1942, Un Grattoir de scribe. *Annales du Service des Antiquités de l'Égypte* 41, 91–95

Dunham, D. 1970, *The Barkal Temples*. Boston: Museum of Fine Arts

Eco, U. 1990, *I Limiti dell'Interpretazione*. Milan: Bompiani

Eco, U. 1992, *Interpretation and Overinterpretation*. Cambridge: CUP

Eddy, S. K. 1961, *The King is Dead: Studies in the Near Eastern Resistance to Hellenism 334–31 BC*. Lincoln, NE: University of Nebraska Press

Edgerton, W. F. and J. A. Wilson 1936, *Historical Records of Ramses III: The Text in Medinet Habu*. Chicago: University of Chicago Press

Eide, T., T. Hägg, R. H. Pierce and L. Török 1998, *Fontes Historiae Nubiorum, Vol. III. From the First to the Sixth Century AD, 896–901*. Bergen: University of Bergen

Eliade, M. 1959, *Cosmos and History, the Myth of the Eternal Return*. New York: Harper

El-Khouli, A. 1993, Stone Vessels, in J. Baines (ed.), *Stone Vessels, Pottery and Sealings from the Tomb of Tutankhamun*, 1–35. Oxford: Griffith Institute

Emery, W. B. 1949, *Great Tombs of the First Dynasty I*. London: Egypt Exploration Society

Emery, W. B. 1954, *Great Tombs of the First Dynasty II*. London: Egypt Exploration Society

Emery, W. B. 1958, *Great Tombs of the First Dynasty III*. London: Egypt Exploration Society

Englund, G. 1987, Gods as a Frame of Reference. On Thinking and Concepts of Thought in Ancient Egypt, in G. Englund (ed.), *The Religion of the Ancient Egyptians. Cognitive Structures and Popular Expressions*, 7–28. Uppsala: Uppsala University

Erman, A. 1899, *Königliche Museen zu Berlin. Ausführliches Verzeichnis der Ägyptischen Altertümer und Gipsabgüsse*. Berlin: W. Spemann

Erman, A. and H. Grapow 1926–1950, *Wörterbuch der Aegyptischen Sprache und Altertumskunde*. Leipzig: Hinrichs

Evers, H. G. 1929, *Staat aus dem Stein. Denkmäler, Geschichte und Bedeutung der Ägyptischen Plastik Während des Mittleren Reichs. I*. Munich: F. Bruckmann

Eyre, C. 1984, Crime and Adultery in Ancient Egypt. *Journal of Egyptian Archaeology* 70, 92–105

Eyre, C. 1996, Is Egyptian Historical Literature "Historical" or "Literary"?, in A. Loprieno (ed.), *Ancient Egyptian Literature: History and Forms*, 415–433. Leiden: Brill

Eyre, C. 1999, The Village Economy in Pharaonic Egypt, in A. K. Bowman and E. Rogan (eds), *Agriculture in Egypt: from Pharaonic to Modern Times. Proceedings of the British Academy* 96, 33–60. Oxford: OUP

Eyre, C. 2002, *The Cannibal Hymn. A Cultural and Literary Study*. Liverpool: Liverpool UP

Fakhry, A. 1959, *The Monuments of Sneferu at Dahshur, I–II*. Cairo: Antiquities Service

Faulkner, R. O. 1962, *A Concise Dictionary of Middle Egyptian*. Oxford: Griffith Institute

Faulkner, R. O. 1977, *The Ancient Egyptian Coffin Texts, II: Spells 355–787*. Warminster: Aris & Phillips

Fazzini, R. A. 1972, Some Egyptian Reliefs in Brooklyn. *Miscellanea Wilbouriana I*

Fecht, G. 1972, *Der Vorwurf am Gott in den "Mahnworten des Ipu-wer"*. Heidelberg: C. Winter

Finkelstein, I. and N. A. Silberman 2001, *The Bible Unearthed. Archaeology's New Vision of Ancient Israel and the Origin of its Sacred Texts*. New York: Free Press

Finnestad, R. 1985, *Image of the World and Symbol of the Creator*. Wiesbaden: Harrassowitz

Firth, C. M. and J. E. Quibell. 1935, *The Step Pyramid*. Cairo: Institut Français d'Archéologie Orientale

Fischer, H. G. 1964, *Inscriptions from the Coptite Nome*. Rome: Pontificium Institutum Biblicum

Fischer, H. G. 1973, Some Emblematic Uses of Hieroglyphs with Particular Reference to an Archaic Ritual Vessel. *Metropolitan Museum Journal* 5, 5–23

Fischer, H. G. 1976, *Egyptian Studies I: Varia*. New York: Metropolitan Museum of Art

Fischer, H. G. 1986, *L'Écriture et l'art de l'Égypte ancienne: quatre leçons sur la paléographie et l'épigraphie pharaonique*. Paris: Presses Universitaires de France

Fischer-Elfert, H-W. 1986, *Die Satirische Streitschrift des Papyrus Anastasi I. Übersetzung und Kommentar*. Wiesbaden: Harrassowitz

Fischer-Elfert, H-W. 1987, Der Pharao, die Magier und der General. Die Erzählung des Papyrus Vandier. *Bibliotheca Orientalis* 44, 5–21

Fischer-Elfert, H-W. 2002a, Hieratische Schriftzeugnisse. *Mitteilungen des Deutschen Archäologischen Instituts, Abteilung Kairo* 58, 48–52

Fischer-Elfert, H-W. 2002b, Quelques textes et une vignette du papyrus magique, in Y. Koenig (ed.), *La Magie en Egypte. A la recherche d'une définition*, 167–184. Paris: Musée du Louvre

Fischer-Elfert, H-W. and F. Hoffmann forthcoming, Die Magischen Texte und Vignetten des Papyrus Nr. 1826 der Nationalbibliothek Griechenlands. *Würzburger Medizinhistorische Mitteilungen*

Friedman, F. D. 1995, The Underground Relief Panels of King Djoser at the Step Pyramid Complex. *Journal of the American Research Center in Egypt* 32, 1–42

Gardiner, A. H. 1932, *Late Egyptian Stories*. Brussels: Fondation Egyptologique Reine Elisabeth

Gardiner, A. H. 1935, *Hieratic Papyri in the British Museum, Third Series*. London: British Museum

Gardiner, A. H. 1937, *Late Egyptian Miscellanies*. Brussels: Fondation Egyptologique Reine Elisabeth

Gardiner, A. H. 1946, Davies's Copy of the Great Speos Artemidos Inscription. *Journal of Egyptian Archaeology* 32, 43–56

Gardiner, A. H. 1957, *Egyptian Grammar. Being an Introduction to the Study of Hieroglyphs*. Oxford: Griffith Institute

Gardiner, A. H. 1959, *The Royal Canon of Turin*. Oxford: Griffith Institute

Gardiner, A. H. 1961, *Egypt of the Pharaohs: An Introduction*. Oxford: Clarendon

Gardiner, A. H. 1973, *Egyptian Grammar: Being an Introduction to the Study of Hieroglyphs*. 3rd edition, Oxford: Griffith Institute

Garstang, J. 1904, *Tombs of the Third Egyptian Dynasty at Reqâqnah and Bêt Khallâf*. London: Archibald Constable

Gasse, A. 1990, *Catalogue des ostraca hiératiques littéraires de Deir el-Médina IV.1*. Cairo: Institut Français d'Archéologie Orientale

Gauthier, H. 1916, *Le Livre des rois d'Égypte: recueil de titres et protocoles royaux, noms propres de rois, reines, princes, princesses et parents de rois, 4: de la XXVe dynastie à la fin des Ptolémées*. Cairo: Institut Français d'Archéologie Orientale

Genette, G. 1993, *Fiction & Diction*. London: Cornell UP

Genette, G. 1997, *Paratexts. Thresholds of Interpretation* (trans. J. E. Lewin). Cambridge: CUP

Gessler-Löhr, B. 1989, Bemerkungen zu Einigen *wbȝw njswt* der Nach-Amarnazeit. *Göttinger Miszellen* 112, 27–34

Ghirshman, R. 1962, *Iran, Parthians and Sassanians* (trans. S. Gilbert and J. Emmons). London: Thames and Hudson

Giddy, L. 1999, *Survey of Memphis II. Kom Rabi'a: The New Kingdom Objects and Post-New Kingdom Objects*. London: Egypt Exploration Society

Glanville, S. R. K. (ed.) 1942, *The Legacy of Egypt*. Oxford: Clarendon

Gnirs, A. M. 1996, Die Ägyptische Autobiographie, in A. Loprieno (ed.), *Ancient Egyptian Literature: History and Forms*, 191–241. Leiden: Brill

Gnirs, A. M. 1999a, Ancient Egypt, in K. Raaflaub and N. Rosenstein (eds), *War and Society in the Ancient and Medieval Worlds*, 71–104. Cambridge, Mass: Harvard UP

Gnirs, A. M. 1999b, Review of D. Pressl, 'Beamten und Soldaten'. *Orientalistische Literaturzeitung* 94, 647–654

Goebs, K. forthcoming, *ḥd.t as Insignia of Divine Royalty*

Goedicke, H. 1968, The Capture of Joppa. *Chronique d'Egypte* 43, 219–233

Goedicke, H. 1971, *Re-used Blocks from the Pyramid of Amenemhet I at Lisht*. New York: Metropolitan Museum of Art

Goedicke, H. 1986, *The Quarrel of Apophis and Seqenenre*. San Antonio: Van Siclen

Gomaà, F. 1973, *Chaemwese, Sohn Ramses' II. und Hoherpriester von Memphis*. Wiesbaden: Harrassowitz

Gordon, D. H. 1939, The Buddhist Origin of the Sumerian Heads from Memphis. *Iraq* 6, 35–38

Graefe, E. 1981, *Untersuchungen zur Verwaltung und Geschichte der Institution der Gottesgemahlin des Amun vom Beginn des Neuen Reiches bis zur Spätzeit*. Wiesbaden: Harrassowitz

Graefe, E. 1990, Die Gute Reputation des Königs "Snofru", in S. Israelit-Groll (ed.), *Studies in Egyptology presented to Miriam Lichtheim, vol. 1*, 257–263. Jerusalem: Magnes

Grandet, P. 1994, *Le Papyrus Harris I*. Cairo: Institut Français d'Archéologie Orientale

Griffith, F. L. 1900, *Stories of the High Priests of Memphis*. Oxford: Clarendon

Griffith, F. L. and W. M. F. Petrie 1889, *Two Hieroglyphic Papyri from Tanis*. London: Trübner and Co

Grimal, N. 1981, *La Stèle Triomphale de Pi('ankh)y au Musée du Caire, JE 48862 et 47086–47089.* Cairo: Institut Français d'Archéologie Orientale

Guglielmi, W. 1983, Eine "Lehre" für einen Reiselustigen Sohn. *Die Welt des Orients* 14, 147–166

Guglielmi, W. 1984, Zur Adaption und Funktion von Zitaten. *Studien zur Altägyptischen Kultur* 11, 347–364

Guksch, H. 1994, Sehnsucht nach der Heimatstadt: Ein Ramessidisches Thema? *Mitteilungen des Deutschen Archäologischen Instituts, Abteilung Kairo* 50, 101–106

Gundlach, R. 1992, Die Religiöse Rechtfertigung des Sturzes der Achten Dynastie, in U. Luft (ed.), *The Intellectual Heritage of Egypt: Studies presented to Làzlo Kákosy,* 245–264. Budapest: Eötvös Loránd

Günther, H. 1993, *Zeit der Geschichte. Welterfahrung und Zeitkategorien in der Geschichtsphilosophie.* Frankfurt: Fischer

Hall, E. S. 1986, *The Pharaoh Smites his Enemies: a Comparative Study.* Munich: Deutscher Kunstverlag

Harle, J. C. 1991, Terracottas from Ancient Memphis: Are They Really Indian?, in G. Bhattacharya (ed.), *Aksayanivi, Essays presented to Dr Debala Mitra,* 55–62. Delhi: Satguru

Harle, J. C. 1992, The "Indian" Terracottas from Ancient Memphis: A Hitherto Unknown Deity?, in C. Jarrige (ed.), *South Asian Archaeology 1989: Papers from the Tenth International Conference of South Asian Archaeologists in Western Europe,* 375–384. Madison, WI: Prehistory Press

Harpur, Y. 1987, *Decoration in Egyptian Tombs of the Old Kingdom: Studies in Orientation and Scene Content.* London: Kegan Paul

Harpur, Y. 2001, *The Tombs of Nefermaat and Rahotep at Maidum: Discovery, Destruction and Reconstruction.* Oxford Expedition to Egypt

Harris, J. 2001, *The New Art History: A Critical Introduction.* London: Routledge

Harvey, J. 2001, *Wooden Statues of the Old Kingdom: A Typological Study.* Leiden: Brill

Harvey, S. 2003, Interpreting Punt: Geographic, Cultural and Artistic Landscapes, in D. O'Connor and S. Quirke (eds), *Mysterious Lands*, 81–92. London: UCL Press

Heinz, S. C. 2001, *Die Feldzugsdarstellungen des Neuen Reiches: Einer Bildanalyse.* Vienna: Österreichische Akademie der Wissenschaften

Helck, W. 1970, *Die Prophezeiung des Nfr.tj.* Wiesbaden: Harrassowitz

Herrmann, S. 1957, *Untersuchungen zur Überlieferungsgestalt Mittelägyptischer Literaturwerke.* Berlin: Deutsche Akademie der Wissenschaften

Herzog, R. 1968, *Punt.* Glückstadt: J. J. Augustin

Higgins, R. A. 1967, *Greek Terracottas.* London: Methuen

Himmelmann, N. 1983, Realistic Art in Alexandria. *Proceedings of the British Academy, London* 67, 193–207. Oxford: OUP

Hoffmann, F. 2000, *Ägypten. Kultur und Lebenswelt in Griechisch-Römischer Zeit.* Berlin: Akademie

Hölbl, G. 1994, *Geschichte des Ptolemäerreiches; Politik, Ideologie und Religiöce Kultur von Alexander Den Grossen bis zur Römischen Eroberung.* Darmstadt: Wissenschaftliche Buchgesellschaft

Hölbl, G. 2001, *A History of the Ptolemaic Empire* (trans. T. Saavedra). London: Routledge

Hölscher, W. 1937, *Libyer und Ägypter: beiteäger zu Ethnologie und Geschichter Libyscher Volkerschaften nacht den Altägypten quellen.* Glückstadt: J. J. Augustin

Holwerda, A. E. J., P. A. A. Boeser and J. H. Holwerda 1905–1908, *Die Denkmäler des Alten Reiches.* Leiden: Brill

Hornung, E. 1965, Zum Äegyptischen Ewigkietsbegriff. *Forschungen und Fortschritte* 39, 334–336

Hornung, E. 1968, *Altägyptische Höllenvostellungen.* Berlin

Hornung, E. 1982a, *Conceptions of God in Ancient Egypt.* Ithaca: Cornell UP

Hornung, E. 1982b, *Tal der Könige. Die Ruhestätte der Pharaonen*. Munich: Artemis

Hornung, E. 1990, *The Valley of the Kings, Horizon of Eternity* (trans. D. Warburton). New York: Timken

Hornung, E. 1991, *Die Nachtfahrt der Sonne*. Munich: Artemis

Huizinga, J. 1936, A Definition of the Concept of History, in R. Klibansky and H. J. Paton (eds), *Philosophy and History. Essays presented to Ernst Cassirer*. Oxford: Clarendon

Hunter, V. 1982, *Past and Process in Herodotus and Thucydides*. Princeton: Princeton UP

Ingham, M. F. 1969, The Length of the Sothic Cycle. *Journal of Egyptian Archaeology* 55, 36–40

Iversen, E. 1963, Horapollon and the Egyptian Conceptions of Eternity. *Rivista* 38, 177–186

Janosi, P. 1999, The Tombs of Officials: Houses of Eternity, in D. Arnold and C. Ziegler (eds), *Egyptian Art in the Age of the Pyramids*, 27–40. New York: Metropolitan Museum of Art

Janssen, R. M. and J. J. Janssen 1996, *Getting Old in Ancient Egypt*. London: Rubicon

Jarosch, V. 1994, *Samische Tonfiguren aus dem Heraion von Samos*. Bonn: Deutsches Archäologisches Institut

Jasnow, R. 1992, *A Late Period Hieratic Wisdom Text (P. Brooklyn 47,218,135)*. Chicago: Oriental Institute

Jasnow, R. 1999, Remarks on Continuity in Egyptian Literary Tradition, in E. Teeter and J. A. Larson (eds), *Gold of Praise. Studies on Ancient Egypt in Honor of Edward F. Wente*, 193–210. Chicago: Oriental Institute

Jeffreys, D. 1985, *The Survey of Memphis Part 1*. London: Egypt Exploration Society

Jeffreys, D. 1996, House, Palace and Islands at Memphis, in M. Bietak (ed.), *Haus und Palast im Alten Ägypten*, 287–294. Vienna: Österreichische Akademie der Wissenschaften

Jeffreys, D. and L. L. Giddy 1989, Memphis 1988. *Journal of Egyptian Archaeology* 75, 1–12

Jequier, G. 1940, *Fouilles à Saqqarah: le monument funéraire de Pepi II*. Cairo: Institut Français d'Archéologie Orientale

Johnson, J. H. (ed.) 1992, *Life in a Multicultural Society: Egypt from Cambyses to Constantine and Beyond*. Chicago: Oriental Institute

Johnson, W. R. 1996, Amenhotep III and Amarna: Some New Considerations. *Journal of Egyptian Archaeology* 82, 65–82

Josephson, J. A. 1992, A Variant Type of the Uraeus in the Late Period. *Journal of the American Research Center in Egypt* 29, 123–130

Josephson, J. A. 1997a, *Egyptian Royal Sculpture of the Late Period 400–246 BC*. Mainz: von Zabern

Josephson, J. A. 1997b, Egyptian Sculpture of the Late Period Revisited. *Journal of the American Research Center in Egypt* 34, 1–20

Junge, F. 1984, Sprache, in W. Helck and W. Westendorf (eds), *Lexikon der Ägyptologie* 5, 1,176–1,211. Wiesbaden: Harrassowitz

Junge, F. 1985, Sprachstufen und Sprachgeschichte. *Zeitschrift der Deutschen Morgenländischen Gesellschaft*, supplement VI, 17–34

Junge, F. 1999, *Neuägyptisch. Eine Einführung*. 2nd edition, Wiesbaden: Harrassowitz

Kahl, J., K. Nicole and U. Zimmermann 1995, *Die Inschriften der 3 Dynastie: Eine Bestandsaufnahme*. Wiesbaden: Harrassowitz

Kaiser, W. 1998, Zur Entstehung der Mastaba des Alten Reiches, in H. Guksch and D. Pohl (eds), *Stationen. Beiträge zur Kulturgeschichte Ägyptens: Rainer Stadelmann gewidmet*, 53–62. Mainz: von Zabern

Kákosy, L. 1964, *Urzeitmythen und Historiographie*. Budapest

Kákosy, L. 1978, Einege Probleme des Ägypteschen Zeitbegriffes. *Oikumene* 2, 95–111

Kammerzell, F. 1995, Die Tötung des Falkendämonen, in O. Kaiser (ed.), *Texte aus der Umwelt des Alten Testaments III.5 Mythen und Epen II*, 970–972

Kamrin, J. 1999, *The Cosmos of Khnumhotep II at Beni Hasan*. London: Kegan Paul

Kasher, A. 1985, *The Jews in Hellenistic and Roman Egypt*. Tübingen: J. C. B. Mohr

Keith-Bennett, J. L. 1981, Anthropoid Busts: II. Not From Deir el-Medineh Alone. *Bulletin of the Egyptological Seminar* 3, 43–72

Kemp, B. J. 1981, Preliminary Report on the el-Amarna Expedition, 1980. *Journal of Egyptian Archaeology* 67, 5–20

Kemp, B. J. 1989, *Ancient Egypt: Anatomy of a Civilization*. London: Routledge

Kitchen, K. A. 1973, *The Third Intermediate Period in Egypt (1100–650 BC)*. Warminster: Aris & Phillips

Kitchen, K. A. 1996, *Rammesside Inscriptions, Translated and Annotated: Translations II*. Oxford: Blackwell

Kitchen, K. A. 1999, Further Thoughts on Punt and its Neighbours, in A. Leahy and J. Tait (eds), *Studies on Ancient Egypt in Honour of H. S. Smith*, 173–178. London: Egypt Exploration Society

Koefoed-Petersen, O. 1956, *Catalogue des bas-reliefs et peintures Égyptiens*. Copenhagen: Fondation Ny Carlsberg

Koenig, Y. 1994, *Magie et magiciens dans l'Égypte ancienne*. Paris: Pygmalion

Koselleck, R. 1979, *Vergangene Zukunft. Zur Semantik Geschichtlicher Zeiten*. Frankfurt: Suhrkamp

Kozloff, A. P. 1997, Statue of Queen Arsinoe II, in *Miho Museum: South Wing*, 34–37. Shigakaraki: Miho Museum

Kozloff, A. P. and B. M. Bryan with L. Berman 1992, *Egypt's Dazzling Sun. Amenhotep III and his World*. Cleveland: Cleveland Museum of Art

Krauss, R. 1999, Wie Jung ist die Memphitische Philosophie auf dem Shabaqo-Stein?, in E. Teeter and J. A. Larson (eds), *Gold of Praise. Studies on Ancient Egypt in Honor of Edward F. Wente*, 239–246. Chicago: Oriental Institute

Kugel, J. L. 1997, *The Bible as it Was*. Cambridge, Mass: Harvard UP

Kuhrt, A. 1995, *The Ancient Near East c. 3000–330 BC*. London: Routledge

La'da, C. 2003, Encounters with Ancient Egypt: The Hellenistic Greek Experience, in R. Matthews and C. Roemer (eds), *Ancient Perspectives on Egypt*, 157–170. London: UCL Press

Lacau, P. 1914, *Sarcophagés anterieurs au nouvel empire, I*. Cairo: Cairo Catalogue

Lacau, P. and H. Chevrier 1956–1969, *Une Chapelle de Sesostris Ier à Karnak*. Cairo: Institut Français d'Archéologie Orientale

Laisney, V. P.-M. forthcoming, *Die Lehre des Amenemope*

Latacz, J. 1997, *Homer. Der Erste Dichter des Abendlandes*. Zurich: Artemis

Latacz, J. 2001, *Troia und Homer. Der Weg zur Lösung eines Alten Rätsels*. Munich and Berlin: Koehler and Amelang

Lauer, J. P. and C. P. Picard 1955, *Les Statues ptolémaïques du Sarapieion de Memphis*. Paris: Institut d'Art et d'Archéologie de l'Université de Paris

Lauffray, J. 1970 Rapport sur les travaux de Karnak. *Kemi* 20, 71

Lauffray, J. 1979, *Karnak d'Égypte. Domain du divin*. Paris: Editions du CNRS

Layton, R. 2003, Mysterious Lands – The Wider Context, in D. O'Connor and S. Quirke (eds), *Mysterious Lands*, 203–214. London: UCL Press

Leahy, A. (ed.) 1990, *Libya and Egypt c. 1300–750 BC*. London: Society for Libyan Studies

Leahy, A. 1992, Royal Iconography and Dynastic Change, 750–525 BC: the Blue Crown and Cap Crowns. *Journal of Egyptian Archaeology* 78, 223–240

Leclant, J. 1954, *Enquêtes sur les sacerdoces et les sanctuaires Egyptiens à l'époque dite 'Ethiopiennes' (XXVe dynastie)*. Cairo: Institut Français d'Archéologie Orientale

Leclant, J. 1961, *Montouemhat, quatrième prophète d'Amon*. Cairo: Institut Français d'Archéologie Orientale

Leclant, J. 1980, La 'Famille Libyenne' au temple haut de Pép Ier, in *Institut Français d'Archéologie Orientale du Caire, Livre de Centenaire*, 49 ff. Cairo: Institut Français d'Archéologie Orientale

Lefebvre, G. 1923–1924, *Le Tombeau de Petosiris*. Cairo: Institut Français d'Archéologie Orientale

Legrain, G. 1906, *Statues et statuettes de rois et de particuliers. I. Catalogue général des antiquités Égyptiennes du Musée du Caire*. Cairo: Institut Français d'Archéologie Orientale

Lepenies, W. 1992, *Aufstieg und Fall der Intellektuellen in Europa*. Frankfurt: Campus

Levi-Strauss, C. 1970, *The Raw and the Cooked. Introduction to Science and Mythology* (trans. J. and D. Weighton). London: Jonathan Cape

Lichtheim, M. 1973, *Ancient Egyptian Literature I: The Old and Middle Kingdoms*. Berkeley: University of California Press

Lichtheim, M. 1976, *Ancient Egyptian Literature II: The New Kingdom*. Berkeley: University of California Press

Lichtheim, M. 1980, *Ancient Egyptian Literature III: The Late Period*. Berkeley: University of California Press

Lillios, K. T. 1999, Objects of Memory: The Ethnography and Archaeology of Heirlooms. *Journal of Archaeological Method and Theory* 6, 235–262

Lilyquist, C. 1988, The Gold Bowl Naming General Djehuty: A Study of Objects and Early Egyptology. *Metropolitan Museum Journal* 23, 5–68

Littauer M. A and J. H. Crouwel 1985, *Chariots and Related Equipment from the Tomb of Tutankhamun*. Oxford: Griffith Institute

Liverani, M. 1993, Model and Actualization. The Kings of Akkad in the Historical Tradition, in M. Liverani (ed.), *Akkad. The First World Empire*, 41–67. Padua: Sargon

Lloyd, A. B. 1975, *Herodotus: Book II. Introduction*. Leiden: Brill

Lloyd, A. B. 1982, The Inscription of Udjahorresnet. A Collaborator's Testament. *Journal of Egyptian Archaeology* 68, 166–180

Lloyd, A. B. 2000a, The Late Period (664–332 BC), in I. Shaw (ed.), *The Oxford History of Ancient Egypt*, 369–394. Oxford: OUP

Lloyd, A. B. 2000b, The Ptolemaic Period (332–30 BC), in I. Shaw (ed.), *The Oxford History of Ancient Egypt*, 395–421. Oxford: OUP

Loprieno, A. 1988, *Topos und Mimesis: zum Ausländer in der Ägyptischen Literatur*. Wiesbaden: Harrassowitz

Loprieno, A. 1995, *Ancient Egyptian. A Linguistic Introduction*. Cambridge: CUP

Loprieno, A. (ed.) 1996a, *Ancient Egyptian Literature: History and Forms*. Leiden: Brill

Loprieno, A. 1996b, Defining Egyptian Literature: Ancient Texts and Modern Theories, in A. Loprieno (ed.), *Ancient Egyptian Literature: History and Forms*, 39–58. Leiden: Brill

Loprieno, A. 1996c, Defining Egyptian Literature: Ancient Texts and Modern Literary Theory, in J. S. Cooper and G. M. Schwartz (eds), *The Study of the Ancient Near East in the Twenty-First Century. The William Foxwell Albright Centennial Conference*, 209–232. Winona Lake, IN: Eisenbrauns

Loprieno, A. 1996d, Linguistic Variety and Egyptian Literature, in A. Loprieno (ed.), *Ancient Egyptian Literature: History and Forms*, 515–529. Leiden: Brill

Loprieno, A. 1998, *Nhzj* "der Südländer"?, in H. Guksch and D. Polz (eds), *Stationen. Beiträge zur Kulturgeschichte Ägyptens: Rainer Stadelmann gewidmet*, 211–217. Mainz: von Zabern

Loprieno, A. 2001, *La Pensée et l'écriture. Pour une analyse sémiotique de la culture Egyptienne*. Paris: Cybèle

Loprieno, A. 2003, Travel and Fiction in Egyptian Literature, in D. O'Connor and S. Quirke (eds), *Mysterious Lands*, 31–52. London: UCL Press

Lorenz, K. 1977, *Die Rückseite des Spiegels. Versuch einer Naturgeschichte Menschlichen Erkennens*. Munich: R. Piper and Co

Lorton, D. 1976, The Treatment of Criminals in Ancient Egypt through the New Kingdom. *Journal of the Economic and Social History of the Orient* 20, 2–64

Louxor 1985, *Musée d'art égyptien ancien de Louxor: catalogue*. Cairo: American Research Center in Egypt

Luft, U. 1993, Asiatics in Illahun: a Preliminary Report, in *Atti del VI Congresso Internazionale di Egittologia, vol. 2*, 291–297. Turin: Italgas

Luft, U. 1998, The Ancient Town of el-Lâhûn, in S. Quirke (ed.), *Lahun Studies*, 1–41. Reigate: SIA

Macadam. M. F. L. 1955, *The Temples of Kawa, II. History and Archaeology of the Site*. Oxford: OUP

Malek, J. 1982, The Original Version of the Royal Canon of Turin. *Journal of Egyptian Archaeology* 68, 93–106

Manniche, L. 1987, *Sexual Life in Ancient Egypt*. London: Kegan Paul

Manuelian, P. der 1983, Prolegomena zur Untersuchung Saitischer 'Kopien'. *Studien zur Altägyptischen Kultur* 10, 221–245

Manuelian, P. der 1987, *Studies in the Reign of Amenophis II*. Hildesheim: Gerstenberg

Manuelian, P. der 1994, *Living in the Past. Studies in Archaism of the Egyptian Twenty-Sixth Dynasty*. London: Kegan Paul

Marciniak, M. 1973, Une Formule empruntée à la sagesse de Ptahotep. *Bulletin de l'Institut Français d'Archéologie Orientale du Caire* 73, 109–112

Marciniak, M. 1974, *Deir el-Bahari I. Les inscriptions hiératiques du temple de Thoutmosis III*. Varsovie: Editions Scientifiques de Pologne

Martin, H-J. 1994, *The History and Power of Writing*. Chicago: University of Chicago Press

Matthews, R. and C. Roemer 2003, Introduction: The Worlds of Ancient Egypt – Aspects, Sources, Interactions, in R. Matthews and C. Roemer (eds), *Ancient Perspectives on Egypt*, 1–20. London: UCL Press

McDowell, A. 1992, Awareness of the Past in Deir el-Medina, in R. J. Demarée and A. Egberts (eds), *Village Voices: Proceedings of the Conference 'Texts from Deir el-Medina and Their Interpretation ...'*, 95–109. Leiden: Leiden University

McDowell, A. 1993, *Hieratic Ostraca in the Hunterian Museum Glasgow (the Colin Campbell Ostraca)*. Oxford: Griffith Institute

McDowell, A. 2000, Teachers and Students at Deir el-Medina, in R. J. Demarée and A. Egberts (eds), *Deir el-Medina in the Third Millennium AD. A Tribute to Jac. J. Janssen*, 217–233. Leiden: Nederlands Instituut voor het Nabije Oosten

Meeks, D. 2003, Locating Punt, in D. O'Connor and S. Quirke (eds), *Mysterious Lands*, 53–80. London: UCL Press

Megally, M. 1981, Two Visitors' Graffiti from Abusir. *Chronique d'Égypte* 56, 218–240

Merrilles, R. S. and J. Winter 1972, Bronze Age Trade Between the Aegean and Egypt: Minoan and Mycenean Pottery from Egypt in the Brooklyn Museum, in B. Bothmer (ed.), *Myscellanea Wilbouriana 1*, 101–133. Brooklyn: Brooklyn Museum

Meskell, L. 1999, *Archaeologies of Social Life: Age, Sex, Class et cetera in Ancient Egypt*. Oxford: Blackwell

Michalowski, P. 1989, *The Lamentation Over the Destruction of Sumer and Ur*. Winona Lake, IN: Eisenbrauns

Milne, J. G. 1916, *A History of Egypt Under Roman Rule*. London: Methuen

Moers, G. 2001, *Fingierte Welten in der Ägyptischen Literatur des 2 Jahrtausends v. Chr.* Leiden: Brill

Moftah, R. 1985, *Studien zum Ägyptischen Königsdogma im Neuen Reich.* Mainz: von Zabern

Momigliano, A. 1990, *The Classical Foundations of Modern Historiography.* Berkeley: University of California Press

Mond, R. and O. H. Myers 1940, *Temples of Armant. The Plates.* London: Egypt Exploration Society

Montet, P. 1952, Chonsou et son serviteur. *Kêmi* 12, 59–76

Montet, P. 1966, *Le Lac sacré de Tanis.* Paris: Imprimerie Nationale

Morelli, G. 1892, *Italian Painters: Critical Studies of Their Works (the Borghese and Doria-Pamfili Galleries in Rome)* (trans. C. J. Ffoulkes). London: John Murray

Morenz, L. D. 1996, *Beiträge zur Ägyptischen Schriftlichkeitskultur des Mittleren Reiches und der Zweiten Zwischenzeit.* Wiesbaden: Harrassowitz

Morenz, L. D. 1997, Ein Wortspiel mit dem Namen Chetys, des Assertors der *Lehre für Meri-ka-re?. Göttinger Miszellen* 159, 75–81

Morenz, L. D. 1998a, Fair Gegenüber dem "Mann von Draußen" (*rwtj*) – zu Einer Passage Einer Inschrift der Ersten Zwischenzeit. *Journal of Egyptian Archaeology* 84, 196–201

Morenz, L. D. 1998b, Die Schmähende Herausforderung des Thebaners *ḥȝrj ꜥn ḥty. Welt des Orients* 29, 5–20

Morenz, L. D. 1998c, Samut/*kyky* und Menna, Zwei Reale Leser/Hörer des *Oasenmannes* aus dem Neuen Reich? *Göttinger Miszellen* 165, 73–81

Morenz, L. D. 1999, Geschichte als Literatur. Reflexe der Ersten Zwischenzeit in den *Mahnworken*, in J. Assmann and E. Blumenthal (eds), *Literatur und Politik im Pharaonischen und Ptolemäischen Ägypten*, 111–138. Cairo: Institut Français d'Archéologie Orientale

Morenz, L. D. 2000, Zum Oasenmann – Entspanntes Feld, Erzählung und Geschichte. *Lingua Aegyptia* 8, 53–82

Morenz, L. D. 2001, Geschichte(n) der Zeit der Regionen (Erste Zwischenzeit) im Spiegel der Gebelein-Region, eine Fragmentarische Dichte Beschreibung. Unpublished Habilitationsschrift, University of Tübingen

Morenz, L. D. forthcoming, Annäherungen an die *Sinuhe*-Dichtung

Morenz, S. 1971, Traditionen um Cheops. Beiträge zur Überlieferungsgeschichtlichen Methode in der Ägyptologie. *Zeitschrift für Ägyptische Sprache und Altertumskunde* 97, 111–118

Morenz, S. 1972, Traditionen um Menes. Beiträge zur Überlieferungsgeschichtlichen Methode in der Ägyptologie. *Zeitschrift für Ägyptische Sprache und Altertumskunde* 99, x–xvi

Morenz, S. 1996, Die Bedeutungsentwicklung von "Das, Was Kommt" zu "Unheil", "Unrecht", in M-L. Bernhard (ed.), *Mélanges offerts à Kazimierz Michalowski*, 137–157. Warsaw: Panstwowe Wydawn

Moret, A. 1919, Monuments Égyptiens de la collection du Comte de Saint-Ferriol. *Revue Égyptologique* 1, 1–5

Morkot, R. G. 2000, *The Black Pharaohs: Egypt's Nubian Rulers*. London: Rubicon

Morkot, R. G. 2003, On the Priestly Origin of the Napatan Kings: The Adaptation, Demise and Resurrection of Ideas in Writing Nubian History, in D. O'Connor and A. Reid (eds), *Ancient Egypt in Africa*, 151–168. London: UCL Press

Morkot, R. G. forthcoming, A Statue of a Kushite Royal Woman, perhaps a God's Wife of Amun, in B. Ockinga and K. Sowada (eds), *Egyptian Art in the Nicholson Museum*. Mainz: von Zabern

Morschauser, S. N. 1988, Using History: Reflections on the Bentresh Stela. *Studien zur Altägyptischen Kultur* 15, 203–223

Müller, H. W. 1975, Der "Stadtfürst von Theben" Montemhêt. *Münchner Jahrbuch der Bildenden Kunst* 26, 8–9

Murnane, W. J. 1995a, *Texts from the Amarna Period in Egypt*. Atlanta: Scholars Press

Murnane, W. J. 1995b, The Kingship of the Nineteenth Dynasty: A Study in the Resilience of an Institution, in D. O'Connor and D. P. Silverman (eds), *Ancient Egyptian Kingship*, 185–217. Leiden: Brill

Murray, M. A. 1905, *Elementary Egyptian Grammar*. London: Quaritch

Murray, M. A. 2000, Viticulture and Wine Production, in P. T. Nicholson and I. Shaw (eds), *Ancient Egyptian Materials and Technology*, 577–608. Cambridge: CUP

Myśliwiec, K. 1988, *Royal Portraiture of the Dynasties XXI–XXX*. Mainz: von Zabern

Myśliwiec, K. 1994, Athribis: Eine Hellenistische Stadt im Nildelta. *Antike Welt* 25, 35–46

Nachtergael, G. 1995, Chronique terres cuites de l'Égypte Gréco-Romaine. A propos de quatre catalogues recent. *Chronique d'Égypte* 139, 254–294

Naville, E. 1886, *Das Aegyptische Todtenbuch der XVIII bis XX Dynastie*. Berlin: A. Asher

Naville, E. 1907, *The XIth Dynasty Temple at Deir el-Bahari*, Vol. I. London: Egypt Exploration Fund

Naville, E. 1910, *The XIth Dynasty Temple at Deir el-Bahari*, Vol. II. London: Egypt Exploration Fund

Nelson, H. 1930, *Medinet Habu I, Earliest Historical Records of Ramses III*. Chicago: University of Chicago Press

Nelson, H. 1932, *Medinet Habu II, Later Historical Records of Ramses III*. Chicago: University of Chicago Press

Nelson, R. S. and R. Schiff (eds) 1996, *Critical Terms for Art History*. Chicago: University of Chicago Press

Niese, B. 1889, *Flavii Iosephi Opera, vol. V: De Iudaeorum Vetustate Contra Apionem*. Berlin: Weidmann

O'Connor, D. 1982, Egypt, 1552–664 BC, and Appendix: The Toponyms of Nubia and of Contiguous Regions in the New Kingdom, in J. D. Clark (ed.), *The Cambridge History of Africa Vol. I: From the Earliest Times to c. 500 BC*, 830–940. Cambridge: CUP

O'Connor, D. 1990, The Nature of Tjemhu (Libyan) Society in the Later New Kingdom, in A. Leahy (ed.), *Libya and Egypt c. 1300–750 BC*, 29–114. London: Society for Libyan Studies

O'Connor, D. 1992, New Kingdom and Third Intermediate Period, 1552–664 BC, in B. G. Trigger, B. J. Kemp, D. O'Connor and A. B. Lloyd, *Ancient Egypt. A Social History*, 183–278. Cambridge: CUP

O'Connor, D. 1993, *Ancient Nubia: Egypt's Rival in Africa*. Philadelphia: University Museum Publications

O'Connor, D. 1997, Egyptian Architecture, in D. Silverman (ed.), *Searching for Ancient Egypt*, 153–161. Philadelphia: University Museum Publications

O'Connor, D. 1998a, The City and the World: Worldview and Built Forms in the Reign of Amenhotep III, in D. O'Connor and E. Cline (eds), *Amenhotep III. Perspectives on his Reign*, 125–172. Ann Arbor: University of Michigan Press

O'Connor, D. 1998b, The Interpretation of the Old Kingdom Pyramid Complex, in H. Guksch and D. Polz (eds), *Stationen. Beiträge zur Kulturgeschichte Ägyptens: Rainer Stadelmann gewidmet*, 135–144. Mainz: von Zabern

O'Connor, D. forthcoming, Sexism and Architecture at Medinet Habu? Eastern High Gate, in P. Janosi (ed.), *Festschrift für Dieter Arnold*, 421–436. Vienna: University of Vienna Press

Omlin, J. A. 1973, *Der Papyrus 55001 und seine Satirisch-Erotischen Zeichnungen und Inschriften*. Turin: Museo Egizio di Torino

Onasch, H-U. 1994, *Die Assyrischen Eroberungen Ägyptens. Agypter und Altes Testimant*. Wiesbaden: Harrassowitz

Osing, J. 1992, *Aspects de la culture pharaonique. Quatre leçons au Collège de France (Février–Mars 1989)*. Paris: Diffusion de Bocard

Osing, J. and G. Rosati 1998, *Papiri Geroglifici e Ieratici da Tebtynis*. Florence: Istituto Papirologico G. Vitelli

Otto, E. 1954, Altägyptische Zeitvorstellungen und Zeitbegriffe. *Die Welt als Geschichte* 14, 135–148

Otto, E. 1960, Der Gebrauch des Königstitels *bjtj*. *Zeitschrift für Ägyptische Sprache und Altertumskunde* 85, 143–152

Otto, E. 1964, *Gott und Mensch nach den Ägyptischen Tempelinschriften der Griechisch-Römischen Zeit. Eine Untersuchung zur Phraseologie der Tempelinschriften.* Heidelberg: Carl Winter University

Panofsky, E. 1939, *Studies in Iconology: Humanistic Themes in the Art of the Renaissance.* New York: OUP

Panofsky, E. 1944, Renaissance and Renascences. *Kenyon Review* 6, 201–233

Panofsky, E. 1960, *Renaissance and Renascences in Western Art, I-II.* Stockholm: Almquist and Wiksell

Parada, C. 1993, *Genealogical Guide to Greek Mythology.* Stockholm: Åströms

Parker, R. A. 1950, *The Calendars of Ancient Egypt.* Chicago: University of Chicago Press

Parker, R. A., J. Leclant and J-C. Goyon 1979, *The Edifice of Taharqo by the Sacred Lake of Karnak.* Providence: Brown UP

Parkinson, R. B. 1991a, The Date of the 'Tale of the Eloquent Peasant'. *Revue d'Egyptologie* 42, 171–181

Parkinson, R. B. 1991b, Teachings, Discourses and Tales from the Middle Kingdom, in S. Quirke (ed.), *Middle Kingdom Studies*, 91–122. New Malden: SIA

Parkinson, R. B. 1995, 'Homosexual' Desire and Middle Kingdom Literature. *Journal of Egyptian Archaeology* 81, 57–76

Parkinson, R. B. 1997a, *The Tale of Sinuhe and Other Ancient Egyptian Poems 1940–1640 BC.* Oxford: Clarendon

Parkinson, R. B. 1997b, The Text of *Khakheperreseneb*: New Readings of EA 5645, and an unpublished Ostracon. *Journal of Egyptian Archaeology* 83, 55–68

Parkinson, R. B. 2000a, Imposing Words: The Entrapment of Language in the Tale of the Eloquent Peasant. *Lingua Aegyptia* 8, 35–36

Parkinson, R. B. 2000b, The Teaching of King Amenemhet I at el-Amarna: EA 57458 and 57479, in A. Leahy and J. Tait (eds), *Studies on Ancient Egypt in Honour of H. S. Smith*, 221–226. London: Egypt Exploration Society

Parkinson, R. B. 2002, *Poetry and Culture in Middle Kingdom Egypt. A Dark Side to Perfection.* London: Athlone

Parkinson, R. B. and L. Scholfield 1993, Akhenaten's Army? *Egyptian Archaeology* 3, 34–35

Peacock, D. 2000, The Roman Period (30 BC–AD 395), in I. Shaw (ed.), *The Oxford History of Ancient Egypt*, 422–445. Oxford: OUP

Peden, A. J. 1994, *The Reign of Ramesses IV.* Warminster: Aris & Phillips

Peden, A. J. 2001, *The Graffiti of Pharaonic Egypt. Scope and Roles of Informal Writings (c. 3100–332 BC).* Leiden: Brill

Pendlebury, J. 1951, *The City of Akhenaten Part III: The Central City and the Official Quarters.* Oxford: OUP

Pestman, P. W. 1961, *Marriage and Matrimonial Property in Ancient Egypt.* Leiden: Brill

Petrie, W. M. F. 1888, *Tanis Part II: Nebesheh (AM) and Defenneh (Tahpanhes).* London: Egypt Exploration Fund

Petrie, W. M. F. 1900, *Dendereh 1898.* London: Egypt Exploration Fund

Petrie, W. M. F. 1900–1901, *Royal Tombs of the First Dynasty, I-II.* London: Egypt Exploration Fund

Petrie, W. M. F. 1907, *Gizeh and Rifeh*. London: British School of Archaeology in Egypt

Petrie, W. M. F. 1909a, *Memphis I*. London: Egypt Exploration Society

Petrie, W. M. F. 1909b, *The Palace of Apries (Memphis II)*. London: Egypt Exploration Society

Petrie, W. M. F. 1910, *Meydum and Memphis III*. London: Egypt Exploration Society

Petrie, W. M. F. 1923, *Social Life in Ancient Egypt*. London: Constable

Petrie, W. M. F. 1953, *Ceremonial Slate Palettes*. London: British School of Egyptian Archaeology

Philipp, H. 1972, *Terrakotten aus Ägypten im Ägyptischen Museum Berlin*. Berlin: Mann

Pinch, G. 1994, *Magic in Ancient Egypt*. London: British Museum Press

Porter, B. and R. L. B. Moss 1978, *Topographical Bibliography of Ancient Egyptian Hieroglyphic Texts, Reliefs, and Paintings, II: Memphis: Saqqâra to Dahshûr*. Oxford: Griffith Institute

Posener, G. 1938–1980, *Catalogue des ostraca hiératiques littéraires de Deir el-Médineh I–III*. Cairo: Institut Français d'Archéologie Orientale

Posener, G. 1955, L'Exorde de l'instruction éducative d'Amennakhte (recherches littéraires, V). *Revue Égyptologique* 10, 61–72

Posener, G. 1956, *Littérature et politique dans l'Égypte de la XIIe dynastie*. Paris: Librairie Ancienne Honoré Champion

Posener, G. 1975, La Piété personelle avant l'âge amarnien. *Revue d'Égyptologie* 27, 195–210

Quack, J. F. 1990, Zwei Ostrakon-Identifizierungen. *Göttinger Miszellen* 115, 83–84

Quack, J. F. 1992, *Studien zur Lehre für Merikare*. Wiesbaden: Harrassowitz

Quack, J. F. 1993, Ein Altägyptisches Sprachtbau. *Lingua Aegyptia* 3, 59–79

Quack, J. F. 1994, *Die Lehren des Ani. Ein Neuägyptischer Weisheitstext in Seinem Kulturellen Umfeld*. Freiburg: Universitätsverlag

Quack, J. F. 1997, Die Klage über die Zerstörung Ägyptens, in B. Pongratz-Leisten, H. Kühne and P. Xella (eds), *Ana Šadî Labnani lu Allik*, 345–354. Neukirchen-Vlyn: Neukirchener

Quack, J. F. 1999, Der Historische Abschnitt des Buches vom Tempel, in J. Assmann and E. Blumenthal (eds), *Literatur und Politik im Pharaonischen und Ptolemäischen Ägypten*, 267–278. Cairo: Institut Français d'Archéologie Orientale

Quaegebeur, J. 1983, Trois statues de femme d'époque Ptolémaïque, in H. de Meulenaere and L. Limme (eds), *Artibus Aegypti: Studia in Honorem Bernardi V. Bothmer a Collegis Amicis Discipulis Conscripta*, 109–127. Brussels: Musées Royaux d'Art et d'Histoire

Quaegebeur, J. 1989, The Egyptian Clergy and the Cult of the Ptolemaic Dynasty. *Ancient Society* 20, 93–116

Quibell, J. E. 1908, *Excavations at Saqqara (1906–1907)*. Cairo: Service des Antiquités

Quibell, J. E. 1913, *Excavations at Saqqara (1911–1912): The Tomb of Hesy*. Cairo: Institut Français d'Archéologie Orientale

Quibell, J. E. 1923, *Excavations at Saqqara (1912–1914): Archaic Mastabas*. Cairo: Institut Français d'Archéologie Orientale

Quirke, S. 1991, Royal Power in the 13th Dynasty, in S. Quirke (ed.), *Middle Kingdom Studies*, 123–139. New Malden: SIA

Quirke, S. 1996, Archive, in A. Loprieno (ed.), *Ancient Egyptian Literature: History and Forms*, 379–401. Leiden: Brill

Quirke, S. and C. Andrews 1989, *The Rosetta Stone*. New York: Harry N. Abrams

Radwan, A. 1969, *Die Darstellungen des regierenden Königs und seiner Familienangehörigen in den Privatgräbern der 18 Dynastie*. Berlin: Bruno Hessling

Raible, W. 1980, Was Sind Gattungen? Eine Antwort aus Semiotischer und Textlinguistischer Sicht. *Poetica* 12, 320–349

Rampley, M. 2000, *The Remembrance of Things Past: On Aby M. Warburg and Walter Benjamin*. Wiesbaden: Harrassowitz

Rather, S. 1993, *Archaism, Modernism, and the Art of Paul Manship*. Austin: University of Texas Press

Raue, D. 1999, *Heliopolis und das Haus des Re. Eine Prosopographie und ein Toponym im Neuen Reich*. Berlin: Achet

Ray, J. D. 1988, Egypt 525–404 BC, in J. Boardman *et al.* (eds), *The Cambridge Ancient History IV*, 254–286. 2nd edition, Cambridge: CUP

Redford, D. B. 1984, *Akhenaten the Heretic King*. Princeton: Princeton UP

Redford, D. B. 1986a, *Pharaonic King-Lists, Annals and Day-Books: A Contribution to the Study of the Egyptian Sense of History*. Mississauga: Society for the Study of Egyptian Antiquities

Redford, D. B. 1986b, Tuthmosis III, in W. Helck and W. Westendorf (eds), *Lexikon der Ägyptologie*, 6, 540–548. Wiesbaden: Harrassowitz

Redford, D. B. 1992, *Egypt, Canaan and Israel in Ancient Times*. Princeton: Princeton UP

Redford, D. B. 1997, Textual Sources for the Hyksos Period, in E. Oren (ed.), *The Hyksos: New Historical and Archaeological Perspectives*, 1–44. Philadelphia: University Museum, University of Pennsylvania

Redmount, C. 1997, Tales of a Delta Site: The 1995 Field Season at Tell el-Muqdam. *Journal of the American Research Center in Egypt* 34, 57–83

Reeves, N. 1990, *The Complete Tutankhamun: The King, the Tomb, the Royal Treasure*. London: Thames and Hudson

Reisner, G. A. 1936, *The Development of the Egyptian Tomb Down to the Accession of Cheops*. Cambridge, Mass: Harvard UP

Ricoeur, P. 1997, Gedächtnis – Vergessen – Geschichte, in K. E. Müller and J. Rüsen (eds), *Historische Sinnbildung*, 433–454. Reinbek: Rowohlt

Ritner, R. K. 1993, *The Mechanics of Ancient Egyptian Magical Practice*. Chicago: Oriental Institute

Robins, G. 1997, *The Art of Ancient Egypt*. London: British Museum Press

Robinson, P. 2003, "As for them who know them, they shall find their paths": Speculations on Ritual Landscapes in the 'Book of the Two Ways', in D. O'Connor and S. Quirke (eds), *Mysterious Lands*, 139–160. London: UCL Press

Roemer, T. (ed.) 2000, *The Future of Deuteronomistic History*. Leuven: Leuven UP

Russmann, E. R. 1974, *The Representation of the King in the XXVth Dynasty*. Brussels: Monographies Reine Elisabeth

Russmann, E. R. 1995, A Second Style in Egyptian Art of the Old Kingdom. *Mitteilungen des Deutschen Archäologischen Instituts, Abteilung Kairo* 51, 269–279

Ryholt, K. S. B. 1997, *The Political Situation in Egypt During the Second Intermediate Period, ca. 1800–1550 BC*. Copenhagen: Carsten Niebuhr Institute of Near Eastern Studies

Sadek, A. I. 1984, *Popular Religion during the New Kingdom*. Hildesheim: Gerstenberg

Schadewaldt, W. 1982, *Die Anfänge der Geschichtsschreibung bei den Griechen*. Frankfurt: Suhrkamp

Schäfer, H. 1928, *Ägyptische und Heutige Kunst und Weltgebäude der Alten Ägypter: Zwei Aufsätze*. Berlin and Leipzig: Walter de Gruyter

Schäfer, H. 1963, *Von Ägyptischer Kunst: Eine Grundlage*. Wiesbaden: Harrassowitz

Scharff, A. 1932, Eine Archaische Grabplatte des Berliner Museums und die Entwicklung der Grabplatten im Frühen Alten Reich, in S. R. K. Glanville (ed.), *Studies Presented to F. Ll. Griffith*, 346–357. Oxford: OUP

Scharff, A. 1939, Ein Porträtkopf der Münchener Sammlung. *Zeitschrift für Ägyptische Sprache und Altertumskunde* 75, 93–100

Schenkel, W. 1984, Sonst – Jetzt. Variationen eines Literarischen Formelements. *Welt des Orients* 15, 51–61

Schenkel, W. 1990, *Einführung in die Altägyptische Sprachwissenschaft*. Darmstadt: Wissenschaftliche Buchgesellschaft

Scheurleer, R. L. 1974, Quelques terres cuites Memphites. *Revue d'Égyptologie* 26, 83–99

Schipper, B. 1999, *Israel und Ägypten in der Königszeit. Die Kulturellen Kontakte von Salomo bis zum Fall Jerusalems*. Göttingen: Vandenhoeck and Ruprecht

Schlögel, A. 1985, *Echnaton, Tutanchamun: Fakten und Texte*. 2nd edition, Wiesbaden: Harrassowitz

Schneider, T. 1987, Die Semitischen und Ägyptischen Namen der Syrischen Sklaven des Papyrus Brooklyn 35,1446 verso. *Ugarit-Forschungen* 19, 255–282

Schneider, T. 1998a, *Ausländer in Ägypten während des Mittleren Reiches und der Hyksoszeit 1: Die Ausländischen Könige*. Wiesbaden: Harrassowitz

Schneider, T. 1998b, Mythos und Zeitgeschichte in der 30 Dynastie. Eine Politische Lektüre des 'Mythos von den Götterkönigen', in A. Brodbeck (ed.), *Ein Ägyptisches Glasperlenspiel. Ägyptologische Beiträge für Erik Hornung aus Seinem Schülerkreis*, 207–242. Berlin: Mann

Schorch, S. 2000, *Euphemismen in der Hebräischen Bibel*. Wiesbaden: Harrassowitz

Schoske, S. 1987, Historisches Bewußtsein in der Ägyptischen Kunst. *Münchner Jahrbuch der Bildenden Kunst* 38, 7–26

Schott, S. 1950, *Altägyptische Festdaten*. Wiesbaden: Akademie der Wissenschaften Mainz

Schreiber, Th. 1885, Alexandrianische Sculpturen in Athen. *Mitteilungen des Deutschen Archäologischen Institutes in Athen* 10, 380–400

Schulman, A. R. 1967, Ex Votos of the Poor. *Journal of the American Research Center in Egypt* 6, 153–156

Schulman, A. R. 1988, *Ceremonial Execution and Public Rewards*. Göttingen: Vandenhoeck and Ruprecht

Scott, G. D. 1986, *Ancient Egyptian Art at Yale*. New Haven: Yale UP

Sellers, J. B. 1992, *The Death of Gods in Ancient Egypt: An Essay on Egyptian Religion and the Frame of Time*. New York: Penguin

Sethe, K. 1906–1957, *Urkunden der 18 Dynastie (Urkunden IV)*. Leipzig: Hinrichs

Sethe, K. 1928, *Dramatische Texte zu Altägyptischen Mysterienspielen: Herausgegeben und Erläutert von Kurt Sethe*. Leipzig: Hinrichs

Sewell, J. W. S. 1942, The Calendars and Chronology, in S. R. K. Glanville (ed.), *Legacy of Egypt*, 13–26. Oxford: OUP

Shaw, I. 1984, Ring Bezels at Amarna, in B. J. Kemp, *Amarna Reports* I, 124–132. London: Egypt Exploration Society

Shaw, I. and P. Nicholson. 1995, *British Museum Dictionary of Ancient Egypt*. London: British Museum Press

Silverman, M. H. 1981, Biblical Name-Lists and the Elephantine Onomasticon: a Comparison. *Orientalia* 50, 265–331

Simpson, W. K. (ed.) 1973, *The Literature of Ancient Egypt*. New Haven: Yale UP

Simpson, W. K. 1974, *The Terrace of the Great God at Abydos: The Offering Chapels of Dynasties 12 and 13*. Philadelphia: University Museum Press

Simpson, W. K. 1984, Sinuhe, in W. Helck and W. Westendorf (eds), *Lexikon der Ägyptologie V*, 950–955. Wiesbaden: Harrassowitz

Simpson, W. K. 1991, The Political Background of the Eloquent Peasant. *Göttinger Miszellen* 120, 95–99

Sliwa, J. 1974, Some Remarks Concerning Victorious Ruler Representations in Egyptian Art. *Forschungen und Berichte* 16, 97–117

Smith, M. 1991, Did Psammetichus I Die Abroad? *Orientalia Lovaniensia Periodica* 22, 101–109

Smith, R. R. R. 1988, *Hellenistic Royal Portraits*. Oxford: OUP

Smith, W. S. 1942, The Origin of Some Unidentified Old Kingdom Reliefs. *American Journal of Archaeology* 46, 509–531

Smith, W. S. 1946, *A History of Egyptian Sculpture and Painting in the Old Kingdom*. Boston: Museum of Fine Arts

Smith, W. S. 1958, *The Art and Architecture of Ancient Egypt*. Harmondsworth: Pelican

Smith, W. S. 1965, *Interconnections in the Ancient Near East*. New Haven: Yale UP

Smith, W. S. 1981, *The Art and Architecture of Ancient Egypt*. 2nd edition, Harmondsworth: Pelican

Smith, W. S. and W. K. Simpson 1998, *The Art and Architecture of Ancient Egypt*. New Haven: Yale UP

Snowden, F. 1983, *Before Color Prejudice: the Ancient View of Blacks*. Cambridge, Mass: Harvard UP

Sourouzian, H. 1988, Standing Royal Colossi of the Middle Kingdom Reused by Ramesses II. *Mitteilungen des Deutschen Archäologischen Instituts, Abteilung Kairo* 44, 229–254

Sourouzian, H. 1991, La Statue d'Amenhotep fils de Hapou, âgé, un chef-d'oeuvre de la XVIIIe dynastie. *Mitteilungen des Deutschen Archäologischen Instituts, Abteilung Kairo* 47, 341–355

Sourouzian, H. 1995a, L'Iconographie du roi dans la statuaire des trois premières dynasties, in *Kunst des Alten Reiches: Symposium im Deutschen Archäologischen Instituts Kairo am 29 und 30 Oktober 1991*, 133–154. Mainz: von Zabern

Sourouzian, H. 1995b, Recherches sur la statuaire royale de la XIXe dynastie, unpublished doctoral thesis, Université de Paris IV

Sourouzian, H. 1998, Concordances et écarts entre statuaire et représentations à deux dimensions des particuliers de l'époque archaïque, in N. Grimal (ed.), *Les Critères de datation stylistiques à l'ancien empire*, 305–352. Cairo: Institut Français d'Archéologie Orientale

Spalinger, A. J. 1978, The Concept of Monarchy During the Saite Epoch. An Essay of Synthesis. *Orientalia* 47, 12–36

Spalinger, A. J. 1986, Two Ramesside Rhetorical Poems, in L. H. Lesko (ed.), *Egyptological Studies in Honor of Richard A. Parker*, 136–164. Hanover and London: Brown UP

Sparks R. T. 2003, Egyptian Stone Vessels and the Politics of Exchange (2617–1070 BC), in R. Matthews and C. Roemer (eds), *Ancient Perspectives on Egypt*, 39–56. London: UCL Press

Spiegelberg, W. 1914, *Die Sogenannte Demotische Chronik des Pap. 215 der Bibliothèque Nationale zu Paris Nebst den auf der Rückseite des Papyrus Stehenden Texten*. Leipzig: Hinrichs

Stadelmann, R. 1965, Die 400-Jahr-Stele. *Chronique d'Egypte* 40, 46–60

Stol, M. 1987–1988, Leprosy: New Light from Greek and Babylonian Sources. *Jaarbericht ex Oriente Lux* 30, 22–31

Tait, G. A. D. 1963, The Egyptian Relief Chalice. *Journal of Egyptian Archaeology* 49, 93–139

Tait, J. 1982, *Game-Boxes and Accessories from the Tomb of Tutankhamun*. Oxford: Griffith Institute

Tait, J. 1994, Egyptian Fiction in Demotic and Greek, in J. R. Morgan and R. Stoneman (eds), *Greek Fiction: The Greek Novel in Context*, 203–222. London: Routledge

Tait, J. 1996, Demotic Literature: Forms and Genres, in A. Loprieno (ed.), *Ancient Egyptian Literature: History and Forms*, 175–187. Leiden: Brill

Tait, J. 2003, The Wisdom of Egypt: Classical Views, in P. J. Ucko and T. C. Champion (eds), *The Wisdom of Egypt: changing visions through the ages*, 23–38. London: UCL Press

Tanis 1987, *Tanis: L'or des pharaons*. Paris: Association Française d'Action Artistique

Tanner, J. 2003, Finding the Egyptian in Early Greek Art, in R. Matthews and C. Roemer (eds), *Ancient Perspectives on Egypt*, 115–144. London: UCL Press

Taylor, J. 1991, *Egypt and Nubia*. London: British Museum Press

Taylor, J. 2000, The Third Intermediate Period (1069–664 BC), in I. Shaw (ed.), *The Oxford History of Ancient Egypt*, 330–368. Oxford: OUP

Terrace, E. L. B. and H. G. Fischer 1970, *Treasures from the Cairo Museum*. London: Thames and Hudson

Thissen, H. J. 1999, Homerischer Einfluss im Inaros-Petubastis-Zyklus? *Studien zur Altägyptische Kultur* 27, 369–387

Thompson, D. J. 1988, *Memphis Under the Ptolemies*. Princeton: Princeton UP

Trigger, B. 1976, *Nubia Under the Pharaohs*. London: Thames and Hudson

Trigger, B., B. J. Kemp, D. O'Connor and A. B. Lloyd 1992, *Ancient Egypt: A Social History*. Cambridge: CUP

Ucko, P. J. 1965, Anthropomorphic Ivory Figurines from Egypt. *Journal of the Royal Anthropological Institute* 95, 214–239

Ucko, P. J. 1969, Ethnography and Archaeological Interpretation of Funerary Remains. *World Archaeology* 1, 262–280

Uhlenbrock, J. 1990, *The Coroplast's Art*. New York: Aristide D. Caratzas

Uphill, E. P. 1965–1966, The Nine Bows. *Jaarbericht van het Vooraziatische-Egyptisch Genootschap Ex Oriente Lux* 19, 393–420

Uphill, E. P. 1984, *The Temples of Per Ramesses*. Warminster: Aris & Phillips

Van Essche-Merchez, E. 1992, La Syntaxe formelle des reliefs de la grande inscription de l'an 8 de Ramsès III à Medinet Habou. *Chronique d'Égypte* 67, 211–239

Van Essche-Merchez, E. 1994, Pour une lecture "stratigraphique" des parois du temple de Ramsès III à Medinet Habou. *Revue d'Egyptologie* 45, 87–116

van Minnen, P. 1998, Boorish or Bookish? Literature in Egyptian Villages in the Fayum in the Graeco-Roman Period. *Journal of Juristic Papyrology* 28, 99–184

Vandier, J. 1950, *Mo'alla. La tombe d'Ankhtifi*. Cairo: Institut Français d'Archéologie Orientale

Vandier, J. 1958, *Manuel d'archéologie Égyptienne, III, les grandes époques: la statuaire*. Paris: Picard

Varga, E. 1960, Contributions à l'histoire des modèles de sculpture en stuc de l'ancienne Égypte. *Bulletin du Musée National Hongrois des Beaux-Arts* 16, 3–20

Vassilika, E. 1989, *Ptolemaic Philae*. Leiden: Peeters

Vasunia, P. 2001, *The Gift of the Nile. Hellenizing Egypt from Aeschylus to Alexander*. Berkeley: University of California Press

Velde, H. te 1967, *Seth, God of Confusion*. Leiden: Brill

Vercoutter, J. 1956, *L'Egypte et le monde Égéen préhellénique*. Cairo: Institut Français d'Archéologie Orientale

Verhoeven, U. 1999, Von Hieratischen Literaturwerken in der Spätzeit, in J. Assmann and E. Blumenthal (eds), *Literatur und Politik im Pharaonischen und Ptolemäischen Ägypten*, 255–265. Cairo: Institut Français d'Archéologie Orientale

Vernus, P. 1989, Supports d'écriture et fonction sacralisante dans l'Égypte pharaonique, in R. Lauffer (ed.), *Le Texte et son inscription*, 23–34. Paris: Editions du CNRS

Vernus, P. 1990, Entre néo-égyptien et démotique. *Revue d'Egyptologie* 41, 153–208

Vernus, P. 1991, Ménès et Achtoès, l'hippopotame et le crocodile – lecture structurale de l'historiographie Égyptienne, in *Religion und Philosophie im Alten Ägypten: Festgabe für Philippe Derchain*, 331–340. Leuven: Peeters

Vernus, P. 1995, *Essai sur la conscience de l'histoire dans l'Egypte pharaonique*. Paris: Honoré Champion

Waddell, W. G. 1940, *Manetho, Ptolemy, Tetrabiblos*. London: Heinemann

Warburg, A. 1999, *The Renewal of Pagan Antiquity: Contributions to the Cultural History of the European Renaissance*. Los Angeles: Getty Research Institute

Warburton, D. 2003, Love and War in the Late Bronze Age: Egypt and Hatti, in R. Matthews and C. Roemer (eds), *Ancient Perspectives on Egypt*, 75–100. London: UCL Press

Warburton, D. and R. Matthews 2003, Egypt and Mesopotamia in the Late Bronze and Iron Ages, in R. Matthews and C. Roemer (eds), *Ancient Perspectives on Egypt*, 101–114. London: UCL Press

Ward, W. A. 1982, *Index of Egyptian Administrative and Religious Titles of the Middle Kingdom*. Beirut: American University of Beirut

Wardley, K. and V. Davies 1999, A New Statue of the Kushite Period. *Sudan and Nubia* 3, 28–30

Weatherhead, F. 1992, Painted Pavements in the Great Palace at Amarna. *Journal of Egyptian Archaeology* 78, 179–194

Weatherhead, F. 1995, Wall-paintings from the King's House. *Journal of Egyptian Archaeology* 81, 95–113

Wegner, J. 2002, A Decorated Birth-Brick from South Abydos. *Egyptian Archaeology* 21, 3–4

Weill, R. 1908, *Les Origines de l'Égypte pharaonique, pt. 1: La IIe et la IIIe Dynastie*. Paris: Ernest Leroux

Weill, R. 1961, *Recherches sur la Ie dynastie et les temps prépharaoniques*. Cairo: Institut Français d'Archéologie Orientale

Wente, E. F. 1973, The Quarrel of Apophis and Seknenre, in W. K. Simpson (ed.), *The Literature of Ancient Egypt: An Anthology of Stories, Instructions, and Poetry*, 77–80. New Haven: Yale UP

Westendorf, W. 1975, Die Lehre von den Zwei Ewigkeiten und ihre Nutzanwendung durch den Toten, dargestellt anhand des 17 Kapitels des Totenbuches, in W. Westendorf (ed.), *Göttinger Totenbuchstudien: Beträge zum 17 Kapitel*, 183–206. Wiesbaden: Harrassowitz

Westendorf, W. 1983, Raum zeit aus Entsprechungen der Baiden Ewigkeiten, in M. Görg (ed.), *Fontes atque Pontes*, 422–435. Wiesbaden: Harrassowitz

Westendorf, W. 1986, Einst-Jetzt-Einst oder: Die Rückkehr zum Ursprung. *Welt des Orients* 17, 5–8

Westendorf, W. 1999, *Handbuch der Altägyptischen Medizin*. Leiden: Brill

Whale, S. 1989, *The Family in the Eighteenth Dynasty of Egypt: A Study of the Representation of the Family in Private Tombs*. Sydney: Australian Centre for Egyptology

Wild, H. 1973, Une Statue de la XIIe dynastie utilisée par le roi hermopolitain Thot-em-hat de la XXIIIe dynastie. *Revue d'Égyptologie* 24, 209–215

Wildung, D. 1969, *Die Rolle ägyptischer Könige im Bewußtsein ihrer Nachwelt*. Berlin: Bruno Hessling

Wildung, D. 1977a, *Egyptian Saints: Deification in Pharaonic Egypt*. New York: New York UP

Wildung, D. 1977b, *Imhotep und Amenhotep. Gottwerdung im Alten Ägypten*. Berlin: Deutscher Kunstverlag

Wildung, D. 1978, *Götter Pharaonen*. Munich: Günter Grimm

Wildung, D. 1984, *Sesostris und Amenemhet. Ägypten im Mittleren Reich*. Munich: Hirmer

Wildung, D. (ed.) 1996, *Sudan. Antike Königreiche am Nil*. Munich: Kunsthalle der Hypostiftung

Wildung, D. (ed.) 1997, *Sudan. Ancient Kingdoms of the Nile*. Paris, New York: Flammarion

Wildung, D. 1999, La Haute-Égypte – un style particulier de la statuaire de l'ancien empire?, in *L'Art de l'ancien empire Égyptien*, 335–353. Paris: Musée du Louvre

Wildung, D. (ed.) 2000, *Ägypten 2000 v. Chr: Die Geburt des Individuums*. Munich: Hirmer

Wildung, D. and S. Schoske 1985, *Entdeckungen. Ägyptische Kunst in Süddeutschland*. Mainz: von Zabern

Wilkinson, T. A. H. 1999, *Early Dynastic Egypt*. London: Routledge

Wilkinson, T. A. H. 2000a, *Royal Annals of Ancient Egypt. The Palermo Stone and its Associated Fragments*. London: Kegan Paul

Wilkinson, T. A. H. 2000b, What a King is This: Narmer and the Concept of the Ruler. *Journal of Egyptian Archaeology* 86, 23–32

Wilkinson, T. A. H. 2001, Social Stratification, in D. B. Redford (ed.), *The Oxford Encyclopedia of Ancient Egypt 3*, 301–305. Oxford: OUP

Wilson, J. A. 1969, Egyptian Myths, Tales, and Mortuary Texts, in J. B. Pritchard (ed.), *Ancient Near Eastern Texts Relating to the Old Testament*, 3–36. Princeton: Princeton UP

Wimmer, S. J. and S. Wimmer-Dweikat 2001, The Alphabet from Wadi el-Hôl: A First Try. *Göttinger Miszellen* 180, 107–112

Winlock, H. E. 1942, *Excavations at Deir el Bahri 1911–1931*. New York: Macmillan

Winlock, H. E. 1947, *The Rise and Fall of the Middle Kingdom in Thebes*. New York: Macmillan

Wood, W. 1978, A Reconstruction of the Reliefs of Hesy-Re. *Journal of the American Research Center in Egypt* 15, 9–24

Wreszinski, W. 1923, *Atlas zur Altaegyptischen Kulturgeschichte*. Leipzig: Hinrichs

Young, E. 1964, Sculptors' Models or Votives? In Defence of a Scholarly Tradition. *Bulletin of the Museum of Fine Arts* 22, 246–256

Zabkar, L. V. 1965, Some Observations on T. G. Allen's Edition of the Book of the Dead. *Journal of Near Eastern Studies* 24, 75–87

Zauzich, K-Th. 1991, Einleitung, in P. J. Frandson (ed.), *Demotic Texts from the Collection*, 1–11. Copenhagen: Museum Tusculanum

Ziegler, C. 1990, *Catalogue des stèles, peintures et reliefs Egyptiens de l'ancien empire et de la première période intermédiare vers 2686–2040 avant J-C*. Paris: Musée du Louvre

Ziegler, C. and F. Tiradritti 2002, *The Pharaohs*. Milan: Bompiani Arte

Index

Note: figure numbers are denoted in bold type.

Giza: archaism in 41

graffiti: ancient tourist graffiti in tombs 131–133; incorporation of elements from instructional texts 132

Grundformen (of artists) 35, 37, 49, 58

Hadra 214–215

Harbes, stela of **4:2**, 63

Hardedef *see* Djedefhor

Harmakhis-Ra-Atum 133

harpers' songs 76, 122, 127, 131; *see also* Papyrus Harris

Harpocrates figurines 189

Hathor 133

Hatshepsut: archaizing statues 97; Deir el-Bahri tomb-chapel **9:13**, 24, 89, 90, 181; erasure from history 12; eternity of 24; foreigners, repelling of 145; lion statues of 84; Myth of Divine Birth 134; Punt expedition 12; Speos Artemidos inscriptions 145

Hawara: Middle Kingdom pyramids 74

heirlooms 197, 198, 199–200; ancestor 'busts' **11:5**, 204; definition of 197, 198, 201, 203, 210, 211; jewellery 204–206; ritual objects 199–200; scarabs 204–207, 210; slaves 204; and social stratification 198–199; tomb furniture 207–208; tools 204

Heracleopolis 153

Herdsman's Tale 103, 104

Heresankh: statue of 193

Hermaios 147, 148

Herodotus 10, 101, 139; Egyptian histories 149–150, 151, 218

Hesiod 108, 153

Hesy, tomb of 12; archaism in 35, 36, 37, 41, 42, 51, 52, 53, 54, 55, 56, 57; architecture, archaizing 41, 42; architectural history 39, 41, 57; dating of 38–39, 42; excavation of 38; modernist elements 51, 52–53; plan of **3:1**, 39, 41; relief panels **3:2–3:8**, 12, 42, 43, 45–46, 48–55, 57, 58; relief panels, arrangement of 43, 45–46, 48; replicatory temporality 50–52, 53, 55, 58; sculpture, archaizing 42; stylistic analyses of its relief panels 36–38, 49–50, 56, 57; swamp scene 42, 43

Hibis: Amun, temple of 216; Ptolemaic patronage of 216

Hierakonpolis: Narmer palette **9:3**, 70, 157; Pepi I's statue 70

Hinduism: Brahma, duration of 22

Hipparchus: discovery of precession 16

history: archival 142; Amarna kings' erasure from 12; chronicle approaches 153; construction of causal links 146; dynastic chronologies 17–19; Hellenistic Egyptian approaches 142–415; history writing, style of 7–9, 10, 11, 101, 139–142; Hyksos, accounts of 143–146; and ideology 140, 141; Jewish presence in Egypt, traditions of 144–145, 146; and legitimation 9, 11–12; mnemohistory 140–141; multi-layered readings 141, 144–145; mythologizing 146; oral traditions 10–11; past, concept of 1, 7–8, 15, 19–20, 22–26; political use of 9, 11–12, 139, 141, 151, 216, 218, 223; reconstructive 142, 152; reproductive 141–142; *see also* king lists

Hittites: Amenophis II's defeat of 156; Egyptian treaties 168–169; Kadesh, battle of **9:4**, 161, 174

Homer 141, 153

Horakhti, Era of 18

Hor-Djedef *see* Djedefhor

Hori: historicity of 123; instructional texts of 121–122, 124

Horus: creation of 25; duration of 19, 20; kingship, relationship with 26

Hyksos: chariot, adoption of 98, 198; defeat of 145; historiographic traditions 143–146, 148, 149; invasion of Egypt 147, 165; in literature 135; Seth-Ba'al, installation of the cult of 136; tomb robbing during 211

Ibi, tomb of 90

ideology: elite 160–161; of foreign relations 160–161; of foreigners 167–171; *see also* cosmology

Illahun: Sesostris II's pyramid 74, 75

Imhotep 17, 131, 133; cult of 128, 131, 207; instructional texts 122; in literature 127, 136, 151; in spells 129; tomb of, its state of preservation 131

Imiseba 90

Instruction of Amenemhet 77, 103, 104; distribution of 121; historicity of 123

Instruction for Kagemni: attributed authorship 127; distribution of 121

Instruction for Merykara 77, 101; distribution of 122

Instruction of Ptahhotep: its incorporation in tomb graffiti 132–133

Intermediates p 141 LOPRIENO 119 Fischer Elfert

pp 107-17 MORENZ +

+ 'TIME OF THE REGIONS' v 'dark age', F. Inter. Period

NB esp 143